The #1 Dream Website

"First of all, let me just say that I absolut[ely love your site.] [I have found it] immensely useful." -

"I am always checking your dream diction[ary ...whenever I had a dream of] something. Keep up the good work and more power to you!" -- *Ken*

"Amazing. Splendid and excellent work by your team. I was astonished when I saw beautiful explanation for even those very hazy dreams. A big and loud applause for whole team working with dreammoods.com -- *Kishore*

"Thank you so much. You have helped me understand my emotions and I have then been able to sort them out. Your meanings are clear and I can relate to them easily. BEST WEBSITE EVER!!!!!!!!!! :) Thanks again for all your help!" -- *Shannon*

"I am impressed with the level of thought that goes into creating something like this and how accurate it has been. I now firmly believe that the unconscious mind reflects our true emotions and feelings. The level of sophistication is unreal!" -- *Keith*

"You guys are the best; just simply incredible. I'm going through a pretty tough time, but the accuracy is amazing at saying what is going on." -- *Alex*

"I've read many books and checked many sites, etc. and have found DREAM MOODS to be the most accurate description ever. I'm intuitive by nature, but looking up my dreams and plugging them into my waking life with the help of your site is really amazing. Keep up the good work." -- *Jill*

"I just want to thank you for your website. I look at a number of them and yours is the best. Thanks for doing this and all the effort you put in." -- *Jenny*

"This site is by far the BEST site and dreams source out there available!!! You guys don't know me at all and it's relating to my life so incredibly much, it's unbelievable and fabulous!!! It's the greatest!!!" -- *April*

"Hi there. I just wanted to let you know how impressed I am with the accuracy of your suggestions. It was truly fascinating to read what you had and how PERFECTLY it corresponded to my life and situation. Thank you". -- *Cameron*

"Your website is astounding. It makes me look forward to dreaming at night. And in such a scary way, your interpretations were always correct. Thank you so much. You guys blow every other physic or dream interpreter away! -- *Amber*

"Just writing in to say that I think it is a fantastic site. Helped me to learn loads more about sleep and dreams. Can't wait until my next dream." -- *Tom*

"Just wanted to send you a quick note to say how much I appreciate the information available on your site. I am always impressed by the amount of definitions. Almost every word I look up is there! Thank you." *--Erica*

"Wow! Your site is AMAZING! It matched perfectly so well with what was going that it was almost kind of creepy in a good way. Nice job. -- *Nichole*

"Please make a book?! I've been trying to find a dream dictionary book and I'm never satisfied. Please, please, please, turn dreammoods.com into a book!!" -- *Katelyn*

"I have looked at other books, but none seem to compare to how accurate the interpretations are dreammoods.com. Many thanks" -- *Emily*

"This is the best, most comprehensive interpretation I have ever seen. I use it often and it makes sense every time I look up a dream. I feel it really taps into the true psychology of dreams." -- *Valerie*

"I rarely email people from web sites but this site is so incredibly thorough, so surprisingly accurate, and has helped me learn so much about myself that I thought the least I could do was mention this fact." -- *Jonathan*

"I just wanted to let you know I was very impressed with your website. I don't usually write to people telling them so, but I found your site so easy to navigate I felt I had to comment." -- *Laura*

"I very much enjoyed your website. It is very complete, concise, thorough, and informative. A great deal of information is offered and it is very well structured and laid out. Thanks for the info". -- *Paul*

"Thank you for this wonderful and insightful website! It makes interpreting my dreams so easy!" -- *Pam*

"I've become a big fan of your website and use it almost every day to help analyze my dreams. Your information is very thorough." -- *Susan*

"I would just like to say thank you for creating such a complete, easy to use dream website! This is the best dream dictionary that I have found online, and it is so easy to navigate your site." -- *Heather*

"Thank you for the dream interpretation. I'd say that was right on the nail." -- *Debra*

"Thank you so much, this was extremely accurate and helpful!" -- *Maggie*

"I give it two thumbs up!! Your explanations are great." -- *Rebecca*

"I wanted to compliment you on your wonderful dream dictionary! You have a much more extensive selection of words to choose from! Thank you." -- *Jennica*

FROM THE CREATOR OF THE #1 DREAM WEBSITE

dream moods™

WHAT'S IN YOUR DREAM? AN A TO Z

DREAM DICTIONARY

Concise Edition

MICHAEL VIGO

Copyright 2010 Dream Moods, Inc.

What's In Your Dream? An A to Z Dream Dictionary – Concise Edition by Michael Vigo is also viewable online at www.dreammoods.com

ISBN 978-0-557-52852-3

Cover design by Dream Moods, Inc.

All rights reserved. No part of this book may be reproduced, duplicated, reengineered, modified, translated or distributed in any form or manner, either mechanically or electronically, including photocopying, recording, or any information storage system, without the prior written permission of Dream Moods, Inc., except for the inclusion of brief quotations in an article, review, forum post, research paper, or blog and as long it is properly cited.

INTRODUCTION

Symbols are the language of dreams. A symbol can invoke a feeling or an idea and often has a much more profound and deeper meaning that any one word can convey. At the same time, these symbols can leave you confused and wondering what that dream was all about.

Acquiring the ability to interpret your dreams is a powerful tool. In analyzing your dreams, you can learn about your deep secrets and hidden feelings. No one is a better expert at interpreting your dreams than yourself. Only you know yourself best.

We realize that your dreams are unique. No other individual can have your background, your emotions, or your experiences. Every dream is connected with your own "reality". Thus, in interpreting your dreams, it is important to draw from your personal life and experiences.

To guide you with your dream interpretations, we have interpreted nearly 3000 keywords and symbols. These meanings are in no way, the final say in what YOUR dream means, but it will hopefully inspire you to explore and offer a suggestive starting point to understanding your own dreams. Can't find your symbol? Please check online at www.dreammoods.com in our continuously updated dream dictionary or email your request to dictionary@dreammoods.com and we will look at adding the symbol to the online dream dictionary.

Every detail, even the most minute element in your dream is important and must be considered when analyzing your dreams. Each symbol represents a feeling, a mood, a memory or something from your unconscious. Look closely at the characters, animals, objects, places, emotions, and even color and numbers that are depicted in your dreams. Even the most trivial symbol can be significant. This dream dictionary, along with your own personal experiences, memories and circumstances, will serve to guide you through a meaningful and personalized interpretation. With practice, you will gain greater understanding of the cryptic messages your dreams are trying to tell you.

So what are you waiting for?! Get ready to discover what's in YOUR dream!

A

To see the letter "A" in your dream, represents the beginning of a new stage. You are moving on to something new and grand. Alternatively, the letter "A" invokes feelings of superiority and grandeur. It may indicate the name or initial of a person.

Abandonment

To dream that you are abandoned, suggests that it is time to leave behind past feelings and characteristics that are hindering your growth. Let go of your old attitudes. A more direct and literal interpretation of this dream indicates you have a fear of being deserted, abandoned, or even betrayed. It may stem from a recent loss or a fear of losing a loved one. The fear of abandonment may manifest itself into your dream as part of the healing process and dealing with losing a loved one. It may also stem from unresolved feelings or problems from childhood. Alternatively, the dream indicates that you are feeling neglected or that your feelings are being overlooked. Perhaps the dream is a metaphor that you need to approach life with "reckless abandon" and live more freely.

To abandon others in your dream, suggests that you are overwhelmed by the problems and decisions in your life.

Abbreviations

To see abbreviations in your dream, may represent the initials of someone in your life. The abbreviations could stand for an organization or a common acronym or it may spell out some hidden message or advice. The dreaming mind likes to make use of puns, as well as shorthand messages. For example, "CD" could be a pun on a "seedy" situation. "AA" could stand for Alcoholics Anonymous and thus point to the dangers or your excesses and negative behaviors. "Inc" may represent an "inkling", hunch or suspicious you have about a situation.

Abortion

To dream that you have an abortion, suggests that you are hindering and blocking your own growth. You may be hesitant in pursuing a new direction in your life due to fear, pressure, personal conflict or moral obligation. The dream may also be a reflection of your own real-life abortion. And thus, serves as a way of healing from the trauma and working towards self-acceptance.

Alternatively, this dream may also be a message for you to take care and look after your health.

Abyss

To dream of an abyss, signifies an obstacle that is creating much anxiety for you. You need to work through the difficulty and overcome this obstacle in your life. Perhaps you are afraid of "taking the plunge".

To dream that you are falling into an abyss, symbolizes the depths of your unconscious. You are afraid and/or uncertain as to what you will discover about yourself and about your hidden feelings and fears. The abyss may also represent your primal fears and feelings of "falling into a pit of despair". Perhaps you are in a state of depression or wallowing in your negative feelings. Alternatively, the dream could denote your lack of spirituality.

Accident

To dream that you are in an accident, signifies pent-up guilt in which you are sub-consciously punishing yourself over. Perhaps you have done something that you are not proud of. Alternatively, the accident may symbolize an error or mistake your have made. Accident dreams also represent your fears of being in an actual, physical accident. You may simply be nervous about getting behind the wheel or that the dream is trying to warn you of some accident.

To dream of a car accident, symbolizes your emotional state. You may be harboring deep anxieties and fears. Are you "driving" yourself too hard? This dream may tell you to slow down before you hit disaster. You need to rethink or re-plan your course of actions and set yourself on a better path.

To dream that a loved one dies in an accident, indicates that something within your own Self is no longer functional and is "dead". It is also symbolic of your own relationship with that person. Perhaps you need to let go of this relationship.

Accordion

To hear the music of an accordion, signifies some saddening and depressing matter. You need to focus on more joyous moments.

To dream that you play the accordion, denotes intense emotions that are causing physical strain to your body. You are feeling weary. Alternatively, the dream suggests that you need to work hard to achieve your goals

Accountant

To see or dream that you are an accountant, represents your objectivity toward some situation. You are taking a step back and looking carefully at the facts.

Ace

To see the ace in the deck of cards, suggests ambiguity in your life. You need some clarity. In particular, the ace of hearts means that you are involved in some love affair. If you see the ace of spades in your dream, then it means that you are involved in a scandal. If you see the ace of diamonds, then it symbolizes your legacy or reputation. And if you see the ace of clubs, then it indicates that you will be involved in some legal matter.

Alternatively, the dream may be a metaphor that you are an "ace". Or the dream is a pun on "acing" a test.

Acne

Please See Pimples.

Acorn

To see an acorn in your dream, symbolizes strength and durability. Seemingly small beginnings will have the greatest potential for growth. Don't underestimate your minor goals. Alternatively, the dream means that you are about to enter a new phase in your life.

To dream that you are eating acorns or picking them from the ground, suggests that you will enjoy the benefits of your success after long and hard work.

To dream that you are shaking acorns from a tree, indicates that you have significant influence on others.

Acrobat

To see or do acrobats in your dream, suggest that you need to better balance aspects of your life. It could also mean that fears will prevent you from achieving your goals. Alternatively, acrobatics in your dream may be a metaphor for sexual intercourse.

Actor/Actress

To see an actor or actress in your dream, represents your pursuit for pleasure. Your admiration of a particular celebrity may lead to a desire to have some of their physical or personality traits. Consider also who this actor/actress is and what characteristics you associate with him or her. These may be the same characteristics that you need to acknowledge or incorporate into yourself. The dream may also be a pun on his or her name.

To dream that you are an actor, denotes that your hard work and labor will be well worth it in the end. It also indicates your strong desires to be recognized and acknowledged. Perhaps you are putting too much emphasis on your outward appearances. Alternatively, the dream may be analogous to the role that you are playing in your real life, whether it be the role of a parent, sibling, co-worker, etc. Or perhaps you are putting on an act or a facade.

To see a particular actor or actress in your dream, look at the role they are playing. Even though you may not know them on a personal level, how you perceive them or the characters they play can provide understanding in how it relates to you. See also Celebrities.

Acupuncture

To dream that you are getting acupuncture, suggests that you are in need of healing. You may need to divert your energies to different pursuits. Alternatively, the dream may be a metaphor for a problem or issue that you need to pinpoint.

Address

To dream of your old address, suggests that you need to take a look back at the past and learn from it. To dream of a new address, indicates the need for change.

To dream that you are addressing an envelope, represents your need to explore more possibilities. Weigh your options carefully before making a final decision. Alternatively, the dream suggests that you have found your direction in life and are ready to pursue your goals.

Adultery

To dream that you commit adultery or have an affair, signifies your sexual urges and desires that are longing to be expressed. Alternatively, it indicates self-betrayal of your subconscious. You may find yourself entangled in a situation that is not in your best interest, perhaps even illegal.

To dream that your mate, spouse, or significant other is cheating on you, highlights your insecurities and your fears of being abandoned. You feel that you are being taken for granted. You are lacking attention in the relationship or that he or she is being less affectionate. Alternatively, you feel that you are not measuring up to the expectations of others.

Age

To dream of your age, signifies you anxiety and concern of growing older. It may also represent some regret or failure in your endeavors.

To dream that you are older than you really are, signifies wisdom. Perhaps you need to be more sensible. Negatively, it may mean your unyielding ways and rigid thinking.

To dream that you are younger than you really are, suggests that you need to be more carefree and be young at heart. Live a little!

If you are a parent and dream that your child is younger than he or she really is, then it means that you are longing for the past. Perhaps you feel that you are no longer important and wish to regress back to a period where you were more needed. Time is passing you by.

Agoraphobia

To dream that you have agoraphobia, signifies a fear of being exposed or seen. You don't like being the center of attention or being the focus. The dream may symbolize a real life phobia or highlight feelings of anxiety.

Agreement

To dream of an agreement, indicates resolution to a conflict or problem. Your unconscious is working in accordance with your conscious.

AIDS

To dream that you have AIDS, indicates that your psychological integrity is being attacked. You are unable to defend your position in some matter.

To dream that your mate has AIDS, suggests that you are in an unhealthy or destructive relationship.

Air

To dream about the air, symbolizes creativity and intelligence. If the air is foggy or polluted, then it suggests that your thought process or mind is clouded.

To feel cold air in your dream, signifies discordance in your domestic relations and setbacks in your business affairs. You may be in danger of losing touch with reality.

To dream that you are breathing hot air, signifies the influence of evil around you.

Air Conditioner

To dream that the air conditioner is not working, suggests that you are not able to relax and breathe freely. You may be overly worried about a situation.

To see or feel the air conditioner in your dream, represents purification and relief. You have cooled off from some heated argument.

Aircraft Carrier

To see an aircraft carrier in your dream, suggests that you are preparing to confront your emotions. You are addressing feelings that you have been ignoring or suppressing for too long.

Airplane

To see an airplane in your dream, indicates that you will overcome your obstacles and rise to a new level of prominence and status. You may experience a higher consciousness, new-found freedom and greater awareness. Perhaps you need to gain a better perspective or wider view on something. If the airplane is taking off, then it suggests that an idea or plan is about to "take off" and be put into action. It may also represent you need to get away and escape from your daily life.

To dream that you are flying an airplane, suggests that you are in complete control of your destination in life. You are confident and self-assured in your decisions and accomplishments.

To dream that you transfer planes, implies an important transitional phase in your life which will take you away from your intended path. These changes will take you to new directions and new heights of status and recognition.

To dream that you miss your connection flight, indicates that you are feeling helpless and trapped by some situation. You feel that you are being held back, either physically or mentally. Alternatively, the dream may also suggest that you are feeling disconnected in some aspect of your life - work, relationship or home life.

To dream that a plane crashes, suggests that you have set overly high and unrealistic goals for yourself. Your goals may be too high and are impossible to realize. You are in danger of having it come crashing down. Alternatively, your lack of confidence, self-defeating attitude and self-doubt toward the goals you have set for yourself is represented by the crashing airplane; you do not believe in your ability to attain those goals. Loss of power and uncertainty in achieving your goals are also signified.

To dream that an airplane is hijacked, signifies disturbing feelings and past emotions in your unconscious mind.

Airport

To see an airport in your dream, symbolizes birth (arrivals) and death (departures). If the airport is busy, then it signifies the desire for freedom, high ideals, ambition, and hopes. It is an indication that you are approaching a new departure in your life. Some new idea is taking off or is ready to take off. You may be experiencing a new relationship, new career path or new adventure.

To dream of a deserted airport, indicates that your plans or goals will be changed or delayed. You are having to put some aspect of your life on hold.

Aladdin

To see or dream that you are Aladdin, represents realization of your goals or dreams.

Alarm

To hear or pull an alarm in your dream, suggests that you are experiencing a conflict in a relationship or situation which is giving your much anxiety. You may be questioning the decisions you have made. Alternatively, the dream may be a pun on an "alarming" situation which needs your immediate attention. You need to spring into action quickly.

Alcohol

To dream that you are enjoying alcohol in moderation, denotes contentment and satisfaction in the decisions that you have made. Success is within your grasp. The dream may also be a metaphor for "spirits" and your need for spiritual enrichment.

To dream that you are consuming alcohol in excess, signifies feelings of inadequacy, worries, regrets and fears of being discovered for who you really are. You are using alcohol as a way to escape or as an excuse for something you did. Alternatively, the dream may be reflective of waking issues and problems of alcoholism.

Aliens

To dream that you are an alien, symbolizes the undiscovered part of yourself. Your manifestation as an alien may be your way of "escaping" from reality. Dreams of this nature also symbolize your outlandish ideas and your wild imagination.

To dream that you are being abducted by aliens, indicates your fear of your changing surroundings or your fear of losing your home and family. You feel that your space and/or privacy is being invaded.

To see aliens in your dream, signify that you are having difficulties adapting and adjusting to your new surroundings. You are feeling "alienated" and disconnected. You may also be having difficulties with how to handle or deal with a certain situation or person. On a psychological level, seeing aliens represent an encounter with an unfamiliar or neglected aspect of your own self.

Alley

To see an alley in you dream, suggests that you have limited options. Consider the phrase "something is right up your alley" to mean that something may be perfect for you. Learn to be more open minded. Alternatively, an alley indicates that you are sidetracked from your goals due to your domestic duties and communal responsibilities. You are experiencing a dilemma in your waking life.

To dream that you are walking through an alley, represents a dead-end. You feel that you have missed out on some opportunity in life. Alternatively, the dream denotes that your reputation is in jeopardy. You feel that you are on the outside.

Alligator

To see an alligator in your dream, symbolizes treachery, deceit, and hidden instincts. It may be a signal for you to take on a new perspective on a situation. It may also represent your ability to move between the physical, material world of waking life and the emotional, repressed world of the unconscious. Alternatively, the alligator represents healing powers and qualities. An alligator also suggests that you are thick-skinned or insensitive.

To dream that you are running away from the alligator, indicates that you are unwilling to confront some painful and disturbing aspect of your unconscious. There is some potentially destructive emotion that you are refusing to acknowledge and owning up to.

To dream that you are raped by an alligator, indicates that you feel violated or taken advantage of in some way. The alligator is symbolic of someone who is ruthless, insensitive and treacherous. This person has a strong hold on you despite your efforts to break free from the unhealthy relationship.

Alone

To dream that you are alone, indicates feelings of rejection. You may be feeling that no one understand you.

Amber

To see amber in your dream, symbolizes the sun and positive energy. Amber is said to have natural healing power. Some believe that the amber can heal sore eyes, sprained limbs or arthritis. Thus the amber in your dream could mean you need to be healed in some way.

Alternatively, to see amber in your dream, represents resurrection. Something in your past will prove to be extremely important to your future. It could mean a situation or relationship in your waking life that was once lively, is now non-existent. You feel trapped or that your life is too rigid and inflexible. You need to change your outdated way of thinking and old ideas.

Ambulance

To see an ambulance in your dream, indicates that your careless activities and indiscretion may lead to major problems and complications. This dream may also stem from your own fears of contracting a disease or your deteriorating health. Perhaps, you should cease what you are doing and pay closer attention to some waking situation.

To see an ambulance full of wounded passengers, signifies a fear of letting go your old Self and making space for the new you. You are projecting your emotional wounds and painful experiences onto others. Alternatively, it may also mean that you are hanging around the wrong crowd and are doing yourself more harm than good.

To dream that someone is hit by an ambulance, suggests that some aspect of your psyche is injured and needs immediate care and attention.

Amethyst

To see an amethyst in your dream, signifies peace of mind and satisfaction in your professional and personal life. You are content with where you are in your life. It does not take much to make you happy.

To dream that you lose an amethyst, signifies heartbreaks and disappointments in love.

Ammonia

To see or smell ammonia in your dream, indicates that there is some distressing or offensive matter that you need to confront.

Amnesia

To dream that you have amnesia, suggests that you are trying to block out the rejected or negative aspect of yourself. You are afraid of change.

Amputation

To dream that your limbs are amputated, signifies abandoned talents and serious, permanent losses. It indicates your feelings of frustration, powerlessness and helplessness. Sometimes amputation may also represent a situation that you have been ignoring and has finally reached a crisis point. In particular, to dream that your arms are amputated, suggests that you lack motivation. Dreaming that you legs are amputated suggests that you are being limited. Something or someone is hindering your progress and where you want to go in life.

Amusement Park

To see or be in an amusement park in your dream, indicates that you need to set some time for more relaxation and enjoyment in your life. The rides, booths and elements in the amusement park are an expression of some aspect of yourself or some area in your life. Look up the symbolism of specific rides for more details. Alternatively, the dream indicates that you are too easily distracted lately.

To dream that the amusement park is empty or abandoned, suggests that you need to open yourself to more fun and adventure.

To dream that the rides at the amusement park are breaking down, means that something in your life is not going as expected.

To dream that the amusement park is closed, suggests that you are denying yourself your time for fun and leisure. You need a break.

Anchor

To see an anchor in your dream, signifies stability and security. You may be in search for a solid foundation or a firmer ground in your life. Alternatively, an anchor indicates that you are someone who stands firmly on your views and opinions.

On the other hand, an anchor may be seen as a symbol for something that is holding you back and restraining your freedom. Consider a relationship that may not be working or a career that is going nowhere for you.

Angels

To see angels in your dream, symbolize goodness, purity, protection, comfort and consolation. Pay careful attention to the message that the angels are trying to convey. These messages serve as a guide toward greater fulfillment and happiness. Alternatively, it signifies an unusual disturbance in your soul. Angels may appear in your dream as a result of your wicked and mean-hearted activities.

To dream that you are an angel, suggests that you are feeling good about something your said or did.

In particular, to see three angels in your dream, symbolize some sort of divinity. It is considered a particularly spiritual and holy dream.

To see an angel holding a scroll in your dream, indicates a highly spiritual dream. Your future and goals are more clearer to you. The message on the scroll is particularly significant.

Anger

To dream that you are holding or expressing anger, symbolizes frustrations and disappointments in your Self. You tend to repress your negative emotions or project your anger onto others. You need to look within yourself.

Being angry in your dream may have been carried over from your waking life. Dreams function as a safe outlet where you can express your strong and/or negative emotions. You are suppressing your anger and aggression, instead of consciously acknowledging them.

Animals

To see animals in your dream, represent your own physical characteristic, primitive desires, and sexual nature, depending on the qualities of the particular animal. Animals symbolize the untamed and uncivilized aspects of yourself. Thus, to dream that you are fighting with an animal signifies a hidden part of yourself that you are trying to reject and push back into your subconscious. Refer to the specific animal in your dream.

To dream that animals can talk, represent superior knowledge. Its message is often some form of wisdom. Alternatively, a talking animal denotes your potential to be all that you can be.

To dream that you are saving the life of an animal, suggests that you are successfully acknowledging certain emotions and characteristics represented by the animal. The dream may also stem from feelings of inadequacy or being overwhelmed. If you are setting an animal free, then it indicates an expression and release of your own primal desires.

To see lab animals in your dream, suggest that an aspect of yourself is being repressed. You feel that you are not able to fully express your desires and emotions. Alternatively, it suggests that you need to experiment with your fears, choices, and beliefs. Try not to limit yourself.

Anime

To dream that you are watching anime, represents your carefree attitude.

To dream that you are an anime character, suggests that you need to be more expressive. You need to convey your emotions more clearly.

Ankle

To dream about your ankles, indicates that you are seeking support and direction in your life. Ask yourself where you want to be headed.

To sprain your ankle in your dream, suggests that you are experiencing some obstacles or difficulties in your progress.

Anniversary

To dream about your anniversary, represents acceptance or appreciation of some aspect of yourself. Consider the type of anniversary. If it is a wedding anniversary, then it symbolizes a celebration of love. You need to accept love into your life. If it is an anniversary of a death or some solemn occasion, then it suggests a new start. The dream may simply mean a reminder of some important date.

Anorexia

To dream that you have anorexia, represents your lack of self-acceptance and self-esteem. You need to learn to love yourself and accept who you are instead of punishing yourself. The dream symbolizes your quest for perfection.

Answering Machine

To see an answering machine in your dream, suggests that you are not listening to a message that someone around you is trying to convey. Perhaps you are experiencing difficulties and frustration in understanding some idea or viewpoint.

Anteater

To see an anteater in your dream, indicates that you need to proceed with caution in some endeavor.

Antenna

To see an antenna in your dream, represents your communication with your surroundings. Consider the condition of the antenna to determine your ability to transmit your ideas and convey your thoughts to others.

Antifreeze

To see or use antifreeze in your dream, suggests that you are being emotionally cold and perhaps need to warm up to others more.

Antique

To see antiques in your dream, represent your time honored values, tradition, wisdom and inherited personal characteristics. It symbolizes something genuine or proven. Certain things in your past are worth holding onto or worth keeping. If you do not like or appreciate antiques, then is suggests that you are moving away from outdated childhood conditioning or old modes of thinking. On a negative note, you may be discarding or rejecting something of value that you should really be embracing and heeding.

Ants

To see ants in your dream, signify your general dissatisfaction in your daily life. You are feeling neglected and insignificant. Or petty things will annoy you throughout the following day. The dream may also be a metaphor on feeling antsy or restless. It may also be a pun on your "aunt".

Ants also symbolize hard work, diligence, cooperation and industry. Increase business activities are expected. On a less positive note, ants symbolize social conformity and mass action. In this regard, you may feel that your life is too structured and orderly.

Apes

To see an ape in your dream, indicates deception, mischievous, and falsehood. Alternatively, it may refer that you or someone have gone "ape". You need to calm down. The ape may also symbolize your wild inner nature, particularly your sexual nature.

Apologize

To dream that you are apologizing to someone, denotes the revolving door of friendships and friends who have come and gone in your life. Perhaps, it is also representative of truth and forgiveness. It is time to let go of past grudges.

Applause

To hear applause in your dream, indicates that you are seeking acclaim and recognition. You need to acknowledge yourself in some area or situation in your life.

To dream that you are applauding another, suggests that you need show more appreciation and praise. Try to be a motivator.

Apples

To see apples growing in a tree in your dream, symbolize knowledge, wisdom and great prosperity. Rewards are on the horizon for you. Consider also the common phrase, "an apple a day keeps the doctor away" which may imply that you need to take better care of your health. Perhaps you need to go to the doctor. Or the dream may also be a metaphor for an apple computer.

To dream that you are eating an apple, denotes harmony, pleasure, and fertility. In a biblical sense, eating an apple symbolizes your sexual appetite, lustful desires, and sexual awareness as associated with the apple in the Garden of Eden.

To see green apples, represents developing love or love that has yet to blossom.

To see rotten or eaten apples in your dream, indicates that whatever you are striving and aiming for may not be fulfilling, and even harmful to you. It may also represent neglect and carelessness.

Appliance

To fix an appliance in your dream, represents your need to work on your relationship and prevent it from falling apart. Consider the significance of the appliance for clues on specific area of the relationship.

Application

To dream that you are filling out an application, indicates that you are lacking something in your life. Consider the significance of what the application is for and how it relates to your waking life. Alternatively, the dream may be a pun that you need to "apply" yourself. You need to put forth some effort in order to excel or succeed.

Appointment

To dream that you are going to an appointment, suggests that you need to be more goal-oriented. If you dream that you miss an appointment, then it indicates that you are not paying enough attention to some minor details and little things in life.

April

To dream of the month of April, denotes pleasure and profit are in store for you. In particular, to dream about April Fool's day, indicates that you are acting like a fool or being foolish.

Apron

To see an apron in your dream, suggests that you or someone is making a commitment to work on some familial task. You are trying to nurture some project. Alternatively, an apron symbolizes protection and secrecy.

To wear an apron in your dream, indicates that you are in a submissive position. You are letting others tell you what to do.

Aquamarine

To see aquamarine in your dream, symbolizes youth, vitality, creativity, and hope. The dream may be telling you that you need to open the line of communication with someone. It may also share some significance with the symbol for water.

Aquarius

To dream that someone is an Aquarius, represents new ideas, individuality and innovation. You are looking ahead and preparing yourself for the future. It also refers to an aspect of yourself that wants everyone within a group to be happy and satisfied.

Arcade

To see or dream that you are at an arcade, suggests that you need to look back to a previous event or experience that brought you much joy and amusement. You want to go back to the good 'ole days. The dream arcade also serves as a temporary escape from reality. You are trying to numb and block out your problems. Alternatively, the dream indicates that you are manipulating others or that you feel manipulated.

Archaeologist

To dream that you are an archaeologist, suggests that you need to learn from past experiences or that you need to look to the past to find answers to present issues.

Arctic

To dream that you are in the Arctic, symbolizes your emotional state. You may be feeling cold and rigid. Alternatively, it suggests that you are feeling isolated and lonely.

Aries

To dream that someone is an Aries, suggests new beginnings and growth. It is representative of your leadership, your courage, your passion and your enthusiasm. As represented by the ram, the dream may be telling you that you need to approach an issue or emotion head on. Alternatively, the dream may indicate some mental problem.

Arm

To see your arms as the emphasis in your dream, indicate your nurturance side and your ability to reach out and care for people. Alternatively, it may represent the struggles and challenges in your life. Consider the pun "arm yourself" which implies that you need to protect yourself, be more aggressive and take a firmer stance on things or the pun "up in arms", representing anger and your readiness to argue.

To dream that your arm has been injured, signifies your inability to care for yourself or your helplessness in reaching out to others. You may have been feeling limited and restricted in terms of your freedom or activities. The right arm signifies your outgoing nature and is associated with masculine energy, while your left arm signifies your supportive or nurturing nature and is associated with feminine qualities. Losing either arm may suggest that you are failing to recognize its respective characteristics.

To dream that you rip someone else's arms out, indicates that you are extremely upset with something that this person has done, but you have not been able to fully express your anger. Because you tend to keep your emotions inside, it is finding expression in your dreams in a violent way.

Armadillo

To see an armadillo in your dream, represents your need to establish certain boundaries. You may be putting up walls between you and those who want to know you better. Alternatively, it indicates codependency. You need to be more assertive and not let others step all over you.

Armageddon

To dream about Armageddon, suggests that you are feeling hopeless and out of control. The dream may be triggered from the deep emotional stress that you are experiencing in your waking life.

Armor

To dream that you are wearing an armor, symbolizes your defense mechanisms. You have developed a way of shielding yourself from things that may hurt you. Alternatively, it means that you are feeling invincible and superior.

To see armor in your dream, indicates insecurity. You are worried about your well being.

Armored Car

To see or drive an armored car in your dream, suggests that you are feeling insecure about the progress you have made so far in life. Perhaps you feel that you are not measuring up to others. You are building a protective barrier or emotional wall around yourself. Alternatively, the dream means that you need to be careful of your spending and that you need to protect your finances.

Armpit

To see/notice your or someone else's armpit in your dream, represents your social connections and your relationships to others. It is the characteristics and personality that you chose to display to the public. Alternatively, the dream may refer to something or some place that is smelly.

To smell your armpit in your dream, indicates that you are making some character adjustments in order to smooth over a situation or relationship. Alternatively, it suggests that you are looking for acceptance.

Army

To see the army in your dream, symbolizes an overpowering force working against you. You may feel outnumbered or pressured and are unable to deal with this situation.

To dream that you join the army, suggests your feelings of superiority. You feel that no one is any match for you.

Arranged Marriage

To dream that you are in an arranged marriage, suggests that you are feeling forced to do something you do not want to do. You are reluctantly moving into a new stage in your life. You feel that you have no voice or no choice in a situation. Consider how a waking situation may be making you feel voiceless.

Arrested

To dream that you are being arrested, indicates issues of control and restraint. Some aspect of your Self may have been prevented from fully developing. Alternatively, it suggests feelings of guilt.

Arrow

To see an arrow in your dream, represents the targets that you are reaching for and the goals you are setting for yourself. Alternatively, the arrow also signifies an end to suffering and the beginning of new-found pleasures and festivities. If you are hit by an arrow, then it symbolizes release or exposure of some tension and pressure. Consider the body part that the arrow hits.

To see an old or broken arrow, symbolizes disappointments and severed relationships. Alternatively, it may indicate that you have changed your mind about some decision.

To see a two-headed arrow in your dream, signifies opposing ideas and viewpoints. You need to consider both sides.

In the Freudian school of thought, an arrow symbolizes the penis and its ability to penetrate.

Arson

To dream about an arson, represents unexpressed rage that has the potential to become destructive. It is best to express your anger instead of keeping it bottled up inside.

Arthritis

To dream that you have arthritis, indicates that you are having difficulties achieving your goals. You are feeling helpless to do anything or are lacking motivation and/or desire to move forward with your plans. Alternatively, it signifies your rigid attitudes.

Artichoke

To see or eat an artichoke in your dream, suggests that you need to get to the heart of some matter. It is also representative of your potential and creativity. Perhaps you are holding back in how you want to express yourself.

Artist

To dream that you are an artist painting a picture, signifies the creative and intuitive side of your character. The picture that you are painting in your dream may symbolize the way that you are visualizing your current situation in your waking life. .

Ashes

To see ashes in your dream, signify bitter changes and disruptions. Ashes may represent a failed relationship or a ruinous business enterprise. You feel that the good times are over and nothing of value is left in your life. Alternatively, ashes may mean that you are dwelling too much on the past. You need to learn to let go.

In particular, to see or clean ashes in a fireplace or stove, indicates that you are unsatisfied with aspects of your life. You may be in a rut and feel trapped by your daily routine.

Ashtray

To see or use an ashtray in your dream, suggests that you are trying to rid yourself of former feelings/memories and your old ways. It symbolizes relationships that have been extinguished and no longer intact. Alternatively, it may be related to feelings of anxieties or connected to your smoking habit, especially if you are trying to quit.

Ass

To see an ass in your dream, signifies a lack of understanding. It also suggests that you will come upon many annoyances. The dream may be a metaphor for someone who is being an ass.

To see an ass carrying burdens in your dream, signifies that after much patience and hard work, you will succeed in your professional and personal life.

Please Also See Donkey.

Asteroid

To see an asteroid in your dream, represents a spiritual message from above. You are about to be enlightened with some knowledge. Alternatively, it signifies a brainstorming of ideas and thoughts. If the asteroid hits the earth, then it indicates that your idealistic notions are deteriorating or being shattered apart.

Astronaut

To see or dream that you are an astronaut, indicates that you are expanding your awareness and consciousness. You are utilizing the information you have and making the best of it. Alternatively, the astronaut symbolizes your ambition. You are reaching for the stars. Or it may mean that you are experiencing some communication issues.

ATM Machine

To see or use an ATM Machine in your dream, represents your desires for financial security. The dream may be trying to offer reassurance; your fears of financial instability are unfounded. If you are withdrawing money from the ATM Machine, then it suggests that you are expending too much energy on fruitless endeavors and are in danger of depleting your inner resources. If you are depositing money into the ATM Machine, then it symbolizes the energies that you are investing into a project.

Atomic Bomb

Please See Nuclear Bomb.

Attack

To dream that you attack someone, represents pent-up frustration and anger. You feel that you have been wronged. Your dream serves as an easy and safe way to express your anger.

To dream that you are being attacked by someone, indicates your character is being questioned. You feel the need to defend yourself. You are feeling stressed, vulnerable and helpless. You may also be facing with difficult changes in your waking life. Dreaming of an attack provides a way for you to confront these situations that you may be avoiding in real life.

To dream that you are being attacked by an animal, is a warning to be careful with those around you. Take notice of who you know in your waking life that shares and exhibits the same qualities of the animal that attacked you in your dream.

To dream that you kill an attacking animal, suggests that you are going against your instincts or gut feeling.

Attic

To see an attic in your dream, represents hidden memories or repressed thoughts that are being revealed. It also symbolizes your mind, spirituality, and your connection to the higher Self. Alternatively, it signifies difficulties in your life that may hinder you from attaining your goals and aspirations. However, after a long period of struggle, you will overcome these difficulties.

To see a cluttered attic in your dream, is a sign to organize your mind and thoughts. Perhaps, you need to rid yourself of the past and let go of the past emotions that are holding you back.

Auction

To dream that you are at an auction, indicates that you may be undervaluing or overvaluing something or some relationship. It may also mean that you have learned from your past experiences and are ready to move on.

To dream that someone outbid you in an auction, suggests that you are being denied something that you have earned.

To dream that no one is bidding at an auction, suggests that your opinions and ideas are not appreciated. Your opinions are being ignored.

Audience

To dream that you are in front of an audience, represents the world around you and how it is paying close attention to your actions. Alternatively, it signifies your fears of having your personal feelings and private thoughts discovered or revealed. If the audience is rowdy or noisy, then it suggests cluttered thoughts and confusion of ideas.

To dream that you have no audience, denotes that you are not being acknowledged for your work or achievements. Perhaps you are feeling ignored or neglected.

Audition

To dream that you are at an audition, indicates feelings of insecurity and vulnerability. You have trouble expressing yourself and feel that you are being put to a test. The attitude and behavior of the audience will also guide you in how you think others perceive you.

August

To dream of the month of August, suggests that there is some misunderstanding in a personal relationship or business situation.

Aunt

To see your aunt in your dream, represents family connection, heritage and value. The aunt may also represent aspects of yourself that you like or dislike. She can also be seen as a substitute mother.

Aura

To see an aura around you or someone else, indicates that some important information is being relayed to you in the dream. You need to pay close attention to the message. You need to draw on this energy for strength.

Autograph

To dream that you are asking for an autograph, indicates your desire to be like the person whose autograph you seek. You may be looking for some form of approval.

To dream that someone is asking for your autograph, suggests that you are giving your consent or approval to someone.

Autumn

To dream of autumn, represents the cycle of life - something is about to come to an end and something new will begin. Alternatively, autumn symbolizes abundance and hospitality. It is time to collect the benefits and rewards that you've worked so hard for.

Avalanche

To see an avalanche in your dream, signifies your raging emotions which have been held back and repressed for a long time. These emotions have not been dealt with in a productive manner and now are being expressed in a sudden and violent anger. Alternatively, the dream symbolizes the inescapable stresses and overwhelming pressures in your life. You are feeling the weight of life's daily demands piled onto you.

Avocado

To see or eat an avocado in your dream, symbolizes lust, sexuality, fertility, potential, and continuity of life. Alternatively, an avocado symbolizes richness and indulgence.

To see an avocado tree in your dream, suggests that you will be well rewarded if you devote some time and effort to some goal or project.

Ax

To see an ax in your dream, indicates that you are overly controlling. It is symbolic of destruction, hostility, and the frustrations that you are experiencing. Perhaps you "have an ax to grind" with someone. Or the dream can be a metaphor that you are ready to "bury the ax" and make amends.

To dream that you are chopping wood with an ax, suggests that you need to divide your problems into smaller, more manageable sizes. Break down your problems into pieces you can handle. Alternatively, it indicates that your strength and power have been cut down to size.

B

To see the letter B in your dream, is a pun on "to be". Perhaps the dream is telling you to "let it be".

Baby

To see a baby in your dream, signifies innocence, warmth and new beginnings. Babies symbolize something in your own inner nature that is pure, vulnerable, helpless and/or uncorrupted. If you find a baby in your dream, then it suggests that you have acknowledged your hidden potential. If you dream that you forgot you had a baby, then it suggests that you are trying hide your own vulnerabilities; You do not want to let others know of your weaknesses. Alternatively, forgetting about a baby, represents an aspect of yourself that you have abandoned or put aside due to life's changing circumstances. The dream may serve as a reminder that it is time for you to pick up that old interest, hobby, or project again.

If you dream that you are on your way to the hospital to have a baby, then it signifies your issues of dependency and your desires to be completely care for. Perhaps you are trying to get out of some responsibility. If you are pregnant in real life, then a more direct interpretation may simply mean that you are experiencing some anxieties of making it to the hospital when the time comes.

To dream of a crying baby, symbolizes a part of yourself that is deprived of attention and needs to be nurtured. Alternatively, it represents your unfulfilled goals and a sense of lacking in your life. If you dream that a baby is neglected, then it suggests that you are not paying enough attention to yourself. You are not utilizing your full potential.

Alternatively, this dream could represent your fears about your own children and your ability to protect and to provide for them.

To dream about a starving baby, represents your dependence on others. You are experiencing some deficiency in your life that needs immediate attention and gratification.

To dream of an extremely small baby, symbolizes your helplessness and your fears of letting others become aware of your vulnerabilities and incompetence. You may be afraid to ask for help and as a result tend to take matters into your own hands.

To see a dead baby in your dream, symbolizes the ending of something that was once a part of you.

To dream that you are dipping a baby in and out of water, signifies regression. You are regressing to a time where you had no worries and responsibilities. Alternatively, such a scenario is reminisce of when the baby is in the fetus and in its comfort zone. In fact, some expectant mothers even give birth in a pool, because the environment in the water mimics the environment in the uterus. It is less traumatic for the baby as it emerges into the world. So perhaps, the dream represents your search for your own comfort zone.

Baby Bottle

To see a baby bottle in your dream, represents your issues of dependency. You are relying too much on others. If you are drinking from a baby bottle, then the dream means that you need are emotionally immature. You need to grow up.

Babysitter

To dream that you are babysitting, suggests that you need to care for the child within yourself.

To see or call for a babysitter in your dream, indicates that you need to acknowledge and work on your inner child.

Back

To dream of your back, represents your attitudes, strengths, burdens and stance in the world. It may also relate to stress and pressure that someone is putting on you.

To see a naked back in your dream, symbolizes secrets that you may have kept from others or aspects of yourself that you have kept hidden and shielded away. Consider the phrase, "watch your back!"; this dream may be telling you to do just that. Traditionally, seeing a back in your dream, forewarns that you should not lend money to anyone. In particular, lending money to friends will cause a rift in your relationship.

To see a person turn their back on you, signifies that you will be deeply hurt as a result of envy and jealousy.

Backbone

Please See Spine.

Backpacking

To dream that you are backpacking, symbolizes your self-sufficiency and survival skills. You may be reflecting on all the obstacles and adversities that you have overcame.

Backstage

To dream that you are backstage, symbolizes opportunities and access. You need to make sure to take advantage of this limited time opportunity. Alternatively, the dream indicates that there are

17

aspects of yourself that you are reluctant to express or show. Or it may also mean that you need to look at some situation or problem from a new perspective.

Backward

To dream that you are walking or moving backwards, indicates that your current course of action may be counter-productive. Whatever you are looking for in life seems to be moving away from you. Thus, you may feel a sense of failure or belief that you are unable to achieve your goals and aspirations. On the other hand, moving backwards in your dream, indicate that you need to back off or retreat from a situation that you are currently facing in your waking life.

Backyard

To dream about your backyard, represents your childhood memories or your unconscious. Alternatively, dreaming of your backyard, refers to the secrets you are keeping. There are some aspects of your life which you want to keep hidden and out of the view of others. The dream also represents some aspect of your life that you have taken for granted. Consider also the phrase "not in my backyard." In other words, everything is okay as long as it does not happen to you or occur in your own home. The condition of the yard is also symbolic of how well you maintain and balance aspects of your life.

Bacon

To see bacon in your dream, symbolizes essentials, staples, and life's supply. It may also be a play on the common phase "being home the bacon" to refer to earning a living.

To see bacon that has gone rancid in your dream, suggests a forbidden situation.

Badge

To see or flash a badge in your dream, represents recognition of your position. You are held in high honor and prestige. You regard yourself highly. Alternatively, it signifies your need to belong and to be part of something.

Badger

To see a badger in your dream, signifies your persistence and final victory over your opponents. The dream may also be a pun on how you are badgering others or vice versa. Perhaps someone, especially someone of power is bothering you and giving you a difficult time.

Bag

To see a bag in your dream, represents the responsibilities that you carry. If the bag is ripped or torn, then it indicates that you are carrying a lot of burden. The symbol may be a metaphor for an "old bag" and refer to someone who is old.

To dream of a bag full of junk, symbolizes that you are burdened with worries and problems; you have to find a way on unloading some of this burden.

Bait

To see bait in your dream, suggests that you may be fishing for a deal or a compliment. It may also indicate your desire to lure or entice someone.

Baking

To dream that you are baking, represents your creative self and you ability to make things happen. If you are mixing ingredients together that you normally would not combine, then it suggests that you need to find a connection between two seemingly different things. Perhaps these things that seem incompatible may yield surprising but positive results.

Balance

To dream that you lose your balance, suggests that you are having difficulty weighing your options and choices in some situation.

Balance Beam

To dream that you are walking on a balance beam, indicates that there is a situation that requires your focus and full attention. Alternatively, the dream may be a metaphor for the various aspects that you are trying to balance in your life.

Balcony

To see or dream that you are on a balcony, refers to your desire to be seen and noticed. You are searching for prestige and higher status. It may also mean that you are on your way up the social ladder. If the balcony is clean, then it indicates that you are looked up to by others. If the balcony is old, then it suggests that your public image is in need of repair. Alternatively, the balcony could signify your ambivalence regarding a situation. You are feeling torn or undecided.

Bald

To dream that you are going bald, suggests a lack of self-esteem or worries about getting older. Alternatively, baldness symbolizes humility, purity, and personal sacrifice. You are at a stage in your life where you are confident in fully exposing yourself.

*Please See Also Hair.

Ball

To see or play with a ball in your dream, symbolizes completeness and wholeness. It may also indicate that you need to be more in tune with the inner child within. The dream may also be a metaphor for the testicles. Consider also the phrase, "he's got balls" to indicate guts and strength.

To dream that you are watching a ball game, indicates that you need to take more initiative. Your lack of action may stem from your shyness which you must overcome. Perhaps you are too overly self-conscious.

Ballerina

To dream that you are a ballerina, suggests that you are moving through the obstacles of your life effortlessly. You feel unrestricted. It is also a symbol of innocence, frailty, and vulnerability. Alternatively, you may feel unable to attain and measure up to society's ideals of beauty.

Balloon

To see balloons in your dream, indicate declining hopes and disappointments in your search for love. A situation in your life will take a turn downward. Balloons also represent arrogance and an inflated opinion of yourself.

To dream that you or someone is blowing up a balloon, represents your aspirations, goals and ambitions. You are experiencing renewed hope.

To see black balloons in your dream, symbolizes depression, especially if the balloons are descending.

To see an ascending balloon in your dream, signifies frustrating conditions in your life in which you are seeking to rise above. You are expressing a desire to escape. On a positive note, balloons symbolize celebration and festivities. You need to acknowledge your inner child.

To see a balloon pop in your dream, symbolizes an unrealized goal or dream. It may also represent the stresses in your life. The pressure may be starting to be too great for you to bear.

To see or dream that you are in a hot air balloon, suggests that it is time to overcome your depression. The dream may be a metaphor indicating that you are losing your ground or your foothold on some situation/problem. Alternatively, it represents the process of individuation and your quest to fulfill some spiritual needs. You feel the need to be elevated in someone's eyes.

Ballot

To see a ballot in your dream, represents a decision that needs to be made. If your name is on a ballot, then it indicates that you are seeking support, approval or acceptance.

Ballroom Dancing

To dream that you are ballroom dancing, indicates success in your endeavors. You have a positive outlook in life and are willing try anything and give it your all.

Baloney

*Please See Bologna.

Bamboo

To see bamboo in your dream, symbolizes trustworthiness, strength and resilience. You are able to easily bounce back from setbacks and disappointments in your life. Alternatively, it refers to strong ties/bonds and fair dealings.

To dream that the bamboo is soft or rotting, suggests that there is imbalance in your waking life.

Bananas

To see bananas in your dream, may be a metaphor for repressed sexual urges and desires. It is a phallic symbol and represents masculine sexuality.

To dream that you are eating bananas, indicate that your hard work will be met with little rewards or gains.

Band

To see a band or play with a band in your dream, represents a sense of community and belonging. The dream may also be a pun on banding together and need for cooperation/unity.

Bandages

To dream that you have bandages, indicate your need to heal. You may be feeling emotionally wounded and are trying to cover/shield your hurt from others. Consider where on the body was the bandage for more additional clues.

To dream that someone is throwing bandages at you, suggests that someone is causing you some emotional pain. You are hurting on the inside, but manage to keep a happy appearance on the outside.

Bandana

To see or wear a bandana in your dream, suggests that you need to look at issue or problem more objectively. You need to think through your options more carefully.

Bandit

To see or dream that you are a bandit, indicates primitive sexuality and primal lust.

Bank

To see a bank in your dream, denotes your desires for financial security. The dream may be trying to offer reassurance and that your fears of financial instability are unfounded.

To dream that you are robbing a bank, signifies that you are expending too much energy and are in danger of depleting your inner resources. Alternatively, it indicates that money that is due to you is being delayed.

Bankrupt

To dream that you are bankrupt, indicates that you need to start taking measures to protect yourself and your resources. You may be feeling emotionally drained or physically overworked. The dream may be a sign of depression. Alternatively, to dream that you are bankrupt, symbolizes feelings of insecurity.

Bar

To dream that you are at a public bar, signifies your desire to escape from the stresses of your daily life and retreat into a light-hearted environment where pleasure abounds. Alternatively, you are seeking acceptance in some aspect of your daily life. The dream may also be a pun on being "barred" from some place or something. You are feeling excluded or held back by circumstances beyond your control.

To see a metal bar in your dream, represents your own inner strength. You have the ability and tools to build a solid foundation and future. Alternatively, metal bars symbolize defiance and aggression.

Barbarian

To see or dream that you are a barbarian, represents the savage and instinctual aspect of your character. Perhaps you are being a little too rough or brash. Alternatively, the dream may also refer to your sexuality and your wild side.

Barbecue

To dream of a barbecue, refers to a minor issue or transformation occurring in your waking life.

To dream that you are barbecuing, symbolizes togetherness, relaxation, and ease.

Barbed Wire

To see barbed wire in your dream, represents difficulty in breaking through or getting your point across to someone.

To dream that you are caught in barbed wire, symbolizes oppression and confinement. You are feeling trapped and restricted in some relationship.

Barber

*Please See <u>Hairdresser.</u>

Barber's Pole

To see a barber's pole in your dream, indicates that you are contemplating a change in your life. Alternatively, the symbol represents some childhood memory or a piece of nostalgia.

Barbie Doll

To see a Barbie doll in your dream, represents society's ideals. You may feel that you are unable to meet the expectations of others. Alternatively, the Barbie doll refers to the desire to escape from daily responsibilities. It may serve to bring you back to your childhood where life was much simpler and more carefree.

Barefoot

To dream that you are barefoot, represents your playful attitudes and relaxed, carefree frame of mind. Alternatively, being barefoot indicates poverty, lack of mobility, or misunderstanding. You have low self-esteem and lack confidence in yourself. Or you may be dealing with issues concerning your self-identity. You are unprepared for what is ahead for you.

Bark

To hear barking in your dream, suggests that you are annoying those around you with grumpiness and fussiness. The dream may also be analogous to your tendency of barking orders at people, instead of asking or talking kindly. Alternatively, barking refers to unhappy and disgruntled companions.

Barn

To see a barn in your dream, signifies the feelings that are kept in your unconscious. There is a possibility that you may be holding back your instinctual action or natural urges.

Barrel

To see an empty barrel in your dream, signifies unfulfilled needs and emotional emptiness. If there is something inside the barrel, consider the significance of the contents. If you are putting a stopper into a barrel, then it suggests that you need to hold onto what you have. Perhaps you are feeling a little instable or insecure about your position or status in life.

Barrette

To see or wear a barrette in your dream, indicates that you are open to a new idea. Alternatively, you are ready to show the world a whole new you.

Barrier

To see a barrier in your dream, represents an obstacle to your emotional growth. You may feel hindered in fully expressing yourself. The dream may also indicate your resistance to change.

Baseball

To dream that you are attending a baseball game, represents contentment and peace of mind.

To dream that you are playing baseball, denotes your need to set goals and achieve them. It is time to stop goofing around and set your sights for the long term. Consider the significance of the position you are playing. Alternatively, playing baseball may be analogous to sexual foreplay as in getting to first, second, or third base on a date. The game of baseball has sexual innuendos, where the masculine aspects is depicted by the bat and the feminine aspects is depicted in the form of the ball or the ballpark.

To dream that you are on a baseball field, indicates that you need to pay attention to opportunities that are coming your way.

To see a baseball field under construction, refers to unresolved sexual issues.

Basement

To dream that you are in a basement, symbolizes your unconscious mind and intuition. The appearance of the basement is an indication of your unconscious state of mind and level of satisfaction. It represents primal urges, animalistic desires and basic needs. The dream may also be metaphor for "abasement" or being "debased". Are you feeling humbled or unworthy?

To dream that the basement is in disarray and messy, signifies some confusion in which you need to sort out. These are things that you have "stored" away or put aside in your mind because you do not know what to do with it or you do not have the time to deal with it. It may also represent your perceived faults and shortcomings.

Basket

To see a basket in your dream, symbolizes the womb and physical body. It also represents the things that you are holding onto. If the basket is full, then it denotes abundance and fertility.

Basketball

To dream that you are playing basketball, indicates teamwork and cooperation. There is a situation in your waking life where you will need the cooperation and assistance of others in order to achieve a common goal. Perhaps you are standing in the way of your own progress and need to ask for help.

To see a basketball in your dream, suggests that you need to make the first move. You also need to concentrate and focus on your goals.

Bath

To dream that you are taking a bath, signifies a cleansing of your outer and inner self. You are washing away the difficult times. This dream may also be symbolic of ridding yourself of old ideas, notions, opinions, and other negativities. Your dream may be pointing toward forgiveness and letting go.

To dream that you are bathing someone, suggests that you are seeking a closer connection with that person. It also points to your nurturing side.

Bathroom

To dream that you are in the bathroom, relates to your instinctual urges. You may be experiencing some burdens/feelings and need to "relieve yourself". Alternatively, a bathroom symbolizes purification and self-renewal. You need to cleanse yourself, both emotionally and psychologically.

To dream that you are in a public restroom with no stalls or that there are a lot of people around while you are trying to do your business, signifies your frustrations about getting enough privacy. You are always putting others ahead of your own needs. As a result, you are lacking a sense of personal space. Alternatively, the dream indicates that you are having difficulties letting go of old emotions. You are afraid that if you reveal these feelings, then others around you will judge and criticize you.

To dream that you are in a bathroom meant for the opposite sex, suggests that you are overstepping your boundaries. You have crossed the line in some situation.

To dream that you cannot find the bathroom or that you have difficulties finding one, indicates that you have difficulties in releasing and expressing your emotions. You are holding back your true feelings about something.

*Please Also See <u>Urination</u>.

Bathtub

To see or be in a bathtub in your dream, suggests a need for self-renewal and escape from everyday

23

problems. You need to rid yourself of the burdens that you have been carrying. Alternatively, it indicates your mood for love and pursuit of pleasure and relaxation.

To dream that you or someone has drowned in a bathtub, indicates that you are not as ready as you had thought you were in facing your fears and emotions. You are feeling overwhelmed in confronting your repressed emotions. You need to take things more slowly, instead of trying to dive right in.

Baton

To see or throw a baton in your dream, represents your need for self expression and recognition in a dramatic way. In particular, to see a police baton, symbolizes male sexuality or power.

Bats

To see a bat in your dream, symbolizes uncleanness, demons, and annoyances. Alternatively, bats represent rebirth and unrealized potential. You need to let go of old habits. Your current path is not compatible with your new growth and new goals. It may also indicate some unknown situation and how you are blindly entering into a situation or deal. You need to evaluate the facts more carefully. The dream may also been a pun on feeling "batty" or feeling crazy.

To dream of a white bat, signifies death of a family member. To dream of a black bat, signifies personal disaster.

To see a vampire bat in your dream, suggests that a person in your life may be draining your of self-confidence and/or your resources.

According to Chinese folklore, if you see five bats in your dream, then it symbolizes good health, longevity, pace, wealth, and happiness.

Battery

To see a battery in your dream, symbolizes life energy and vitality. If the battery is dead, then it suggests that you are emotionally exhausted or feeling low.

Battle

To be in or see a battle in your dream, suggests that you are overworked. You need to give yourself a break. There is a conflict between your rational thinking and your irrational impulses. Alternatively, it represents eroticism. You may be overly stimulated or you are trying to suppress your instinctual urges.

Beach

To see the beach in your dream, symbolizes the meeting between your two states of mind. The sand is symbolic of the rational and mental processes while the water signifies the irrational, unsteady, and emotional aspects of yourself. It is a place of transition between the physical/material and the spiritual.

To dream that you are on the beach and looking out toward the ocean, indicates unknown and major changes that are occurring in your life. Consider the state of the ocean, whether it is calm, pleasant, forbidding, etc.

To dream that you are looking toward the beach, suggests that you are returning to what is familiar to you. Alternatively, you may be adapting or accepting to the changes and circumstances in your life.

To dream that you are relaxing on a beach, signifies that the coming weeks will be calm and tranquil for you. Your stress will be alleviated and you will find peace of mind.

To dream that you are working on the beach, signifies a business project that will consume most of your time.

Beads

To see beads in your dream, indicate your tendency to please others and put their needs in front of your own. Alternatively, you have a need to strive for perfection.

To dream that you are stringing beads, suggests that you have laid the groundwork for your success. You will be recognized and/or rewarded for your achievements.

To dream that you are counting beads, symbolizes pleasure, calmness and joy.

Beaker

To see or use a beaker in you dream, signifies your need to integrate various aspects of your life together. Alternatively, the dream represents logic and objectivity. Perhaps you need to try looking at a problem from a completely different perspective.

Beanbag

To see or toss a beanbag in your dream, signifies a carefree or lackadaisical attitude.

Beanbag Chair

To see or sit on a beanbag chair, indicates temporary setbacks. You are not fully settled in your life.

Beanie Baby

To see a beanie baby in your dream, suggests that you are able to adapt to most situations. Consider the animal or the name of the beanie baby. The dream may have an underlying message or a pun.

Beans

To see or eat beans in your dream, signify your connection to your roots and to humanity. Consider what binds you to your community. Alternatively, beans are symbolic of the soul and of immortality. They also relate to fertility.

Bear

To see a bear in your dream, symbolizes independence, the cycle of life, death and renewal, and resurrection. You are undergoing a period of introspection and thinking. The dream may also be a pun on "bare". Perhaps you need to bare your soul and let everything out into the open.

To dream that you are being pursued or attacked by a bear, denotes aggression, overwhelming obstacles and competition. You may find yourself in a threatening situation or domineering relationship.

To see a polar bear in your dream, signifies a reawakening.

Beard

To see a long beard in your dream, is representative of old age and insight, and wisdom. If you dream that you have a beard, but you do not have on in real life, then the dream means that you are trying to conceal your true feelings. You are being deceptive about some matter. Alternatively, the dream represents your individualistic attitude. You do not care what others think or say about you.

If you are a woman and you dream of growing a beard, signifies the masculine aspect of your personality. You want to be more assertive and wield more power.

Beast

To see a beast in your dream, signifies foolishness and ignorance.

To see faceless beasts in your dream, indicate a situation you are refusing to see or confront, but are aware of it in some passive way. This dream also suggests that something in your life is bringing up feelings of fear and insecurities.

Beating

To dream that you are beaten, indicates that you need to make some fundamental changes to your character. You need to make some conscious adjustments and evaluations. Alternatively, it suggests that someone is pushing you beyond your limits.

To see others being beaten, suggests that some part of your life is out of balance.

To dream that you are beating someone, indicates that you are shoving your own views and opinions on others.

Beauty Contest

Please See Pageant.

Beaver

To see a beaver in your dream symbolizes energy, ambition and productivity. It is time to put your ideas into action. Hard work is necessary to achieve your own goals.

Bed

To see your bed in your dream, represents your intimate self and discovery of your sexuality. If you are sleeping in your own bed, then it denotes security and restoration of your mind. You may be looking for domestic bliss, for peace or for some form of escape. If you are waking up in a different and/or unknown bed, then it represents the consequences of the decisions you have made. The dream may also be a pun on the completion of a project and "putting it to bed." Consider the condition of the bed. If the bed is made, then it symbolizes security. If the bed is unmade, then it indicates that certain secrets will soon be exposed or revealed. Or that you are exhibiting some carelessness in your sexual behavior.

To dream that you are searching for a bed, suggests that you are having difficulties acknowledging your intimate self. You may be feeling inhibited in expressing your sexuality. Alternatively, it may mean that you are looking for domestic security and happiness. Or you just need more sleep.

To dream that you are floating or lifting up into the air from your bed, suggests that you are feeling helpless and disconnected from those around you. Your ideas may be alienating people. You might need to tone down your personality a bit.

Bed Wetting

To dream that you wet the bed, represents a lack of control in your life. You are experiencing a lot of anxieties. You may be concerned with not being accepted because of your beliefs or behaviors. The dream may also point to issues in your sexual relationships or sexuality.

Bedbugs

To dream of bedbugs, indicate that you are uneasy or annoyed about some situation or relationship. You are keeping these negative feelings to yourself instead of verbalizing it.

Bedroom

To dream that you are in the bedroom, signifies aspects of

yourself that you keep private and hidden. It is also indicative of your sexual nature and intimate relations.

Beef

To see or eat beef in your dream, signifies your animal instinct and animalistic energy. The dream may also be a pun on your "beef" or grudge with someone. Are you trying to pick a fight?

Beehive

To see a beehive in your dream, denotes that there are many opportunities for you to get ahead in life. Don't let them escape from your grasp. The beehive symbolizes hard work and the importance of teamwork. A promotion may be in store for you.

To see an empty beehive, signifies sorrow over love affairs and financial losses.

To dream of destroying a beehive, symbolizes losses and bad luck.

Beer

To see or drink beer in your dream, represents happiness, fogginess, or inspiration. It also indicates that you have quite a social life.

*Please Also See <u>Alcohol</u>.

Bees

To see bees in your dream, symbolize wealth, good luck, harmony, creativity and bliss. Bees are also symbolic of hard work and industry as represented by the common phrase "busy as a bee." Your hard work will pay off in the end with sweet results. Alternatively, the dream represents the things that are happening in your life or something that is buzzing with activity. Is there a lot going on in your life?

To dream that you are stung by a bee, indicates that you have been wronged. Maybe you have been hurt by some stinging remark.

Beetle

To see a beetle in your dream, indicates that some destructive influences may be at work in your waking life. You may also feel that your values and beliefs are being compromised. If you dream that beetles are crawling all over you, then it indicates that a lot of minor issues are bugging you.

Beets

To see or eat beets in your dream, symbolize success and abundance. You are reaping the benefits of your hard work.

Beg

To dream that you are begging for something, represents your unhappiness and dissatisfaction with your current waking situation. You are afraid to accept help or do not want to admit that you need help.

Beggar

To see or dream that you are a beggar, represents your sense of insecurity and lack of self-worth. You feel that you are undeserving. Alternatively, the dream may be telling you that "beggars can't be choosers". Perhaps you are being too picky about something that you should not be picky about.

To dream that you are helping a beggar, indicates that you will overcome your hardships and inadequacies.

Behind

To dream that you are behind someone, suggests that you are offering your support and encouragement for someone.

27

Alternatively, it refers to emerging unconscious thoughts and feelings.

To dream that you are left behind, represents feelings of rejection or not fitting into a group. It may also highlight fears of not being able to keep up. You are questioning your abilities and/or may not be utilizing your full potential. If you left something or someone behind, then it indicates that you are ready to let go of the past and move forward.

Beige

Beige represents the basics, the essentials and the barest form. It may also indicate your neutral or unbiased position in some matter.

Belch

*Please See <u>Burp.</u>

Bell Pepper

To see or eat a bell pepper in your dream, represents your tenacity, your defense mechanism and your ability to put up a fight. In general, it is a positive symbol indicating a change for the better. Consider the color of the bell pepper. If it is green, then it suggests that you are still feeling fresh and energetic about your fight. If it is red, then it indicates that there is anger behind your wall of defense. If the bell pepper is yellow, then it means that you are using your energy wisely.

Bells

To hear a bell in your dream, represents a warning or a call to order. The ringing of the bell signals the beginning of something new. It may also be a way for your unconscious to prepare you for whatever is happening next. If the bell rings and never stops, then it suggests that you are experiencing extreme anxiety.

To see a silver bell in your dream, means that you are trying to keep negative forces at bay. Alternatively, it signals the holidays.

Belly

To see your belly in your dream, indicates that your are processing and integrating your ideas and feelings from the unconscious to the conscious level. The belly symbolically holds repressed emotions and unexpressed feelings. Your dream may also be telling you to trust your gut feeling and intuition.

To see a pregnant belly, represents emotions that are due to come to the surface. They can no longer remain suppressed.

To dream that you are stroking or touching a belly, indicates that you are coming to terms with certain feelings. You are slowly confronting and acknowledging your repressed emotions.

To dream that you or someone has a belly piercing, denotes your deep connection with your mother. Perhaps the dream is telling you to reconnect with your mother or that you need to be in touch with your maternal instincts.

Belly Button

*Please See <u>Navel.</u>

Below

To see something below you in your dream, indicates that you are looking down on others. You feel that you are too good for someone or for a situation. Alternatively, the dream suggests that you are delving into your unconscious.

Belt

To see a belt in your dream, signifies a constricted flow of life energy and issues of morality. You may be feeling conflicted between what you think (your intellectual reasoning) and what you feel (your instinctual nature). Alternatively, a belt may symbolize punishment and discipline.

Bench

To see or sit on a bench, signifies your tendency to procrastinate and put things aside. It also suggests that you often take on a passive role instead taking initiative.

Beret

To see or wear a beret in your dream, symbolizes the military. It could mean either peace or war. Consider the color of the beret for additional significance. In particular, if the beret is green or red, then it signifies successful strategy in battle.

Berries

To see or eat berries in your dream, indicate that you will be involved with a fulfilling relationship or experience. In particular, if the berries are poisonous, then it suggests that you are in danger of becoming negatively influenced by something or someone.

Bet

To dream that you are making a bet, suggests that you are taking a risk in a relationship or work situation which may not be such a wise choice. Use your judgment and proceed cautiously.

Betrayal

To dream that you have been betrayed, represents your suspicions about a particular person, relationship or situation. This dream often occurs when you are having feelings of insecurity and are faced with major commitments in your life at the same time.

To dream that someone has betrayed you, indicates self-pity. You are feeling sorry for yourself.

Beverage

To drink a beverage in your dream, represents your ability to understand and take in a new idea or concept. The dream may be analogous to your thirst for knowledge. Consider the type of beverage for additional meaning.

Bible

To see or read the bible in your dream, symbolizes truth, belief, inspiration and knowledge. You are seeking some form of comfort. The bible may also refer to your fundamental belief system. Perhaps you need to turn to the bible more.

To buy a bible in your dream, suggests that you are trying to justify your actions.

Bicycle

To dream that you are riding a bicycle, signifies your desires to attain a balance in your life. You need to balance work and pleasure in order to succeed in your current undertakings. If you have difficulties riding the bicycle, then it suggests that you are experiencing anxieties about making it on your own.

To see a bicycle in your dream, indicates that you need to devote time to leisurely pursuits and recreation.

To dream that you are riding tandem in a bicycle, suggests that you are more accepting with aspects of yourself or of your partner that you have previously rejected.

Big

To dream that someone or something is bigger than normal, indicates that you either have an inflated opinion of yourself or of someone. You may be expressing a desire to be more dominant in some situation or relationship.

To see a big figure in your dream, represents authority and power.

Bigfoot

To see bigfoot in your dream, symbolizes the unknown and the unconscious. Alternatively, it suggests that you are misrepresenting yourself in some way or that you are misleading others.

To see or drive a bigfoot truck in your dream, indicates that you have total control over the path that your life is taking. You do not let anybody stand in your way, especially toward your goals.

Billboard

To see a billboard in your dream, is a sign or message that you need to take note of in your path toward your goals. Consider what advice the billboard is trying to convey to you.

Bills

To see bills in your dream, suggest that your mind is preoccupied with financial and money matters. You may be feeling overwhelmed with life's demands.

To receive a bill in your dream, represents something that you have done is now costing you in some way or other.

Binder

To see a binder in your dream, represents things that you need to keep track and stay on top of. It may indicate emotions and issues that you have overlooked in your waking hours. Consider the contents inside the binder. Alternatively, the dream may be a pun on "binding" something

together. Perhaps you need to integrate, incorporate or combine certain qualities within yourself. Or the binder could also symbolize your obligations and responsibilities.

Bingo

To see or play bingo in your dream, symbolizes a sudden revelation. Pay special attention to the dream content as there is something significant and profound that you have learned or discovered about yourself.

Binoculars

To dream that you are looking through a pair of binoculars, suggests that you need to take a long and close look at a situation. You need to carefully evaluate your choices and decision.

Bird

To see birds in your dream, symbolize your goals, aspirations and hopes. To dream of chirping and/or flying birds, represent joy, harmony, ecstasy, balance, and love. It denotes a sunny outlook in life. You are experiencing spiritual freedom and psychological liberation. It is almost as if a weight has been lifted off your shoulders.

To dream of dead or dying birds, indicates disappointments. You will find yourself worrying over problems that are nagging on your mind.

To see bird eggs in your dream, symbolize money.

To see birds hatching in your dream, symbolize delayed success.

To see a bird nest in your dream, symbolizes independence, refuge and security. You need something to fall back on. Alternatively, it may signify a prosperous endeavor, new opportunities, and fortune.

Bird Of Paradise

To see a bird of paradise in your dream, represents your hard shell and cold exterior. You need to be more receptive and open yourself to love. Alternatively, the dream symbolizes relaxation. It is time for a vacation.

Birth

To dream of giving birth or see someone else giving birth, suggests that you are giving birth to a new idea or project. It also represents a new attitude, fresh beginnings or a major event. Alternatively, the dream may be calling attention to your inner child and the potential for you to grow. A more direct interpretation of this dream, may represent your desires/ anxieties of giving birth or the anticipation for such an event to occur.

To dream that you are giving birth to a non-human creature, signifies your overwhelming (and unfounded) fear in the health of your baby. You are overly concerned that your baby may have birth defects. This type of dream is common in expectant mothers in their second trimester. If you are not expecting, then it refers to your fear in the outcome of some decision or project. You are trying to overcome difficulties in your life and achieve inner development.

In particular, if you dream that you are giving birth to a monster, then it implies that your inner creative energy has yet to blossom and grow into expression. You may have some hesitation in releasing this "monster" for fear that others will judge you or that they will not accept your ideals.

To dream that the mother dies during birth, represents transformation. The dream represents the ending of one thing (death) and the new beginning of another thing (birth). You may be making life changes or getting rid of your old habits and ways.

*Please See Also Pregnant.

Birthday

To dream about your birthday, denotes acceptance of yourself. You are celebrating who you are and coming to terms with who you are as a person. Alternatively, the dream may mean you are afraid of getting old.

To dream that your birthday was forgotten, suggests that you are feeling lonely, overshadowed, and underappreciated.

Bison

*Please See Buffalo.

Bites

To see a bite in your dream, forewarns of danger from someone who wish you harm, either physical or financial. Be careful of people who surround you.

To dream that you are being bitten, represents your vulnerability regarding some unresolved issues or emotions. You may be pestered by a problem or obstacle. The dream may also be a metaphor indicating that you have bitten off more than you chew. Perhaps you have too much to handle.

To dream that you are being bitten by a vampire, signifies your need to shut out a person in your life who has been using you. It is time to open your eyes and stand up for yourself. Do not let yourself be manipulated and played for a fool.

To dream of biting someone in your dream, signifies the pressure you are putting on some people causing them great distress. You may have unexpressed, perhaps even childish, feelings of anger or resentment that need to be recognized. This dream is a message for you to lighten up and alleviate the stress that you are putting on others.

Black

Black symbolizes the unknown, the unconscious, danger, mystery, darkness, death, mourning, rejection, hate or malice. The color invites you to delve deeper in your unconscious in order to gain a better understanding of yourself. It also signifies a lack of love and lack of support. More positively, black represents potential and possibilities. It is like a clean or blank slate.

If the feeling in the dream is one of joy, then blackness could imply hidden spirituality and divine qualities.

To dream in black and white, suggests that you need to be more objective in formulating your decisions. You may be a little too unyielding in your thought process and thus need to find some sort of balance between two opposing views. Consider the views and opinions of others. Alternatively, black and white dreams is a sign of depression or sadness. You may feel that there is not enough excitement in your life.

Black Hole

To see the black hole in your dream, indicates that there is no turning back on a decision that you have made. You may be feeling stuck in a situation. Alternatively, the hole symbolizes the unconscious and the unknown.

Blackboard

*Please See <u>Chalkboard.</u>

Blackmail

To dream that you are blackmailing someone, indicates your issues with power and domination. You may be letting your competitive nature get the best of you.

To dream that you are being blackmailed, represents inner weaknesses and helplessness. You may not have confidence in your own ability. It may also be a pun on a "black male" you may know in your life.

Blackout

To dream that there is a blackout, indicates your lack of insight and perspective on a situation. You may be feeling frustrated or experiencing failure in some work that you are attempting. The blackout may also symbolize ignorance, the unconscious, evil, death, or fear of the unknown.

Blanket

To see a blanket in your dream, symbolizes warmth, love, security and protection. You may be seeking for some form of shelter from the outside world. Consider also how your dream may be calling attention to a "cover-up" in some situation or circumstance in your waking life.

To dream that you are wrapped in a blanket, indicates your fear of the unknown. You may feel some sort of threat/chaos or sense some coldness from those around you.

To dream that you are covering or wrapping someone in a blanket, indicates your desire to care for that person.

Bleach

To see or use bleach in your dream, signifies a time of healing and cleansing. You are ready to mend past hurts and resolve any unexpressed emotions.

Blender

To see a blender in your dream, symbolizes your ability to blend various ideas into a harmonious whole.

Blind

To dream that you are blind, represents your refusal to see the truth or your lack of awareness to a problem. Perhaps you are rejecting something about yourself or your situation. Are you refusing to see any other point of view except your own? Consider the pun, "turning a blind eye".

To see a blind person in your dream, suggests that you are letting opportunities pass you by.

Blinking

To dream that you are blinking, indicates that there is something you fear in seeing. You are refusing to see the obvious.

Blister

To dream that you have a blister, indicates that some minor annoyance or problem is draining your energy and time. Consider how you may have gotten the blister. If you got the blister from manual and hard labor, then it indicates that you need to put forth more effort in order to overcome your little problems. To dream that you got the blister from a burn, suggests an emotional or relational problem.

Where the blister is located is also significant. If the blister is on you hand, then it suggests that you are having issues related to power and competency. If the blister is on your face, then it indicates issues related to your identity, self-image, and self-identity.

Blizzard

To dream about a blizzard, suggests that you are feeling emotionally cold and frigid. You feel excluded and left out. It may indicate a lack of love and the absence of warmth within your own family circle.

Blocks

To see a block or blocks in your dream, represent obstacles that you need to overcome. These are things that try to hinder you from achieving your goals. Alternatively, it symbolizes a vision and making something out of nothing.

Blog

To read or write a blog in your dream, suggests that you are trying to change or rewrite the past to suit your own needs. Consider what is written in the journal and how it is similar or dissimilar to actual events in your waking life. Alternatively, it symbolic of some memory or something that you need to always remember.

To dream that someone is reading your blog, indicates your popularity. You are experiencing life to the fullest.

Blood

To see blood in your dream, represents life, love, and passion as well as disappointments. If you see the word "blood" written in your dream, then it may refer to some situation in your life that is permanent and cannot be changed. If something else is written in blood, then it represents the energy you have put into a project. You have invested so much effort into something that you are not willing to give it up.

To dream that you are bleeding or losing blood, signifies that you are suffering from exhaustion or that you are feeling emotionally drained. It may also denote bitter confrontations between you and your friends. Your past actions has come back to haunt you. Women often dream of blood or of someone bleeding, shortly before or during their periods or while they are pregnant.

To dream that others are bleeding, signifies an emotional cry for help.

To dream that you are drinking blood, indicates that you have a fresh burst of vitality and power.

To dream that you are giving or donating blood, suggests that you are feeling physically drained due to stress.

Blow Dry

To dream that you are blow drying your hair, suggests that you are clearing out your thoughts and getting some fresh ideas. It may also be a pun on something that blows your mind.

Blue

Blue represents truth, wisdom, heaven, eternity, devotion, tranquility, loyalty and openness. Perhaps you are expressing a desire to get away. The presence of this color in your dream, may symbolize your spiritual guide and your optimism of the future. You have clarity of mind. Alternatively, the color blue may also be a metaphor for "being blue" and feeling sad.

If you are wearing light blue in your dream, then it symbolizes your creativity. You like to pace yourself in whatever you are doing.

Blueprint

To see a blueprint in your dream, indicates that you need to pay closer attention at the details before proceeding forward with some plan or relationship. It may also mean that you are in the process of going through some inner changes in your life. You are working on expanding your way of thinking.

Blurry

To have a blurry dream, indicates that there is something you are not confronting or are refusing to see. Life may be passing you by if you do not participate in it. It also represents secrets and confusion. Perhaps you think that someone is trying to keep something from you.

Blush

To dream that you are wearing blush, indicates that you want to be more expressive and loving. Alternatively, the dream may be highlighting an embarrassing situation.

Boar

To see a boar in your dream, indicates that you need to look inside to find the answers and secrets about yourself and the people around you. The dream may also be a pun on " a bore" or something or someone that is "boring".

Boat

To dream that you are in or see a boat, signifies your ability to cope with and express your emotions. Pay particular attention to the condition and state of the waters, whether it is calm or violent, clear or murky, etc. Are you "smooth sailing"? Alternatively, you may be ready to confront your unconscious and unknown aspects of yourself. The dream could be telling you not to rock the boat and to stay out of harm's way.

To dream that you are trying to jump off a boat, suggests that you want to confront those difficult emotions and approach your problems head on.

Bobble Head

To see a bobble head in your dream, represents your tendency to go along with what other people do or say. You need to start thinking for yourself. Alternatively, the bobble head indicates indecision.

Body

To dream about your own body, signifies your level of self-worth and self-esteem. Often times, these qualities are dependent on your physical appearance or how your perceive yourself. The dream body also reflects your conscious identity or is representative of your state of health.

Body Bag

To see a body bag in your dream, indicates that you are feeling distant or disconnected. You are out of touch.

Body Builder

To see a body builder in your dream, suggests that you need to develop a better sense of power or be more flexible in some situation.

To dream that you are a body builder, means that you are feeling empowered.

Body Paint

To dream that you are covered in body paint, represents acceptance of yourself. You are proud of your body.

Body Piercing

*Please See Piercing.

Bodyguard

To dream that you have a bodyguard, indicates that you are uneasy about some situation in your waking life. You are feeling insecure, either physically or emotionally. Perhaps you have been hurt recently.

To dream that you are a bodyguard, represents your desire to protect others from emotional hurt. It highlights your sympathetic and nurturing side.

Boiling

To dream that something is boiling, represents transformation and/or sacrifice. There is something that you need to get down to the heart of. In particular to dream that water is boiling, suggests that you are expressing some emotional turmoil. It also may mean that feelings from your unconscious are surfacing and ready to be acknowledged.

Bologna

To eat bologna in your dream, indicates financial insecurities. Alternatively, the dream may be a pun on something that is phony or nonsense.

Bolt

To see a bolt in your dream, suggests that you are protecting yourself from difficult emotions and experiences. The dream may also be a pun on your tendency or desire to flee from a situation.

Bomb

To see a bomb in your dream, indicates that you are going through a potentially explosive situation in your waking life. The bomb could represent repressed desires and unexpressed emotions that are on the verge of exploding or bursting if not dealt with soon.

To dream that you are unable to disarm a bomb, suggests that your anger is out of control.

To dream of a bomb threat, suggests that you are experiencing some inner anger and/or pressures which are on the verge of exploding into violence.

Bondage

To dream that you are in bondage, signifies that aspects of your emotions and/or character are too tightly controlled or that are repressed. You may be restricting your need for self-expression or feel that you are a prisoner of your circumstances.

In a sexual sense, dreams of bondage represents your desires to be more sexually submissive. Perhaps you have not acknowledged these sexual passions.

Bones

To see bones in your dream, represent the discovery of your personal, family, or cultural secrets. It is also symbolic of your underlying strengths that you have not yet recognized. Consider the symbolism of getting to the "bare bones" or the significance of "having a bone to pick with someone."

To dream of broken bones, represents the discovery or realization that that there is a weakness in your plans or in your thinking. Your dream may call for your immediate attention to a particular situation or relationship.

To see a dog eating or chewing a bone, represents your basic desires and instincts.

Bonfire

To see a bonfire in your dream, suggests that you need to find a new path and set forth toward a different goal. It is time to express yourself more freely and let go of the old outdated ways of thinking.

Bonsai Tree

To see a bonsai tree in your dream, indicates the limitations of your own conscious mind. You need to consider what your instincts are telling you.

Booing

To hear booing or dream that you are being booed, indicates that you are seeking approval and affirmation from others. Alternatively, you may find yourself in an embarrassing or shameful situation.

Books

To see books in your dream, indicate calmness. You are moving toward your goals at a slow and steady pace. Books also symbolize knowledge, intellect, information and wisdom. In particular, to see an open book in your dream, means that you are able to grasp new ideas with ease. If the book is closed, then it represents your allure and mysteriousness. Consider the type of book for additional clues. The dream may represent your calling into a specific field of work or an area that you need to devote more study to. Alternatively, the dream could be telling you not to judge a book by its cover.

To see dusty books in your dream, denotes forgotten knowledge or previous "chapters" of your life.

To see children's books in your dream, symbolize memories from your own childhood. It may also suggest your desire to escape from reality and retreat into some fantasy world.

To see a satanic book in your dream, represents your one-sided way of thinking and looking at things. You are trying to denounce any responsibility in your actions and are putting forth as little effort as possible.

Boomerang

To see or throw a boomerang in your dream, indicates that what you do to others will come back to you, whether it is positive or negative.

Booster Cables

To see or use booster cables in your dream, suggests that you need to get a jumpstart on your goals. Stop wasting your life away and start getting a move on.

Boot Camp

To dream that you are in a boot camp, represents your need for discipline and rigid rules. You need to have a better focus on your goals. If you have been through boot camp, then the dream may represent the feelings you were going through at the time. Something in your current life is triggering those similar feelings. Alternatively, the dream may represent your need for a new start or fresh beginning.

Boots

To see or dream that you are wearing boots, refers to the power in your movement and the boldness of your position. You are taking a firm stance. The dream may also be a metaphor that you are getting the boot. Are you getting kicked out somewhere?

Borrow

To dream that you are borrowing something, suggests that you need to let go of your pride. It is okay to ask for help and lean on the support of friends and family. Alternatively, the dream indicates that you need to incorporate a certain quality into your own life that you are not utilizing currently.

Boss

To see your boss in your dream, represents the bossy or authoritative side of your own personality. Your boss may reveal self-confidence and the assertive aspect of yourself. It is telling of your issues of control and authority. Alternatively, to see your boss in your dream may indicate your over-involvement or obsession with your work. Negatively, the boss in your dream may symbolize your limitations and lack of freedom/originality.

To dream that you are afraid of your boss, indicates your fear of authority. You may feel that someone else is running your life or dictating what you can and can not do.

Consider also the relationship you have with your boss. This may provide clues to work-related stress or issues that need to be resolved.

Bottle

To see a bottle in your dream, indicates that you are pushing your feelings back inside, rather than expressing them. The contents of the bottle represent the nature of the emotions. A bottle of champagne shows your need to socialize, while a bottle of poison signifies evil thoughts and a wine bottle symbolize sexuality.

To see an empty bottle, denotes that you have exhausted your inner resources. You may be feeling drained and empty inside.

Bow

To see or tie a bow in your dream, symbolizes femininity. Alternatively, the bow can stand for a social cause. Consider the color the bow for additional significance.

To see an archer's bow in your dream, refers to the pursuit and accomplishment of your goals.

Bow And Arrow

To see a bow and arrow in your dream, represents a combination of female and male energies. It may refer to your libido or some sexual energy/desire. Alternatively, it symbolizes anger, aggression, or tension. This dream symbol may also be a metaphor that you are aiming for perfection.

Bowel Movement

To dream that you have a bowel movement, signifies that you are successfully getting rid of your old habits/ways and thinking patterns. It is usually analogous to the release of strong emotions, such as anger or hatred.

To dream that you have a bowel movement in a public place, suggests that you are expressing regret about something that you said. You may have spoken your mind a little too loudly.

*See Constipation or Diarrhea.

Bowl

To see a bowl in your dream, symbolizes the womb and sense of security. Consider the condition of the bowl and how it is treated or handled in the dream. This may offer clues as to how you feel you are being treated in a particular relationship.

Bowling

To dream that you are bowling, represents the strikes, hits, and misses in your life. If you are bowling a bad game, then you may be expressing some regrets. If you are bowling strike after strike, then it suggests that you are on your way toward a successful future. The dream may also be a pun on your striking performance and/or stellar ability.

To dream that you bowl a gutter ball, suggests that you are stuck in a rut and need to make some changes of where your life is headed.

Alternatively, bowling and bowling alleys may also be a metaphor for sexual conquest. Consider the sexual innuendos that are at play in the bowling alley. The pins and bowling balls can be viewed as masculine symbols. The pin deck is symbolic of the womb or vagina (as is with any dark receptacle like caves, bowls, containers, etc.).

Box

To see a box in your dream, signifies your instinctual nature and destructive impulses. Alternatively, you may be trying to preserve and protect some aspect of yourself. The box may also symbolize your limitations and restrictions. Consider the pun of "being boxed in".

To dream that you are opening a box, indicates an aspect of yourself that was once hidden is now being revealed. It symbolizes self discovery. Consider your feelings as you open the box. If opening the box fills you will fear, you may be uncovering aspects of yourself that cause you to feel anxious.

Boxing

To watch boxing or dream that you are a boxer, suggests that you are experiencing some internal struggle or conflict. The dream may also be a pun on "boxing" things up. It suggests that you are limiting yourself and your goals/ideas. It may also indicate that you keep your emotions inside.

Boy

If you are female and dream that you see or are a boy, then it indicates that you are developing the masculine aspects of character. Alternatively, it may represent your feelings about a real-life boy who is important and significant to you. You may have a crush on this boy and your waking thoughts of him has carried over into the dream world. Your motherly instincts may be taking over.

If you are an adult male and dream that you see or are a boy, then it suggests your playful, innocent, childlike nature. Alternatively, it can symbolize the immature aspects of yourself that still needs to grow. Your inner child may be trying to draw your attention to parts of yourself that you need to recognize and acknowledge.

Boy Scout

Your own experience as a boy scout will definitely affect this dream symbol. If you were never a boy scout and dream that you are, then it signifies your commitment and discipline toward some task. The dream may emphasize a sense of community, belonging, and helpfulness.

To see a boy scout in your dream, denotes that you or someone else has displayed exemplary behavior. You will gain the ranks necessary to achieve your goals and success.

Boyfriend

To see your boyfriend in your dream, represents your waking relationship with him and how you feel about him.

To dream that your boyfriend is dead, indicates that something in your own Self that is no longer functional and is "dead". You are not being allowed to fully express yourself. It is also symbolic of your own relationship with that person. Perhaps you need to let go of this relationship.

If your boyfriend is away and your dreams of him involve a lot of touching, then it signifies how much you are missing his presence and having him nearby. The dream is telling you not to take the day to day things for granted. Learn to cherish the smaller things in life.

To dream that your boyfriend tells you that he is gay or that he doesn't love your anymore, represents your own insecurities with the relationship. It may also mean that the relationship is moving to a new level to which you are expressing some anxiety and fears about the changing situation. You may feel left out it in his life or that you are unable to share in all his experiences. It boils down to trust and communication.

Bra

To dream that you are wearing a bra, signifies support and protection. Perhaps you need to have your spirits uplifted. Alternatively, it may represent your nurturing side and maternal feelings.

To dream that you are not wearing a bra, indicates that you have no discipline or control. Alternative, it may reflect your sexual nature.

Bracelet

To see or wear a bracelet in your dream, refers to an expression of deep passion and fire. The dream also highlights your need to reach out to others. It is a sign that you need to rekindle old friendships and to call up an old friend that you haven't heard from in awhile.

To see a broken bracelet in your dream, suggests that you tend to sacrifice your own comfort and happiness for others.

Braces

To dream that you have braces, indicates your brashness and critics of others. You should not be so quick to criticize. You need to stop talking too much and listen to what others have to say. The dream may also be a pun on "brace yourself".

Brain

To dream of your brain, suggests that you are under severe intellectual stress. You need to put your problem-solving abilities to use. Alternatively, it implies that your ideas are not receiving enough attention and validation. You are concerned that your knowledge and teachings are not be transmitted clearly.

To dream that you are undergoing brain surgery, indicates that you need to rethink some important issue. You need to change your way of thinking and put aside any misconceived notions you have.

Brainwash

To dream that you are being brainwashed, suggests that you need to think for yourself. Stand up for yourself and do not let others tell you what to do.

Brakes

To dream that you are applying your brakes, signifies that you should slow down in your business and/or personal affairs. You have been living on the fast lane and you need to take it easy.

To dream that your brakes failed, forewarns that you lack stability in your life. Now is not the time to take risks. Your life is out of control and you need to make some significant changes. It may also not a bad idea to check out the brakes in your car, as you mind might have picked up subtle cues and is manifesting the problem in your dream.

Bread

To see bread in your dream, represents the basic needs of life. Bread may signify the positive qualities and great things you have learned on your journey of life. Alternatively, it suggests that you need to rise above the situation or rise for the occasion.

Break

To dream that you break something, indicates that changes are ahead for you. You need to "break" away from some situation and change the direction that your life is headed in. Alternatively, to break something suggests that you need to take things slower as in "take a break". Or the dream may be a pun on being broke. Are money matters weighing on your mind?

To dream that objects around you are breaking, suggests that you are under tremendous stress. The dream could be a metaphor that you are literally at your breaking point.

Break-Up

To dream that you break up with your significant other, indicates that there is something in your life that you need to let go no matter how hard it may be.

To dream that your boyfriend or girlfriend is breaking up with you, indicates that your relationship is moving to the next level. In a way, it is an end to something; you are leaving some past behind. At the same time, it is the start of something new or better. It is important to remember that such a dream is not an omen that the relationship is not working out. As a relationship evolves and grows, it also changes.

To dream that you did not break up with your boyfriend or girlfriend, suggests that you are still in denial about the break-up. Your mind many not have accepted the notion that the relationship is over.

Breakfast

To dream about breakfast, indicates the start of a new project or the beginning of a new stage in your life. Alternatively, your mind may already be thinking ahead on what to make for breakfast in the morning. It is not uncommon for your fleeting thoughts to be incorporated into your dream.

Breast Feeding

To dream that you are breast feeding, symbolizes tenderness, love, nurturance, and motherly love. Good things will be at your grasp. Alternatively, the dream suggests that you need to be careful in who you confide in.

Breasts

To see breasts in your dream, symbolize primal nourishment and your need to be nursed and care for. The breasts represent motherhood, nurturance, and infantile dependency. Alternatively, breasts indicate sexual arousal and raw energy.

Seeing naked breasts can also denote a feeling of exposure and invasion of privacy. In particular, for a woman, the dream may indicate anxieties about becoming a woman/mother.

Breath

To dream that you are trying to catch your breath or that you are out of breath, indicates that you are experiencing some anxiety, tension, or fear concerning a new situation in your waking life.

To dream that you have bad breath, suggests that you are feeling enclosed or crowded in. Perhaps someone is invading your personal space.

To dream that you are holding your breath, indicates your stubborn state of mind. Your views are too one-sided. The dream is telling you to be more open to the opinions of others.

Breathalyzer Test

To dream that you are being administered a breathalyzer test, indicates that your misdeeds or bad behavior will catch up with you. The dream may be telling you to slow down.

Brick

To see a brick in your dream, represents your individual ideas and thoughts. Experience and/or heartbreak may have hardened you.

To dream that you are building a brick wall, signifies a wall that you are putting up to protect yourself against hurt. You are trying to isolate yourself. Alternatively, a brick may also indicate that you may be hard on the outside but still sensitive on the inside.

Bride

To see a bride in your dream, symbolizes a union or partnership.

To dream that the bride is shot at her wedding, suggests that a feminine aspect of yourself has come to an abrupt end.

If you are single and dream that you are a bride, represents your desires for marriage. Alternatively, it may represent the most feminine

41

qualities about yourself. The dream may also symbolize purity and virginal qualities.

Bridesmaid

To dream that you are a bridesmaid, signifies a looming romance. Also consider the old adage "always a bridesmaid, never a bride". You could be expressing your desire to be in a committed relationship.

Bridge

To dream that you are crossing a bridge, signifies an important decision or a critical junction in your life. This decision will prove to be a positive change filled with prosperity and wealth in the horizon. Bridges represent a transitional period in your life where you will be moving on to a new stage. If the bridge is over water, then it suggests that your transition will be an emotional one. If you fall off the bridge and into the water, then the dream indicates that you are letting your emotions hold you back and prevent you from moving forward. Alternatively, the bridge may indicate that you are trying to "bridge" or connect two things together.

To dream of a run-down bridge, indicates that you should not contemplate any major changes in your life at this time.

To see a bridge collapse in your dream, implies that you have let an important opportunity pass you by.

Briefcase

To see or carry a briefcase in your dream, represents your level or preparedness in some situation or circumstance. It also refers to your concerns and worries about work and travel.

Bright

To dream that something is bright, represents divinity, a higher consciousness, and spirituality. You need to show your honor toward an important an person or situation. The dream may also be a metaphor for intellect and someone who is smart. If your dream is particularly bright and vivid, then it could indicate a prophetic or epic dream.

If the brightness is blinding, then it suggests that you are not paying attention to some new insights.

Broccoli

To see or eat broccoli in your dream, suggests that you are in need of spiritual nourishment. Or it could just mean that you are lacking a particular nutrient. You need to eat a more well balanced diet. Alternatively, the dream indicates that you are putting up your defenses about a situation.

Broom

To see a broom in your dream, denotes that it is time to clean up your act and resolve your past issues. You need to discard what is no longer useful to you. Alternatively, brooms symbolize domesticity and the establishment of a household. Perhaps it is time to settle down. Also, brooms are sometimes associated with witches and thus broomsticks may refer to the female shadow aspect of yourself.

Brother

To see your brother in your dream, symbolizes some aspect of your relationship with him. It can also serve to remind you that someone in your waking life has certain characteristics or behaviors similar to your brother.

If you do not have a brother and dream that you have one, then he may symbolize characteristics that you need to acknowledge within yourself. The brother in your dream can also be synonymous with a close friend or buddy. Brother also has religious implications and thus represents spiritual issues. Consider also the familiar phrase "big brother is watching you" which indicate that your dream has to deal with issues of authority and oppression.

To dream that you are mad or angry at your brother, signifies repressed anger that you are feeling but afraid to express in your waking life.

Brown

Brown denotes worldliness, practicality, domestic bliss, physical comfort, conservatism, and a materialistic character. Brown also represents the ground and earth. You need to get back to your roots.

Bruise

To dream that you have a bruise, represents stress and mounting pressure that you are dealing with in your waking life. It may also refer to a reawakening of old, family wounds that have not been properly addressed. Alternatively, the dream is telling you that you need to accept the consequences of your actions. Consider the symbolism of the specific part of your body that is bruised.

Brush

To see a brush in your dream, symbolizes your desire to "brush" away problems or something in your life that needs to be cleaned up. Perhaps you are taking a nonchalant attitude to circumstances that need serious consideration.

If you lose or can't find your brush, then suggests that you are unable to sort out your problems.

To dream that you are brushing your hair, suggests your need to organize and sort your thoughts. You need to search for some elements that are not clear. Brushing your hair may also highlight your preoccupation with appearances and beauty over substance and quality.

Bubble

To see bubbles in your dreams, represent merriment, fun, and childhood joys. It may also symbolize wishes or unrealistic expectations. In deciphering this dream symbol, consider also the phrase of having your bubble burst and the resulting disappointment.

Bubble Bath

To dream that you or someone is taking a bubble bath, represents ultimate relaxation. You have rid yourself of your worries/difficulties and release all the negative emotions you have been keeping inside.

Bubble Wrap

To see or use bubble wrap in your dream, indicates that there is a problem that you need to be cautious in the way you handle it. Alternatively, the dream suggests that you are looking to shield yourself from some emotional hurt.

To dream that you are popping the bubble in the bubble wrap, represents your satisfaction with the way your life is going. You have an effective outlet to release stress.

Buckle

To dream that you are fastening a buckle, represents your acceptance of certain responsibilities. The dream may also be a pun to on "buckling" under the pressure. A fancy or expensive looking buckle symbolizes status and honor.

Buffalo

To see a buffalo in your dream, symbolizes survival, strength, and power. The dream may also warn that you are deviating from your life path and goals. Alternatively, the dream represents your heritage and your roots. In particular, if you see a white buffalo in your dream, then it means that your desires or wishes will be fulfilled.

To see an injured or killed buffalo, forewarns that you need to carefully think through any new ventures and projects that you are undertaking.

To see a herd of buffalo in your dream, signifies tranquility and plentitude.

Bug

To see a bug in your dream, suggests that you are worried about something. It is symbolic of your anxieties and/or fears. What is literally bugging you? Consider also the popular phrase "bitten by the bug" to imply your strong emotional ties or involvement to some activity/interest/hobby. Alternatively, the bug may be representative of your sexual thoughts.

Bugle

To see or hear a bugle in your dream, represents some sort of warning. It signals an end to something and the beginning of another. Alternately, hearing a bugle symbolizes remembrance, mourning and solemnity.

Building

To see a building in your dream, represents the self and the body.

How high you are in the building indicates a rising level of understanding, awareness or success. If you are in the lower levels of the building, then it refers to more primal attitudes and/or sexuality.

To see a building in ruins or damaged, indicates that your approach toward a situation or relationship is all wrong. You need to change. Your own self-image may have suffered and taken some blow.

To dream that a building collapses, indicates that you are losing sight of your ambitions and goals. Your pursuit for material gains is failing.

To dream that you or someone fall off a building, suggests that you are descending into the realm of unconscious. You are learning about and acknowledging aspects of your unconscious. Alternatively, it symbolizes your fear of not being able to complete or succeeding in a task.

To dream that you are scaling or climbing a building, indicates that you are getting carried away by your ambitions.

Bulimia

To dream that you have bulimia, represents your lack of self-acceptance, self-esteem and your quest for perfection. You feel alone and cut off from others. Learn to love yourself and accept who you are instead of punishing yourself. The dream symbolizes your quest for perfection.

Bull

To see a bull in your dream, symbolizes stubbornness, strong will, strength, and power. The dream may be telling you that it is time to take a stand and be more assertive. Alternatively, the bull indicates a rich, prosperous, and abundant life. Consider also the metaphor, "being bull-headed". You need to learn to compromise in a situation. Or it could be a pun on something that is "bull", as in crap or worthless.

Bulls are also symbolic of repressed sexual energies, fertility and virility. To see an untamed, raging bull represents that your passions may be out of control. The bull may also represent a person in your life who is born under the Taurus sign.

To dream that you are bathing in bull's blood, represents immortality and eternal life.

Bulldozer

To see a bulldozer in your dream, suggests that you are feeling pushed away from what you want. Or that you are being diverted away from the path toward your goals. You may be feeling helpless and bullied. Alternatively, it suggests that you need to organize and clear away the clutter in your life.

Bullets

To see a bullet or bullets in your dream, indicate anger and aggression directed at you or someone else. You need to be cautious on what you say and do. Your actions and words may easily be misinterpreted. Alternatively, the dream may be telling you that you need to "bite the bullet" and accept some difficult situation.

To dream of being hit by a bullet, suggests that you need to persevere and endure the difficult times.

Bulletproof Vest

To wear a bulletproof vest in your dream, suggests that you are a overprotecting yourself from emotional hurt. You don't want to get hurt from a personal relationship again.

Bullfight

To dream that you are watching a bullfight, symbolizes the struggle between your animalistic desire and your spiritual side.

To dream that two bulls are fighting, represent an imbalance in some area of your life.

Bum

To dream that you are a bum, indicates that you are feeling like failure or an outcast. You are losing control of a situation in your life.

To see a bum in your dream, signifies laziness. You need to take more initiative.

Bumper Car

To dream that you are riding in a bumper car, represents your resilience. You are able to bounce back from adversity. Alternatively, the dream suggests that you are going nowhere with your life.

Bungee Jumping

To dream that you are bungee jumping, represents your ability to bounce back from adversities and setbacks in your life. The important thing to remember is that you took the initial risk.

Bunsen Burner

To see or use a Bunsen burner in your dream, suggests that you need to be more expressive and focus your energies on more fruitful or worthwhile endeavors. The dream may also be symbolic of a developing awareness, truth or enlightenment.

Buoy

To see a buoy in your dream, represents your ability to hold your head up even amidst your emotional distress. It may also indicate a renewed state of mind and emotional calm. Alternatively, it suggests that some of your repressed thoughts or unconscious material has come to the surface and is making itself known.

Burglary

To dream that you have been burglarized, indicates that you are feeling violated or that personal space has been invaded. You feel helpless in some situation or relationship. This could be due to a major change in your life. Give yourself some time to adjust to your new environment. The dream may also occur as a result of being burglarized in real life and a symptom of post traumatic stress.

Burrito

To see or eat a burrito in your dream, symbolizes your efficiency in some matter.

Bus

To dream that you are waiting for a bus, indicates a temporary setback in achieving your personal goals. If you miss the bus, then it indicates that an aspect of your life is out of control. You need to slow down and map out a new plan. If you get on the wrong bus, then the dream indicates your fears of making the wrong choice and going on the wrong path. You are conflicted between what you want and what others want for you.

To dream that you are at the bus station, suggests that you have reached some new level or stage in your emotional or physical life.

To dream that you are riding a bus, implies that you are going along with the crowd. You are lacking originality and control over where your life is taking.

To dream that you are in a bus accident, suggests that it is time for you to move away from a group setting and venture out on your own. You need to be more independent.

Butcher

To see a butcher in your dream, represents your raw emotions or immoral behaviors. You may be testing the limits of your physical strength. The dream may be a metaphor that you are "butchering" or ruining some project or situation.

To dream that you are a butcher, signifies pent up anger and hostility.

Butler

To see a butler in your dream, suggests that you are depending too much on others for their help. You need to be more independent and tend to your own needs. Alternatively, the dream may symbolize your desire for wealth or material possessions.

To dream that you are a butler, represents your feelings of subservience. Perhaps you need to take on a more submissive role.

Butter

To see or taste butter in your dream, suggests that you are looking to be gratified in some area of your life. You need to indulge yourself in life's pleasure. The dream may be a metaphor that you need to "butter" up to someone, in order to ease the situation.

To dream that you are churning butter, represents hard work and difficult task.

Butterfly

To see a butterfly in your dream, denotes your need to settle down. Butterflies signify creativity, romance, joy and spirituality. You may be experiencing a transformation into a new way of thinking. Or you may be undergoing a transitional phase. Consider the term "social butterfly" to describe someone who is popular and outgoing. Does this describe you? Perhaps you need to be more outgoing. Alternatively, the butterfly is symbolic of longevity.

To see two butterflies in your dream, represent a long and happy marriage.

To catch or kill a butterfly, suggests that you are being too superficial.

To dream that you are mounting a butterfly on frame, symbolizes sexual oppression.

Buttocks

To see your buttocks in your dream, represent your instincts and urges. It may also indicate feelings of insecurity and reveals your struggles with some situation.

To dream that your buttocks are misshaped, suggest undeveloped or wounded aspects of your psyche.

Buzzer

To hear a buzzer in your dream, indicates that you are experiencing a conflict in a relationship or situation. You are questioning the decisions you have made. Perhaps you feel you made the wrong choice and are now expressing regret. Alternatively, there is something in your dream that needs your immediate attention.

C

To see the letter "C" in your dream, symbolizes being average. It may also be a pun on "seeing". The dream is drawing your attention to something that you need to see or take notice. Pay attention! Alternatively, it may indicate the name or initial of a person.

Cab

To dream that your are hailing a cab, suggests that you need to ask for help in order to be able to move forward in some waking situation.

To dream that you are in a cab, indicates that you are being taken for a ride. Someone is taking advantage of you.

Cabin

To see or dream that you are in a wood cabin, indicates that you will succeed via your own means. It suggests that you are self-reliant and independent, yet still remain humble. You prefer the simpler things in life.

To dream that you are in a ship cabin, indicates that are seeking some refuge from your emotions.

Cabinet

To see a cabinet in your dream, symbolizes the female body and/or the womb. Alternatively, you may be hiding some family or personal secret. Consider the contents and condition of the cabinet for more clues.

To dream that someone rearranged your cabinets, suggests that somebody is overstepping your boundaries.

Cactus

To see a cactus in your dream, suggests that you are feeling invaded, that your space is being crowded into and that you are being suffocated. The prickly spines of the cactus represent the boundary you are trying to establish between your personal and private. Or you feel the need to defend yourself in some way. Alternatively, the dream implies that you have found yourself in a sticky situation. Perhaps you need to adapt to your existing circumstances instead of trying to change them.

Cage

To dream that you are in a cage, indicates that you are experiencing inhibitions and powerlessness in some areas of your life. You are feeling restricted, confined and restrained in a current relationship or business deal. Somebody may be keeping a short leash on you, where you are lacking the freedom to act independently.

To dream that you are putting a wild animal into a cage, signifies that you will succeed in overcoming your rivals and fears. It is also symbolic of your ability to control you animalistic rages and anger.

To see a bird in a cage, suggests that you are feeling limited in your expression and a sudden lost of freedom. You may be experiencing frustrations and an inhibited spirituality. The dream may also imply that you are feeling like a "jail bird".

Cake

To see a cake in your dream, indicates that you need to learn to share and allocate your workload instead of trying to do everything yourself. Cakes also symbolize selfishness or the feeling of not getting your fair share. More positively, the dream may represent your accomplishments and achievements. Consider also the metaphor a "piece of cake" or some situation that is easy.

To see a partially eaten cake in your dream, signifies missed and lost opportunities.

To dream that you are buying a cake, suggests that you have accepted the rewards and recognition your are getting for our work. You are learning to be comfortable in the spotlight.

Calculator

To see a calculator in your dream, suggests that you need to thoroughly think through some problem and carefully evaluate your choices. You need to lay out some sort of plan or outline. The symbol may also be a metaphor for someone who is "calculating", cunning and scheming.

Calendar

To see a calendar in your dream, represents the passing of time and past events. The dream may also be a reminder of a special event, appointment or important date in your waking life.

Calluses

To dream that you have calluses, symbolize hard work. You have be laboring over a difficult task or situation.

Calves

To see your calves in your dream, symbolize movement and your ability to jump from situation to situation. In particular, if you are admiring your own calves, then it denotes a needy or codependent relationship.

Camcorder

*Please See <u>Video Camera</u>.

Camel

To see a camel in your dream, denotes that you need to be more conservative; you are carrying too many responsibilities, burdens and problems on your shoulders. Consider the common phrase, "the camel that broke the camel's back". You tend to hold on and cling on to your emotions instead of expressing and releasing them. Learn to forgive and forget. Alternatively, the camel represents your stamina.

Camera

To see a camera in your dream, signifies your desires to cling on and/or live in the past. Alternatively, it may indicate that you need to focus on a particular situation. Perhaps you need to get a clearer picture or idea.

To dream that the camera is broken, indicates that you are ignoring an issue or refusing to see the big picture.

To see or dream that you are on a hidden camera, indicates that you feel that you are being scrutinized. All eyes are on you.

Camouflage

To dream that you are in camouflage, suggests that you are hiding your true self and feelings. You are concealing who you really are.

Camper

To dream that you are living in a camper, indicates that you need to move on with some situation or some aspect of your life. You may be dwelling on a situation and it is time to move forward. Alternatively, you may be expressing your desire to be more independent and self-sufficient.

Camping

To dream that you are camping, indicates a need for relaxation and a long-deserved break. You need to be more in touch with nature and go back to a more basic and simpler life. Alternatively, it refers to your social circle and support group. You are looking for a sense of belonging, but at the same time be self-sufficient and independent.

Can

To see a can in your dream, indicates that there is something in your past that you need to hold on to and preserve. The dream may also be a pun on how you "can" do something. Don't underestimate your abilities and talents.

To see canned foods in your dream, symbolizes the emotions that you are keeping inside.

Can Opener

To see a can opener in your dream, indicates your willingness to accept new ideas and new concepts. It may also be a symbol of reassurance and a way to tell yourself that "I can" do something.

Canary

To see a canary in your dream, represents happiness and harmony. Alternatively, the dream could indicate your desires for a relationship or that a new relationship is blossoming.

Cancer

To dream that you have cancer, denotes hopelessness, grief, self-pity, and unforgiveness. You feel you are wasting your life away. This dream also represents areas in your life which are bothering you, disturbing you, and hurting you in some emotional way.

To dream that you are being treated for cancer, signifies a positive change in your life.

To dream that someone has cancer, indicates that you need to change your negative way of thinking before it eats away at you. Start being more positive.

To dream that someone is a Cancer sign, symbolizes your tendency to keep and hold on to everything. You have a lot of power and influence. The Cancer sign also indicates that you tend to be sensitive, moody and emotional. You are also very family oriented.

Candle

To see a burning candle in your dream, signifies that good luck and hope will be coming your way in small and steady amounts. You are in a comfortable stage in your life and may be seeking spiritual enlightenment. Lit candles are also symbolic of intellect, enlightenment, awareness or the search for truth.

To see an unlit candle, denotes feelings of rejection or disappointments. You are not utilizing your fullest potential. If you try to light the candle, but it won't light, then it represents grief. You are in denial about something.

To see a candle blow out in your dream, indicates that you are surrendering a significant aspect of yourself. You are letting go of something that used to be important to you.

To watch the candle burn down to nothing in your dream, signifies your fears of aging and dying. Alternatively, it represents a fear of sexual impotence.

To see a red colored candle in your dream, symbolizes some intimate or romantic relationship. You may not be giving the relationship a fair chance and are dismissing it before you invested sufficient time to learn more about the other person. On the other hand, you may just not be feeling any chemistry or passion.

Candy

To see or eat candy in your dream, symbolizes the joys and the special treats in life. It also represents indulgence, sensuality and/or forbidden pleasure. You may be devoting too much time to unimportant issues. A more direct interpretation suggests that you are eating too much candy and sweets.

Cane

To see or use a cane in your dream, suggests that you are in need of some support and advice. The cane may also represent someone you trust and can rely on.

To dream that you are being caned, indicates that you are being forced into submission or obedience. Someone is trying make an example of you. Alternatively, the dream symbolizes self-guilt.

To dream that you are caning someone, signifies pent up aggression. Pay attention at who you are caning. You may harbor some ill feeling or anger toward this person. This person could also represent an aspect of your own self.

Cannibalism

To see cannibalism in your dream, symbolizes a destructive and forbidden desire or obsession. In a literal sense, cannibals consume people's lives, along with their energy. Thus, this dream may then denote an aspect of your life (career, relationship, children, etc), which is consistently draining your enthusiasm and vitality.

To dream that you are a victim of cannibalism, represents feelings of being "eating alive" by work, a relationship. or a situation in your waking life.

Cannon

To see a cannon in your dream, suggests that there is something drastic that needs to be done immediately. According to the Freudian, school of thought, the cannon symbolizes the penis.

Canoe

To see a canoe in your dream, represents serenity, simplicity, and independence. It is also a reflection of your emotional balance. You are moving ahead via your own power and determination.

Cape

To see or dream that you are wearing a cape, indicates that you are trying to shield yourself from being emotionally hurt. It may also mean that you are trying to cover-up or hide something.

Capricorn

To dream that someone is a Capricorn, signifies fears of inadequacy. You are afraid that you are not measuring up. Alternatively, it denotes your drive, tenacity and ambition.

Capsize

To dream that your boat has capsized, represents your avoidance in confronting uncomfortable feelings and/or situations.

Captain

To dream that you are a captain, indicates that you are taking charge of your emotions and confronting the issues that are bothering you.

To see a captain in your dream, represents your powerful influence over others.

Car

To dream that you are driving a car, denotes your ambition, your drive and your ability to navigate from one stage of your life to another. Consider how smooth or rough the car ride is. If you are driving the car, then you are taking an active role in the way your life is going. However, if you are the passenger, then you are taking a passive role. If you are in the backseat of the car, then it indicates that you are putting yourself down and are allowing others to take over. This may be a result of low self-esteem or low self-confidence. Overall, this dream symbol is an indication of your dependence and degree of control you have on your life.

To dream that your car won't start, indicates that you are feeling powerless in some situation.

To dream that you forgot or can't find where you parked your car, indicates that you are dissatisfied or unhappy with an aspect of your waking life. You do not know what you really want to do with your life or where you want to go. To dream that you car has been stolen, indicates that you are being stripped of your identity. This may relate to losing your job, a failed relationship, or some situation which has played a significant role in your identity and who you are as a person.

To dream that your car is overheating, suggests that you are expending too much energy. You need to slow down or run the risk of being burnt out. You are taking on more than you can handle. It is time to take a breather.

To see a parked car in your dream, suggests that you need to turn your efforts and energies elsewhere. You may be needlessly spending your energy in a fruitless endeavor. Alternatively, a parked car may symbolize your need to stop and enjoy life.

To dream that you are almost hit by a car, suggests that your lifestyle, beliefs or goals may be in conflict with another's. It may also be symbolic of a jolting experience or injured pride.

To dream that you are unable to roll up the windows of your car, suggests that you are showing some hesitation and reservation about the direction that you are taking in life or the path that you have chosen.

To see a haunted car in your dream, represents unfinished goals. You had started off on a path or journey, but never reached the end. Perhaps life had taken you on a different direction that you had planned or intended.

Cards

To dream that you are playing a game of cards, represents your ability to strategize in various areas of your life. In particular, diamonds indicate wealth and materialism, clubs indicate work and industry, hearts indicate happiness in love, and spades indicate troubling times and disappointments.

To dream that you are shuffling cards, signifies indecision. You need to reevaluate your choices.

Carjack

To dream that you have been carjacked, suggests that you have lost your direction in life. You feel that circumstances in your life has lead you on a different course.

Carnation

To see carnations in your dream, symbolize light-heartedness, vitality and joy. Alternatively, it may represent bachelorhood. Consider the color of the carnation for additional significance.

Carnelian

To see a carnelian in your dream, represents passion, lust, sexuality, or matters of the heart. It also indicates a need for spiritual healing.

Carnival

To dream that you are at the carnival, represents falsehoods and deception. If you observe freakish sights, then it denotes a lack of harmony in your domestic life. Much sorrow will arise in what were thought to be pleasant times.

To dream that you are on a carnival ride, suggests that you are going in circles. It may also symbolize cheap thrills.

To dream that you run away with the carnival, denotes that you will be involved in or closely connected to the entertainment field.

Caroling

To dream that you are caroling, signifies joy, harmony and tranquility. You are in a festive and upbeat mood. The dream may also be a pun on someone who is named "Carol".

Carousel

*Please See <u>Merry Go Round.</u>

Carpet

To see a carpet in your dream, represents your way of protecting yourself from life's harsh realities. Alternatively, a carpet symbolizes luxury, comfort or richness. Consider the condition and designs of the carpet and how it parallels the foundation that you have laid for yourself in life. Perhaps the dream is telling you that you are refusing to confront some issue and instead are sweeping it under the carpet?

To dream that you are installing or laying down carpet, suggests that you are trying to make your life more comfortable. The dream may also be analogous to the planning of something. You are laying out some new project or endeavor.

To dream of a magic carpet, implies your desires and wishes to escape from a situation, relationship, or responsibilities. The dream is similar to a flying dream, so you may want to look up flying.

Carriage

To see an old-fashioned carriage in your dream, suggests that your ways of thinking may be too outdated and antiquated. The carriage is also a symbol of power and status.

Carrot

To see a carrot in your dream, signifies abundance and fertility. It may also symbolize a lure as in the pun "dangle a carrot".

To eat a carrot in your dream, indicates clarify. You are seeing something more clearly.

Cartoon

To dream that your real life is depicted in a cartoon world, suggests that you are perceiving the world in a comical and unserious manner. This dream may also serve as an escape from the stressful realities of your life. It is your way of obtaining moments of lightheartedness and fun. Additionally, you need to learn to laugh at yourself and at your mistakes.

To dream that you are watching cartoons, indicates that you are not taking life seriously.

To see others as cartoon characters in your dream, indicate that you are not taking them seriously and are shrugging them off. You tend to overlook their opinions and feel that what they have to say is unimportant. Alternatively, seeing others as a cartoon character may be an easier, less tense, and a non-confrontational way for you to deal with others. They appear more harmless.

To see a specific cartoon character in your dream, consider the qualities and traits you associate with that particular character and how those traits come into play in some aspect of your waking life or situation. For example, to see Bugs Bunny in your dream may suggest your slyness and sneakiness. To see the Roadrunner may refer to something you are running from and not confronting.

Cartwheels

To dream that you are doing cartwheels, represent poise and balance in your life or the need to regain balance. You need to handle life's obstacle and stress with more fortitude.

To dream that you have difficulties doing cartwheels, suggest that you do not have confidence in your own abilities. It may also mean that you are lacking discipline and are exhibiting some struggles in your life. There is an imbalance between work and pleasure.

Carwash

To dream that you are at a carwash, indicates that you need to clean up your self-image. You are ready for a fresh start.

Cash

Please See Money.

Cashier

To see or dream that you are a cashier, indicates that you are re-evaluating your life and what you have accomplished. Alternatively, it suggests that you have removed yourself out of some situation. You have "checked out".

Casino

To dream that you are in a casino, signifies the risk-taker within you. If you are a reserved or passive person, then the dream suggests that you should take a chance. If you are not, then it implies that you need to make a more informed decision instead of relying on fate.

Cast

To dream that you are wearing a cast, suggests that your motion is being inhibited in some way. Or that you need to show some restraint in an area of your life. Consider which part of the body is in a cast. Alternatively, a cast symbolizes a time of healing and discipline.

Castanets

To see, hear or play with castanets in your dream, represent little annoyances and irritations in your waking life. Alternatively, the dream may be a metaphor that you need to "cast-a-net". Perhaps you are looking for some assistance.

Castle

To see a castle in your dream, signifies reward, honor, recognition, and praise for your achievements. You are destined to a position of power, wealth, and prestige. Alternatively, the dream indicates your desire to escape from life's daily problems.

To dream that you live in a castle, represents your extreme need for security and protection to the point where you may be isolating yourself from others. Perhaps the dream parallels a waking situation where it has put you on the defensive.

Cat

To see a cat in your dream, symbolizes an independent spirit, feminine sexuality, creativity, and power. It also represents misfortune and bad luck. The dream symbol has different significance depending on whether you are a cat lover or not. The cat could indicate that someone is being deceitful or treacherous toward you. If the cat is aggressive, then it suggests that you are having problems with the feminine aspect of yourself. If you are afraid of the cat in your dream, then it suggests that you are fearful of the feminine. The dream may be a metaphor for "cattiness" or someone who is "catty" and malicious. If you see a cat with no tail, then it signifies a loss of independence and lack of autonomy.

To dream that a cat is biting you, symbolizes the devouring female. Perhaps you are taking and taking without giving. You may be expressing some fear or frustration especially when something is not going as planned.

To dream that a cat is scratching you, suggests that you are feeling threatened.

To see a black cat in your dream, indicates that you are experiencing some fear in using your psychic abilities and believing in your intuition. You may erroneously associate the black cat with evil, destruction, and bad luck. In particular, if the black cat is biting, clawing or attacking you, then the dream means that you must acknowledge what your intuition is trying to tell you. You can no longer ignore it. Do not be afraid to face the situation. If you see a white cat, then it denotes difficult times.

To dream that a cat killed a spider, suggests that you are expressing your femininity in a seductive and cunning manner rather than in an overtly and almost destructive way.

Catapult

To see a catapult in your dream, indicates that you will overcome your obstacles through ingenuity and determination. Alternatively, the dream implies that you know no limit. You are on the fast track to success.

Catch

To catch something in your dream, suggests that you need to incorporate something into your life. Consider the object you are trying to catch and look up its meaning. If you are trying to catch a ball, then it indicates that you want to feel whole or you need to be more well-rounded. If you catch a fish, then it suggests that you need to be more spiritual.

To dream that you are playing catch, signifies your carefree attitude. You are enjoying life. Consider who you are playing catch with. If you are playing catch with mother or father, then it represents your bond and closeness to them.

The dream may also be a metaphor to indicate something that is "catchy" or contagious.

Caterpillar

To see a caterpillar in your dream, signifies a stage in your own personal growth and development where you are on your way, but have not yet reached your goal.

Cathedral

Please see <u>Church</u>.

Cattle

To see a cattle in your dream, indicates that you need to proceed with caution in some situation or relationship.

To see a herd of cattle in your dream, represents a lack of individuality. You generally go with the flow of things. Alternatively, it symbolizes prosperity.

To see a stampede of cattle in your dream, suggests that something in your life is out of control.

Catwalk

To see or dream that you are walking a catwalk, represents your new found confidence. It may also mean that you enjoy being the center of attention. You are being recognized for your talents or creativity. Alternatively, the dream could mean that you are using your appearance to get your way. You need to start looking within yourself.

Cauldron

To see a cauldron in your dream, implies that you are undergoing some transformation, It also indicates destiny or some magical, spiritual force. Alternatively, the cauldron symbolizes fertility and the womb. Consider the symbolism of what is inside the cauldron and its importance.

Cauliflower

To see or eat cauliflower in your dream, symbolizes spiritual nourishment, purity and perfection. It also represents sadness and a need to be uplifted. Your dream indicates that the tough times you are experiencing will soon be over. Alternatively, the cauliflower represents the brain and your mental capabilities.

Cavities

To dream that you have a cavity, indicates feelings of fear and insecurity over a situation. You are lacking self confidence.

Cave

To see or dream that you are in a cave, symbolizes the womb and thus signify refuge, protection and concealment.

To dream that you are walking in a dark cave, represents an exploration of your unconscious mind. It signals self discovery.

CD

To see a compact disc in your dream, represents a need for enjoyment or a distraction. It also points to the opportunities and possibilities within your grasp. Consider the type of music and the title of the compact disc. If you are giving away the CD, then you may be trying to convey a message to that person within the songs. Alternatively, the CD is analogous to the meaning of a circle.

Consider also if the initial "CD" have any additional significance to you. Perhaps it represents a person or may even be a pun on something that is "seedy".

Ceiling

To see a ceiling in your dream, represents a mental or spiritual perspective. It may also symbolize the limit you have set for yourself. If you see vaulted ceiling in your dream, then it signifies your askew perspective or view.

Celebrities

To dream that you are a celebrity, signifies your high aspirations that may be way beyond your reach at the present moment. You may just be setting yourself for a let-down.

To dream that a friend or lover becomes a celebrity, denotes your fear of losing the friendship and loyalty of this person.

To see a celebrity in your dream, represents your beliefs and understanding about him or her. Consider what the celebrity is famous or known for and how you relate to that quality. Something in you waking life has triggered these similar beliefs and feelings. It is not uncommon that your obsession with a certain celebrity may carry over onto your dream world. Celebrities are often seen as heroes and all that is mighty. Also consider any puns within the name.

To dream that you are good friends with a celebrity, represents your idealized version of someone you know in your life. Perhaps you hope that a real-life friend can act more like a particular celebrity. Consider the qualities that you see in this celebrity and how you want your friends to have those qualities. Alternatively, the dream may be trying to compensate for your own lack of self-confidence. You want to escape from your own reality and live the high life. You want to fit in.

To dream that you are having sex with a celebrity, indicates your drive to be successful. Consider what movies you associate this celebrity with or what makes this celebrity famous for clues as to where and what you want to achieve success in.

*See Also <u>Actor / Actress.</u>

Celery

To see or eat celery, represents your need to be cleansed, either physically or emotionally. The dream may also be a pun on "salary" and thus indicate your financial concerns.

Cell Phone

To see or use a cell phone in your dream, indicates that you are being receptive to new information. It also represents your mobility. Alternatively, the dream signifies lack of understanding. Perhaps you are having difficulties getting through to someone.

To dream that you lost your cell phone, represents a lack of communication. You have lost touch with some aspect of your feelings or your Self. If you find a cell phone, then it symbolizes reconnection and reopened communication.

*Please See Also Telephone.

Cellar

To dream that you are in a cellar, represents a part of your subconscious mind where you have kept your fears and problems hidden.

To dream that you are going down the cellar, signifies that you are digging deep into your own past and facing your fears.

Cello

To see or hear a cello in your dream, represents sensual or creative achievements. You are displaying much strength and stability.

Cement Truck

To see a cement truck in your dream, represents firm and "concrete" ideas or plans that are being set into motion.

To dream that you are mixing cement, suggests that you are fusing ideas or aspects of yourself together.

* Please See Also Concrete.

Cemetery

To dream that you are in a cemetery, indicates an end to a habit or behavior. You are experiencing a rebirth. More directly, the dream may symbolize sadness, unresolved grief or your fears about death.

Centaur

To see a centaur in your dream, symbolizes the duality of human nature. It indicates that you are trying to balance your intellectual/mental nature with your physical nature. The centaur also represents humanity, wisdom, and compassion.

Center

To dream that you are at the center of something, represents your belief that everything revolves around you. The dream may also be a metaphor that you are in the middle of some situation that you cannot get out of. If you are off centered, then it indicates that something in your life is out of balance.

Cereal

To dream that you are eating cereal, denotes the start of a new project or new stage in your life. It may also indicate your need to restore yourself in some basic way. Alternatively, your mind may already be thinking ahead to breakfast. It is not uncommon for your fleeting thoughts to be incorporated into your dream.

Chains

To see chains in your dream, signify your need to break free from a routine, old idea, or a relationship. If you are being chained, then some part of you is being forcefully put in check. You are being held back from what you really want to do.

Chainsaw

To see a chainsaw in your dream, indicates that something drastic is about to happen. Success will only come about through willpower. Alternatively, it suggests that you get right to the heart of the matter quickly. The chainsaw may be seen as a phallic symbol and can refer to your sexual drives.

Chair

To see a chair in your dream, symbolizes your need to sit down and take time out to contemplate a situation before proceeding. Or you just need to relax. Alternatively, it indicates that your feelings or ideas are being dismissed or cast to the side.

To dream that someone is offering you a chair, suggests that you need to be open to taking and accepting advice.

Chalkboard

To see a chalkboard in your dream, represents the classroom and the difficulties you may have experienced in school. There is a lesson to be learned from this dream. You may feel that you are being put to the test. Consider what is being written on the chalkboard. Alternatively, it signifies your debts.

To dream that you are writing on the chalkboard, indicates you will need to get your hands dirty in some situation.

Chameleon

To see a chameleon in your dream, represents your ability to adapt to any situation. You are versatile and are well-rounded. Alternatively, you feel you are being overlooked.

Champagne

To see the opening of a bottle of champagne, symbolizes a sexual act. Alternatively, it represents extravagance and overindulgence. Or it indicates a celebration or a personal achievement that you are proud of.

Chanting

To dream that you are chanting, symbolizes your camaraderie and oneness with others toward a common cause. It also suggests that you are in touch with a Higher plane and an elevated sense of spirituality.

Charades

To dream that you are playing charades, indicates that there is something that you are not able to put into words or articulate. Try to decipher what message you are trying to convey.

Chariot

To dream that you are riding in a chariot, indicates that you need to exercise control in your life.

To dream that you or someone else fall from a chariot, denotes failure.

Charlie Chaplin

To see or dream that you are Charlie Chaplin, suggests that you are searching and looking for some direction in your life. You need some variety from your daily routine.

Chase

To dream that you are being chased, signifies that you are avoiding a situation that you do not think is conquerable. It is a metaphor for some form of insecurity. In particular, to dream that you are chased by an animal, represents your own unexpressed and unacknowledged anger which is being projected onto that animal.

Alternatively, you may be running away from a primal urge or fear.

To dream that you are chasing someone, signifies that you are attempting to overcome a difficult goal or task. You may also be expressing some aggressive feelings toward others.

Chasm

Please See Abyss.

Chauffeur

To dream that you are a chauffeur, indicates that you are helping someone with their goals. You are trying to steer them on the right direction.

To dream that you are being chauffeured, signifies extravagance and luxury. You have a high sense of self worth. Alternatively, the dream represents your dependence on others. You are not in control of your life.

Cheating

To dream that you are cheating on your spouse, mate, fiancé, or significant other, suggests feelings of self-guilt and self-betrayal. You may have compromised your beliefs or integrity and/or wasting your energy and time on fruitless endeavors. Alternatively, cheating dreams reflect the intensity of your sexual passion; you are exploring areas of your sexuality. In this scenario, the dream may actually serve as a reaffirmation of your commitment. Furthermore, if you are approaching your own wedding date, then it is not uncommon to have dreams about erotic experiences with partners other than your intended spouse. Most likely, such a dream represents the newness of your sexual passion. It may also signify anxieties of changing your identity - that of a spouse.

To dream that your mate, spouse, or significant other is cheating on you, indicates your fears of being abandoned. You may feel a lack of attention in the relationship. Alternatively, you may feel that you are not measuring up to the expectations of others. This notion may stem from issues of trust or self-esteem. The dream could also indicate that you are unconsciously picking up hints and cues that your significant other is not being completely truthful or is not fully committed in the relationship.

To dream that you are cheating at a game, suggests that you are not being honest with yourself. You feel inadequate and insecure.

Check

To see a check in your dream, suggests that you may feel indebted to others. The dream may also be a pun on checking things out.

To see a blank check in your dream, symbolizes your unused potential. It may also indicate unclaimed rewards.

To see a check mark in your dream, indicates approval and acceptance. Your hard work has paid off.

Checkers

To see or play checkers in your dream, suggests that you need to have a clear strategy in order to overtake your opponents. The dream may also be a pun on "check her". Perhaps you need to reevaluate this female person.

Cheeks

To see your cheeks in your dream, symbolize commitment, intimacy, and closeness. It also reveals your strength of character and your opinions. Alternatively, cheeks can also be a slang for the buttocks.

To see rosy-colored cheeks in your dream, signifies life energy, enthusiasm and vitality. If the cheeks are sunken in, then it symbolizes sadness, hunger, poverty and/or struggles. The emphasis of cheeks in your dream could also point to health issues.

To dream that your checks are painted, represents your attitudes of courage and violence/passivity.

Cheerios

To see or eat Cheerios in your dream, indicates that there is something missing from your life. You do not feel completely whole. Alternatively, the dream may be a pun on "farewell" or "good bye".

Cheerleader

To see a cheerleader in your dream, represents competition and triumph. Your dream may be telling you to offer more praise and encouragement toward others.

To dream that you are a cheerleader, signifies your self-confidence and self-esteem. You need to be more active and more positive in some waking situation in your life.

Cheese

To see cheese in your dream, symbolizes gains and profits. Alternatively, the dream may be a metaphor for something that is "cheesy" or lame. Or it could be saying that you need to smile more.

Chemicals

To see or use chemicals in your dream, suggest that you are undergoing some transformation and individuation process.

To dream that you are mixing or combining chemicals, represent creativity, manipulation and/or intellectual power.

Cherry

To see cherries in your dream, symbolize honesty and truthfulness or sweetness and good fortune. Alternatively, the dream may be telling you that "life is like a bowl of cherries". In other words, don't take life so seriously; take it easy.

To see a cherry tree in your dream, represents luck, spring, femininity, and youth.

Chess

To see or play chess in your dream, indicates that you need to carefully think through the situation before making a decision. The light and dark squares of the chess board symbolizes the positive (pro) and negative (con) of a situation. The dream may also comment on how you have met your match in love or in business.

To dream that your king chess piece is in danger, suggests that you are being stifled by some female character in your life.

Chest

To see your chest in your dream, signifies confidence, conquest and vitality. Alternatively, it represents feelings of being overwhelmed and being dangerously confronted by something. Consider also if the dream is telling you that there is something that you need to "get off your chest".

To dream that you are beating on your chest, indicates triumph and a great accomplishment.

It is common for those who experience real life chest pains to have dreams where they are being shot in the chest or feel heavy pressure on their chest.

Chickens

To see chickens in your dream, symbolize cowardliness and a lack of willpower. The dream may be a pun on being a chicken or chickening out of some situation. Chickens also represent excessive chatter and gossip. Listen closely to what people may be saying about you or what you are saying about others.

To see a rubber chicken in your dream, indicates that you are being too serious and need to lighten up. It is okay to be silly sometimes.

Chihuahua

To see a Chihuahua in your dream, represents someone around you who is unexpectedly vocal. It may also represent someone who is insecure. Alternatively, the dream may refer to a situation or relationship where the bark is larger than the bite.

Childhood

To dream of your childhood, indicates your wish to return to a life where you had little responsibility and worries. It also represents innocence. Alternatively, it suggests that certain aspects of your childhood has not yet been integrated into your adult personality. On the other hand, some childhood anxiety has yet to be resolved in your adult life.

Children

To see children in your dream, signify an aspect of yourself and your childlike qualities. You may be retreating back to a childlike state and longing for the past. You are trying to still satisfy repressed desires and unfulfilled hopes. Perhaps there is something that you need to see grow and nurture. Take some time off and cater to the inner child within. Alternatively, the dream may be highlighting your innocence, purity, simplicity, and carefree attitude. If you are fighting with children, then it implies that you are repressing your inner child. The children could represent someone in your waking life (coworker, mate, sibling, etc.) who is acting like a child. If you see children fighting in your dream, then it means that your sense of morality and character are in conflict.

To forget about your child or children, suggests that you are feeling overwhelmed by your waking responsibilities. The dream is telling you that you are overly fixating on minor details and overlooking the important things on your life. You need to re-prioritize your time and focus on what matters. To dream that your own grown children are still very young, indicates that you still see them as young and dependent. You want to feel needed and significant.

To dream that you are watching children but they do not know you are there, is a metaphor for some hidden knowledge or some latent talent which you have failed to recognize.

To save a child in your dream, signifies your attempts to save a part of yourself from being destroyed. If you dream that you are separated from your children, then it symbolizes failure in some personal endeavor or a setback in some ideal you had.

Chili

To see or eat chili in your dream, symbolizes intense passion and raw emotion. The dream may also be a metaphor for being "chilly".

Chills

To get the chills in your dream, signify fear. Alternatively, it represents your indifference to some situation or person. The dream may be an actual physical reaction; perhaps the blankets have fallen off of you. Or the dream may be a metaphor indicating that you need to "chill out" or calm down.

Chimera

To see a chimera in your dream, represents a feeling of confusion. You need to sort out your thoughts and emotions.

Chimney

To see a chimney in your dream, represents warmth, tradition, and family values. Alternatively, a chimney symbolizes the phallus. So if the chimney is smoking, then it represents sexual release. If it is not smoking, then it signifies sexual tension or your need for sexual release. If the chimney collapses, then it implies impotence.

To dream that you are sweeping the chimney, indicates your need to vent off your frustrations and get things out in the open. You need to release all that negativity and/or guilt that you are holding in.

Chin

To notice your chin in your dream, refers to your resilience and your ability to bounce back from adversity. The chin often symbolizes character, strength, and resolve. Perhaps you need to "keep your chin up" and remain optimistic.

Chipmunk

To see a chipmunk in your dream, suggests that you are holding on to the past and need to learn to let go.

Chisel

To see or use a chisel in your dream, indicates that you need to forcibly break through the surface or barrier in order to get to the core of the situation or problem.

Chocolate

To see chocolate in your dream, signifies love, celebration and self-reward. It also suggests that you may be indulging in too many excesses and need to practice some restraint.

To eat chocolate in your dream, indicates that you are embracing your own sensuality.

Choir

To dream that you are singing in a choir, symbolizes spiritual harmony and balance. It also refers to your ability to work and cooperate with others. If you are singing out of tune, then it suggests that you are not fitting into some group situation.

Choking

Choking dreams are often a fearful experience and it is not uncommon for dreamers to awaken from them. To dream that you are choking on an object, suggests that you may find some advice/remarks/situation hard to swallow or difficult to accept. Alternatively, you may feel that you are unable to completely express yourself in a situation. In particular, if you are choking on food, then it may be an expression of self-guilt and unnurtured feelings. If you are choking on smoke, then it indicates something you are unwilling to confront.

To dream that someone is choking you, indicates that you are suppressing your emotions. You have difficulties in expressing your fears, anger, or love. Consider the phrase "being all choked up". Alternatively, you may feel that you are being prevented or restricted from freely expressing yourself.

To dream that you are choking someone, signifies feelings of aggression. You may be trying to prevent something from being said or revealed.

Chopping

To dream that you are chopping something, indicates that you are trying to cut your problems into smaller, more manageable sizes. You need to break up the issues and attack them piece by piece. Consider also the significance of the object that you are chopping. Alternatively, the dream may be a metaphor for having the chops or the guts and fortitude to do something.

Chopsticks

To see or use chopsticks in your dream, indicates that you are trying to manipulate some situation. Alternatively, it represents an extension of your reach.

If you are using chopsticks for its unintended function, then it suggest that you are in a sticky situation.

Chores

* Please See <u>Housework.</u>

Christening

To dream of a christening, symbolizes a renewal and fresh beginning. You may be undergoing a transformation where you want to better yourself as a person.

Christmas

To dream of Christmas, symbolizes family togetherness, reunions, celebration, peace, goodwill, generosity, and human kindness. It is also representative of new beginnings and fresh starts. Consider also your own associations with this holiday.

Christmas Tree

To see a Christmas Tree in your dream, symbolizes family celebrations, gatherings, and familial relationships. You may be experiencing some anxieties and stress in your domestic life. It also signifies a passage of time, self-development, and spiritual enlightenment. Consider also the feelings and emotions you experience during this holiday season to help you decipher this dream symbol.

If your dream of a Christmas Tree occurs in December, it may indicate the expected pleasures, demanding responsibilities, and growing anxieties associated with the holiday season.

Chrysanthemums

To see chrysanthemums in your dream, represent abundance, prosperity, humility, longevity, and gratitude. Alternatively, it may suggest that you need to keep silent about some situation.

Church

To see the outside of the church in your dream, signifies sacredness and spiritual nourishment. It is representative of your value system and the things you hold sacred.

To dream that you are inside a church, suggests that you are seeking for spiritual enlightenment and guidance. You are looking to be uplifted in some way. Perhaps you have made some past mistakes which have set you back on your path toward your goals. With proper support, you will get on the right track again. Alternatively, the dream may also mean that you are questioning and debating your life path and where it is leading. You are reevaluating what you want to do.

Cicadas

Please See Locusts.

Cigar

To see or dream that you are smoking a cigar, represents a relaxed state of mind. You are in control of your own emotions and passions. According to Freud, a cigar is a phallic symbol and is representative of masculinity and raw energy. This dream symbol may also serve as a symbol for someone you know who smokes cigars.

To see dried or shriveled cigars may be a pun on your lack of a sex life.

Cigarettes

To dream that you are smoking or offering a cigarette, signifies your need for a break. It may also points to issues of dependency . However if you are against smoking and have this dream, you need to analyze aspects of your waking life and what you are doing that may adversely affect your health.

Cinderella

To see or watch Cinderella in your dream, indicates that a seemingly bad situation will work out for the best in the end. There is such thing as "happily ever after".

To dream that you are Cinderella, suggests that you are feeling overburdened. You are taking on too much. Alternatively, the dream means that you are feeling overshadowed, overlooked or neglected. You are not being recognized for your work.

Cinnamon

To see or smell cinnamon in your dream, suggests that you need to introduce a little spice into your life. You need to do something that is out of your character. Alternatively, the dream signifies renewal and purification.

Cinema

Please See Theater.

Circle

To see a circle in your dream, symbolizes perfection, completeness, immortality and/or wholeness. On a less positive note, it may also mean that you are going around in circles in some situation. Or the circle can indicate monotony and endless repetition.

To see circles within circles in your dream, indicate that you are well protected or that you are being overly guarded. You may need to let down your defenses. Alternatively, the dream may highlight the notion that you are going around in a vicious circle. You need to somehow find a way to break this circle.

To see an imperfect or incomplete circle in your dream, suggests that you will face many obstacles and setbacks toward achieving your goals. You need to work on your inner self and develop more knowledge. Eventually, you will overcome these obstacles and find that your struggles are well worth it.

To see a circle with a cross, symbolizes earth. It may also serve as guidance toward the center and self-orientation.

Circuit Breaker

To see or trigger a circuit breaker in your dream, suggests that you are overloaded and overwhelmed. You are no longer functioning efficiently or properly. The dream may be metaphor telling you to take a break. Learn to prioritize and reorganize your tasks.

Circumcise

To dream that you are being circumcised, suggests that you are getting rid of an essential part of yourself. Alternatively, it may mean that you are regressing and cutting yourself off from feeling emotions.

Circus

To dream that you are at the circus, indicates your desires for a more exciting life. Alternatively, it suggests that you are easily influenced or lured into dangerous situations. Sometimes you are giving off the wrong impression to others. Consider the significance of the various acts you see in your dream.

To dream that the circus is abandoned or empty, suggests that you are feeling excluded in some situation. You are feeling lonely.

To dream that there is chaos at the circus, signifies that your life is out of control.

Citation

To dream that you get a citation, suggests that you need to reevaluate how you are going about your life as it might get you into trouble.

City

To see a city in your dream, signifies your social environment and sense of community. If you dream of a big city, then it suggests that you need to develop closer ties and relationships. You are feeling alienated and alone. To dream that you are in a deserted city, indicates that you feel rejected by those around you.

To dream of a city in ruins, denotes that you are neglecting your social relationships and allowing them to deteriorate.

To dream of an underground or underwater city, represents your unconscious and how through deeper understanding of yourself, you find commonality and shared experiences with others.

Claddagh

To see a claddagh in your dream, symbolizes love, loyalty and friendship. In particular, to give or wear a claddagh ring in your dream, signifies your commitments and convictions when it comes to love, loyalty and friendship.

Clam

To see a closed clam in your dream, suggests that you are emotionally cold. You are shutting others out and not letting them in on your problems and feelings.

Clapping

*Please See <u>Applause</u>.

Clarinet

To see or play a clarinet in your dream, suggests that you need to adjust your tone of voice.

Class

To dream that you are in class, is a metaphor that you need to have more class.

To dream that you forget to attend a class you signed up for, indicates your anxieties and fear of failing. You may also be lacking self-confidence in your ability to handle new responsibilities or projects.

Classmates

To see old classmates in your dream, indicate that you need to draw on your old associations with your former classmates to gain insight in some current relationship. It represents a past lesson that you have learned and is applicable in some aspect of your waking life now.

Claustrophobia

To dream that you have claustrophobia, suggests feeling of self-guilt. You fear that you will be punished for your past's actions.

Clay

To see or work with clay in your dream, represents creativity, flexibility and the ability to shape your mind or mold yourself to fit into a situation. It may also mean that you are able to manipulate things to your advantage. Alternatively, it indicates your need to set some goals and plans for yourself. You have some growing up to do and need to plan for the future. According to Freudian perspective, clay symbolizes feces.

To see a clay pot in your dream, signifies devotion, virtue or purity. The clay pot is also a healing symbol.

Cleaners

To dream that you are at the cleaners, warns that someone may be "taking you to the cleaners." Someone may be taking advantage of your. Alternatively, you may need to clear up a matter without getting overly emotional.

Cleaning

To dream that you are cleaning, implies that you are removing some negativity in your life and overcoming major obstacles. You are moving ahead toward a new stage in your life. In particular, if you are cleaning your house, then it means that you need to clear out your thoughts and get rid of your old ways and habits. You are seeking self-improvement. Alternatively, the dream may be a metaphor that you need to "come clean" or tell the whole truth about some situation or matter.

To dream that you are cleaning an object, represents an aspect of yourself that is not working or functioning as well as it should. If you are cleaning the refrigerator or oven, then it indicates that you are getting to root of a matter or situation. It may also indicate feeling so negativity and inferiority. You feel stuck in some area of your life.

To dream that you are cleaning out a desk, suggests that you are getting rid of the burdens that has been weighing you down. You are acknowledging your new choices, decisions, and a new sense of freedom.

Cleopatra

To see Cleopatra in your dream, indicates that you are in danger of being seduced by some uncontrollable force.

To dream that you are Cleopatra, suggests that you are acknowledging your own beauty and sexual appeal.

Cliff

To dream that you are standing at the edge of a cliff, indicates that you have reached an increased level of understanding, new awareness, and a fresh point of view. You have reached a critical point in your life and cannot risk losing control. Alternatively, it suggests that you are pondering a life-altering decision.

To dream that you or someone falls off a cliff, suggests that you are going through a difficult time and are afraid of what is ahead for you. You fear that you may not be up for the challenge or that you cannot meet the expectations of others.

To dream that you are climbing to the top of a cliff, symbolizes your ambition and drive. The dream may parallel your desires to achieve success and to be the at the top of your profession. It is analogous to climbing the corporate ladder.

Climate

Please See <u>Weather</u>.

Climb

To dream that you are climbing up something (ladder, rope, etc.), signifies that you are trying to or you have overcome a great struggle. It also suggests that your goals are finally within reach. Climbing also means that you have risen to a level of prominence within the social or economic sphere.

To dream that you are climbing down something, indicates that you need to acknowledge and take notice of your unconscious. You are expressing some hesitance and reservation with delving into your more negative feelings. Alternatively, it suggests that you may be feeling low or emotionally drained.

Cloak

To dream that you are wearing a cloak, signifies the need for security and warmth. You want to be protected. It may also mean that you are trying to cover-up or hide something.

If see a torn or ragged cloak in your dream, signifies a separation between you and a friend or lover.

Clock

To see a clock in your dream, signifies the importance of time in some waking situation. You may be feeling some anxiety of not being on top of things. Your mind may be preoccupied with a deadline that you have to meet or some other time-sensitive issue. It is time for you to tread on and speed up your actions. If the clock is chiming, then it suggests that time is running out. Alternatively, clocks symbolize the ticking of the human heart and thus is indicative of the emotional side of your life. If the clock has stopped, then it signifies death. This is a common theme for the terminally ill or the dying. Consider the time shown on the clock and determine the significance of the numerals or of the time.

To dream that the time on a clock is moving or speeding out of control, symbolizes some overwhelming task or emotion that you are going through in your waking life. Time is not on your side.

To dream that a clock is moving backwards, parallels the way that your life is going. Instead of moving forward and progressing toward your goals, you feel that you have not made any significant accomplishments. You feel you are stuck in a rut.

To dream that you are winding or setting a clock, suggests that you need to put more effort toward a task in order to obtain the desired result or outcome.

Clock Tower

To see a clock tower in your dream, indicates that you will be recognized for your work.

Clogs

To wear clogs in your dream, signify your firm and solid foundation. The dream may also be a pun on feeling clogged. Perhaps you are feeling overloaded or overwhelmed. On the other hand, you are not expressing your feelings and harbor some pent up anger.

To dream that you are clogging or clog dancing, signifies the beat and rhythm of your life. You are expressing your enthusiasm and zest for life.

Clone

To dream that you have a clone, suggests that you are either in harmony with or in conflict between ideas and decisions. Alternatively, the dream indicates that you are overburdened. You are spread to thin and feel that you need to clone yourself in order to get what you need to get done.

To dream that you have many clones, represent your lack of originality. You have a tendency to copy other's ideas/beliefs. You need to start thinking things through for yourself.

Closed

To dream that a door is closed, represents an aspect of your life or an opportunity that is closed off to you. It may also refer to sexual secrets or activities.

To dream that the store is closed, signifies your inability to consider other alternatives and other viewpoints. You may be biased in your judgment and opinion. Alternatively, it also represents feelings of inadequacy and frustration. Something is missing from your life.

Closet

To see a closet in your dream, symbolizes something in your life that you have kept hidden. It may also signify an unveiling of previously hidden aspects of yourself, as in "coming out of the closet."

Clothesline

To dream that you are hanging clothing on a clothesline, suggests that you are revealing hidden aspects of yourself, especially if they are underwear. The dream may also signify your hang-ups. In particular, if you are hanging white clothes in the backyard, then it indicates your desire for pureness and to be cleansed. You may also be proclaiming your innocence in some situation. Or perhaps the dream is telling you not to "air out your dirty laundry."

Clothing

To dream of your clothes, is symbolic of your public self and how you are perceived. It is indicative of the act you put on in front of others. Clothes are also an indication of your condition and status in life. Thus, if you wear clothes that do not suit you or that you normally would not wear, then it suggests that you are putting up a front and trying to deceive others. Something in your life is "unsuitable". It may be a symbol of hypocrisy and being someone that you are not. Alternatively, it could also mean that you are revealing a hidden part of yourself to the world.

To dream that your clothes are soiled and you are trying to clean them, signifies your attempts to change something about your character. You may need to change your old habits and old ways of thinking.

To dream that you are wearing brand new clothes, signifies new attitudes and a new persona. You are finding a different way of expressing yourself. If the price tags are still attached to the clothes, then it suggests that you are trying too hard to adapt to this new attitude. Perhaps it is not who you really are and you are not quite fitting in.

To dream that you are constantly changing your clothes, represents the need for change and your need to fit into a new situation or role. You need to establish a new self-image.

To dream that your clothes fit too tightly, denote that you feel restricted in some way. You may feel constrained in a relationship or held back at work. If you are wearing inappropriate clothes for a situation, then it means that you are unprepared for the task at hand.

To dream that your clothing is torn or ripped, indicates that there are some flaws in your thinking or thought process. Your logic is not making sense. You need to alter your reasoning and make a stronger argument.

To dream that you are shopping for or buying clothes, represents your anxieties about trying to fit in or being "well-suited" for your changing role.

To dream that all your clothes in the closet are white, suggests that you need to lighten up. You may have recently been feeling a little depressed. Perhaps you are going through some crisis. It is time to move on. and change your attitude. You need to better get a grip of your inner emotions.

To dream that your clothes are worn inside out, represents your non-conformist attitude. You like to go against what everybody else says. If you turn your clothes inside out in your dream, then it suggests that you are trying to protect yourself against something. You don't want to get hurt.

Clouds

To see fluffy, white clouds in your dream, signify inner peace, spiritual harmony and compassion. An issue in your waking life may be clearing up.

To see dark or stormy clouds in your dream, symbolize depression or anger. It indicates an impending eruption of emotions. Alternatively, it represents a lack of wisdom or confusion in some situation. Thus, the dream may be a metaphor for your "clouded" way of thinking.

Clover

To see a three-leaf clover in your dream, symbolizes the past, present, and future.

To see a four-leaf clover in your dream, represents good luck and happiness. The four leaves symbolize fame, wealth, good health, and faithful lover. Alternatively, the dream suggests that you have successfully come to a resolution of some problem.

Clown

To see a clown in you dream, symbolizes absurdity, light-heartedness, and a childish side to your own character. The countenance of the clown is a reflection of your own feelings and emotions. Whether it is a happy clown or a sad clown, that will help guide you through how you may be feeling. The actions of the clown signifies your uninhibited nature. Alternatively, a clown is an indication of your thoughtless or insincere actions.

If you have a fear or phobia of clowns, the clown may represent a mysterious person in your life who mean you harm. Somebody you know may not be who they appear to be. Or somebody may be pretending to be somebody they are not and are hiding under a facade.

Club

To see a club in your dream, denotes feelings of aggression or submission depending if the club is used by or against you. You may have some unexpressed anger that is on the verge of boiling over. It is also symbolic of virility and combativeness.

To dream that you are in a night club or dance club, represents the social aspects of your life and your sense of belonging. The dream could be a commentary on your lifestyle. Perhaps you need to settle down a little.

To see the clubs of a deck of card in your dream, indicate work and industry.

Clubbing

To dream that you are clubbing, represents your sense of belonging. More directly, the dream suggests your need to relax and let loose or that you need to settle down a little.

Clumsy

To dream that you or someone is clumsy, suggests that some situation or relationship is not going smoothly in your life. You need to take it easy and not be too hard on yourself.

Clutter

To see clutter in your dream, indicates that you need to clean up and organize a certain aspect of your life. The dream could be telling you that you need to let go of the past.

Coach

To see or dream that you are a coach, indicates that you need to be more self-disciplined.

Coal

To see a coal in your dream, represents wealth and prosperity. It also points to your unused potential. Alternatively, it indicates that you have been misbehaving and have been caught in the act.

To dream that you or someone is walking on coals, indicates that you will overcome adversity. Nothing is impossible if you put your mind to it.

Coast

To see the coast in your dream, suggests that you are on a spiritual quest. The coast symbolizes the meeting between your two states of mind - the rational and the irrational. Alternatively, the dream may be a metaphor of how you are "coasting". through life. You may need to take things more seriously. Or the dream may be telling you that "the coast is clear". You are free to move ahead.

Coat

To see or wear a coat in your dream, symbolizes your protectiveness and defensive persona. You may be isolating yourself. Consider also the color, appearance, and type of coat for additional significance.

To dream that a coat is old, worn, or shabby, then it suggests that you are feeling down on yourself.

To see or wear a fur coat in your dream, symbolizes prosperity and luxury. It also indicates your need for attention and your need to be admired.

Cock

To see a cock in your dream, symbolizes masculinity, pride, valor, cockiness and arrogance. It indicates that you or someone is being a show-off. You have little or no regards for others. The dream may also be a pun on the penis.

To hear a rooster in your dream, signifies bragging and self-glorification.

To see cocks fighting in your dream, indicate rivalry and quarreling.

Cockroach

To see a cockroach in your dream, symbolizes uncleanness. It also signifies longevity, tenacity and renewal. You need to reevaluate major aspects of your life. Alternatively, the dream represents an undesirable aspect of yourself in which you need to confront. A roach may also be a pun on smoking marijuana.

Coconuts

To see a coconut in your dream, foretells of unexpected rewards.

Cocoon

To see a cocoon on your dream, signifies a place of safety and solitude. It may also represent transformation or healing.

To dream that you are in a cocoon, represents your need to rejuvenate and restore your body, mind and spirit. You may be recreating new paths of expression and perhaps a rebirth. Alternatively, it symbolizes your unrealized potential and possibilities.

Coffee

To dream that you are drinking or need your coffee, suggests that you need to gain some insight and knowledge before making a decision or tackling some project/relationship. You may be acting too hasty and need to slow down. Alternatively, it may imply a need for you to change your routine.

To dream that you are drinking coffee with someone, indicates that you might have feelings for that person. Alternatively, having coffee with someone denotes your hospitality and sociability.

To see a coffee pot in your dream, signifies hospitality and sharing of knowledge, hopes, concerns and/or ideas. It may also represent neighborliness, comfort, and companionship.

Coffee Maker

To see a coffee maker in your dream, represents a disturbance in your psyche and well-being. You are feeling off-balanced. Alternatively, the dream could also mean your level of alertness. Consider the phrase "wake up and smell the coffee".

Coffin

To see a coffin in your dream, symbolizes the womb. It also signifies your thoughts and fears of death. If the coffin is empty, then it denotes irreconcilable differences. Alternatively, the coffin represents ideas and habits that you are no longer of use and can be buried.

To see a body in a coffin in your dream, signifies that you are going through a period of depression. You may feel confined, restricted and that you are lacking personal freedom. There may be a dead or decaying situation or issue in your life that you need to address. It is time to end this situation or relationship.

Coins

To see coins in your dream, indicate missed or overlooked opportunities that have come your way. To see gold coins in your dream, represent success and wealth. Silver coins represent spirituality, intuition, values, and your sense of self-worth. Copper coins indicates healing.

To see coins stacked in your dream, symbolize masculine power, dominance, and energy.

To dream that you are flipping a coin, represents your casual attitude about making some decision. You may also not be taking responsibility for your decisions. Alternatively, it indicates your irrational thoughts.

Cola

*Please See <u>Soda</u>.

Cold

To dream that you are cold, indicates that you are experiencing a breakthrough in some area in your life. Alternatively, you may be feeling isolated or emotionally restrained. Your sense of coldness could reflect your feelings about a lover or a certain person. The dream may also occur as a result of your immediate environment in which you are really feeling cold.

To see the word cold in your dream, suggests that you need to be more neutral or objective in your decision making. You need to remain emotionally detached.

To dream that you touch something cold, suggests that you should avoid that object or what that object represents in your waking life

Collar

To see a collar in your dream, signifies confinement and restraint. You may be going through a frustrating work situation or a confining relationship.

To dream that you have ring around the collar, indicates that you need to clean up your language and the way you talk to others.

Colleague

*Please See <u>Coworker.</u>

College

To dream that you are in college, indicates that you are going through some social or cultural changes. You want to expand your knowledge and awareness. It also suggests that now is a good time for you to experiment and try new things. If you had gone to college in your past, then also consider your personal experiences and memories of your college days. However, if you are currently in college, then it may be a reflection of your current surroundings. Alternatively, the dream suggests that you will achieve your goals through perseverance and hard work. You may be going through a period of stress in your life.

Coloring Book

To see or color in a coloring book, symbolizes childhood. It indicates that you have a carefree attitude free from any responsibilities. Alternatively, the dream may be warning you against being idle and wasting time on fruitless pursuits. Consider the significance of the color you are using and what you are coloring.

Colors

Colors in dreams represent energy, emotions, and vibes. First consider what that single color in your dream means to you and your own personal associations and relationship with that color. In general, pale pastel colors indicate weakness or subtlety. Dark colors represent passion and intensity. Bright colors mean awareness.

To dream in color and then dream in black and white, suggests that you are starting to look at a situation from a more objective perspective instead of from an emotional standpoint. You are subconsciously reacting to events in the dream.

Look up the specific color for additional significance.

Coma

To dream that you are in a coma, indicates your helplessness and inability to function in some given situation. You are not prepared for the major changes that are happening around you. Alternatively, your dream coma state may reflect what is really happening to your body when you are in the dream stage of sleep. In this stage of sleep, your body remains immobile as if it was paralyzed; commonly referred to as REM paralysis.

Comb

To dream that you are combing your hair, suggests your need to organize and sort your thoughts. You need to search for some elements that are not clear to you in a situation or relationship. Alternatively, combing you hair may highlight your preoccupation with appearances and beauty over substance and quality.

*Please See Also Hair.

Comedian

To see or dream that you are a comedian, suggests that you need to be more carefree. You are feeling overburdened from your daily problems and need an outlet to release all that tension. You need to learn to laugh at yourself and not take yourself so seriously.

Comet

To see a comet in your dream, indicates that you need to move on and free yourself from emotional and physical burdens. Charge forward toward your goals.

Comforter

To see or use a comforter in your dream, symbolizes warmth, love, security and protection. You may be seeking for some form of shelter from the outside world. Alternatively, the dream may be a metaphor that you are looking for "comfort" or that you need to be "comforted" by someone. You feel depressed.

Comics

To see or read comics in your dream, suggest that you need to learn to not take yourself so seriously. You need to have more of a sense of humor.

To dream that you are collecting comics, indicate that you refuse to see the problems that exist in your life and only want to focus on the good times. Perhaps you are in denial about something.

Commercials

To dream that you are watching TV commercials, signify your tendency to jump from one thing to another without completing your initial responsibilities and tasks. You have a tendency to emotionally distance yourself and remain objective about the situations you are faced with.

If the commercials quickly jump from one to another, then the dream symbolizes your flightiness.

Compact Disc

To see a compact disc in your dream, represents a need for enjoyment or a distraction. It denotes opportunities and possibilities. Consider the type of music and the title of the compact disc. If you are giving away the CD, you may be trying to convey a message to that person within the songs.

Consider also if the initial "CD" have any additional significance to you. Perhaps it may even be a pun on something that is "seedy".

Compass

To see a compass in your dream, is a way of your subconscious to show you the way. The dream may be telling you to reconsider the direction in your life and to rethink the path you are taking.

Compost

To see compost in your dream, suggests that you need to channel and transform your outdated ideas or past experiences into something you can learn from.

Computer

To see a computer in your dream, symbolizes technology, information, and modern life. New areas of opportunities are being opened to you. Alternatively, computers represent a lack of individuality and lack of emotions and feelings. Too often, you are just going along with the flow, without voicing your own opinions and views. You may also feel a depreciated sense of superiority.

To dream that your computer has a mind of its own, denotes anxiety about technology and loss of control. You are feeling overwhelmed and that you are at the mercy of another.

To dream that a computer has a virus or has crashed, suggests that something in your life that is out of control. It may parallel something in your life that has come to a crashing end.

Concentration Camp

To see or live in a concentration camp in your dream, indicates that you are afraid of differences. You are having difficulties accepting others and their differences. Learn to appreciate diversity and the uniqueness in yourself and in others around you. If you actually lived in a concentration camp, then the dream may signify a situation in your waking life which is triggering similar feelings felt at the time.

Concert

To dream that you are at a concert, represents harmony and cooperation in a situation or relationship in your waking life. You are experiencing an uplift in your spirits.

To dream that you are holding a concert, symbolizes your untapped talents and hidden potential. You need to show of your creative side.

Concrete

To see concrete in your dream, represents your solid and clear understanding of some situation. The dream may also mean that you are too unyielding and inflexible.

To see wet concrete in your dream, suggests that some issue or some aspect of your life still remains unresolved.

Condom

To see a wrapped condom in your dream, represents your one-sided viewpoints. You are not allowing others to voice their opinions. It also symbolizes sexual possibilities.

To see an unwrapped condom in your dream, indicates sexual frustration. Additionally, it may also indicate that you are experiencing some anxiety about pregnancy or sexually transmitted diseases.

To dream that you or your partner is wearing a condom, suggests that you feel emotionally protected.

Condor

To see a condor in your dream, signifies your close connection with your spirituality and to the supernatural. You possess a lot of insight.

Cone

To see a cone in your dream, represents a flow of ideas and feelings.

Confession

To dream that you or someone is confessing, represents feelings of guilt and self-blame. Alternatively, it suggests a form of healing. You are heralding new changes into your life.

Confetti

To see or throw confetti in your dream, represents achievement and success. You have achieved a higher level of growth and learning and are at a turning point in your life. Alternatively, it symbolizes much festivity and fanfare. You may be expressing joy, victory, and freedom from restraint.

Confucius

To see Confucius in your dream, indicates that you need to utilize your common sense. Perhaps you are acting stupid and need to wise up. Alternatively, it represents the importance of loyalty and duty to your family.

Confusion

To dream that you are confused, reflects your true confused state of mind and the nonsensical events of your waking life. Isolate the single element in your dream that is confusing to you and analyze the meaning of that particular symbol. Alternatively, dreams of confusion indicate that you are being pulled in opposite directions or you do not know which viewpoint is right.

Conman

To see a conman in your dream, indicates that you are being taken advantage of in some way. The dream may highlight fears that you are being played. Perhaps you need to trust your instincts.

To dream that you are a con artist, represents your ability to manipulate some situation or relationship. The dream may be calling attention to your lacking conscience and low character.

Constellation

To see a constellation in your dream, indicates that something in your life is coming together in a complex way. It represents a mental process. Consider what the constellation is depicting.

Constipation

To dream that you have constipation, denotes that you are unwilling to part with your old ways. You continue to grasp onto your old ways and fail to let go, forgive, and forget. You may be dwelling on past problems and previous difficulties.

Construction

To dream that a building is under construction, suggests that you need to work on some aspect of yourself and better your mind or body.

To see construction in your dream, signifies a new surge of energy, growth, ambition and renewed confidence. It may also represent the rebuilding of your own life.

Contest

To dream that you enter or are in a contest, indicates the need to prove yourself as worthy and deserving. If you win the contest, then it represents your self-confidence, pride, and/or conceit. If you lose the contest, then it indicates a lack of self-esteem. You may not be fully applying yourself to the task at hand.

Contortionist

To see or dream that you are a contortionist, suggests that you are literally getting all twisted and wound up over a problem or situation in your life. Alternatively, it represents flexibility in your thinking or fluidity in your emotions. The dream may also be a metaphor in how you are able to stretch or twist the truth or facts of a situation.

Contraceptive

To see or use contraceptive in your dream, suggests that you are refusing to let your creativity emerge from beneath the surface. You are holding back some aspect of yourself. The contraceptive may be a metaphor for protection against emotional hurt. Alternatively, it signifies your anxieties about pregnancy or sexually transmitted diseases.

Contract

To dream that you are signing a contract, indicates that you are ready to commit to a long term relationship or project.

To dream that you enter into a bad contract, suggests that you need to think twice about committing to a relationship. Carefully examine what you are getting into.

Contrail

To see a contrail in your dream, symbolizes hope, pride and possibilities. Alternatively, the dream may seek to tell you that no matter how far or how fast you go, you will always leave an impression on those you left behind. You will not be forgotten.

Control Tower

To see or dream that you are in a control tower, may be a metaphor that you need to get a better handle on your waking life situation. You need to take things one at a time and evaluate the situation individually. Alternatively, the dream symbolizes complete control over your emotions. You may be too overly rational and not let feelings get in the way.

Convent

To dream that you are at a convent, represents your need for spiritual support and nurturance. You need to isolate yourself and block out any external forces that may cloud your judgment. Alternatively, the dream indicates that you are being restricted from fully expressing yourself.

Convertible

To see or dream that you are in a convertible, refers to your glamorous attitude. You are showing off your power and influence.

Conveyer Belt

To see a conveyer belt in your dream, suggests that you are stuck in a rut. Your daily routine has become predictable and unchallenging.

Convict

To dream that you are a convict, suggests that some situation or relationship is making you feel restricted. You may be experiencing a loss of freedom in some area of your life. Alternatively, the dream represents your feelings of shame and guilt. This dream image is trying to tell you to stop punishing yourself.

To see a convict in your dream, indicates that an aspect of yourself is unable to freely express itself.

Cookie Cutter

To see or use a cookie cutter in your dream, symbolizes monotony and sameness. The dream may be telling you to deviate from the norm. Do something or say something unexpected.

Cookie Monster

To see Cookie Monster in your dream, indicates that you need to eat more healthier and have a more balanced diet. Alternatively, the dream means that you need to show restraint and control.

Cookies

To dream that you are eating, giving, receiving, or stealing cookies, signify that you will let trivial problems and minor disputes annoy you.

To dream that you are baking cookies, signifies feelings of optimism and increases You may also experience a rise in status.

To see or eat chocolate chip cookies, symbolizes your guilty indulgences. If you are baking chocolate chip cookies, then it represents your connection to someone in an intimate and emotional way.

To dream that you are eating an oatmeal cookie, suggests that it is okay to indulge once in a while.

Cooking

To dream that you are cooking, signifies your desire to influence others in such a way so that they will like you or become dependent on you. Alternatively, it represents your nurturing side. You want to be loved. Or the dream could mean that you need to express your creativity.

To dream that you have difficulties cooking, indicates that you are trying too hard.

Cooler

To see a cooler in your dream, represents someone who is frigid or who has cold personality. As the cooler is a feminine symbol representing the womb, the dream could mean a female in your life who is emotionally cold. Alternatively, the dream may be telling you that you need to cool off or that you need to "keep your cool". Consider also what is inside the cooler.

Cop

*Please See <u>Police</u>.

Copier

To see or use a copier in your dream, represents your lack of originality and your tendency to copy other's ideas/beliefs. You need to start thinking things through for yourself. Alternatively, the dream may indicate a desire to spread some idea and circulate the word out.

Copper

To see copper in your dream, represents the power of healing. It also indicates a flow of ideas, your connection to a situation to others, and flow of information.

Copycat

*Please See <u>Mimic</u>

Coral

To see coral in your dream, symbolizes protection and the beauty of life. Acknowledging your feelings is the key to a happy and rewarding life. Alternatively, it represents purification and blood.

Cork

To see cork in your dream, represents your versatility and adaptability in different situations. You have the ability to stay afloat in times of turmoil and rise above your circumstances.

To see a cork pop in your dream, symbolizes male sexuality and climax.

Corkscrew

To see or use a corkscrew in your dream, suggests that some aspect of your life is spinning out of control, especially if you are having difficulties using the corkscrew. Alternatively, the dream may indicate the beginning of a fresh new idea.

Corn

To see corn in your dream, signifies abundance, prosperity, growth and fertility. Also consider the pun that something is "corny".

To see a field of corn in your dream, represents domestic bliss and harmony.

Corner

To dream that you are in a corner, signifies feelings of frustration and lack of control in making decisions. You may feel trapped and "cornered". Alternatively, it indicates self-punishment.

Corpse

To see a corpse in your dream, represents an aspect of yourself that has died. Or it may mean that you are unexpressive. You have shut yourself down and are dead inside.

Correction Tape

To see or use correction tape in your dream, represents your desires for a fresh new start. Alternatively, the dream maybe telling you are suppressing past mistakes into your subconscious, instead of learning from them.

Corset

To see or wear a corset in your dream, indicates submission, restraint and restrictions. You may be feeling limited. Alternatively, it may mean that you have a tendency to hold in your displeasure in order to please others.

Cosmetics

*Please See Makeup.

Cost

To see or notice the cost of something in your dream, represents the value you are placing on yourself, your time and your abilities. If the cost is high, then it indicates that you value yourself highly. If the cost is low, then you are undervaluing yourself or taking somebody else for granted. The dream also relates to your self esteem.

Costume

To dream that you are wearing a costume, indicates that you are putting on a facade toward others. You do not want to reveal your true self and are not being completely honest with people around you.

Costume Party

To dream that you are at a costume party, suggests that you are trying to escape from the demands of real life. You want to enjoy life and not worry about your daily responsibilities.

Cotton

To dream that you are picking cotton, suggests that you are seeing little benefits from all your long hard work. It may also mean that aspects of yourself are in harmony.

To dream that you are wearing cotton, symbolizes simplicity.

Cotton Candy

To see or eat cotton candy in your dream, represents childhood pleasures or rewards. You are content with the way things are going in your life.

Couch

To see or dream that you are on a couch, represents rest, relaxation, laziness or boredom. It may also mean you need to clear you mind and thoughts. Consider also who is on the couch with you as the dream may also have sexual connotations.

Cougar

To see a cougar in your dream, symbolizes wild beauty, power, grace, and raw emotion. It often refers to feminine power and aggression. Thus, the dream may represent a woman. Alternatively, it indicates lurking danger and death.

Coughing

To dream that you are coughing, represents your fear or dissatisfaction of the future. You need to put some distance between yourself and others. Alternatively, it indicates that you have made a negative choice in some important matter.

Counselor

To see or dream that you are a counselor or dream that you are one, suggests that you are seeking for some support and direction in your life. Pay important attention to what the counselor is saying and/or doing. Your dream is trying to convey a message that you need to think about and possibly act upon.

Counting

To dream that you are counting, suggests that you are too rigid, obsessive-compulsive and overly disciplined. You need to relax a little. Alternatively the dream may be a metaphor for being the one that others can "count on". You are reliable and dependable.

Courage

To dream that you have great courage, indicates that you are willing to confront rejected aspects of your unconscious head on. You are about to come to a whole new understanding. The dream may be training you for what you need to do in your waking life.

Coupons

To see or clip coupons in your dream, suggest that you are doing your best to maximize your resources. You need to be more frugal or conserve your energy.

Court

To dream that you are in court standing up for charges against you, signifies your struggle with issues of fear and guilt. A situation or circumstance in your life is giving you much distress and worry. You feel that you are being judged in some way and need to defend yourself.

Cousins

To see your cousin in your dream, represents something or some aspect of your character that is somewhat familiar. Perhaps you need to spend more time in cultivating and developing some emerging ability or character. In particular, if you dream that your cousin is ignoring you, then it indicates that you are not acknowledging some aspect of yourself that is represented by your cousin.

To dream that you or your sibling is in love with a cousin, represents your acceptance of each other. You are acknowledging and embracing key qualities in one another.

Cow

To see a cow in your dream, symbolizes your passive and docile nature. You obey others without question. Alternatively, a cow represents maternal instincts or the desire to be cared for. For some cultures, the cow represents divine qualities of fertility, nourishment and motherhood.

To see the skeleton of a cow, suggests that your mother or motherly figure in your waking life is displaying a lack of emotions. She is being unresponsive to your needs.

To see a herd of cows, indicates your need to belong.

To dream that you are milking a cow, represents your willingness and drive to work hard. In the end, you will benefit from your hard work.

Cowboy

To see or dream that you are a cowboy, symbolizes masculinity, ruggedness, and toughness. You are in control of your animalistic and instinctual side.

Coworker

To see your coworkers in your dream, highlights aspects of your waking relationship with them, including difficulties/support. It signifies your ambition, struggles and competitive nature. If the coworkers in your dream are not your actual coworkers, then they may pertain to some psychological business that you need to work on.

Work-related dreams can also often be linked to stress at work.

To dream that you are training someone to take your place, suggests that you are moving toward deeper inner development. You are leaving behind old attitudes and are looking toward the future.

Please See Also Office.

Cowrie Shells

To see or wear cowrie shells in your dream, signify your laid back and easy going attitude. Alternatively, a cowrie shell symbolizes fertility, womanhood, and reproduction. The dream may also be a metaphor for the value that you assign to certain things.

Coyote

To see a coyote in your dream, denotes deception and weakness.

CPR

To dream that you are performing CPR on someone, indicates that you have resolved some anxiety, fear or tension in your life. Alternatively, the dream signifies creativity and intelligence.

To dream that someone is giving you CPR, suggests that you are feeling exhausted or emotionally drained. You are seeking advice.

Crab

To see a crab in your dream, signifies you perseverance and tenacity. On an extreme note, you maybe be too clingy and dependant. You are hanging on to a hopeless endeavor or relationship. Alternatively, the dream may indicate that you are trying to avoid some issue. You are being evasive. Crabs are also symbolic of your irritable personality, as in the pun, being "crabby".

Crack

To dream of a crack in some object, indicates that something in your life is imperfect. Nobody is perfect. Or there could be a flaw in your thinking or relationship. The dream may also be a pun on "cracking under pressure". You may be experiencing difficulties in trying to maintain your composure and keeping it together.

Crackers

To see or eat a cracker in your dream, suggests that you tend to care for the needs of others before your own. You spend your time looking after other people and as a result, neglect your needs. The dream may also be a pun on "crack her". Perhaps you are trying to get someone to reveal certain information or secrets.

Cradle

To see a cradle in your dream, symbolizes a dependent relationship. You may feel the need to be protected and cared for. Your dream may be telling you to regain some control and independence in your life. Alternatively, it represents a new project or fresh start.

Crane

To see a crane in your dream, represents happiness, maternal love, and your gestures of good will. You look out for those who are near and dear to you. Alternatively, a crane signifies tact, immortality or vigilance.

Crank Call

To dream that you are making a crank call, signifies your frustrations about not being taken seriously.

To dream that someone is crank calling you, indicates that you are feeling out of the loop. You feel that some information is being hidden from you.

Crash

To dream that you are in a car crash, indicates that your beliefs, lifestyle, or goals are clashing with another's. It may also represent a shocking situation or painful experience. Alternatively, car crashes may forewarn of your dangerous or careless driving habits.

To dream that a plane crashes, signifies that you have set overly high and unrealistic goals for yourself. You are in danger of having those goals come crashing down. Alternatively, the crashing airplane represents your lack of confidence, self-defeating attitude and self-doubt. You do not believe in your own ability to achieve those goals. Loss of power and uncertainty in achieving your goals are also signified.

Crater

To see a crater in your dream, indicates that aspects of your unconscious are being slowly revealed to you. This dream symbol is also symbolic of past memories and experiences.

Crawling

To dream that you are crawling, indicates that you are approaching your goals with careful forethought and preparation. Alternatively, the dream may indicate that you are lowering yourself and your standards. You may be doing less than your best.

To dream that you are crawling out of a wreck or ruins, represents your willpower.

To dream that someone is crawling towards you, signifies your need for

81

power, revenge, superiority, or control.

Crayons

To see crayons in your dream, represent some childhood memory or a period of time where you were more carefree. It is also symbolic of creativity. You may need to think outside the lines into more unconventional thoughts and ways of doing things. Consider the symbolism of the color of the crayon.

Crazy

To dream that you are going crazy, suggests that you have lost sight of your goals. You may feel that you are no longer able to depend on someone. Alternatively, you feel that your opinions, viewpoints or decisions are being unaccepted or being ignored. You may feel like an outsider.

Cream

To see or eat cream in your dream, indicates that you appreciate the minor and sweet things in life. It is symbolic of nurturance and richness.

To see or apply face cream in your dream, represents a beautiful soul. It may also represent the character and personality you are portraying to others in your waking life.

Credit Cards

To dream about credit cards, relate to your worth, value and/or credibility. Depending on your waking experiences, the credit cards may symbolize being in debt and your attitudes about money, work, and thrift.

To dream that you lose your credit cards, indicate your carelessness in some aspect of your waking life.

To dream that someone is stealing your credit cards, suggest that something or someone is robbing you of vital energy.

Cremation

To dream that someone is being cremated, represents purification and your strive for perfection. It symbolizes the ending to a phase in your life and the beginning of something else. If the person being cremated has passed away in real life, then the dream may be a way of grieving or coping with the loss. You want to always remember them in a positive light.

Crib

To see a crib in your dream, suggests that you are harvesting or "babying" a new idea, creation or project. Alternatively, it may refer to your nurturing, protective, and caring nature. A more literal interpretation of this symbol, suggests that you may be yearning for a baby or that you are expecting a baby. The dream may also be a pun on "your home".

Crickets

To see crickets in your dream, represents introspection. You are seeking guidance.

To hear crickets in your dream, suggests that you are letting minor things bother you.

Criminal

To dream that you are a criminal, indicates that you are looking for a short cut in life. You are selling yourself short and underestimating your own potential. Alternatively, the dream means that you feel you are entitled to certain things.

Cripple

*Please See <u>Handicap</u>.

Crochet

To see crochet in your dream, indicates that you will find yourself entangled in some situation

To dream that you are crocheting, symbolizes your creativity and artistic abilities.

Crock Pot

To see or use a crock pot in your dream, suggests that you need to look at various sources to attack a problem. Alternatively, it means that patience, hard work, and tenacity will pay off in the long run. Hang in there and don't let difficulties and obstacles discourage you.

Crocodile

To see a crocodile in your dream, symbolizes freedom, hidden strength and power. It also forewarns of hidden danger. Someone near you is giving you bad advice and is trying to sway you into poor decisions. Because crocodiles can live in water and on land, they also represent your conscious and unconscious and the emotional and rational. Perhaps something is coming to the surface and you are on the verge of some new awareness.

Alternatively, the crocodile may be an aspect of yourself and your aggressive and "snappy" attitude. Or it may reveal that are being insincere, displaying false emotions and shedding "crocodile tears".

To dream that you are chased or bitten by a crocodile, denotes disappointments in love and in business.

Cross

To see a cross in your dream, signifies suffering, martyrdom, death, and/or sacrifice. It is a symbol of your religious faith. Perhaps your dream is telling you that you have a cross to bear or that you are acting "crossed" and annoyed. Ask yourself what is causing you to suffer or what is causing you great difficulties.

Cross-Dressing

To dream that you or someone is cross-dressing, indicates that you need to express and acknowledge your masculine side if you are female or your feminine side if you are male.

Crossword Puzzle

To see or do a crossword puzzle, suggests that you are being faced with a mental challenge. The dream may be a pun on "cross words" directed at your or aimed toward someone.

Crow

To see a crow in your dream, represents death and the darker aspects of your character. The dream could also be pointing out your annoying habits. Alternatively, the crow may be conveying a message from your unconscious.

Crowd

To dream that you are in or part of a crowd, suggests that you need some space for yourself. You need solitude to reflect on a situation and recharge your energy. Consider also the familiar phrase of "going along with the crowd" which implies conformity and lack of individuality. Perhaps you feel that your own opinion doesn't count or matter. Alternatively, dreaming of a crowd means that you need to incorporate the various aspects of the crowd into your own persona.

To see an unruly crowd in your dream, signifies that the worries and problems around you are pressing in on you. You are expressing great distress.

To see a happy, orderly crowd in your dream, indicates that you have a strong social support system.

Crown

To see a crown in your dream, symbolizes success and prominence.

To dream that you are wearing a crown, suggests that you are in a position of power. Alternatively, you may be basking in your own achievements. You are recognizing your talents and accomplishments.

Cruise

To dream that you are on a cruise, represents some emotional journey that you are going through. The dream may also be a pun on "cruising" through situations in your life with ease and little effort.

Crumbs

To see or make crumbs in your dream, suggest that you are feeling left out. Do you feel like an outsider in some situation?

Crush

To dream that you are crushing something, denotes that you are under tremendous stress over a decision that you need to make. If you dream that a part of your body is being crushed, then it suggests that you are being prevented to full express yourself.

To dream that you have a crush on somebody, is a literal reflection of your attraction and fascination for that person. To see your crush in your dream, represents your current infatuation with him or her. If you find yourself thinking about him during the day, then it is not surprising that his image will appear in your dream during the night. If you dream of your crush frequently, then your dream maybe be telling you that it is time to let this person know how you feel, especially if you are dreaming of him or her in a good way. Only good things can happen from you telling your crush. Even if he or she is not interested, at least you can move on and stop wasting time on him or her.

If you dream that somebody has a crush on you, then it represents you own sense of worthiness and esteem.

To dream about a former crush, refers to a particular period in your life and what you were feeling then. Perhaps a waking relationship is repeating the same pattern.

To dream that your crush rejects you or stands you up, represents your feelings of insecurities and anxieties. The idea of not knowing how your crush feels about you is driving you nuts. Assuming that he or she rejects you, before you actually know how he or she feels, saves you from getting hurt. Because you are afraid to find out how he or she really feels about you, it may just be easier to move on if you think that they don't like you back.

Crutches

To dream that you are on crutches, signify your need to lean on others for help. Perhaps you are acting helpless in order to get out of some situation or obligation.

Cry

To dream that you are crying, signifies a release of negative emotions that is more likely caused by some waking situation rather than the events of the dream itself. Your dream is a way to regain some emotional balance and to safely let out your fears and frustrations. In your daily lives, you tend to ignore, deny, or repress your feelings. But in your dream state, your defense mechanisms are no longer on guard and thus allow for the release of those feelings that you have repressed during the day.

To see someone else crying in your dream, may be a projection of your own feelings onto someone else. If you do not cry in your waking life, then seeing someone else cry may be a little easier to deal with then seeing yourself cry.

To wake up crying, represents some suppressed hurt or previous trauma that is coming up to the surface. You can no longer suppress these emotions. They need to be dealt with head on.

To dream that no one hears or responds to your cries, represents your helplessness, difficulties and frustrations in trying to communicate with others. You feel that your words are falling on deaf ears. Perhaps your dream is telling you to be more vocal and work harder to get your point across.

Cryopreservation

To dream that you are being cryopreserved, indicates that you may be stuck in the past. You are dwelling on how things used to be.

Crystal

To see a crystal in your dream, signifies wholeness, purity, healing. development and unity. It represents your higher Self. The dream may be a metaphor for something in your life that is crystallizing or taking shape.

To dream that you are looking into a crystal, represents how you are looking within yourself to find your true destiny. Alternatively, it indicates your outlook of the future.

Crystal Ball

To see or look through a crystal ball in your dream, suggests that you are looking for guidance and direction in your life. It represents your outlook of the future.

Cuckoo

To see a cuckoo in your dream, symbolizes unfaithfulness. Or there may be someone in your life whose presence is unwelcome. Perhaps you are the one who is intruding on other people's business. Alternatively, a cuckoo represents timing and fate. You need to change your direction or alter your approach in how your pursue some situation. The dream may also be a metaphor for someone who is behaving crazily.

Cult

To dream that you are in a cult, suggests that you are in some destructive and/or manipulative relationship. You are being exploited. On a more positive note, you have the desire to strive for a better Self. It implies devotion and sense of community.

To see a cult in your dream, indicates that you are lacking any spiritual freedom.

To dream that you are a leader of a cult, signifies your authoritarian attitude. No one should question your motives or choices.

Cup

To see a cup in your dream, represents love, nurturance and the womb. The cup may also signify rejuvenation and healing. Alternatively, it indicates a transcendence into a realm of higher consciousness. Is the cup half-full or half-empty? Do you see life from an optimistic or pessimistic point of view.

To see a cup with a broken handle, indicates your feelings of inadequacy and anxieties of being unable to handle a particular situation.

To see a broken cup in your dream, denotes feelings of powerlessness, guilt and/or low self-esteem. Perhaps you feel unqualified or inadequate in dealing with a situation.

Cupcake

To see or eat a cupcake in your dream, suggests that you are treating yourself to a little sweet reward. You feel that you are deserving of some sort of gift of prize. Alternatively, a cupcake represents your need to downsize some aspect of your life in order to make it more palatable or manageable. Take it a little bit at a time.

Cupid

To see cupid in your dream, represents a love relationship in your waking life. Its appearance in your dream may mean that you need to take a risk in love.

Curfew

To dream that you have a curfew, symbolizes some time-sensitive situation. You are feeling burdened by the expectation of others.

To dream that you miss curfew, then it denotes your fear of change. You are feeling unprepared, unworthy, or unsupported in your current circumstances. Alternatively, the dream suggests that time has ran out and you do not have time to accomplish all the things you want.

Curlers

To see curlers in your dream, suggest that you are thinking in circles. You may be going over the same problem/situation again and again without any conclusion.

Curse

To dream that you or someone is under a curse, suggests that you are getting caught up in your own guilt. You also need to proceed with caution in some situation or relationship.

To dream that you or someone is cursing, refers to your inner fears. It also means that you are becoming a hardened person.

Curtains

To see or dream that you are shutting the curtains, signify secrecy and a repression of thoughts. You are concealing some personal matter or some aspect of yourself. On the other hand, to dream that you are opening the curtains, indicates that you are ready to reveal something hidden about yourself.

To dream that a stage curtain is going up, indicates personal development and growth. You have learned something significant about yourself. If the stage curtain is coming down, then it suggests that you need to accept some decision. You have to come to terms with the end.

Curtsy

To curtsy in your dream, suggests that you are acknowledging something that is greater than you and deserves your respect. You are submitting to a power larger than you.

Cushion

To see or use a cushion in your dream, suggests that you are in need of more rest and relaxation. Alternatively, the dream may be a metaphor that you need to "cushion" or distance yourself against a hurtful situation or some offensive remarks.

Cut

To dream that you have a cut, suggests that you are being let down or being undermined. Alternatively, it refers to feminine sexuality and feminine attitudes toward sex. In particular, if the cuts are on your legs, then it symbolizes an imbalance. You are unable to stand up for yourself.

To dream that you are cutting yourself, indicates that you are experiencing some overwhelming turmoil or problems in your waking life. You are trying to disconnect yourself from the unbearable pain you are experiencing.

Cymbals

To dream that you are playing with cymbals, indicate that you are overreacting in some situation. You are making too much fuss over a small thing. Alternatively, the dream refers to your connection to your spirituality.

Cyst

To dream that you have cyst, suggests that you have something that needs to be expressed and get out in the open. You may be harboring some prejudices, attitudes, or some other negative emotion that attempting to be released. You need to acknowledge these feelings and deal with them. Also consider the symbolism of where on the body the cyst is located.

D

To see the letter "D" in your dream, signifies mediocrity. Alternatively, the letter D refers to receptiveness and joy. As a Roman Numeral, it could represent the number 500.

Dad

*Please See Father.

Daffodil

To see daffodils in your dream, symbolize self-love, renewal, inner growth, optimism, inspiration, and hope. It may signal a fresh start, a new beginning or a new project.

To give someone daffodils in your dream, represent unrequited love. Someone that you are interested in may not feel the same way about you. The dream is telling you that it is time to move on.

Daisy

To see daisies in your dream, symbolize freshness, beauty, innocence, simplicity, friendliness, and cleanliness. If you are plucking the petals of a daisy, then it denotes the purity of love.

To dream that someone gives you a bouquet of daisies, symbolizes sorrow and/or lost love.

To dream of walking in a field of daisies, represents good luck and prosperity. Someone will be there to offer you a helping hand and some guidance for your problems.

Dam

To see a dam in your dream, signifies repressed emotions or feelings that needs to be released. To dream of a bursting dam, denotes that you have lost control of your anger and are overwhelmed with emotions.

Dance

To dream that you are dancing, signifies freedom from any constraints and restrictions. Your life is in balance and in harmony. Dancing also represents frivolity, happiness, gracefulness, sensuality and sexual desires. You need to incorporate these qualities in your waking life.

To dream that you are dancing with a partner, signifies intimacy and a union of the masculine and feminine aspects of yourself. If you are leading, then it indicates that you are in control of your personal life. It could also mean that you are being overly aggressive and assertive.

To dream that you are attending or going to a dance, indicates a celebration and your attempts to achieve happiness. Consider the phrase the "dance of life" which suggests creation, ecstasy, and going with what life has to offer you.

To see children dancing in your dream, indicates a happy home life.

To see ritualistic dancing in your dream, denotes your need to get in touch with the spirit within.

Dandelion

To see dandelions in your dream, represent pleasant and joyous surroundings. You are content with where you are at in life. Alternatively, the dream seeks to bring your back to your childhood and past memories.

To dream that you are blowing on dandelions, symbolize fleeting moments. You are trying to recapture a certain time in your life. You feel that time is passing you by.

To dream that you are eating dandelions, signify that you need to take better care of your health or suffer unpleasant consequences.

Dandruff

To dream that you have dandruff, indicates that you are misusing your energy. You may have been under a lot of stress and tension. You should rethink the way you are approaching any of your current problems. Alternatively, this dream may suggest a lack of self-esteem.

Danger

To dream that you are in danger, suggests that you need to be more cautious in some aspect of your life. Alternatively, your negativity and pessimistic attitude is causing you to be depressed about the future.

To dream that you escape from danger, signifies that you will rise to a place of high position and honor in your business and social circle.

Darkness

To dream that darkness comes upon you, signifies failure in some work that you are attempting. Darkness is synonymous with ignorance, the unconscious, evil, death, and fear of the unknown. If the sun breaks through the darkness, then you will overcome your failures. If you feel safe in the dark, then it suggests that you like not knowing about certain things. As some might say, ignorance is bliss.

To dream that you cannot find someone in the darkness, signifies that you need to keep your temper in check. You have the tendency to let your emotions get out of control and lose your temper.

To dream that you are lost in the darkness, denotes feelings of desperation, depression, or insecurity.

To dream that you are groping around in the darkness, indicates that you have insufficient information to make a clear decision. Do your research and do not rush into making choices.

Darts

To dream that you are throwing darts in your dream, refers to some hurtful or harmful remarks that you or someone have said. Alternatively, it represents your goals and your "go-getter" attitude.

Date

To dream that you are on a date, represents your need for self-discovery and self-awareness. You are getting to know some hidden aspects of yourself and acknowledging your hidden talents. Alternatively, it may reflect your anxieties about dating or finding acceptance. The dream may also be a "rehearsal" for an actual date you have. It serves to overcome anxieties you may have.

To dream of a date, as in a particular, month, day and year, represents the passing of time and past events. The dream may also be a reminder of a special event, appointment or important date in your waking life. Also consider the significance of the numbers in the date.

Daughter

To see your daughter in your dream, represents your waking relationship with your daughter and the qualities that she projects. If you do not have a daughter, then it symbolizes the feminine aspect within yourself.

Day

To dream of a sunny day, symbolizes clarity and/or pleasantness. You are seeing things clearly. To dream of a gloomy or cloudy day, signifies sadness. If you dream of a particular day, then you may need to look closely at that day for any significance. Consider the number associated with that day. A certain date could highlight a special anniversary, appointment or occasion.

To dream of the passing of a day, indicates that you need to manage your time better and plot out your goals in a more deliberate manner.

Dead

To see the dead in your dream, forewarns that you are being influenced by negative people and are hanging around the wrong crowd. This dream may also be a way for you to resolve your feelings with those who have passed on. Alternatively, the dream symbolizes material loss.

If you dream of a person who has died a long time ago, then it suggests that a current situation or relationship in your life resembles the quality of that deceased person. The dream may depict how you need to let this situation or relationship die and end it.

To see and talk with your dead parents in your dreams, represent your fears of losing them or your way of coping with the loss. You are using your dream as a last opportunity to say your final good-byes to them.

To see your dead sibling, relative, or friend alive in your dream, indicates that you miss them and are trying to relive your old experiences you had with them. In trying to keep up with the pace of your daily waking life, you dreams may serve as your only outlet in coping and coming to terms with the loss of a loved one.

*Please See Also <u>Death</u>.

Dead End

To dream that have reached a dead end, indicates that you have come to an abrupt end in the pursuit of your goals. You must find another way to achieve your goals because the current path is not working out. Alternatively, the dream may be telling you that you are going nowhere. Perhaps, the dream is symbolic of a dead end job or a dead end relationship. You need to reevaluate your options.

Deadline

To dream of a deadline, signifies your preoccupation with time. You feel that time is running out for you and that will not be able to meet your goals by a set time. You need to learn to prioritize and balance aspects of your life.

Deaf

If you are not deaf in real life and dream that you are deaf, then it suggests that you are feeling secluded from the world, You may be closing yourself off from new experiences or shutting yourself out. Alternatively, the dream could indicate that your defenses are up. There is something that you are refusing to hear. Perhaps you have problems taking criticism. The dream could just mean that you are in need of some peace and quiet.

To dream that someone else is deaf, suggests that someone close to you is withdrawn.

Death

To dream about the death of a loved one, suggests that you are lacking a certain aspect or quality that the loved one embodies. Ask yourself what makes this person special or what you like about them. It is that very quality that you are lacking in your own relationship or circumstances. Alternatively, the dream indicates that whatever that person represents has no part in your own life anymore. In particular, to dream about the death of your parents, indicates that you are undergoing a significant change in your waking life. Your relationship with your parents has evolved into a new realm.

To dream that you are faking your own death, suggests that you are looking for a new start. You need some change in your life.

To dream that you die in your dream, symbolizes inner changes, transformation, self-discovery and positive development that is happening within you or your life. You are undergoing a transitional phase and are becoming more enlightened or spiritual. Although such a dream may bring about feelings of fear and anxiety, it is no cause for alarm as it is often considered a positive symbol. Dreams of experiencing your own death usually means that big changes are ahead for you. You are moving on to new beginnings and leaving the past behind. These changes does not necessarily imply a negative turn of events. Metaphorically, dying can be seen as an end or a termination to your old ways and habits. So, dying does not always mean a physical death, but an ending of something.

On a negative note, to dream that you die may represent involvement in deeply painful relationships or unhealthy, destructive behaviors. You may feeling depressed or feel strangled by a situation or person in your waking life. Perhaps your mind is preoccupied with someone who is terminally ill or dying. Alternatively, you may be trying to get out of some obligation, responsibility or other situation. You are desperately trying to escape from the demands of your daily life.

To see someone dying in your dream, signifies that your feelings for that person are dead or that a significant change/loss is occurring in your relationship with that person. Alternatively, you may want to repress that aspect of yourself that is represented by the dying person.

Decay

To see something decay in your dream, signifies the degradation of a situation or circumstance. It may also represent the death of an old situation before the rebirth into a new stage.

December

To dream of the month of December, signifies togetherness, friendships, and happy reunions. Consider your own personal associations with this month. Is it someone's birthday? Does it invoke the holiday spirit? Is the dream telling you to be more giving? Does December signify a closure to something?

Deer

To see a deer in your dream, symbolizes grace, compassion, gentleness, meekness and natural beauty. It has feminine qualities and may point to the feminine aspect within yourself. It also represents independence, alertness, and virility. Consider the symbol to be a pun for someone who is "dear" to you. Alternatively, the dream represents vulnerability and naiveté. As a result, others may take advantage of you and your gullibility.

If the deer is black, then it means that you are not acknowledging or are rejecting the feminine qualities in you. You may not be in tune with your feminine side.

To dream that you kill a dear, suggests that you are trying to suppress those feminine qualities.

Defibrillator

To dream that someone is using a defibrillator on you, implies that you need to be reenergized. You need to literally get a jumpstart on your goals.

Deformed

To dream that you or someone is deformed, represents undeveloped aspects of yourself that you may have ignored. You refusal to acknowledge these characteristics may be affecting your performance and creative flow.

Defriend

To dream that you are defriending someone, suggests that your friendships are drifting apart. You are feeling socially disconnected or withdrawn. Alternatively, the dream indicates aspects of your own self that you are rejecting or refusing to acknowledge.

To dream that you have been defriended, indicates that you are feeling betrayed.

Déjà Vu

To dream of Déjà Vu, indicates some unresolved issue which you are not addressing or are refusing to acknowledge. It may also represent a message or word of advice that you need to heed.

Demons

To see demons in your dream, represent ignorance, negativity, distress or your shadow self. It also forewarns of overindulgence and letting lust give way to your better judgment. As a result, your physical and mental health may suffer.

To dream that you are possessed by demons, indicates ultimate helplessness.

Dent

To see a dent in your dream, signifies self-doubt in your thinking. You are second guessing your decisions. It also represents a blemish in your personality.

Dentist

To dream that you are at the dentist, represents your concerns about your appearance. Alternatively, it suggests that you are having some doubt over the sincerity and honor of some person in your life. You are experiencing some momentary anxiety or pain, but you will be a better and stronger person for it in the long run.

Deodorant

To see or put on deodorant in your dream, represents your inner strength and your ability to rid yourself of harmful and destructive behaviors.

Depression

To feel depressed in your dream, refers to your inability to make connections. You are unable to see the causes of your problems and consequences of your decisions. People who are depressed in their waking life often have dreams about being depressed. Pay attention to what is depressing you in your dream and see how it relates to your waking life.

Derrick

To see derricks in your dream, symbolize the obstacles that you need to overcome in order to succeed. The dream may also be a pun on someone who is named "Derek" in your waking life.

Desert

To dream that you are walking through a desert, signifies loss and misfortune. You may be suffering from an attack on your reputation. The desert is also symbolic of barrenness, loneliness and feelings of isolation and hopelessness. The desert landscape may also be a metaphor for feeling deserted and left behind.

Dessert

To see or eat a tasty dessert in your dream, represents indulgence, celebration, reward, or temptation. You are enjoying the good things in life.

Detective

To see a detective in your dream, signifies the thrills and dangers in some aspect of your waking life.

To dream that you are a detective, indicates that you are searching for your hidden abilities and talents. You may be trying to solve a problem and seek out the truth about some worrisome issue.

To dream that you are being followed by a detective, signifies guilt. Your character will be put under scrutiny and called into question.

Detention

To dream that you are in detention, suggests that you need to reflect on your negative actions and bad behavior. Learn from your past mistakes.

Detour

To see a detour in your dream, suggests that you have encountered an obstacle in some aspect of your life. You are not wanting to confront something directly, and thus are trying to find a way around it.

Devil

To see the devil in your dream, signifies fear, limitations, and negative aspects of yourself. You may be harboring feelings of guilt. It is time to release these feelings. Alternatively, the devil represents intelligence, cunningness, deception, and cleverness.

To dream that you fight off the devil, indicates that you will succeed in defeating your enemies.

To dream that the devil talks to you, suggests that you will find certain temptations hard to resist even though you know it is not in your best interest.

To dream that you and the devil are friends, suggests that you are easily influenced and can be persuaded into doing something you do not necessarily want to do. Alternatively, you may be dealing with issues of morality.

Diamonds

To see diamonds in your dream, signify the wholeness of the Self. You may be finding clarity in matters that have been clouding you. Alternatively, it represents vanity, conceit, and your unchanging or unyielding nature. You may be distancing yourself from others.

To receive diamond jewelry in your dream, signifies love, commitment and dedication. If you lose the diamond jewelry, then it indicates difficulty in your love relationship. It may also be analogous to financial hardships.

To dream that a diamond is fake, suggests that you are trying to be someone that you are not. Alternatively, the dream may indicate that you that you are living beyond your means.

Diaper

To see or wear a diaper in your dream, symbolizes your childish or babyish attitudes/actions. You may be too dependent on others.

To dream that you are changing diapers, suggests a need to clean up you behavior and change your childish ways. Perhaps you need to change your attitude and approach regarding a new idea or project.

To see dirty diapers in your dream, indicate that you need to clean up the mess you have created as a result of your childishness.

Diarrhea

To dream that you have diarrhea, signifies that some part of your life is going out of control. You can no longer contain your strong emotions and need to get it out of your system quickly. Alternatively, the dream indicates that you have not analyzed a situation long enough or that you do not want to deal with the problem at all.

*Please See Also <u>Bowel Movement.</u>

Diary

*Please See <u>Journal.</u>

Dice

To see or play dice in your dream, suggests that you are taking chances and playing with fate. It refers to the unpredictability of life. The dream may also be a pun on a situation that may be getting too "dicey". Consider the significance of the numbers reflected on the dice or how many dice were thrown.

Diet

To dream that you are on a diet, suggests that you are punishing yourself. You feel restricted from what you really want to do. Alternatively, it indicates self-control and self-discipline. You are giving up the things that are unhealthy in your life. The key is balance and moderation.

Digging

To dream that you are digging, indicates that you are working hard to uncover the truth in a problem that is haunting you. You are overly preoccupied with trying to find out something about yourself, your reputation, or your self-identity. Alternatively, the dream suggests that you are trying to get to the root of some issue. Or the dream may be a metaphor to imply an insult.

To dream that you dig a hole and find something, may be a pun that you "dig something", as in you like it or appreciate it. Or it may also refer to someone that you might be "digging" or like. Alternatively, the dream suggests that you need to be more open minded and welcome new ideas.

To dream that you dig a hole and fill it with water, denotes that no matter how hard you try, your efforts will not sway things your way. You need to learn to compromise.

Dim

To dream that it is dim, indicates that you are lacking clarity in a waking situation. You need to shed some light or perspective on the issue. Alternatively, the dream may be a metaphor for someone who is dumb or stupid.

Dime

To see a dime in your dream, represents the number 10 and thus means closure, strength and big gains. Alternatively, the dream indicates money issues. You need to do some serious saving! Also consider the phrases, "stop on a dime" to mean ending something abruptly or quickly or "drop of a dime" to mean dropping everything to tend to someone else's needs without hesitation.

Dining Room

To dream that you are in a dining room, represents your quest for knowledge and understanding. You may be reaching an important decision in your life.

Dinner

To dream that you are eating dinner alone, indicates that you need to do some serious thinking about your goals and directions in life. Alternatively, it may represent independence or lack of social skills.

To dream that you are eating dinner with others, signifies your acceptance or others, your interpersonal relationships, and how you behave in your social life. It is a time to reflect and share past experiences. It also suggests that you see everyone as an equal.

Dinosaur

To see a dinosaur in your dream, symbolizes an outdated attitude. You may need to discard your old ways of thinking and habits.

To dream that you are being chased by a dinosaur, indicates your fears of no longer being needed or useful. Alternatively, being chased by a dinosaur, may reflect old issues that are still coming back to haunt you.

Diploma

To see or receive a diploma in your dream, symbolizes completion and/or recognition for a job well done.

Dirty

To dream that you or something is dirty, represents your anxieties and feelings toward sex. The dream stems from low self-esteem and feelings of being unworthy. You need to purify your mind, heart and body.

Disability

To dream that you have a disability, indicates that you are experiencing a lowered self-esteem. You have lost your power or direction in life. Perhaps you are not utilizing your full potential and skills. Consider the symbolism of the part of your body that is disabled.

Disappear

To dream that people or objects are disappearing right before your eyes, signify your anxieties and insecurities over the notion that loved ones might disappear out of your life. You feel that you cannot depend on anyone and that you will end up alone. You need to work on your self-image and self-esteem.

Alternatively, to dream that someone is disappearing, suggests that you may not have given sufficient attention to those aspects/qualities of that person within your own self. Have you lost touch with some aspect of yourself? If your lover is disappearing, then it suggests that your love or interest for them is fading.

Disco

To dream that you are a disco, suggests that you need to get out and be more sociable.

To dream that you are listening or dancing to disco music, represents your free spirit.

Disc Jockey

To listen to a disc jockey in your dream, represents a message from your unconscious. The disc jockey may be trying to give you some advice about a waking situation. Alternatively, the dream may symbolize someone in your life with the initials "DJ".

Disco Ball

To see a disco ball in your dream, symbolizes your fun and free spirit. It is a reflection of the various components of your life.

Disease

To dream that you are inflicted with a disease, forewarns of some illness or physical ailment. Sometimes your dreams are able to diagnose an illness before you are aware of the symptoms. Alternatively, the disease in your dream may be symbolic of some fear or tension that you are experiencing in your waking life.

Disguise

To dream that you are in a disguise, indicates that you are hiding from something or someone in your waking life. It is time to face reality and stop hiding behind a facade. Alternatively, the dream suggests that you are being someone you are not.

Dishes

To see dishes in your dream, represent ideas, concepts, and attitudes. The dream may be a pun on the things you are "dishing" out to others. Or it could describe someone you are interested in as in someone who is a "dish". Perhaps it is time that you make the first move. If the dishes are dirty and unwashed, then it signify dissatisfaction and an unpromising outlook. You may have overlooked some problems in your life or you have not confronted your emotions.

To dream that you are washing dishes, suggest that you are moving on and planning for the next thing that comes your way. Alternatively, it represents your daily routine. Perhaps you are in a rut.

To see shelves of polished dishes, suggest that you are doing your best and making the best out of a situation. You are trying to make a good impression.

To see broken dishes or break dishes in your dream, signify feelings of poverty, lack, and inadequacy. You may feel that you are not meeting the expectations of others.

Disneyland

To dream that you are at Disneyland, indicates that you need to take some time off, especially after all the hard work that you have been involved in. Known as the "happiest place on earth", the dream may suggest a lack of happiness in your life. You are looking for that happiness.

Dismemberment

To dream that you are dismembered, suggests that some situation or circumstance is falling apart in your waking life. You feel cut off, isolated and disempowered. You may also be experiencing some great and significant loss. Consider also which part of your body is dismembered as that body part may offer additional significance or needs special attention. Alternatively, the dream may coincide with some significant life change as in a new job, new school, marriage, moving, etc. You are feeling a loss of power, potential, or identity.

Dissection

To dream that you are dissecting something, suggests that you are trying to get to the core of some situation. You are trying to peel away at the layers in order to get to the heart of the matter.
Alternatively, the dream may indicate that you are overanalyzing a situation. Consider also what you are dissecting.

In particular, to dream that you are dissecting a frog, indicates that you are trying to figure out if the guy you are interested in is just a frog or is a real prince. Alternatively, the dream seeks to bring you back to your high school science class and how you felt when you had to dissect a frog.

To dream that you are dissecting a human cadaver, suggests that you are trying to reveal or expose an aspect of yourself that you have kept hidden.

Diving

To dream that you are diving into clear water, indicates that you have overcome your obstacles and setbacks. You have a new sense of confidence. Things are looking up. Alternatively, the dream indicates that you are trying to get to the bottom of a current situation or the root of your problems or feelings. It may also refer exploration of your unconscious.

To dream that you are diving into muddy water, suggests that you are feeling anxious about how you have handled certain issues in your waking life.

To see others diving in your dream, represents psychological and emotional balance.

To see animals diving in your dream, suggest that are exploring your instinctual and sexual urges which have been previously suppressed into your unconscious.

Divorce

To dream that you are getting a divorce, indicates that you need to differentiate between things in your life and prioritize them. Perhaps you need to separate yourself from some issue or some aspect of yourself. Alternatively, the dream suggests that you have a fear of separation or fear of being alone. You may be unsatisfied with your present relationship.

Divorce dreams may reflect real-life events and the stress that it brings. You may be wondering if you have made a mistake in some situation or decision Divorce dreams suggest a transitional phase. It is time to change your old habits.

DNA

To dream about DNA, suggests that you need to focus your energy. Carefully plot out your goals so you can move ahead in life. Learn from the negativity that you have experienced. DNA symbolizes life, humanity and science. The dream may also represent the initials "D" and "A". Consider who or what in your life has these initials.

Doctor

To dream that you are seeing the doctor, indicates your need for emotional and spiritual healing. The dream could also highlight medical concerns. Perhaps it is time to go and get a physical check up.

To dream that you are a doctor, suggests that there is some problem that you need to patch up or some emotional wound that you need to bandage up. Alternatively, it signifies your ability to offer your support to others.

Dog

To see a dog in your dream, symbolizes intuition, loyalty, generosity, protection, and fidelity. The dream suggests that your strong values and good intentions will enable you to go forward in the world and bring you success. The dream dog may also represent someone in your life who exhibits these qualities. Alternatively, to see a dog in your dream, indicates a skill that you may have ignored or forgotten. If the dog is vicious and/or growling, then it indicates some inner conflict within yourself. It may also indicate betrayal and untrustworthiness. If the dog is dead or dying, then it means a loss of a good friend or a deterioration of your instincts.

To dream that a dog bites you on the leg, suggests that you have lost your ability to balance aspects of your life. You may be hesitant in approaching a new situation or have no desire to move forward with your goals. Alternatively, it symbolizes disloyalty.

To see a happily barking dog in your dream, symbolizes pleasures and social activity. You are being accepted into some circle. If the dog is barking ferociously, then it represents your habit of making demands on people and controlling situations around you. Are you "barking" too many orders? Alternatively, it could also indicate unfriendly companions.

To dream that you are buying a dog, indicates your tendency to buy your friends or buy compliments and favors. Alternatively, it suggest a need for you to find companionship. If you are being guided by a dog, then it suggests that you are having difficulties in navigating out of a situation or problem.

To dream that you give or send your dog away, indicates that the decisions and choices you are making now may be misinterpreted as disloyalty. You have to do what is right for you and not worry about what others think of the decision. Alternatively, it signifies rejection of friendship.

To dream that you are dressing up your dog, signifies your attempts to cover up your own character flaws and habits.

To see a black colored dog in your dream, symbolizes the shadow aspect of a friend. The dark side of someone close to you is being revealed and you are able to see through to their true intentions.

Also consider the notions associated with the word dog, such as loyalty ("man's best friend") and to be "treated like a dog".

Dog House

To see a dog house in your dream, suggests that you are in big trouble. You are being punished for your actions.

Dodgeball

To play dodgeball in your dream, parallels a situation in your waking life where you are either on the offensive or on the defensive. If you are throwing the ball, then it represents pent up anger and aggression. If you are hit by the ball, then it suggests that you are feeling victimized by a situation. Alternatively, the dream may be a metaphor that you are "dodging" or avoiding a situation or question.

Doll

To dream that a doll comes to life, signifies your desires to be someone else and escape from your present problems and responsibilities. The doll serves as a means to act out your wishes.

To see a doll in your dream, symbolizes childhood innocence and light-hearted fun. The dream may also be a metaphor for someone that you call or refer to as "doll".

To dream that you are playing with a doll, represents a lack of communication between your conscious and unconscious mind. The dream also indicates an immature attitude towards the opposite sex.

Dollhouse

To see or play with a dollhouse in your dream, suggests that you are idealizing family life. You have the notion that everything is perfect or problem-free. Perhaps you are in denial about any problems. Alternatively, the dollhouse in your dream may serve as an indirect way to solve and work out waking problems with family members.

Dolphins

To see a dolphin in your dream, symbolizes spiritual guidance, intellect, mental attributes and emotional trust. The dream is usually an inspirational one, encouraging you to utilize your mind to its capacity and move upward in life. Alternatively, it suggests that a line of communication has been established between the conscious and unconscious aspects of yourself. Dolphins represent your willingness and ability to explore and navigate through your emotions.

To dream that you are riding a dolphin, represents your optimism and social altruism.

To dream that a dolphin is dying, indicates feeling of despair. You are feeling disconnected.

Dominatrix

To dream that you are a dominatrix, represents your need for power and control. Alternatively, it suggests that you are experiencing an elevated sense of spirituality.

Dominoes

To see or play dominoes in your dream, suggests that your actions are sure to affect those around you. Consider the phrase "fall like dominoes".

Donkey

To see a donkey in your dream, represents your stubbornness and unyielding personality. You are unwilling to cooperate with others. The donkey also symbolizes menial work. You may be feeling overburdened or stressed. If the donkey is dead, then it denotes that your party hearty attitude will lead to unrestrained immorality. Alternatively, the donkey is representative of the United States democratic party. Consider your personal associations and feelings about the democrats.

To dream that you fall off or are thrown from a donkey, signifies separation and disharmony in love..

To dream that you are kicked by a donkey, suggests that you are afraid of being caught in some illicit activity. There is a cloud of suspicion over you.

To dream that you are leading a donkey by a halter, signifies your leadership abilities. You have the gift of convincing people to see things your way.

Donuts

*Please See <u>Doughnuts</u>.

Door

To dream that you are entering through a door, signifies new opportunities that are presented before you. You are entering into a new stage in your life and moving from one level of consciousness to another. In particular, a door that opens to the outside, signifies your need to be more accessible to others, whereas a door that opens into the inside, denotes your desire for inner exploration and self-discovery.

To see an opened door in your dream, symbolizes your receptiveness and willingness to accept new ideas/concepts. In particular, to see a light behind the door, suggests that you are moving toward greater enlightenment/spirituality.

To dream that the door is closed or locked, signifies opportunities that are denied and not available to you or that you have missed out on. Something or someone is blocking your progress. It also symbolizes the ending of a phase or project. In particular, if you are outside the locked door, then it suggests that you have anti-social tendencies. If you are inside the locked door, then it represents harsh lessons that need to be learned.

To dream that you are locking the door, suggests that you are closing yourself off from others. You are hesitant in letting others in and revealing your feelings. It is indicative of some fear and low self-worth. If someone slams the door in your face, then it indicates that you are feeling shut out or some activity or that you are being ignored.

To see revolving doors in your dream, suggests that you are literally moving in circles and going nowhere. You may feel that your opportunities and choices lead to a dead end.

Doorbell

To dream that you hear or ring a door bell, indicates that you are open to new experiences. The dream may also be calling attention to something that you have overlooked.

99

Perhaps you do not yet realize that an opportunity is open to you.

Dormitory

To dream that you are in a dormitory, represents the value you place on knowledge and education. You believe that you are constantly learning, even when you are in the classroom. If you are currently a college student who live in a dormitory, then this symbol may just be a reflection of your current surroundings and hold similar meaning as a house.

Dots

To see dots in your dream, symbolize routine and monotony.

Double

To see your own double in your dream, suggests that you are attempting to recapture the past and the good old times. Alternatively, the dream may indicate that you are needlessly working twice as hard or doing double duty.

Dough

To see or work with dough in your dream, signifies potential, possibilities and the ability to create. The dream may also be a metaphor to symbolize money.

Doughnuts

To see a doughnut in your dream, represents the Self. It suggests that you may be feeling lost and still trying to find yourself and your purpose in life. Alternatively, it refers to growth, development and nurturance. You are not yet completely whole.

Doves

To see a dove in your dream, symbolizes peace, tranquility, harmony, affection and innocence. In particular, to see a white dove in your dream, represents loyalty, love, simplicity, gentleness and friendships. It may also signify a message and blessing from the Holy Spirit. You have let go of your thoughts of hate and revenge.

To dream that doves are mating and building a nest, symbolize a joyous home life filled with love, tranquility, pleasure and security.

Down

To dream that you are moving down, suggests that you have made a wrong decision or headed toward the wrong direction in life. Alternatively, the ream may be a pun on "feeling down" or depressed. "Going down" may also sexual connotation and be a metaphor for oral sex.

Dracula

*Please See Vampire.

Drafted

To dream that you have been drafted, indicates that the opinions and beliefs of others are being forced upon you. You are feeling pressure from those around you who want you to do something that you are not comfortable with. Alternatively, it indicates your need for more self discipline in your life.

Dragon

To see a dragon in your dream, represents your strong will and fiery personality. You tend to get carried away by your passion, which may lead you into trouble. You need to exercise some self-control.

In the eastern cultures, dragons are seen as spiritual creatures symbolizing good luck and fortune.

To dream that you are a dragon and breathing fire, suggests that you are using your anger to get your own way.

Dragonfly

To see a dragonfly in your dream, symbolizes change and regeneration. It may also indicate that something in your life may not appear as it seems. Alternatively, the dream represents instability, flightiness or activity. You are always on the go.

To dream that you are eating a dragonfly, suggests that you are consumed by some sort of passion even at the risk of offending or hurting other's feelings.

Drain

To see a drain in your dream, signifies your need to release and channel your emotions. You should not keep your feelings inside. Consider the condition and appearance of the drain for clues on how you are feeling. Alternatively, it may represent some wasted effort or loss. The dream may also be a pun on something or someone that is "draining" you of your energy or resources.

To dream that you are unclogging the drain, indicates that you need to remove some obstacle or blockage that is hindering your progress.

Drawing

To dream that you are drawing, represents an expression of your latent artistic abilities. You need to show more of your creativity in your waking life. Alternatively, the dream may be a pun on a "draw" to mean a tie or some undecided decision or argument. "It's a draw.".

Dreams

To dream that you are dreaming, signifies your emotional state. You are excessively worried and fearful about a situation or circumstance that you are going through.

Dress

To see or wear a dress in your dream, represents a feminine outlook or feminine perspective on a situation. You are freely expressing your femininity. If you are a man and dream that you are wearing a dress, suggests that others are questioning your sexuality. Or that you are feeling sexually insecure.

To dream that you are wearing a white dress, implies that you want to appear pure and angelic toward others. Perhaps you are trying to look "innocent". If the dress is another color, look up the specific color for additional significance.

Dressing Room

To dream that you are in a dressing room, suggests that you are trying to fit into some new situation or role. You are working on a fresh self-image. If the clothes do not fit, then it implies a feeling of insecurities. You feel you don't fit in. Alternatively, the dream represents your changing roles and the various personas you have.

Drift

*Please See <u>Floating.</u>

Drill

To see a drill in your dream, indicates that you are headed toward a new direction in life. You are opening yourself up to new experiences and insights.

Drinking

To dream that you are drinking water, represents spiritual refreshment. You will find resolution by looking within yourself and your past. Alternatively, the dream may indicate that you are really thirsty.

101

To dream that you are drinking alcohol, denotes that you are seeking either pleasure or escape. In particular, if you are drinking wine, then it is symbolic of a divine power.

Drinks

Please See <u>Beverage.</u>

Driving

To dream that you are driving a vehicle, signifies your life's journey and your path in life. The dream is telling of how you are moving and navigating through life. If you are driving and cannot see the road ahead of you, then it indicates that you do not know where you are headed in life and what you really want to do with yourself. You are lacking direction and goals. Similarly, to dream that you are driving at night, suggests that you are unsure of where you are headed in life. You are experiencing obstacles toward your goals. Perhaps you do not want to see what is ahead for you or you are afraid to confront certain issues. You may be feeling apprehensive about the future. If your view is blocked or obstructed while you are driving, then it symbolizes your lacking awareness of something in your life. You are overlooking certain aspects in your life. Alternatively, the dream indicates dangers or problems that are not yet made known to you. If you are driving on a curvy road, then it indicates that you are having difficulties in achieving your goals and accepting the changes associated with it. Metaphorically, driving a car in your dream, is analogous to your sex life and sexual performance. Consider how you are driving and what kind of car you are driving and how it relates to your waking sex life. Or the dream may be a pun on your "drive" or ambition.

To dream that someone else is driving you, represents your dependence on the driver. You are not in control of your life and following the goals of others instead of your own. If you are driving from the passenger side of a car, then it suggests that you are trying to gain control of the path that your life is taking. You are beginning to make your own decisions.

To dream that you are driving a cab or bus, suggests that menial tasks are providing little opportunities for advancement.

To dream that you are driving a car in reverse, suggests that you are experiencing major setbacks in your goals. In particular, if you drive in reverse into a pool of water, then it means that you emotions are literally holding you back.

To dream that you are driving drunk, indicates that your life is out of control. Some relationship or somebody is dominating you.

To dream that you drive off a mountain road, suggests that the higher you climb in life, the harder it is to stay at the top. You feel that your advanced position is a precarious one. It takes hard work to remain at the top. You may also feel that you are not able to measure up to the expectations of others.

To dream that you are a backseat driver, means that you have problems relinquishing control. You have power issues.

Driving Test

To dream that you are taking a driving test, suggests that your goals and aspirations are being put to the test. You may be questioning what you really want to do with your life. If you fail the driving test, then it indicates that you do not have the necessary tools to move toward your goals. You may be lacking confidence. If you pass the driving test, then it represents your motivation and confidence in your ability.

Drooling

To dream that you are drooling, suggests that you are feeling foolish or embarrassed by some situation. On the other hand, you may be taking things to seriously and need to let loose.

Drought

To dream of a drought, indicates that you are void of emotions. You are withdrawn and depressed. The dream may be a result of a major loss in your life. Alternatively, the dream suggests that you are not drinking enough water and staying well hydrated.

Drowning

To dream that you are drowning, indicates that you are feeling overwhelmed by emotions. Repressed issues may be coming back to haunt you. You may be proceeding too quickly in trying to discover your unconscious thoughts. You should proceed more cautiously and slowly. If you drown to death, then is refers to an emotional rebirth. If your survive the drowning, then it means that a waking relationship or situation will ultimately survive the turmoil.

To see someone drowning in your dream, suggests that you are becoming too deeply involved in something that is beyond your control. Alternatively, it represents a sense of loss in your own identity. You are unable to differentiate who you are anymore.

To dream that you rescue someone from drowning, indicates that you have successfully acknowledged certain emotions and characteristics that is symbolized by the drowning victim.

Drugs

To dream that you are in possession of or taking drugs, signifies your need for a "quick fix" or an escape from reality. You may be turning to a potentially harmful alternative as an instant escape from your problems. Ask yourself why you need the drugs. What do you hope the drugs will achieve for you?

To dream that you or someone overdoses, suggests that you do not know your limits. You may be pushing yourself too hard. Alternatively, the dream means that you are on a self-destructive path and need to make some significant changes.

To dream that you are dealing or selling drugs, represents changes.

To dream that you have been drugged, indicates that you are refusing to take responsibility for your actions.

Drums

To dream that you are playing the drums, indicate that you progress through life by your own terms. You are strong willed and stick by the decisions you make. The dream may also be a metaphor to indicate you are "drumming up" business. You need to be more aggressive with your new ideas.

To hear a drum in your dream, symbolizes the rhythm of life and the need to keep a steady pace in the pursuit of your goals.

Drunk

To dream that you are drunk, suggests that you are acting careless and insensible. You are losing control of your life and losing a grip on reality. Perhaps you are trying to escape from a waking situation.

Duck

To see ducks in your dream, represent your spiritual freedom (if flying) or the unconscious (if swimming). They serve as a connection between the spiritual realm and the physical world. Ducks are multi-talented animals in that they can walk, swim and fly. Thus, a duck indicates your flexibility and your ability to blend and adapt in various situations. Alternatively, the dream suggests that you are setting yourself up or being set up for the kill as associated by the phrase "sitting duck". Are you being targeted? Also, the duck may be a pun on "ducking" some issue or situation, instead of confronting it head-on. Consider the phrase, "if it looks like a duck, walks like a duck, quacks like a duck, it's a duck". Some things are too obvious to deny.

To see a white duck in your dream, signifies falsehood and deceit.

To see a two-headed duck in your dream, suggests that you need to be more grounded. You need to thoroughly think through some emotional issue.

Duel

To dream that you are in a duel, signifies internal disagreements or inner conflicts in which you need to find a middle ground. You need to stop seeing things in black and white.

Dump Truck

To see or drive a dump truck in your dream, suggests that you need to get rid of the burden that you have been carrying around with you. This dream symbol may be related to some major change.

Dummy

To see a dummy in your dream, indicates that a critical component is lacking in your relationship. You are feeling unchallenged and unfulfilled. The relationship is making you feel empty. The dream may also point to how you or someone has acted foolishly and stupidly in a situation.

Dumpling

To see or eat dumplings in your dream, signify dietary balance. You need to take better care of your health.

To make or wrap dumplings in your dream, symbolizes tradition, family, and togetherness.

Dumpster

To dream that you are at a dumpster, implies that you may that you are being dumped on. You feel rejected. Alternatively, it indicates that you are trying to rid yourself of old, negative habits and bad characteristics.

To dream that you are secretly throwing something away in a dumpster, suggests that you are not taking responsibility for something.

Dungeon

To dream that you are in a dungeon, represents your unconscious thoughts and wishes. Consider what you see or do in the dungeon. Alternatively, it indicates that you will overcome the obstacles in your waking life by continuing to struggle and utilizing your wisdom.

Durian

To see or eat durian in your dream, indicates that you should not judge others based on the outside. You never know what you will find if you get pass the exterior appearances. Alternatively, the dream may mean that some unpleasant memory or obstacle is trying to hinder your path to self discovery.

Dust

To see dust in your dream, suggests that certain aspects of yourself have been ignored or neglected.

To dream that you are covered in dust, signifies that the failure of others will adversely affect you.

To dream that you are dusting, implies that you are clearing out all your past mistakes and starting fresh on a new slate.

To dream that gold dust is running through your fingers, indicates regrets with the ending of some personal relationship. You feel that you've made a terrible mistake.

Dye

To dream that you or someone is dyeing cloths and garments, suggests that you are expressing a desire to project a new identity. Depending on the color of the dye, it could be positive or negative. Consider the specific color for further significance.

To dream that you are dyeing your hair, indicates that you are trying to project a new persona. If you are dyeing your hair to a darker color, then it suggests that you want to be more serious. If you are dyeing your hair to a lighter color, then you are looking to be more livelier.

Dynamite

To see dynamite in your dream, symbolizes danger. There is a significant change that is quickly approaching. Alternatively, you may be harboring aggression that is about to blow up.

E

To see the letter "E" in your dream, implies ease and relaxation. The drug ecstasy is often referred to as "E".

Eagles

To see an eagle in your dream, symbolizes nobility, pride, fierceness, freedom, superiority, courage, and powerful intellectual ability. It also represents self-renewal and your connection with your spirituality. You will struggle fiercely and courageously to realize your highest ambitions and greatest desires. Alternatively, if you live in the United States, then the national bird could represent your patriotism and devotion to country.

To see a chained or trapped eagle in your dream, represents a desperate situation where you are feeling restricted and confined. You are unable to express yourself and be who you really want to be. Consider also what the eagle is chained down to for additional clues as to what might be holding you back.

To see a nest of young eagles in your dream, represents your achievements and your climb to the top of the social ladder.

To dream that you kill an eagle, signifies your ruthlessness. You will let nothing stand in your way of ambitions and obtaining your goals, even if it means hurting those around you. If someone else kills an eagle, then it indicates that your fame, fortune and power will be ruthlessly taken from you.

To dream that you eat the flesh of an eagle, implies that your strong and powerful character will lead you to great wealth and influence.

Earlobe

To dream that your earlobes are long, represent your spiritual or ancestral connection. It is also indicative of royalty and your social status in life.

To dream that you are stretching your earlobes, indicates your desires to be more connected with your ancestors and understanding of where you came from. Alternatively, it means that you want to stand out and be different. You want to go against the norm.

Earphones

*Please See Headphones.

Earrings

To dream that you or someone is wearing earrings, suggests that you need to listen more carefully and pay attention to a message that someone is conveying to you.

To see broken earrings in your dreams, suggests that someone is talking about you.

To dream that you are buying earrings, represents your desire for acceptance and affection.

To dream that you lost an earring, indicates that you are being misguided.

Ears

To see ears in your dreams, suggest that you need to be more responsive or receptive to guidance and assistance from others. You may be relying too much on your own judgment and intuition. You need to listen more closely to what you are being told. Alternatively, it signifies your immaturity and lack of experience. If you dream that your ears are weird or oddly shaped, then it indicates deception.

To dream that you are cleaning wax from your ears, suggests that you are not listening to those around you. There may be something that you are refusing to hear. Are you turning a deaf ear?

To dream of pain in your ear, indicates that you will be receive some bad or offensive news.

To dream that your ear is being pulled, indicates dissent and disagreements. If you are pulling someone else's ear, then it suggest that you have a tendency to force your opinions on others.

To dream that your ears are getting red, symbolizes shame or guilt.

To dream that someone is whispering in your ear, suggests that you need to pay closer attention to something or listen to someone more carefully. Alternatively, it represents your insecurities and anxieties that people are talking about your behind your back.

To dream that you are getting your ears pierced, represents some stinging remarks or insults.

Earth

To notice the earth in your dream, indicates that you need to be "grounded" and realistic. Perhaps your sense of stability and security is lacking. Consider the consistency of the earth for additional significance on how you are feeling. If the earth opens or separates, then it represents a project or relationship that you are afraid of falling into.

To see the planet Earth in your dream, signifies wholeness and global consciousness. You are interconnected with the world.

Earthquake

To dream of an earthquake, suggests that you are experiencing a major "shake-up" that is threatening your stability and foundation. The dream highlights your insecurity, fears and sense of helplessness. Is there something in your life that you feel at "fault" for?

If you find cover from the quake, you will overcome these challenges. If you become trapped or injured during the quake, you will suffer some sort of loss in your life. According to the bible, earthquakes symbolize God's anger and power.

Earwax

To dream that you have excessive earwax, suggests that there is something you are refusing to hear.

East

To dream that you are headed east, represents inner wisdom, rejuvenation, and spiritual enlightenment. You need to dedicate yourself to your goals, family, career, etc. The direction east also symbolizes the sun. Since east is related to the direction right, it can suggest that you are headed in the right direction.

Easter

To dream about Easter, suggests that the worst of your problems are over. Things will look up for you after a period of darkness and sadness. It is time to walk with your head held high and stop being ashamed. Alternatively, the dream symbolizes resurrection and spiritual rebirth.

Eating

To dream that you are eating alone, signifies loss, loneliness, and depression. You may feel rejected, excluded, and cut off from social/family ties. Eating may be a replacement for companionship and provide a form of comfort. Alternatively, eating alone reflects independent needs. Also consider the pun, "what's eating you up?" in reference to anxiety that you may be feeling.

To dream that you are eating with others, signifies harmony, intimacy, merriness, prosperous undertakings, personal gain, and/or joyous spirits.

To dream that you are overeating or not eating enough, signifies a lack of spirituality and fulfillment in your waking life. Food can represent love, friendship, ambition, sex or pleasure in your life. Thus, food is a metaphor to fulfill and gratify your hunger for love and desires. If you are refusing to eat, then it indicates that you want to be more independent and not rely on others so much. If you dream that you are a picky eater, than it indicates that you are holding back something. If you are currently dieting in your waking life, then the dream may serve to compensate for the sustenance that you are lacking.

To dream that someone clears away the food before you finish eating, foretells that you will have problems and issues from those beneath you or dependent upon you.

Eating Contest

To dream that you are in an eating contest, suggests that you are lacking a social life. You are turning to food as a companion. Consider also the type of food you are eating to determine which area of your life is severely lacking. Alternatively, the dream highlights your ability to process emotions quickly.

Eavesdropping

To dream that you are eavesdropping, signifies the coming of bad news. You will not like what you hear. Alternatively, it indicates that you are left out on something or someone is hiding information from you. As a result, you are feeling insecure

Echo

To hear or make an echo in your dream, symbolizes your need to repeat yourself in order to be heard and for others to believe you. Pay attention to the power and impact of your own words. You are waiting and hoping for a reaction from those around you. It is also symbolic of the soul. Alternatively, to hear your own voice echo, indicates that someone is mocking you. Or it could mean that your past actions will come back to haunt you. You need to confront those old memories and past issues.

Eclipse

To dream of an eclipse of the sun, indicates self-doubt and fears of not achieving your goals. You feel you are being overshadowed and are underestimating your abilities. Your level of confidence is fading or lost. You may be undergoing some difficult times and unable to remain optimistic.

To see the eclipse of the moon in your dream, signifies that your feminine side is being overshadowed. Or it may mean that some hidden aspect of yourself is coming to the surface.

To dream that the eclipse has passed, symbolizes new light and knowledge. You need to look at a problem from a different perspective.

Eel

To see an eel in your dream, indicates that you have issues with commitment. It also means that you have problems holding on to things. Consider the phrase "slippery as an eel" to mean someone who escapes responsibility or culpability. Alternatively, the eel may be a phallic symbol and thus have erotic connotations.

Eggs

To see or eat eggs in your dream, symbolize fertility, birth and your creative potential. Something new is about to happen. If the eggs are scrambled, then the dream represents your commitment on a set coarse. It may also mean that you need to accept the consequences of your actions.

To find a nest filled with eggs in your dream, signify some financial gain; the more abundant and bigger the eggs, the more significant the gain.

To see cracked or broken eggs in your dream, represent feelings of vulnerability or a fragile state in your life. Consider the phrase, walking on eggshells. Alternatively, you may be breaking out of your shell and being comfortable with who you are.

To see bright colored eggs in your dream, symbolizes celebration of a happy event.

To dream of rotten eggs, signify loss. You may have allowed some situation to take a turn for the worse. Alternatively, the dream is telling you that something may look fine on the outside, but as you delve deeper, you find that it is not what it appears to be. Perhaps, something is too good to be true.

To see fish eggs in your dream, represent an idea that has emerged from your unconscious.

Eight

Eight stands for power, authority, success, karma, material gains, regeneration, and wealth. When the number eight appears in your dream, trust your instincts and intuition. Alternatively, the number eight may be a pun on "ate". Perhaps there is some information that you need to digest.

Eight Ball

To see the eight ball in your dream, indicates that you tend to leave things to chance or fate. Consider the phrase, to be "behind the eight ball". Perhaps you feel that you are stuck or that you are in a hopeless situation. You need to remain strong. Also consider the significance of the number eight in your waking life.

Eighteen

Eighteen symbolizes the conflict between materialism and spirituality. It also warns of treachery, deception, lies, and selfishness. Alternatively, being eighteen means your gateway to adulthood and the responsibilities that go along with it.

Elastic

*Please See Rubber Band

Elbows

To see your own elbow in your dream, indicates that you need to make a space for yourself. Your dream may express hesitance or fear in creating your own space for fear of being scrutinized. Alternatively, the dream may be a pun on your need to put more "elbow grease" on some task.

To dream that your elbow is wounded, suggests your inability to function in some waking situation. It may also refer to some sexual anxiety. The right elbow relates to moral and ethical issues while the left elbow represents passiveness and your undeveloped characteristics.

Election

To dream that you are at an election, represents a choice that you need to make which may affect others.

Electricity

To dream of electricity, symbolizes vigor and life energy. You need to be revitalized. Alternatively, the dream suggests that you need to conserve your energy.

To dream that the electricity is out, indicates your lack of insight and perspective on a situation.

Electrocution

To dream of an electrocution, indicates that the current course of your actions will lead to disaster. The dream also represents fear and the consequences of your actions. You need to be more aware of your surroundings and those around you.

Elephant

To see an elephant in your dream, indicates that you need to be more patient or more understanding of others. Or perhaps there is a memory that you are holding on to for too long. You need to let go of the past. The elephant is also a symbol of power, strength, faithfulness and intellect. Alternatively, the elephant's introverted personality may be a reflection of your own personality. In particular, if you see a white elephant, then it symbolizes royalty.

To dream that you are riding an elephant, indicates that you are in control of your unconscious and aspects that you were once afraid of.

To dream that you are afraid of the elephant, suggests that there is an enormous problem that you are afraid to confront.

To dream that you are an elephant, suggests that you need to make your opinions and views known. You need to be more vocal and voice your ideas. Express yourself. Alternatively, dreaming that you are an elephant may be reflective of your conservative views. The elephant is the symbol of the United States Republican party. Perhaps you are sharing the same views as the Republican party.

Elevator

To dream that you are ascending in an elevator, represents a rise to status and wealth. You may have risen to a higher level of consciousness and are looking at the world from an elevated viewpoint. If the elevator is moving upward in an out of control fashion or it crashes through the roof, then it indicates that you are being catapulted to a position of power in which you do not yet know how to deal with. You are afraid of the new responsibilities ahead for you. Descending in an elevator, suggests that you are being grounded or coming back down to reality. It also signifies setbacks and misfortunes.

In general, the up and down action of the elevator represents the ups and downs of your life. It also symbolizes emotions and thoughts that are emerging out of and submerging into your subconscious. Alternatively, the dream may have sexual connotations.

To dream that the elevator is out of order or that it is not letting you off, symbolizes that your emotions have gotten out of control. It may be a reflection of your life or your career. You are feeling stuck in some aspect of your life, whether it is your career, relationship, etc.

To dream that the elevator is moving sideways, means that your efforts are counterproductive. You are going nowhere in your work, relationship or other situation.

Eleven

Eleven stands for intuition, mastery in a particular domain, spirituality, enlightenment, and capacity to achieve. It is symbolic of your creativity and your vision. Since the number 11 is represented by two parallel lines, then it may represent two individuals or a partnership. If you turn the 11 on its side, then it symbolizes the equal sign. Perhaps you are looking for some balance and equality.

Elf

To see an elf in your dream, refers to some imbalance and disharmony in your life. The elf often serves as a guide of the soul. Alternatively, it suggests that you need to be more carefree, worry-free, and light-hearted.

Email

To dream about email, indicates that you need to reach out to people who may not necessarily always physically be around. It could also very well mean that you have been spending too much time in front of the computer and this has carried over into your dreams.

Embarrassment

To dream that you are embarrassed, signifies hidden weaknesses, fears and lack of self-confidence. This dream also suggests that you are also harboring some insecurities about your sexuality.

Embryo

To dream of an embryo, symbolizes the emergence of a fresh idea. Also, your unconscious feelings may be surfacing. Alternatively, the dream may refer to your feelings of vulnerability and your need to be protected. However if you are pregnant, it is quite common to see an embryo in your dream.

Emerald

To see an emerald in your dream, represents strength, longevity, immortality, faithfulness, durability, and fertility. You may be entering the healing stages of some situation.

Emotions

Emotions expressed in dreams is a way for people to act out the feelings that they normally would not express if they were awake. The dream provides a "safe" outlet for these emotions instead of letting them get pent up.

Emptiness

To dream of emptiness, suggests that there is something missing or lacking in your life. It symbolizes fruitless labor, an emotional void, or loneliness. There is nothing to show for all the effort that you have dedicated to a project or relationship. In particular, to dream that a container is empty, represents optimism.

End

To dream of an end to something, represents an achievement or goal that has been reached. It may also mean that the bad times are coming to an end. Or perhaps your time is running out and you need to come to a decision about some issue. The end of something also signals the beginning of something new.

Enemy

To see your enemy in your dream, represents opposing ideas and contradictory attitudes. You are in denial about something or you are rejecting someone. Enemies may also represent the enemies within yourself and the inner conflict you have with yourself. Consider the phrase "I am my own worst enemy." Perhaps you are trying to rid yourself of certain aspects of your character.

To dream that you are dealing with an enemy, represents a resolution to some inner conflict or waking life problem.

Engine

To see an engine in your dream, represents your heart and its power. Consider the condition of the engine and how it is running. If the engine does not start, then it symbolizes some obstacle that is hindering your progress and goals.

To dream that you engine is blown or disabled, indicates that you have been betrayed. Alternatively, your old habits and old ways of doing things is hindering your progress.

Envelope

To see an envelope in your dream, signifies anticipation or opportunity. If you are opening an envelope, then it represents a message that you or someone is trying to convey to you. Alternatively, the dream means that you are "pushing the envelope." You are testing the limits or boundaries.

To see unopened envelopes, indicate sorrow news and missed opportunities.

Environment

To dream about the environment, symbolizes freedom, tranquility, and renewal.

To dream about environmental issues, represents the important role you play in the overall big picture. Do not underestimate yourself and your abilities. Alternatively, it signifies a sense of powerlessness. You are feeling overwhelmed by things that are out of your control.

Equal Sign

To see the equal sign in your dream, represents balance and symmetry. You are looking for order in your life. As two parallel lines, the equal sign may also symbolize the number 11.

Equator

To dream about the equator, indicates the search for Self. You are exploring aspect of yourself in order to become more whole.

Eraser

To see or use an eraser in your dream, suggests that you need to clear up some mistakes that you have made.

Erection

To dream that you have an erection, symbolizes your creative power and energy. You want to take action. Alternatively, if you are a man and dream of an erection, then it suggests a fear of impotence or sexual dysfunction.

Escalator

To see an escalator in your dream, indicates movement between various levels of consciousness. If you are moving up in the escalator, then it suggests that you are addressing and confronting emotional issues. You are moving through your spiritual journey with great progress and ease. If you are going down the escalator, then it implies repression and descent back into your unconscious. You may be experiencing a setback.

Espresso

To make or drink espresso in your dream, signifies your need to react quickly. The dream is a pun on "express". You need to get moving and act, before the opportunity passes you by.

Evacuation

To dream of an evacuation, suggests that you are isolating yourself and holding back your emotions.

To dream that you are in a town that has been evacuated, indicates that you are feeling rejected by those around you. You are feeling unaccepted.

Evil

To dream that someone or something is evil, denotes a repressed and/or forbidden aspect of yourself. This part of yourself may be seeking recognition and acknowledgment. Alternatively, evil may also be a reflection of your strong, negative emotions like hate, anger, etc.

Ex

To dream about your ex-boyfriend/girlfriend or ex-husband/wife or that you and your ex got back together again, suggests that something or someone in your current life is bringing out similar feelings you felt during that relationship with your ex. The dream may be a way of alerting you to a similar behavioral patterns in your current relationship. What you learn from that previous relationship, may need to be applied to the present one so that you do no repeat the same mistakes. Alternatively, you may be reflecting on the positive experiences and good times that you shared with your past love.

In particular, to see your ex-husband/wife in your dream, indicates that you are currently finding yourself in a situation that you do not want to be in. It suggests that you are experiencing a similar relationship or situation which makes you feel unhappy and uncomfortable. Alternatively, dreaming that you are together with your ex-husband/wife, implies that you are unconsciously repeating the same old patterns from that relationship to your current relationship. You are making the same mistakes and reacting the same way.

To dream that your ex-boyfriend or ex-girlfriend is missing you, suggests that you "miss" some aspect of that past relationship. A situation in your current life may be reminding you of your relationship with your ex. Alternatively, the dream may mean that you have moved on with your life. The notion that your ex is missing you may be a pun on that he has "missed" his opportunity or "missed" his chance with you.

To see your mate's ex in your dream, suggests that you are comparing yourself to the ex. The dream is telling you not to make the same relationship mistakes that ended that relationship.

To dream that you ex has died, indicates that your feelings for you ex are completely dead now. The dream is a metaphor of how you have let go of the past and are ready to move on and fully devote yourself to new relationships.

Metaphorically, seeing your ex in your dream may also signify aspects of yourself that you have x'd out or neglected.

Exam

To dream that you are taking an exam, signifies insecurities, fear of not meeting others' expectations, and fear of failure.

Exclamation Point

To see an exclamation point in your dream, symbolizes excitement, vigor, surprise or disbelief. You are seeing a positive outlook on life. Alternatively, the dream is an expressing an urgency in some matter.

Exercise

To dream that you are exercising, signifies your worries about your health. You may be concerned about fitting into society's ideals of beauty. Alternatively, the dream may also indicate that you need to exercise your rights and power in some situation.

Exit

To see an exit in your dream, indicates that you are looking for a way out of a waking situation.

Exorcism

To dream that you or others are being exorcised, symbolizes your initiative to regain control and take steps toward the direction of your goals. Alternatively, you may not be taking responsibility for your actions and are looking for a scapegoat.

Expelled

To dream that you are expelled, represents rejection. Consider what you did in your dream to get expelled and how it may parallel your actions in your waking life.

Explosion

To see explosions in your dream, symbolize your repressed anger. The rage that you have been holding in has come to the surface in a forceful and violent manner. Your unconscious is trying to get your attention.

To dream that your face becomes blackened or mutilated by the explosion, indicates that will be confronted with unjust accusations. As a result, you may suffer from the consequences.

To dream that you are enveloped in flames or blown up into the air by an explosion, suggests that you are being taken advantage of in some situation. Your trust has been compromised.

To hear the sound of a loud explosion, but you did not see it, indicates that something is about to be exposed or come into consciousness.

Exterminator

To see or call an exterminator in your dream, indicates that you need to cut off ties from those who try to pull you down.

To dream that you are an exterminator, suggests that you need to confront your weakness and stand up to the challenges ahead.

Eyebrows

To notice eyebrows in your dream, represent expressions of amazement, disbelief, surprise, or doubt. It may also indicate concern or disapproval.

To dream that you have no eyebrows, suggests that you are lacking emotions. You are not expressing yourself enough.

To dream that you or someone is getting their eyebrow pierced, may be a metaphor for your "piercing eyes". Alternatively, the dream is drawing your attention to something disturbing or significant that you saw. Perhaps you saw something you that shouldn't have.

Eyeglasses

To dream that you are wearing eyeglasses and you do not normally wear them, suggests that you need a clearer view on a situation. There may have been a misunderstanding or a situation was misperceived and needs to be clarified.

To see broken eyeglasses in your dream, indicates that your vision and perception is impaired. You are not seeing the facts correctly.

Eyelashes

To notice your eyelashes or dream that they are growing, indicates that you are trying to express yourself in some subtle or covert way. It also signifies good luck.

To dream that all your eyelashes fall off, suggests that you are having difficulties expressing yourself. It may also mean a loss in your feminine power. If only one eyelash falls off, then it also signifies good luck.

Eyes

To see your own eyes in your dream, represent enlightenment, knowledge, comprehension, understanding, and intellectual awareness. Unconscious thoughts may be coming onto the surface. The left eye is symbolic of the moon, while the right eye represents the sun. It may also be a pun on "I" or the self. If you dream that your eyes have turned inside your head and you can now see the inside of your head, then it symbolizes insight and something that you need to be aware of. This dream may be literally telling you that you need to look within yourself. Trust your intuition and instincts.

To dream that you have something in your eye, represents obstacles in your path. Alternatively, it may represent your critical view and how you tend to see faults in others.

To dream that you have one eye, indicates your refusal to accept another viewpoint. It suggests that you are one-sided in your ways of thinking.

To dream that you have a third eye, symbolizes inner vision, insight, instinct or some psychic ability you have yet untapped. You are able to see what others cannot. Or you need to start looking within yourself and trust your instincts.

To dream that your eyes are injured or closed, suggests your refusal to see the truth about something or the avoidance of intimacy. You may be expressing feelings of hurt, pain or sympathy.

To dream that you have crossed eyes, denotes that you are not seeing straight with regards to some situation. You may be getting your facts mixed up.

To dream that your eyes are bleeding, symbolizes the sacrifices your have made and the difficulties you have endured. Alternatively, the dream signifies some very deep pain or internal conflict within your soul. Although you may not feel any physical pain, you are hurting inside. Perhaps you have been hiding the pain for so long that you forgot what pain feels like. There is some unrest or uneasiness within which needs to be addressed and resolved immediately.

F

To see the letter "F" in your dream, symbolizes failure. It may also denote an expletive as in "F you".

Face

To see your own face in your dream, represents the persona you show to the world as oppose to the real you. It may refer to how you confront problems and deal with issues in your life.

To dream that your face is flawed or pimply, symbolizes erupting emotions. You may be suffering an attack on your persona or your reputation. According to folklore, if you dream that your face is swollen, then it means that you will see an improvement to your financial situation.

To dream that you or someone has two faces or that the faces changes quickly from one person to another, indicates untrustworthiness. You or someone in your life is acting "two-faced".

To dream that you are washing your face, suggests that you need to come clean about some matter.

Facebook

To dream about your Facebook page, represents your desires to expand your social circle. You need to reach out to others in a more direct and personal way. It is time to get out there and experience life.

Faceless

To see a faceless figure or person in your dream, indicates that you are still searching for your own identity and finding out who you are. Perhaps you are unsure of how to read people and their emotions. Therefore, you are expressing a desire to know and understand these people on a deeper level.

115

Facelift

To dream that you have a facelift, suggests that you are seeking a new self-identity and self-image. You may have experienced a surge in your confidence levels. Alternatively, it symbolizes vanity and you concerns about appearances rather than what is inside.

Factory

To dream that you are at a factory, represents repetitious thinking and an old way of doing things. It is symbolic of predictability and unchanging habits. Alternatively, it signifies business, productivity, energy and bustling activity. You are a person that can get things done.

Fainting

To dream that you are fainting, suggests your inability to confront some unconscious issues or feelings. You need to be more aware and acknowledge those feelings.

To see a family member faint in your dream, signifies that you will hear some indiscreet activities from that person.

Fairy

To see a fairy in your dream, indicates that you are in search of some help or advice for a problem or decision, but may not want to directly admit you need help. In particular, if the fairy is evil, then it suggests that an aspect of yourself needs to be set free. The fairy is also symbolic of your soul and the feminine aspects of yourself.

Fairy Tale

To dream that you are a character in a fairy tale, suggests your need to be rescued or to be swept off your feet. It also indicates that you are exploring your limits and trying to awaken your fullest potential.

To dream that you are reading a fairy tale, indicates that you are a romantic at heart.

Fall

To dream that you fall and are not frightened, signifies that you will overcome your adversities with ease.

To dream that you fall and are frightened, indicates a lack of control, insecurity, and/or lack of support in your waking life. You may be experiencing some major struggle and/or overwhelming problem. It may also imply that you have failed to achieve a goal that you have set forth for yourself.

To dream that you are free-falling through water, indicates that you are feeling overwhelmed with emotions. You may feel that it is easier to give up, then to try to stay afloat or prevent yourself from going under.

To dream of the fall season, indicates that something is about to come to an end and something new will begin. Alternatively, the dream is symbolic of the cycle of life. It is time to collect the benefits and rewards that you've worked so hard for.

Family

To see your own family in your dream, represents security, warmth and love. It could also symbolize bitterness, jealousy, or rivalry, depending on your relationship with your family. Alternatively, it could mean that you are overly dependent on your family, especially if the family members are in your recurring dreams .Consider also the significance of a particular family member or the relationship you have with them.

Fan

To see a fan in your dream, refers to the changes in your life. It may also signifies your need to calm down after a highly charged emotional situation or state.

To dream that you are fanning yourself or that someone is fanning you, represents your lack of self-confidence. Alternatively, the dream symbolizes secret desires.

Farm

To see or live on a farm in your dream, suggests that you need to develop an aspect of yourself and utilize your potential. You are ready for growth.

Farting

To dream that you are farting, suggests that you are being passive aggressive. You need to express your feelings in a more direct manner.

Fast Food

To see or eat fast food in your dream, indicates that you are not taking the time to cater to your emotions. You are not taking good care of your physical or mental health.

Fast Forward

If your dream is in fast forward, then it suggests that you are living life in the fast lane. You need to slow down. Alternatively, it may indicate that life is passing you by if you do not jump in and participate in it.

Fasting

To dream that you are fasting, represents self-renewal and self-cleansing. Fasting may also be way to draw attention to some consciousness or problem. Are you trying to punish yourself? Are you feeling guilty about something?

Fat

To dream that you are fat, signifies a fortunate change in your life. You are experiencing abundance in some area of your life. Alternatively, the dream means that you are being overindulgent. You need to learn moderation. A more literal interpretation of this dream is your fears of gaining weight. You have an skewed perception of your own image which may stem from low self-esteem.

To dream that others are fat, signifies prosperity. Consider also the phrase "it ain't over till the fat lady sings" and how you need to wait for the final result and not assume the outcome.

Father

To see your father in your dream, symbolizes authority and protection. It suggests that you need to be more self-reliant. Consider also your waking relationship with your father and how aspects of his character may be incorporated within yourself.

To dream that your father is dead, forewarns that you need to proceed with caution in conducting your business.

To dream that you are hitting your father, represents a desperate need for greater closeness with your father. You feel that he is not listening to you. In particular, if you are hitting your father with a rubber object, indicates that whatever you are doing or telling him has no significant effect on him. Things just literally bounces off him.

Faucet

To see a faucet in your dream, signifies control of your emotions. You are conscious of what emotions you allow yourself to be

117

expressed. In other words, you have great self control and an ability to turn your emotions on and off at will. If the water is too hot or too cold, then it may be analogous to a situation or relationship in your waking life.

To dream that you cannot turn the faucet on or that no water comes out of the faucet, indicates that you need to be more careful when offering emotional support as your may be overextending yourself. Alternatively, it may also be indicative of sadness and depression.

To see a leaky or dripping faucet in your dream, represents sexual issues and problems. Alternatively, the dream suggests that you are feeling emotionally drained. Something or someone is draining your emotionally.

Fax Machine

To see or use a fax machine in your dream, indicates that you are receiving some message from your unconscious. This message will prove to be the real deal.

Feast

To see a feast in your dream, denotes your emotional needs or sexual appetite. There is a lack of balance in your life. If you are gorging yourself at the feast, then it suggests that you are making too much demands of others. It also indicates greediness and selfishness. If you are the only one who did not get any food at the feast, then it indicates your tendency to always put others ahead of your own needs. As a result, you are compromising your own emotional well being and happiness.

To arrive late to a feast, signifies of a bothersome event that will occupy your mind.

Feather

To dream of a feather floating in the air, signifies a life of ease, comfort, warmth and of financial gains. It may describe your lightheartedness and enjoyment for life. Alternatively, a feather may represent confusion, hastiness, and loss of dignity.

To see a feather in you dream, symbolizes warmth. You are expressing your tender side and a desire to be close to someone. Consider also how the dream may relate to the proverb "birds of a feather flock together". Perhaps you need to break away from the masses or you need to make new friends.

In particular, to see chicken feathers in your dream, signify minor annoyances. Eagle feathers represent the realization of your goals and aspirations. To see peacock, ostrich, or any other ornamental feathers, denotes advancement up the social ladder. You will be met with much success in your future.

To dream that you are selling or buying feathers, symbolize frugality and thriftiness.

February

To dream of the month of February, signifies sadness, gloom and ill health. The dream may also symbolize love or you need for love.

Feces

To see or come in contact with feces, signifies aspects of yourself that are dirty and negative and which you believe to be undesirable and repulsive. You need to acknowledge and express these feelings, even though it may be shameful. Release the negativity in your life. Alternatively, it may also refer to someone who is anal retentive.

To dream that you are unable to dispose of the feces, suggests that you are unwilling to let go of your emotions. You have a tendency to hold in and keep your feelings to yourself.

According to Freud, feces is related to possession, pride, shame, money/financial matters, or aggressive acts. So to dream that you are playing with feces, symbolizes your anxiety over money matters and financial security.

Feelings

*Please See Emotions.

Feet

To see your own feet in your dream, symbolizes your foundation, stability and sense of understanding. It signifies your need to be more practical and sensible. Keep both feet on the ground. Alternatively, feet represents mobility, independence and freedom. Perhaps you have taken a step in the right direction and are contemplating your goals or your next step. The sole of the foot may be a pun of being or feeling like the "sole" or only support of some person or situation.

Consider also the pun of "putting your foot in your mouth".

To dream that you are washing your feet, indicates that others can easily take advantage of you. For Christians, washing your feet symbolizes forgiveness and compassion. If someone is kissing your feet, then it symbolizes humbleness, humility, or devotion.

In particular for the people of India, to dream of the feet may symbolize divine qualities since the feet are considered the holiest part of the body.

Female

*Please See Woman.

Fence

To see a fence in your dream, signifies an obstacle or barrier that may be standing on your path. You may feel confined and restricted in expressing yourself. Are you feeling fenced in some situation or confined in some relationship? Alternatively, it may symbolize a need for privacy. You may want to shut off the rest of the world.

To dream that you are climbing to the top of a fence, denotes success. If you climb over the fence, then it indicates that you will accomplish your desires via not so legitimate means. If you dream that you are on the fence, then the dream may be a metaphor indicating that you undecided about something.

To dream that you are building a fence, suggests that you are building a solid foundation for success. Alternatively, it indicates that you are blocking something out or you are shutting yourself out.

To dream that you fall from a fence, denotes that you are in way over your head in regards to some project which you are dealing with.

Feng Shui

To dream about feng shui, represents your search for spiritual balance, understanding and harmony. You are looking for positivity in your life.

Ferry

To dream that you are riding on a ferry, indicates that you are going through some transitional phases in your life. It also means that you are setting your sights on a new goal.

To dream that you are waiting for a ferry, signifies unforeseen circumstances might hinder your desires and wishes.

Ferris Wheel

To see or ride on a Ferris wheel in your dream, suggests that you are going around in circles. You are headed nowhere. Alternatively, it is symbolic of wholeness and the circle of life. Life is full of ups and downs.

Feud

To dream that you are in the middle of a feud, suggests that aspects of your personality are in conflict. In particular, if you dream of a family feud, then it indicates that you are struggling with your identity. The dream may also be a reflection of a waking strife between you and your family members.

Fever

To dream that you have a fever, suggests that feelings of anger or hatred are threatening to come to your consciousness. You need to find a safe way to express these feelings. Alternatively, the dream may be analogous to blushing and thus represent some embarrassing situation.

Fez

To see or wear a fez in your dream, signifies leisurely pursuits, ease and relaxation,

Field Trip

To dream that you are on a field trip, indicates that you need to incorporate what you have learned with your experiences. The dream represents a transitional phase. Consider the symbolism of what you see and how your felt during the field trip.

Fifteen

Fifteen represents a dissolution of difficult conditions.

Fifty

Fifty stands for all that is holy. It also represents joy and celebration. Alternatively, the dream represents your fair share of something, as in 50:50.

Fighter Jet

To see or dream that you are in a fighter jet, indicates that you are involved in some fast pace project.

Fighting

To dream that you are in a fight, indicates inner turmoil. Some aspect of yourself is in conflict with another aspect of yourself. Perhaps an unresolved or unacknowledged part is fighting for its right to be heard. It may also parallel a fight or struggle that you are going through in your waking life. If you are fighting to the death, then it refers to your refusal to acknowledge some waking conflict or inner turmoil. You are unwilling to change your old attitudes and habits.

To see others fighting in your dream, suggests that you are unwilling to acknowledge your own problems and turmoil. You are not taking any responsibility or initiative in trying to resolve issues in your waking life.

Figs

To see or eat figs in your dream, represent a positive turn of events. Figs are also often associated with sex, conception and eroticism.

Figurehead

To see the figurehead of a ship in your dream, suggests that you are seeking protection for your emotional well being. Consider what the figurehead resembles for additional clues.

File

To dream that you are filing away your bills or other important documents, indicates that you need to keep your life in order.

To see files in your dream, symbolize your responsibilities and burdens. There is something important that that you need to tend to.

Filer

To see a nail file in your dream, suggests that you need to smooth out the rough edges of your personality or your relationship with others. You may be a little too harsh and too abrasive toward others.

Find

To dream that you find something, suggests that you are coming into contact with some aspect of your psyche or unconscious. You are recognizing a part of yourself that was previously repressed or undeveloped. Alternatively, it represents change.

To dream that you find someone, indicates that you are identifying new facets of a relationship. You may be taking the relationship to a new level and/or direction.

Fingernails

To notice your fingernails in your dream, indicate that your defenses are up. Consider the length of the nails, the color (if applicable), the condition, and the cleanliness of the nails for additional meaning to your dream. If you dream that your nails are long, then it signify your idleness. You are not taking action. If you are wearing fake fingernails, then it suggest that you are reaching out to others, but do not have their best interest in mind. You may be acting in a disingenuous way.

To dream that you broke a fingernail, suggests that you are trying to avoid some situation or trying to get out of a responsibility. Alternatively, the dream may reflect yourself image. You are overly concerned with how others perceive you.

To dream that you are polishing your fingernails, represent glamour.

To dream that you are chewing your nails, indicate that a problem is too tough to handle. You are not sure how to go about resolving a situation in your waking life.

To dream that your fingernails are growing rapidly, refer to your desires to reach out to someone. You want to be able to extend a part of yourself to others.

To dream that a man has long red fingernails, suggest that he is very in touch with his sensitivity and emotions. It may also relate to issues of sexuality and sensuality.

Fingerprints

To dream that you are being fingerprinted, indicates guilt. You are expressing some regret in your actions. Alternatively, the dream represents your identity and individualism.

To see someone else's fingerprints in your dream, suggest that you are suspicious about something or someone.

Fingers

To see your fingers in you dream, symbolize physical and mental dexterity. They indicate manipulation, action and non-verbal communication. If you dream that your fingers fall off, then it suggests that you are letting a situation dominate you or dictate how you behave. You may be literally losing your grip on life. To dream that you are crossing your fingers, symbolize optimism, success, luck and hope.

To dream that your fingers are injured or have been chopped off, denote your anxieties about your ability to accomplish some demanding task or perform in some waking situation.

To dream of a finger pointing at you, signifies self-blame or guilt. Perhaps you have done something and are afraid that you will be exposed.

To dream about your little finger, represents mental power, intellect, memory, and the power of communication.

To dream of your index finger or forefinger, symbolizes the number one. It also signifies authority, direction, and judgment. Your dream may be trying to make a point.

To dream of your middle finger, denotes prudence, practicality, caution, responsibility, and hard work. Alternatively, the middle finger symbolizes the phallus or some insult.

To dream of your ring finger, represents success, popularity and creativity, It also has associations with marriage, union, commitments and issues of the heart. In 15th century England, it was the ring finger that doctors used to mix and taste their concocted medicines and thus, the ring finger can be symbolic of healing or the need to be healed.

Fir

To see a fir tree in your dream, indicates your need for clarity in some situation. It also symbolize an end to some aspect of your life and the beginning of something new.

Fire

Depending on the context of your dream, to see fire in your dream can symbolize destruction, passion, desire, illumination, purification, transformation, enlightenment, or anger. It may suggest that something old is passing and something new is entering into your life. Your thoughts and views are changing. In particular, if the fire is under control or contained in one area, then it is a metaphor of your own internal fire and inner transformation. The dream may be a metaphor for someone who is "fiery". It represents your drive, motivation, and creative energy. Alternatively, the dream may be warning you of your dangerous or risky activities. You are literally "playing with fire".

To dream that you are being burned by fire, indicates that your temper is getting out of control. Some issue or situation is burning you up inside.

To dream that a house is on fire, indicates that you need to undergo some transformation. If you have recurring dreams of your family house on fire, then it suggests that you are still not ready for the change or that you are fighting against the change. Alternatively, it highlights passion and the love of those around you.

To dream that you put out a fire, signifies that you will overcome your obstacles in your life through much work and effort. If you are setting a fire to something or even to yourself, then it indicates that you are undergoing some great distress. You are at the brink of desperation and want to destroy something or some aspect of yourself.

Fire Eater

To see or dream that you are a fire eater, indicates that you are able to keep your anger and aggression under control. Alternatively, the dream may also be a metaphor that you are literally being consumed by your anger.

Fire Engine

To see a fire engine in your dream, suggests that you are tending to the needs of others and overlooking your own needs. You worry and stress out in situations that are beyond your control. Stop trying to be in the middle of things and stop trying to fix things. Trust that things will work itself out in the end. Use more discretion.

Fire Extinguisher

To see or use a fire extinguisher in your dream, suggests that you are trying to get your emotions under control. Alternatively, the dream means that you need to let go of whatever anger you are still holding on to.

Firecracker

To see a firecracker in your dream, represents your outbursts. Your anger is being misdirected.

To light a firecracker in your dream, suggests that you are trying to divert the negativity and bad karma away from you. You have a fresh new outlook on life.

Fired

To dream that you are fired from your job. indicates that you are wanting to end some relationship or situation in your waking life. It also suggests that you are repressing what you really desire most.

Firefighters

To see a firefighter in your dream, represents your higher Self. You are experiencing a period of cleansing and purification. The firefighter is the symbol of a true hero and of hope.

To dream that you are a firefighter, suggests that you need to cool off or douse a heated situation before it gets out of hand. You need to remain level headed even in the heat of the moment.

Firefly

To see a firefly in your dream, represents bright ideas that are coming out of your unconscious.

Fireplace

To see a lit fireplace in your dream, symbolizes contentment, warmth, and comfort.

To dream of lighting or stirring a fireplace, suggests a burning a desire. You need to get to the heart of some matter or situation.

To see an unlit fireplace, is indicative of low energy, disinterest, or disheartenment.

Fireworks

To see fireworks in your dream, symbolizes enthusiasm, creativity, and talent. It may also indicate that you are showing off and making a spectacle of yourself. Alternatively, fireworks represents release of some pent up or repressed feelings.

Fish

To see fish swimming in your dream, signifies insights from your unconscious mind. Thus to catch a fish, represents insights which have been brought to the surface. Alternatively, a fish swimming in your dream may symbolize conception. Some women dream of swimming fish when they get pregnant. The fish is also an ancient symbol of Christianity and Christian beliefs. Consider the common phrases "like a cold fish", "fish out of water" or something that is "fishy" about a situation. It may also imply a slippery or elusive situation. Perhaps your dream could be telling you that "there are plenty of other fish in the sea", with regards to some relationship issue.

To dream that you are eating fish, symbolizes your beliefs, spirituality, luck, energy and nourishment. It is food for the soul.

To dream of cooking fish, indicates that you are incorporating your new realizations with your spiritual feelings and knowledge.

To dream that you are cleaning fish, suggests that you are altering your emotional expression in a way that will be presentable to others. You are censoring yourself and not expressing how you completely feel.

Fish Tank

To see or clean a fish tank in your dream, indicates how you have full control of your emotions. You keep your feelings in check. If you are watching the fish in the fish tank, then you may feel that your life is going nowhere or that you are going in circles with your life.

To dream that you are living in a fish tank, indicates that you are detached from society. You are withdrawn. Alternatively, the dream may mean that you are feeling the pressure of those around you. Consider the phrase of "living in a fishbowl". You feel that you are being judged, criticized and scrutinized.

Fishing

To dream that you are fishing, indicates that you are confronting and bringing your repressed emotions to the surface. In particular, to dream that you are ice fishing, suggests that you are breaking through a hardened emotional barrier and confronting difficult feelings from your unconscious. Alternatively, it represents your need for leisure and relaxation.

Consider the common phrase "fishing for compliments". Perhaps you are looking for attention.

Fishnet Stockings

To see or wear fishnet stockings in your dream, symbolizes sexiness, lust, and allure. The dream may be telling you that you need to be more daring.

Fist

To see a fist in your dream, symbolizes anger, power and aggression. It is also indicative of your readiness to fight and defend yourself.

Fitting Room

*Please See Dressing Room.

Five

Five represents your persuasiveness, spontaneity, boldness, daring nature, action, and humanity. The number five represents the five human senses and thus may be telling you to be more "sensitive" and be more in tune to your senses. Alternatively, the number five may reflect a change in your path or that you need to alter your course. It is also the link between heaven and earth.

Flag

To see your national flag in your dream, signifies peace and/or prosperity. It may also bring about feelings of patriotism and duty to country. Or the dream is highlighting some political issue. If you see a flag of another nation, then it represents worldly issues.

To wave a flag in your dream, symbolizes a warning or distress signal of sorts. An issue may be weighing on your mind. In particular, a white flag indicates surrender. You are giving up. Seeing a red flag, suggests your mercilessness and danger. The dream may be telling you to stop something that you are doing. To see a checkered flag in your dream, represents success and completion.

To see a flag at half mast in your dream, indicates that you are mourning. You are unable to let go of the past.

Flamingo

To see a flamingo in your dream, represents you sense of community and cooperation. It also indicates new experiences or situations. Alternatively, you may be overly concerned with your physical appearance.

Flannel

To see or wear flannel in your dream, represents comfort, relaxation and warmth. The dream could be telling you that you are in a comfortable place in your life. Consider the color or the type of flannel item for additional significance.

Flashlight

To see a flashlight in your dream, suggests that you are questioning certain issues about yourself. You may be trying to shed light on your deeper thoughts and/or unconscious feelings. It symbolizes sudden awareness, insight, and the ability to find your way in a situation. Alternatively, the flashlight may imply sexual activities.

Fleas

To see fleas in your dream, signify that you will be provoked into anger and manipulated into retaliation by someone close to you.

To dream that fleas bite you, signify that vicious rumors by false friends will slander your character.

Fleur De Lis

To see a fleur de lis in your dream, symbolizes spiritual power and control.

Flies

To see flies in your dream, symbolize filth and dirtiness, either physical or emotional. It indicates feelings of guilt or a breakdown of a plan. Flies may also forewarn of a contagious sickness. Alternatively, the fly could represent an irritating and annoying person in your life. Perhaps someone does not know who to mind their business.

To dream that you kill or exterminate the flies, indicate that you will redeem yourself and regain your honor after your fall from grace.

Flight Attendant

To see a flight attendant in your dream, indicates travel plans in your future. Alternatively, the dream suggests that you are seeking help in a new project.

To dream that you are a flight attendant, represents a new project that you need to take care of.

Flip Flops

To see or wear flip flops in your dream, indicate that you are feeling relaxed and at ease. Or perhaps you need to find time to relax. Alternatively, the dream may be a metaphor that you are unable to commit to something. You are going back and forth over some issue or decision.

Floating

To dream that you are floating on air, indicates satisfaction, contentment and acceptance of some situation. You are letting go of your problems and rising above obstacles. You are experiencing new-found freedom and gaining a new perspective on things. Nothing seems overwhelming or too difficult to handle. Alternatively, floating in your dream suggests that you are wandering through life aimlessly with no goals. You are just going with the flow.

To dream that you are floating in water, suggests that you have a handle on your emotions.

To dream that you are floating, but are afraid to move, suggests that you are questioning your own abilities. You are experiencing doubts in yourself.

Flood

To dream that you are in a flood, represents your need to release some sexual desires. If the flood is raging, then it represents emotional issues and tensions. Your repressed emotions are overwhelming you. Consider where the flood is for clues as to where in your waking life is causing you stress and tension. Alternatively, the dream indicates that you are overwhelming others with your demands and strong opinion. Still another interpretation could be your desire to wipe everything clean and make a fresh new start.

To see a gentle flood in your dream, indicates that your worries over a certain matter will soon be swept away.

Floor

To see the floor in your dream, represents your support system and sense of security. You have a firm foundation that you can depend on. The floor in your dream may also symbolize the division between the unconscious and conscious. Alternatively, the dream may be a pun on being "floored" or being completely surprised. Perhaps you have been caught off guard about something.

To see a polished, wooden floor in your dream, indicates that you are fully aware of your unconscious and keeping it suppressed. Consider the condition of the floor for further analysis.

To see a slanted floor in your dream, indicates that you are deviating too far from your original plans and goals.

To dream about the floors of a building, represents your level of understanding, awareness or success. The higher floors signify higher accomplishments and achievements. If you are in the lower floors, then it refers to more primal attitudes, the unconscious and/or sexuality. It also denotes failures. Consider the significance of the floor number and the type of building the floors are on.

Floss

To floss in your dream, suggests that you are trying to get to the root of some matter. Alternatively, the dream may be a metaphor that you are showing off and flaunting your material things. If your gums become bloody as a result of flossing, then it represents your fears and the negative consequences of your actions.

Flour

To see flour in your dream, symbolizes a frugal but happy way of life. It also indicates hard work. This dream symbol may also be a pun on "flower".

Flower

To see colorful flowers in your dream, signify kindness, compassion, gentleness, pleasure, beauty, and gain. It is also symbolic of perfection and spirituality. Your dream may be an expression of love, joy and happiness. Alternatively, flowers in dream, especially if they are blooming, represent your hidden potential and latent talents. Flowers can also denote a particular time or season. If the flowers are white, then it symbolizes sadness. Consider the color of the flower and the type of flower for additional analysis.

To see withered or dead flowers in your dream, denotes disappointments and gloomy situations. It may signal an end to a love relationship. Or it could indicate that you may not be utilizing your full potential and talents and letting it go to waste.

To dream that you receive a bouquet of flowers, represents respect, approval, admiration, and rewards.

To see flowers blooming in barren soil, signify that energy and cheerful nature will enable you to overcome your grievances. If you are picking flowers, then the dream symbolizes blooming love or a new developing relationship.

Flute

To hear or play the flute in your dream, indicates harmony in your life. Things are going smoothly for you. Alternatively, hearing the sound a flute, suggests sorrow and longing. You are experiencing a spectrum of emotions. The flute also symbolizes the phallus or a masculine component in your waking life.

Flying

To dream that you are flying, signifies a sense of freedom where you had initially felt restricted and limited.

To dream that you are flying with black wings, signifies bitter disappointments.

Flying Saucer

Please See UFO.

Fog

To dream that you are going through a thick fog, symbolizes confusion, troubles, scandal, uncertainty and worries. You may not be seeing things the way they really are. You may have lost your sense of direction in life. Alternatively, a fog represents mystery, secrecy and protection.

Foil

To see or wrap something in foil in your dream, indicates that you are trying to protect or insulate yourself from the harsh realities. Alternatively, wrapping something in foil is analogous to some pent up anger. You internalize your emotions and keep things inside. The dream may also be a pun on "foiling" or thwarting someone's plans.

Folder

To see a folder in your dream, suggests that you need to sort out your feelings and re-organize some issues in your waking life, especially if you've experienced some trauma or turmoil recently. Consider the contents of the folder for additional clues.

Food

To see food in your dream, represents physical and emotional nourishment and energies. The different types of food can symbolize a wide range of things. Generally, fruit is symbolic of sensuality. Frozen foods may imply your cold emotions and frigid ways. Eating certain foods also refers to qualities that you need to incorporate within your own self.

To dream that you are hording or storing food, indicates a fear of deprivation. You do not trust what you already have.

To see or eat stale food in your dream, suggests that you are feeling sluggish and emotionally drained. You need to be invigorated and revitalized.

To eat bad-tasting food in your dream, indicates some sourness or resentment in your emotional state of mind.

*Please Also See Eating.

Food Fight

To dream that you are in a food fight, suggests that there is a conflict between your physical and emotional well being. There is some issue that you need to resolve in your waking life.

Football

To dream that you are watching football, indicates that you have great satisfaction in your work. You will achieve your goals as you progress through your life.

To dream that you are playing football or on a football field, represents your competitive nature. Alternatively, you are not getting enough cooperation or support in some area of your life. You are being faced with many demanding challenges.

Forehead

To see a smooth forehead in your dream, indicates that you are fair and show good judgment. It is also indicative of your intellectual capacities.

To see a wrinkled forehead in your dream, symbolizes worries and burdens. You may be deep in thought.

To dream that you feel the forehead of your child, denotes sincere praises.

Foreign Land

To dream that you are in a foreign land, represents change in your life. Consider how you feel about the surrounding. If you are afraid or lost, then it indicates that you are not ready for the change. You are not willing to leave the past behind. If you are excited or happy in this unknown place, then it suggests that you are ready for change.

Foreign Language

To hear or speak a foreign language in your dream, indicates a message from your unconscious that you do not yet understand. Alternatively, you may not be making yourself clear to others.

To dream that you are studying a foreign language, suggests that you are having difficulties expressing your thoughts. You are confronted with some unfamiliar problem that you do not know how to approach and resolve in your waking life.

Forest

To dream that you are in or walking through the forest, signifies a transitional phase. Follow your instincts. Alternatively, it indicates that you want to escape to a simpler way of life. You are feeling weighed down by the demands of your life.

To dream that you are lost in a forest, indicates that you are searching through your unconscious for a better understanding of yourself.

To dream of a forest fire, indicates that transformation and regeneration is only possible through some hardships. Alternatively, it suggests that your anger is out of control; it is affecting those around you.

*Please See Also Woods.

Forget Me Not

To see forget me not flowers in your dream, symbolize your lover and your relationship with him or her. You are feeling neglected in your waking relationship or that your feelings are being overlooked. Open communication is key to the relationship. Alternatively, the dream could be telling you not to forget about someone or something. Or it may denote yearning.

Forgetting

To dream that you are forgetting things, signify life's anxieties. You are expressing an overwhelming amount of stress in your life. You feel the need to tend to everything and everyone's needs. Alternatively, forgetting something may represent your unconscious desire to leave that something behind. On a more direct level, the dream could just be your subconscious telling you or reminding you of a forgotten appointment or date.

To dream that you forget where you live, suggests that you do not want to go home. Is there a domestic conflict or argument?

To dream that you forget the baby, indicates that you are feeling burdened by the responsibility of taking care of someone else.

Fork

To see a fork in your dream, represents an extension of your reach. You are on the right track toward pursuing your goals. Alternatively, it may be a pun on "fork it over". Do you feel that you are being coerced or forced?

To dream of being stabbed with a fork, indicates that you are too picky with the ideas/suggestions presented to you.

To see someone eating with a fork, denotes that all your current worries will be cleared up through the help of a friend.

Fork In The Road

To see a fork in the road in your dream, represents an important decision that you need to make. It may indicate your choices or ambivalence about some situation. Alternatively, a fork symbolizes the union of opposites. Opposing views/aspects are coming together.

To see an oak tree at the fork in the road, signifies a life-changing decision.

Forklift

To see or use a forklift in your dream, suggests that you need to rearrange some of your ideals in order to find a solution to a problem. It may also mean that you need to clear out your old emotions and/or memories.

Fort

To dream that you are defending a fort, indicates that you are always on guard. You are constantly put on the defensive. If your fort is under attack, then it suggests that feel emotionally attacked. Or your dream could be prepping you up for a difficult or demanding situation.

Fortune Cookie

To see or eat a fortune cookie in your dream, suggests that you are putting your fate in someone else's hand. The fortune inside the cookie may also be some sort of advice or message from your unconscious.

Fortune Telling

To dream that you are having your fortune told, signifies fears and anxieties about the future. You have issues of control and the desire to know the unknown.

Fossils

To see fossils in your dream, symbolize longevity and wisdom. Some relationship or situation is standing the test of time. The dream may also be a metaphor for someone who is stuck in the past or have outdated ways of thinking. Also consider the object that has been fossilized for hints as to what is outdated in your life.

Foundation

To see the foundation of a building, represents your belief system. You are well-prepared for any situation before you.

To dream that the foundation is shifting, suggests that you are changing your beliefs about something.

Fountain

To see a fountain in your dream, represents joy, renewed pleasure or increased sensitivity. You are experiencing an outburst of positive emotions. Perhaps you are entering into a new relationship or a new phase in that relationship. Alternatively, the fountain may be analogous to sexual climax.

To see a dry fountain in your dream, indicates that you are coming down from the "high" of a passionate relationship.

Four

Four denotes stability, physical limitations, hard labor and earthly things, as in the four corners of the earth or the four elements (earth, wind, fire and water). It also stands for materialistic matters and how you get things done. Alternatively, the dream may be a pun on being "for" a position. In Asian cultures, the number four is a metaphor for death.

Fowl

To see a fowl in your dream, denotes temporary worries and disagreements. The dream may also be a pun on a situation or a conversation that is "foul".

Fox

To see a fox in your dream, represents insight, cleverness, cunningness and resourcefulness. Perhaps the dream is telling you that you need to exhibit more of these qualities in your waking life. Or that you need to conceal your thoughts and be more discrete about some situation. The fox may also symbolize someone in your waking life who is sly and sneaky. Alternatively, seeing a fox in your dream, indicates a period of isolation or loneliness. You need to take this time to ponder some issue or reflect upon your life. The dream could be a metaphor for someone who is a "fox", as in a foxy lady.

Fraction

To see fractions in your dream, indicate that you are not feeling whole. You are looking for some completion or closure in some matter.

Frankenstein

To see or dream that you are Frankenstein, indicates that you are tormented or rejected by society. You feel alone and that no one understands you. Alternatively, the dream represents some fear that you do not know how to deal with.

Freckles

To dream that you have freckles on your face, represent your distinct and unique character. You will stand out in crowd.

Freddy Krueger

To see Freddy Krueger in your dream, represents your fears and the rejected aspects of yourself. You are refusing to acknowledge those negative parts. Alternatively, the dream indicates that you are desperate to get a grasp of a problem or situation. Dreaming of Freddy Krueger also implies that you are feeling neglected.

Freeway

To dream that you are on a freeway, indicates that you are feeling liberated and free. You are well on your way to achieving your goals. If the freeway is slow moving or blocked, then it suggests frustrations or obstacles that are hindering your path toward your goals.

French Fries

To see or eat French Fries in your dream, suggests that you should not overlook the frivolous and seemingly minute things in life.

French Toast

To see or dream that you are eating French toast, indicates that you are satisfied with your current situation in life.

Friday

To dream that it is Friday, represents an end to some difficult task. Things are looking up for you. TGIF as the saying goes. In particular, to dream of your significant other on a Friday, indicates that this is a meaningful day between the two of you. This may be the day you met, the day your broke up, or perhaps the day you two always went out. Whatever the significance, there is something personal between this particular day and which only you can correlate.

Fridge

*Please see Refrigerator.

Friend

To see friends in your dream, signify aspects of your personality that you have rejected, but are ready to incorporate and acknowledge. The relationships you have with those around you are important in learning about yourself. Alternatively, dreaming of a friend, indicates positive news.

To see your childhood friend in your dream, signifies regression into your past where you had no responsibilities. Things were much simpler and carefree. You may be wanting to escape the pressures and stresses of adulthood. Consider the relationship you had with this friend and the lessons that were learned. Alternatively, the childhood friend suggests that you have been acting in a childish manner. You need to start acting like an adult.

To dream that your best friend is dying, suggests that some aspect or quality that your best friend possess is dying within your own self.

Frisbee

To see or play Frisbee in your dream, represents an easy-going attitude or a lack of competitive spirit. It also serves to remind you that situations and relationships in life are give and take.

Frog

To see a frog in your dream, represents a potential for change or the unexpected. The frog may be a prince in disguise and thus, signify transformation, renewal or rebirth. Alternatively, the frog symbolizes uncleanness or fertility.

To see frogs leaping in your dream, indicate your lack of commitment. You have a tendency to jump from one thing to another. Alternatively, it may suggest that you are taking major steps toward some goal. It parallels your progress.

To dream that you are catching a frog, signifies your carelessness concerning your health.

To hear the sounds of a frog in your dream, indicates that you have not accomplished what you wanted.

To eat a frog in your dream, represents some unsavory or unpleasant task that you need to perform. If you swallow a whole frog in your dream, then there is something that you need to do or say, that is literally difficult to swallow. Consider the phrase "a frog in your throat" to suggest that you are unable to speak. You feel you have lost your voice.

Front

To see the front of something in your dream, indicates that you expressing a desire to keep your distance. The dream may also be a pun on "fronting". Are you being someone that you are not? Are you overly concerned about how you come across to others and how they see you?

Frosting

To see or taste frosting in your dream, represents the results of your creativity and/or hard work. You have renewed confidence and self-assurance. New opportunities are now opened to you. Alternatively, the dream may point to how you are looking at things on a superficial level. You need to delve deeper in order to find the truth.

Frozen

To dream that something is frozen, represents something that has been suppressed, rejected, or denied. It could represent something this is not fully developed. Alternatively, the dream may refer to your emotions and cold or bitter feelings.

To dream that someone is frozen, indicates your coldness toward that person or vice versa.

Fruit

To see fruit in your dream, signifies growth, abundance and financial gain. They also symbolize lust and sexuality. In particular, green fruit in your dream, denotes your hastiness and disappointed efforts. You need to work harder and longer in order to achieve your goals. If the fruit is ripe, then it represents fertility and conception. You desire a child or you are ready to have a child.

To see or eat rotting/bitter fruit, represents your missed opportunities for growth and pleasure. Alternatively, it indicates a situation or relationship that ended prematurely. You are expressing some regret.

To dream that you buy or sell fruit, indicates that your efforts are being wasted in a fruitless endeavor.

See Dream Moods' entries on specific fruits for more information.

Fudge

To make or eat fudge in your dream, indicates that you are enjoying life to the fullest. However, be careful not to overindulge in too many excesses. Alternatively, the dream may be a pun on how you are "fudging" some records or answers.

Funeral

To dream of your own funeral, symbolizes an ending to a situation or aspect of yourself. You may be repressing some of your feelings or parts of yourself. Thus, the dream may be a signal for you to recognize and acknowledge those feelings. Instead of confronting a situation, you are dealing with it by burying it and trying to forget about it. If you are nearing death, a funeral dream may relate to your feelings/anxieties about your own death.

To dream that you are at somebody else's funeral, signifies that you are burying an old relationship and closing the lid on the past. You may be letting go some of the feelings (resentment, anger, hostility toward someone) that you have been clinging onto.

To dream that you are attending a funeral for a still-living parent, suggests that you need to separate yourself from your parent's restrictions and confines. The symbolic death may give you the courage you need to take the next step toward your independence and autonomy.

To dream that you are at the funeral of an unknown person, suggests that something in your life needs to put to rest or put aside so that you can make room for something new. You need to investigate further what aspect or component of your life you need to let go.

Fungus

To see fungus in your dream, represents negative emotions that are expanding and growing in your unconscious. You need to find a productive way to express them before it grows out of control.

Furniture

To see furniture in your dream, represents how you feel about yourself and your family. It refers to your relationships with others and how they fit into your life.

To dream that you are moving furniture, indicates that you are going out of your way to please others. Also, you may be changing your ways and trying to reevaluate your relationships/attitudes. Consider how easy or how difficult it is to move the furniture as they may indicate the level of burden or responsibility you are feeling.

To see old or worn furniture in your dream, symbolizes outdated attitudes, former relationships, and/or old ways of thinking.

*Please also refer to specific pieces of furniture.

Furs

To see or wear furs in your dream, represent prosperity, status, and luxury. You are shielded from the cold or from poverty. To others, furs can signify cruelty and torture. Alternatively, the dream may also be symbolic of your animalistic and instinctual nature.

If you are against wearing fur in real life, but dream that you are wearing fur, suggests that someone is not who you thought they were. Or you are less than proud of yourself with something that you did.

G

To see the letter "G" in your dream, may be a pun on money.

Gambling

To dream that are gambling, suggests that you are too impulsive and relying too much on fate. You are not taking responsibility for your own decisions or actions. Alternatively, the dream symbolizes risk-taking activities.

If you are not a gambler and dream that you are gambling, denotes that you need to take a chance or let up on yourself. Be a little more spontaneous!

Game Show

To dream that you are on a game show, suggests that you need to change some aspect of your life around. You may be experiencing feelings of uncertainty and what the future may hold. Consider the type of game show or the name of the game show. What are you playing for and what is its significance relative to your waking life.

Games

To dream that you are playing games, indicates that you need to take a break from your daily life. It is time to relax. Alternatively, the dream symbolizes the spirit of competition and the rules you live by. Consider the type of game you are playing for additional significance.

Gang

To dream that you are a gang member, signifies your need to achieve and accomplish things through force and intimidation. The dream draws attention to the primitive, unruly aspect of yourself.

To dream that you are confronted or threatened by a gang, signifies circumstances or situations in your waking life that are becoming overwhelming. You feel that you are being "ganged" up on.

Garage

To dream that you are in a garage, signifies a period of inactivity and idleness in your life. You feel that you are lacking direction or guidance in achieving your goals.

To dream that you are pulling your car into the garage, represents security and stability brought about by your accomplishments and efforts.

To dream that you are opening the garage door, denotes that you have made a decision about a matter. You have decided on the path you want to take to reach your opportunities and goals. On the other hand, if you are closing the garage door, then it suggests that you are putting off your goals for the sake of others around you.

Garage Sale

To hold or be at a garage sale in your dream, indicates that you are recycling past experiences and finding use for your old skills and ideas. You are learning from your past and making productive use of the lessons you have learned.

Garbage

To dream that you are throwing away garbage, suggests that you are kicking your old negative habits and throwing away your bad characteristics and unwanted traits. Alternatively, garbage indicates that you are not taking responsibility for something.

To see piles of garbage in your dream, represent rejected or unwanted aspects of yourself.

To find something valuable in the garbage, suggests that you can find value in the least expected of places. Do not undervalue or underestimate things. The dream may also be telling you that one man's trash is another man's treasure. Perhaps you need to view things from a different perspective.

Garden

To see a vegetable or fruit garden in your dream, indicates that your hard work and diligence will pay off in the end. It is also symbolic of stability, potential, and inner growth. You need to cultivate a new skill or nurture your spiritual and personal growth.

To see a flower garden in your dream, represents tranquility, comfort, love and domestic bliss. You need to be more nurturing.

To see a sparse, weed-infested garden, suggests that you have neglected your spiritual needs. You are not on top of things.

Gargoyle

To see a gargoyle in your dream, signifies hidden and embarrassing fears over some secret matters that you have not shared with anyone.

Garlic

To dream that you are eating garlic, signifies your practicality and sensibility in matters of the heart; you look for security over love.

To see a clove of garlic in your dream, indicates protection against some danger. You will overcome your barriers.

Garnet

To see a garnet in your dream, symbolizes loyalty, vitality and devotion. Alternatively, the dream suggest that you are overcoming your negative feelings.

Garter

To see or dream that you are wearing a garter, represents seduction and titillation. You are looking to be more sexual adventurous.

Gas

To smell or see gas in your dream, indicates that you need to be reenergized. There may be a situation in your life that you are having difficulty in getting a handle on.

Gas Mask

To see or wear a gas mask in your dream, suggests that the information that you are receiving from others is being filtered. You are not getting the full information. Others may perceive you as fragile or vulnerable.

Gas Station

To dream that you are at a gas station, indicates a need to reenergize and revitalize yourself. You may be running low on energy and need to take time out to refuel. The dream also represents your ability to convert outside resources and use it for your own needs. Alternatively, dreaming that you are in a gas station means that you need to reach out to others and offer your help.

Gasoline

To see gasoline in your dream, represents energy and spirituality. Thus, to dream that you run out of gas, suggests that you are wearing yourself out. Take a time out.

To dream that you are filling your car with gasoline, symbolizes your need to take better care of your Self. You need to be revitalized.

135

Gate

To see or pass through a gate in your dream, suggests that you are walking through a new phase of life. It also represents new opportunities and possibilities, especially if the gate is opened or swinging.

To see a closed gate in your dream, signifies your inability to overcome current difficulties. If you are unable to open the gate, then it indicates that your hard work will be seen as unsatisfactory. It may also mean that you are not ready or not prepared to move on to the next step.

Gavel

To see a gavel in your dream, symbolizes justice, authority and absolute power. It may refer to a problem that you need to acknowledge and confront.

To dream that you are using a gavel, represents a resolution to a problem. A decision has been made.

Gay

*Please See Homosexual.

Gazebo

To see or dream that you are in a gazebo, represents your openness and receptiveness toward some relationship. It also symbolizes your idealistic notions, contentment, and satisfaction.

Gecko

To see a gecko in your dream, represents an agreement or affirmation. The answer to a decision that you need to make is "yes". Alternatively, the dream signifies renewal.

Gemini

To dream that someone is a Gemini, represents your quick thinking ability and keen wit. You are versatile and able to adapt to any situation. Alternatively, it signifies your connections and your ability (or inability) to reach out to others.

Genie

To see a genie in your dream, represents your creativity and mind power. Alternatively, the dream may mean that you have let the genie out of the bottle and are unable to control the consequences.

Germs

To have a dream about germs, represent small and irrational fears that you are feeling in your waking life. You may be lacking energy and motivation. Focus on your purpose and goals in life.

Geyser

To see a geyser in your dream, symbolizes an outburst of emotion. You need to acknowledge and express your pent up anger and feelings before they explode.

Ghost

To see your own ghost in your dream, symbolizes aspects of yourself that you fear. This may involve a painful memory, guilt, or some repressed thoughts. Or you may be afraid of death and dying. Alternatively, ghosts are representative of something that is no longer obtainable or within reach. It indicates that you are feeling disconnected from life and society. Try to figure out what the ghosts wants or what it is looking for. The dream may also be a calling for you to move on and abandon your outdated modes of thinking and behavior.

To dream that you reach out to touch a ghost, but it disappears, indicates that you are taking steps to acknowledging some painful or repressed thoughts even though you are not ready to fully confront them.

To see the ghost of a living relative or friend in your dream, signifies that you are in danger of malice acts by that person.

To see the ghost of a dead friend/relative in your dream, suggests guilt and regrets concerning the past relationships with that particular person.

Ghoul

To see a ghoul in your dream, suggests that your habits and negative ways are hindering your growth. The dream may also represent a fresh beginning.

Giant

To see a giant in your dream, indicates a great struggle between you and your opponents. You are trying to overcome an overwhelming obstacle. Alternatively, a giant symbolizes an issue, a person or a feeling that is dominating you. You are having an inferiority complex.

To dream that you turn into a giant, indicates feelings of inferiority.

Gift

To dream that you are giving a gift, signifies your generosity towards others. Alternatively, you may be trying to express some feeling or have something awkward to say that has to be carefully packaged. If you are showering someone with gifts, then it indicates that you are being overly pushy with your advice. Or that you are trying to hard to be accepted. If you are buying or giving someone expensive gifts, then it symbolizes the sacrifices you are making for that person. You want to make them feel important.

To dream that you receive a gift, indicates that you are being rewarded and recognized for your generosity and giving nature. You are held in high esteem by those around you. If someone gives you an inappropriate gift, then it suggests that you are the subject of unwelcome attention from someone. If you dream that you give someone an inappropriate gift, then it suggests that your true nature will eventually be exposed. Analyze the gift you give or receive for additional significance.

To see a pile of gifts, symbolizes unutilized or unrecognized skills and talents.

To open a gift and find something disgusting inside, symbolizes disappointments or unexpected failures.

Ginger

To see ginger in your dream, indicates security and comfort in your life. However, you need to add a little more excitement and variety to you life.

Ginseng

To see ginseng in your dream, represents virility, longevity and life.

Giraffe

To see a giraffe in your dream, suggests that you need to consider the overall picture. Take a broader view on your life and where it is headed. The dream may also be a metaphor on how you are "sticking your neck out" for someone.

To dream that you are riding a giraffe, represents your desire to stand up amongst the crowd. You want attention, but aren't getting it.

Girdle

To dream that you are wearing a girdle, suggests that you are feeling restricted and limited in the expression of your ideas and feelings. Alternatively, the dream points to your tendency to bear pain in order to please others.

Girl Scout

To dream that you are a girl scout, symbolizes sisterhood, camaraderie, characters and strong values. You need to exemplify these qualities.

To see a girl scout in your dream, suggests that you need to be more dedicated to your goals and achievements. Alternatively, a girl scout may represent model behavior which you are trying to emulate.

Girlfriend

To see your girlfriend in your dream, represents your waking relationship with her and how you feel about her.

Girls

To see a girl in your dream, represents your playful, innocent, and childlike nature. Perhaps you are behaving immaturely in some situation. Alternatively, a girl represents the feminine qualities of your character.

To dream about a girl that you just met, represents your anxieties and thoughts of whether you had made a good impression on her and what she thought of you. If she told you that she disliked you in the dream, then it may be an excuse for you to dismiss her and not pursue a relationship further.

Giving

To dream that you are giving something away, indicates that you need to give more in some relationship or situation. To be able to give, helps fulfill your need to share and to belong. Consider also how you were received.

To dream that something is given to you, suggests that you need to appreciate the gifts you have.

Glacier

To see a glacier in your dream, refers to your cold feelings. You are shutting down emotionally. Alternatively, glaciers denote evitable changes.

Gladiolas

To see gladiolas in your dream, represent heartaches and issues of the heart. It serves to remind you that sometimes love hurts.

Glass

To see glass in your dream, symbolizes passivity or protection. You may be putting up an invisible barrier to protect yourself in a situation or relationship. If the glass is dirty, cloudy or discolored, then it suggests that you are not seeing something clearly. You need more clarity in a situation. To dream that you are drinking from a glass, is an omen of good luck.

To dream that you are looking through glass, represents your openness and non-defensiveness. Alternatively, you may be putting up an invisible emotional barrier around yourself.

To see broken glass in your dream, signifies disappointments and negative changes in your life. Alternatively, it could be symbolic of an aspect of your life that is in pieces. A relationship or situation has come to an abrupt and untimely end. If you are walking on broken glass, then it suggests that you will be experiencing some heartache or pain. You are unsure with how to proceed with your life.

To dream that you are eating glass, highlights your vulnerability, confusion and frailty. You may have difficulties in communicating your thoughts across and getting the right words out. Alternatively, it may symbolize your hurtful and cutting comments. Perhaps you have been hurt or disappointed by something that someone had said. Or you need to be careful in how you phrase and word things or run the risk of offending others.

Glass Slipper

To see or wear glass slippers in your dream, symbolize truth and transformation.

Glitter

To see or throw glitter in your dream, suggests that you need to be more outgoing. Express yourself! The dream may also be a metaphor for fame, glitz, and glamour, as in the glitter of Hollywood.

To dream that something is glittering, indicates that something or someone is trying to get your attention. Alternatively, the dream may indicate that things are not always what it seems. Consider the phrase "all that glitters is not gold." Don't be fooled by what is on the outside or how things may appear to be.

Gloves

To see or wear gloves in your dream, represent the way you handle things. You are getting a handle on a problem. Consider the phrase "handle with kid gloves" and how you need to be more cautious in some situation. Or perhaps you are overly cautious. Alternatively, wearing gloves may mean that your creative abilities are still latent. You need to acknowledge and express that creative side.

To dream that you are taking off gloves, symbolize respect.

To dream that you are wearing work gloves, represent a difficult situation that may get your hands dirty. If you are wearing driving gloves, then it means that you need to take control of your life. If you are wearing boxing gloves, that it indicate that you are involved in a some sort of conflict. Is there something in your life that you are struggling with? To wear white gloves in your dream, signify luxury and richness.

To dream that you throw a glove on the floor, suggests that you need to challenge or address someone about an issue that is bothering you.

Glow

To see a glow in your dream, symbolizes enlightenment and understanding. New light has been shed onto a situation. You have gained a fresh perspective.

Glow Stick

To see a glow stick in your dream, indicates a new direction that you are taking. You may also be seeking some guidance in the course of your actions.

Glue

To see glue in your dream, indicates a fear of being trapped in some situation and not being able to get out of it. You have a fear of partnership or commitment and a general distrust of people around you. On the flip side, you may be too clingy. Alternatively, you are holding on to some false hope.

To dream that you are gluing something together, suggests that you are piecing together aspects of yourself and acknowledging those previously rejected
parts. Alternatively, the dream may be a metaphor for a sticky situation.

Gnaw

To dream that you are gnawing at something, suggests that you are trying to attack or confront a situation or problem that has been menacing you. The dream may also be a metaphor to mean "nah" or "no".

Gnome

To see a gnome in your dream, signifies the inner child and its fantasies. Alternatively, a gnome represents protection, luck, fruitfulness and fertility.

Go-Kart

To see or drive a go-kart in your dream, represents your ability to navigate through life's twists and turns. The dream may also be a pun on your "drive" and ambition.

Goat

To see a goat in your dream, represents your lack of judgment and your gullibility. Alternatively, goats are symbolic of sexuality, sexual desire, and lechery. Also consider the associations with the goat as in "scapegoat" or "getting someone's goat". Do you feel that you have been blamed for someone else's deed?

To dream that a billy goat butts you, forewarns of deceit, underhandedness, and lies.

Goblin

To see a goblin in your dream, refers to a negative person who is working against you. Or it may mean that you have a self-defeatist attitude. You are already setting yourself up for failure.

God

To see God in your dream, signifies your spirituality and expression of your feelings about divinity. God also symbolizes an untouchable, unreachable, and unattainable notion of perfection. Thus such a dream may highlight your struggles and attempts with trying to be perfect.

To dream that you are worshipping God, signifies repentance of your actions and errors.

To dream that God speaks to you, signifies feelings of guilt, eternal punishment, and damnation.

To dream that you are a god, implies your own special talents which you have not yet recognized or fully developed. Alternatively, it refers to your feelings of superiority over others. You think you are above others and have a tendency to look down on people.

Goggles

To see or wear goggles in your dream, suggest that you are trying to protect yourself from emotional harm. Perhaps you need to confront something in your waking like that you know is hurting you.

Goiter

To dream that you have a goiter, indicates that you are overlooking some minor issue that will have significant consequences. Alternatively, a goiter represents a situation that you are having difficulty confronting or accepting.

Gold

To see gold in your dream, symbolizes wealth, riches, natural healing, illumination and/or spirituality. It is also a symbol of love, longevity and domestic bliss. Negatively, gold may represent greed, corruption and temptation.

To find gold in your dream, indicates that you have discovered something valuable about yourself.

This may be some hidden talent or knowledge.

To bury gold in your dream, suggests that you are trying to hide something about yourself.

The golden color reflects a spiritual reward, richness, refinement and enhancement of your surroundings. It also signifies your determination and unyielding nature.

Golden Retriever

To see a golden retriever in your dream, represents your family ideals. The dream may also be a pun on something that you need to "retrieve" or regain control of.

Golf

To dream that you are playing or watching golf, signifies pleasant indulgences. It may also indicate that you are idling and wasting time. Alternatively, the dream symbolizes your individual accomplishments and your drive to succeed.

To dream that you are on a golf course, represents your desires for freedom. You want to escape the grind of your occupation. Alternatively, the dream may be a pun of how you are green or environmentally conscious.

Goodbye

To dream that you are saying goodbye to someone, indicates an end to your worries, to a relationship or and to a chapter in your life. You are moving on into a new stage of your life.

To dream that someone is saying goodbye to you, suggests that you are going on a journey of self-discovery. You are entering a new phase in your life.

Goose

To see a goose in your dream, symbolizes fertility and motherly love. The goose may also represent a message from your unconscious. Alternatively, the dream suggests that you are on a "wild goose chase". Perhaps you are going about a problem all wrong.

Goosebumps

To dream that you have goosebumps, indicate validity and truth to what you have just said or heard. Alternatively, it may symbolize fear and/or your frigid attitude.

Gopher

To see a gopher in your dream, means that you are being used and manipulated by others. Alternatively, the dream may be a pun on "go for" it. You need to take initiative and act now.

Gorilla

To see a gorilla in your dream, suggests that you may be too "over the top" in your behavior. Perhaps you are compensating for your rigidity and stiffness in your waking life. Alternatively, the gorilla symbolizes your primitive impulses, wild nature and repressed sexual energy.

Gout

To dream you have gout, represents obstacles. Something may be hindering or slowing your progress.

Gown

To see or wear an evening gown in your dream, represents enjoyment, social pleasures, grace and culture. It also represents the image that you are projecting to others. Consider the color and design of the gown for additional significance. If the gown is very fancy or ornate, then it signifies an elaborate and luxurious lifestyle. If the gown is plain or simple, then it suggests a simplified lifestyle. Alternatively, to dream you are wearing an evening gown, indicates that you are looking for happiness.

GPS

To dream that you are using a GPS, indicates that you are on a path of self discovery. It symbolizes your goal and purpose in life.

Grade

To see your grade in your dream, represents how well you are doing in life's lesson and how your are progressing through each stage in your life. Consider the significance of the letter. Perhaps it refers to someone's initials.

Graduation

To dream that you are at a graduation, represents your achievements. You are successfully transitioning to a higher level. And you are ready to move forward with your accomplishments and perform more important things.

To dream that you do not have enough units or credits to graduate, suggests that you are not giving yourself enough credit about your successes and achievements. You are short-changing yourself for your accomplishments.

Graffiti

To see graffiti in your dream, indicates that you have low self-worth. If the graffiti in your dream is a positive symbol, then it suggests that you see the good in everything and everyone.

Grandfather

To see your grandfather in your dream, symbolizes tradition, protection, wisdom, and a caring nature. Consider the qualities and characteristics that exist in your own grandfather.

Grandmother

To see your grandmother in your dream, represents nurturance, protection, and unconditional love. Consider the qualities and characteristics that exist in your own grandmother. She may also be the archetypal symbol of the wise old woman.

Grapefruit

To see or eat a grapefruit in your dream, represents a sense of well-being and a refreshed state of mind. Your are experiencing an uplift in your spirits and a rejuvenation of your body.

To see a grapefruit tree in your dream, is symbolic of your talents, belief system and good deeds. It may also represent the fruits of your labor.

Grapes

To see grape vines in your dream, symbolize opulence, wealth, and decadence. It also indicates fortitude and your ability to offer happiness to others.

To see or eat grapes in your dream, represent wealth and prosperity. In the end, your hard work will pay off and you will be rewarded for your labor. Alternatively, grapes refer to immortality and sacrifices.

To dream that you are picking and gathering grapes, signify profit and the realization of your desires.

Grass

To see green grass in your dream, suggests that there is a part of yourself that you can always rely on. The dream is also symbolic of natural protection. Also consider the phrase "the grass is always greener on the other side." Do you always compare yourself with others and look at what other people have?

To dream that you are planting grass, indicates that your hard work and efforts will pay off in the end.

Grasshopper

To see a grasshopper in your dream, symbolizes freedom, independence or spiritual enlightenment. Alternatively, it indicates your inability to settle down or commit to a decision.

Gray

Gray indicates fear, fright, depression, ill health, ambivalence and confusion. You may feel emotionally distant, isolated, or detached. Alternatively, the color gray symbolizes your individualism.

Green

Green signifies a positive change, good health, growth, fertility, healing, hope, vigor, vitality, peace, and serenity. The appearance of the color may also be a way of telling you to "go ahead". Alternatively, green is a metaphor for a lack of experience in some task.

To "be green", means that you are environmentally conscious. Green is also symbolic of your strive to gain recognition and establish your independence. Money, wealth and jealousy are often associated with this color.

Dark green indicates materialism, cheating, deceit, and/or difficulties with sharing. You need to balance your masculine and feminine attributes.

Greenhouse

To see or dream that you are in a greenhouse, represents transformation. You are experiencing some changes in your life brought about mainly as a result of your own doing. It also suggests that you may be too overly controlling. You want things done your way, but in the process you may be isolating yourself.

Grenade

To see a grenade in your dream, suggests that your suppressed emotions are about to explode. It also points to some pent up anger and violence.

Greyhound

To see a greyhound in your dream, symbolizes fortune, pleasant surprises, and friendships.

Grief

*Please See <u>Bereavement.</u>

Grim Reaper

To see the grim reaper in your dream, signifies the negative, rejected aspects of your personality. It represents aspects of yourself that you have repressed. Alternatively, it symbolizes death. The dream may parallel an end to some situation, habit, or relationship in your waking life.

Grinch

To see the Grinch in your dream, suggests that you are no longer centered. You are going along a crooked path. You need to get down to the core of some matter. Alternatively, the Grinch indicates that you need to treat yourself to something special instead of constantly catering to the needs of others.

Groom

To dream that you are a groom, represents your commitment to a relationship or situation. Alternatively, it suggests that your strong assertive side is getting ready

143

to merge with your intuitive nurturing side.

If you are female and see a groom in your dream, then it represents your desire to be in a committed relationship or to be married. Maybe you are ready to enter into a partnership.

Ground

To dream that you are on the ground, represents your foundation and support system. It is also the boundary between your conscious and unconscious. You may be getting closer in confronting and acknowledging your unconscious thoughts. The dream may be a pun on being well-grounded and down to earth or that you have been grounded. Perhaps you are feeling restricted in some aspects of your life.

Grounded

To dream that you have been grounded, indicates that you need to reflect on your negative actions and bad behavior. Learn from your past mistakes.

To dream that an airplane is grounded, indicates that your idea or plan is not taking off. You feel you are being held back, either physically or mentally.

Groundhog

To see a groundhog in your dream, represents unconscious material that is coming to the surface. You are ready to confront some news.

Growing

To see something growing in your dream, indicates that you have reached a new level of maturity or spiritual enlightenment.

Guard

To see an armed guard in your dream, represents rational thinking. You are being cautious and practical. The dream may also be on pun that you need to be "on guard" or alert about a situation.

To see a prison guard in your dream, suggests that your belief and/or your way of thinking is restricting your own growth. Your fear of making mistakes is preventing you from experiencing life.

Guillotine

To see a guillotine in your dream, symbolizes anger, hostility and the eruption of some strong emotions. You are not using your head and your better judgment. You need to think things through before you act.

Guitar

To see or play a guitar in your dream, represents passion and emotion. It also relates to sexual connotations and may signal an erotic or sensual dream.

To see an unstrung or broken guitar, signifies disappointments in love.

Gum

To dream that you are chewing gum, suggests that you are unable to express yourself effectively. You may feel vulnerable. Alternatively, it symbolizes a sticky situation that you are involved in.

To dream that you are unable to get rid of your gum, suggests that you are experiencing some indecision, powerlessness or frustration. You may lack understanding in a situation or find that a current problem is overwhelming. The gum in your mouth is a metaphor for something that you are trying to process or digest. Perhaps you feel that you have bitten off more than you can chew.

Gun

To see a gun in your dream, symbolizes aggression, anger, and potential danger. You may be dealing with issues of passiveness/aggressiveness and authority/dependence. Alternatively, a gun represents the penis and male sexual drive. Thus, the gun may mean power or impotence, depending on whether the gun went off or misfired.

To dream that you are loading a gun, forewarns that you should be careful in not letting your temper get out of control.

To dream that a gun jams or fails to fire, indicates that you are feeling powerless in some waking situation. Perhaps you need to attack your problems from a different approach. Alternatively, a malfunctioning gun represents sexual impotence or fear of impotence.

To dream that you shoot someone with a gun, denotes your aggressive feeling and hidden anger toward that particular person.

To dream that someone is shooting you with a gun, suggests that you are experiencing some confrontation in your waking life. You feel victimized in some situation.

Guts

To see guts in your dream, represent fortitude, strength, and stamina. Consider the common phrase "you have a lot of guts"

Gutter

To notice the gutter in your dream, signifies degradation and unhappiness. You are feeling low and sad. The dream may also be a metaphor telling you to "get your mind out of the gutter."

To find valuables in the gutter in your dream, suggest that you can find value in the least expected of places. Do not undervalue or underestimate things.

Gymnasium

To dream that you are in a gymnasium, indicates that you need to apply what you learned and incorporate it into your daily life. Alternatively, the gym may be telling you that you need to get more exercise.

Gymnast

To see a gymnast in your dream, signifies agility, strength, and grace.

Gynecologist

To see a gynecologist in your dream, indicates that there is something that you do not want to know. There is a situation that you are dreading. Alternatively, the dream may just represent your anxiety about seeing the gynecologist. Perhaps you are concerned about issues with fertility, cancer, venereal diseases or sex.

Gypsy

To see a gypsy in your dream, signifies your desire to roam freely without responsibility and obligation. Alternatively, this symbol may suggest that you need to look toward the future.

H

To see the letter "H" in your dream, symbolizes cooperation, balance and teamwork.

Hack

To dream that someone is hacking into your computer or files, symbolizes your vulnerabilities and weaknesses. The dream may be a way of telling you that you need to work on building up your self esteem.

To dream that you are hacking into someone else's computer, indicates that you are overstepping your boundaries in some situation or relationship.

Hair

To see hair in your dream, signifies sexual virility, seduction, sensuality, vanity, and health. It is indicative of your attitudes. If your hair is knotted or tangled, then it is symbolic of uncertainty and confusion in your life. You may be unable to think straight. If you dream that you make a drastic change to your hairstyle, then it means that you are making a drastic, new approach to some issue in your waking life.

To dream that you are cutting your hair, suggests that you are experiencing a loss in strength. You may feel that someone is trying to censor you. Alternatively, you may be reshaping your thinking or ambitions and eliminating unwanted thoughts/habits.

To dream that you are combing, stroking or styling your hair, suggests that you are taking on and evaluating a new idea, concept, outlook, or way of thinking. You may be putting your thoughts in order and getting your facts straight. A more literal interpretation suggests your concerns about your self-image and appearance.

To dream that you have long hair, indicates that you are thinking long and carefully before making some decision. You are concentrating on some plan or situation.

To dream that you are losing your hair, denotes that you are concerned with the notion that you are getting older and losing your sex appeal or virility. You are preoccupied with aging and your appearance. Losing your hair also signifies a lack of strength. You feel you do not possess the power to succeed in some undertaking. You may be feeling weak and vulnerable.

To dream that someone is smelling your hair, indicates sexual curiosity and your need for some sensual stimulation. You have a lot to learn about a relationship. The way yours or someone else's hair smell may remind your of a particular person.

To dream that you are reaching for someone's hair, suggests that you are trying to connect with that person on a spiritual or intellectual level. It also refers to sympathy, protectiveness, and fraternal love.

To dream that the wind is blowing through your hair, signifies freedom to express uninhibited feelings. You are "letting your hair down".

To dream that your hair is white or turns white, indicates that something important has just been made aware to you. It is a symbol of wisdom and insight. The dream may also be a metaphor suggesting that you are feeling "light-headed".

Hairpiece

To dream that you are wearing a hairpiece, indicates some sort of deception. You may be giving off a false impression and passing the views of others as your own.

To dream that you lose your hairpiece, suggests that you are beginning to lose your mind. The dream may also be a pun on losing your "peace" of mind.

Half

To dream about half of something, indicates that something in your waking life is incomplete or unresolved. It may also indicate that you are only partially acknowledging your feelings. You or someone else is limiting or restricting you. Alternatively, the dream suggests that you need to be open to compromise and meet halfway.

Halloween

To dream of Halloween, signifies death and the underworld. Halloween also represents the temporary adoption of a new persona where you feel less inhibited and more comfortable to freely express yourself.

Hallucination

To have a hallucination in your dream, symbolizes an image from your unconscious. They can also represent repressed emotions and feelings that you do not want to confront. Your dream may be telling you to be more alert and to express yourself more clearly. Alternatively, it refers to self-deception. What are you trying to hide?

Hallway

To see a hallway in your dream, symbolizes self exploration. It is the beginning of the path that you are taking in life. You are going through a transitional phase and journeying into the unknown. It also signals spiritual enlightenment, emotional growth physical prowess, new opportunities and mental passages in your life.

Ham

To dream that you are eating ham, indicates that you need to preserve your energy.

To see a ham in your dream, indicates that you are experiencing some emotional difficulties. The symbol may also be metaphor to suggest your desire for attention.

Hammer

To see a hammer in your dream, signifies power, strength, virility, and masculine attitudes. It also symbolizes growth and construction. Alternatively, the dream may also be a pun on "being hammered" or intoxicated.

To dream that you are using a hammer, represents your determination and drive in pursing your goals. You will accomplish your tasks with great success. However be careful not to be too forceful. Alternatively, it suggests that you may be dealing with old demons and inner struggles.

Hammock

To see a hammock in your dream, implies that you need to devote more time to pleasure and leisurely activity.

To dream that you are lying in a hammock, indicates that you may be pushing people away.

To dream that you fall off a hammock, suggests that you are taking your friends and loved ones for granted.

Hamster

To see a hamster in your dream, represents underdeveloped emotions. You are distancing yourself from others so that you won't end up getting hurt. It may also indicate that issues of sexuality are trivial to you. You are able to separate sex and love.

Hand

To dream of your hands, represent your relationships with those around you and how you connect with the world. Hands serve as a form of communication and can represent authority, hate, protection, justice, etc depending on the gesture. Perhaps you need to lend a helping hand to someone. In particular, the left hand symbolizes your graciousness and your feminine, receptive qualities, while the right hand symbolizes the masculine and active attributes. The right hand may also be a pun for some decision or something being "right". If you dream that your hands are detached or see disembodied hands, then it indicates that you are not getting your point of view across. You are not being understood. The dream may also symbolize feelings of loneliness.

To dream that you are holding hands with someone, represents love, affection and your connection with that person. Your dream may also reflect anxieties about losing touch with him/her or that you are drifting apart.

To dream that you hands are injured, denote an attack on your ego.

To dream that your hands are clasped or closed, signify unity, completeness, acceptance or agreement. On a more negative note, it may suggest that you are close-minded, ungiving or unwilling to help.

To dream that you have unusually large hands, denote success in achieving your goals.

To dream that your hands are hairy or rough, imply your lack of gentleness in dealing with others. You may be too brash and abrasive.

To see blood on your hands, signifies that you are experiencing some sort of guilt.

To dream that you are washing your hands, represent a worrisome issue that you need to work through. Alternatively, it suggests that you are in denial or no longer taking responsibility of some matter. You are letting go and getting things out of your system.

To dream that your hands are itchy, indicate issues with money. If the left hand is itchy, then it signifies money being received. If the right hand or both hands are itchy, then it signifies money being given or lost.

Handcuffs

To dream that you are in handcuffs, suggest that something or someone is holding back your success. Opportunities are shut off to you. You are experiencing a loss of power and effectiveness. Alternatively, your own fears and doubts may be holding you back.

To see others in handcuffs or to put handcuffs on others, indicate that you are being overly possessive.

Handicap

To dream that you or someone is handicap, symbolizes your own weakness and neediness. You are being confronted with many challenges and need to maximize your full potential. Consider which part of your body is handicap and its symbolism. Alternatively, it suggests that you are becoming too arrogant for your own good. You need to be more humble.

Handwriting

To see or dream about your handwriting, represents your self-expression and creativity. Consider the symbolism of what you are handwriting and how it relates to your waking life. The dream may be trying to warn you against something as in "the handwriting is on the wall".

Hang Gliding

To dream that you are hang gliding, symbolizes freedom in your personal life. It also represents trust. You believe in destiny.

To dream that you crash a hang glider, represents a lack of self confidence. You do not have enough faith in yourself.

Hanger

To see a hanger in your dream, suggests that you are getting the hang of some situation or some task. Or it may mean that you are just hanging in there. You need more motivation and encouragement.

Hanging

To watch a hanging in your dream, represents feelings of insecurity. The hanging may symbolize aspects of yourself that you want to eliminate.

To dream that you are hanging yourself, suggests that you are trying to escape from some guilt or fear. Consider also the image as a pun for something in your life which you have left hanging or unfinished.

To dream that you are hanging up clothes, suggests that you are clarifying your thoughts and elevating yourself to a new state of awareness.

Hangover

To dream that you have a hangover, signifies unresolved problems.

Hanukkah

Also known as the festival of lights, thus to dream about Hanukkah, signifies enlightenment, knowledge and spiritual guidance.

Happy

To dream that you are happy, may be a compensatory dream and is often a dream of the contrary. You may be trying to compensate for the sadness or stress in your waking life.

Harbor

To see a harbor in your dream, signifies shelter from a stormy relationship or chaotic situation. You may be seeking refuge until you can recollect your thoughts and prepare for the challenges ahead. The dream may also be a metaphor suggesting that you are "harboring" some ill feelings.

Hard Drive

To dream that your hard drive crashed, indicates that you are being overwhelmed with information. Perhaps something is taking a emotional toll on you. Alternatively, the dream may be a metaphor that your unusually strong will and drive will set you on a crash course.

To see a hard drive in your dream, is analogous to your hard driving demeanor and attitude.

Harmonica

To see or hear a harmonica in your dream, suggests that you need to let more joy and pleasure come into your life. It is also symbolic of a harmonious situation.

To dream that you are playing a harmonica, indicates that there is some emotions that you need to release and integrate into your daily life.

Harp

To see or play a harp in your dream, represents spiritual harmony. It is a healing symbol. Alternatively, the harp may be a pun on how you are "harping on" someone and getting on their case about something.

Harry Potter

To see Harry Potter in your dream, indicates that you have the potential to accomplish amazing things in the face of insurmountable hardships. Harry Potter reflects a more modern, atypical version of a movie hero with glasses and a quiet yet immensely strong personality.

To dream that you are Harry Potter, represents your desires to escape from reality. You are living in your own fantasy world.

Hat

To see or wear a hat in your dream, indicates that you are hiding an aspect of yourself or that you are covering up something. Alternatively, it represents your attitude or the various roles and responsibilities you have in your waking life.

To dream that you are wearing different hats, symbolize the many different roles you have in your waking life. Perhaps you feel you are stretched too thin and overburdened by daily responsibilities.

To dream that you are changing hats, represent your changing opinions and thoughts.

To dream that you are wearing a top hat, denotes your aspirations for wealth. It is also symbolic of male elegance and formality. If the top hat is knocked off your head, then it suggests a loss in your status of a fear that you will be stripped of your authority.

Haunted

To dream that you are being haunted, indicates early unpleasant traumas and repressed feelings or memories. You are experiencing some fear or guilt about your past activities and thoughts.

To see a haunted car in your dream, represents unfinished goals. You had started off on a path or journey, but never reached the end. Perhaps life has taken you on a different direction than you had planned or intended.

Haunted House

To dream of a haunted house, signifies unfinished emotional business, related to your childhood family, dead relatives, or repressed memories and feelings.

Hawk

To see a hawk in your dream, denotes that suspicions are lurking around you and your activities. You need to proceed with caution. Alternatively, a hawk symbolizes insight. Consider the phrase "hawk's eye" to mean that you need to keep a close watch on someone or some situation.

Hay

To see hay in your dream, represents the necessity of hard work; nothing in life comes easy. You may also be feeling hopeless about a situation. Alternatively, hay indicates the need to nurture your maternal instincts, masculine energy, and/or your sexual urges. Consider also the symbol as a pun on "hey". Your dream may be trying to call your attention to something.

Head

To see a head in your dream, signifies wisdom, intellect, understanding and rationality. It may also represent your accomplishments, self-image, and perception of the world. The dream may also be metaphor to indicate that you are "ahead" in some situation or that you need to get ahead.

To dream that someone is trying to rip your head off, suggests that you are not seeing a situation or problem clearly. Perhaps you are refusing to see the truth. You have to confront the situation or the person despite the pain and discomfort you might feel in doing so.

To dream that you have two heads, indicate that you need to learn to ask for help and accept assistance. Consider the metaphor "two heads are better than one". Do not try to do everything yourself.

Headache

To dream that you have a headache, suggests that you are heading in the wrong direction. You are ignoring your intellect and rational thinking. You need to utilize your mind and not let your emotions get out of control.

Headphones

To dream that you are wearing headphones, indicate that you are the only one getting the message. Furthermore, it means that you are in tune with your intuition.

Headlights

To see a car's headlights in your dream, indicate your inability to look beyond the past. You are dwelling on old issues. Alternatively, the dream suggests that you are being caught off guard or caught by surprised as in a "deer in the headlights."

If your headlights are on high beam, then it means that you are forcing your opinions and views on others.

Health Club

*Please See <u>Gymnasium.</u>

Hear

To dream that no one hears you, refers to a waking situation where you feel that no one is listening to you or paying attention to what you are saying. You feel you are being overlooked or overshadowed.

Hearing Aid

To see or wear a hearing aid in your dream, suggests that you are not paying enough attention to what someone is trying to tell you. You are not picking up on certain cues.

Hearse

To see a hearse in your dream, indicates that you are moving into a new phase. You need to carry away and let go of some unfinished issues. Start taking action and making the necessary changes that will carry you into a new transitional level.

Heart

To see your heart in your dream, signifies truth, courage, love, and romance. It is representative of how you are currently dealing with your feelings and expressing your emotions. Also consider the saying "the heart of the matter" which implies that you may need to get down to the core of a situation before proceeding.

To see a winged heart in your dream, represents the power of love and its ability to penetrate through to anyone.

To dream that your heart is bleeding or aching, represents desperation, despair, extreme sadness and sympathy. You are lacking support or love in some a situation in your life.

To dream that you have a heart transplant or heart surgery, indicates a huge change in your personal relationship. Perhaps you are involved in a rebound relationship.

Heart Attack

To dream that you have a heart attack, refers to a lack of support and acceptance. Perhaps you also feel a loss of love.

Heaven

To see heaven in your dream, signifies your desires to find perfect happiness. You may be trying to escape from the difficulties you are experiencing in your life. The dream serves as a medium in which you can restore your faith, optimism, and hope.

Heavy

To dream that something is too heavy, symbolizes your burdens, work load and responsibilities. You are carrying too much on your shoulders and need to prioritize. Take a break and lighten up.

Hedgehog

To see a hedgehog in your dream, suggests that you are being overly sensitive. You are taking everything too personally. Alternatively, it refers to losing your soul.

Heel

To see your heel in your dream, signifies oppression, lowliness, and vulnerability. The dream may also be a pun on "heal". Perhaps the dream is telling you that you need time to heal and recovery, either emotionally or physically.

Heimlich Maneuver

To perform the Heimlich Maneuver on someone in your dream, suggests that you are trying to get that person to open up to you.

To dream that someone is performing the Heimlich Maneuver on you, indicates that you are beginning to open up to others. All the emotions that you have been holding back are coming to the surface.

Helicopter

To see a helicopter in your dream, represents your ambitions and achievements. You are in full pursuit of your goals.

To dream that you are in a helicopter, indicates that you are living beyond your means. You need to slow down and not try to please everyone. Alternatively, you may be experiencing a higher level of consciousness, new-found freedom and greater awareness.

Hell

To dream of hell, suggests that you are suffering from a seemingly inescapable situation. You may have placed your decision or course of action into someone else's hand. Alternatively, you may be possessing a guilty conscious, some inner fears or repressed negative feelings. It is time to quit punishing yourself and take it easy for awhile.

Helmet

To see a helmet in your dream, symbolizes protection. It also indicates that you need to keep your thoughts and ideas closely guarded.

Help

To dream that you are helping someone, indicates your willingness to compromise your beliefs toward a greater accomplishment. It also represents your efforts to combine your talents or energies to achieve a mutual goal. In particular, if you are helping an enemy or someone you do not like, then it suggests that you need to come to an understanding or some sort of middle ground in order to move forward with your life.

To dream that you are calling or signaling for help, suggests that you are feeling lost, overwhelmed, and/or inadequate.

Hen

To see a hen in your dream, symbolizes gossip and calamity. You have a tendency to brag about minor things. The hen is also a maternal figure. Consider the metaphor of being "hen-pecked" or that you feel being picked on.

Henna

To dream that you have a henna tattoo, signifies good luck. You are transitioning into a new phase in your life.

Hercules

To see Hercules in your dream, suggests your individual struggle for freedom and immortality.

Herd

To see a herd in your dream, indicates that you are a follower. You tend to go along with the crowd. Learn to make your own decision and take initiative. The dream may also be a pun on "heard". Perhaps you heard something that was not meant for your ears. Consider also the specific animal in the herd.

Hermaphrodite

To see or dream that you are a hermaphrodite, represents the union of opposites and balance. Alternatively, the dreams suggest that you are trying to conceal your sexuality. Perhaps you are feeling ambiguous about your sexuality.

Hero

To dream that you are a hero, signifies your inner strength and weaknesses. The dream refers to your ability, determination and level of confidence. You have the power to bravely face the secrets of your unconscious and confront life's challenges.

Herpes

To dream that you or someone has herpes, refers to your sexual anxiety and worries. Perhaps you have practiced unsafe sex and are expressing your regrets.

Hexagon

To see a hexagon in your dream, signifies your direction or position in life as represented by each of the six corner and sides. The dream may be telling to you move up or down, forward or backward and left or right. Alternatively, a hexagon symbolizes death.

Hiccup

To dream that you have hiccups, symbolize minor interruptions and annoyances. You need to pace yourself and take your time in moving toward your goals.

Hickey

To dream that you have a hickey, represents a split between your rational thinking and your emotional thinking. You may be acting with your heart instead of thinking things out more clearly. Alternatively, you may be feeling emotionally or physically drained. You feel that you are giving too much of yourself in a relationship or situation.

Hide 'N Seek

To dream that you are playing hide 'n seek, means that you are keeping some information or secret that you cannot keep inside any longer. Consider whether you were the one hiding or the one seeking. If you were the one hiding, then it indicates that there is something that you are not revealing or sharing. If you are the one that is seeking, then it represents your inquisitive mind and your desire to find more information about a particular situation. Alternatively, the dream may be a regression of your childhood where the times were more carefree and simpler.

Hiding

To dream that you are hiding, suggests that you are keeping some secret or withholding some information. You may not be facing up to a situation or dealing with some issue. However, you may be getting ready to reveal something and confess before somebody finds out. In particular, to dream that you are hiding from some authority figure (police, parent, teacher...), implies feelings of guilt.

To dream that someone is hiding, indicates that you are looking for a sense of security and protection.

Hieroglyphics

To see hieroglyphics in your dream, denote that you will face many obstacles as you try to figure out your path in life.

High Chair

To see a high chair in your dream, indicates that you are trying to gain a better perspective on some issue.

To dream that you are sitting on a high chair, suggests that you have a tendency to look down on others. You expect others to be at your feet. It represents your elevated sense of self and high ambition.

High Five

To dream that you high five someone, indicates that you are looking for approval, validation and acknowledgement for your work. Also consider the significance of the number five.

High School

To dream about high school, refers to the bonds and friendships that you made while you were in high school. What spiritual lessons have you learned? The dream may also be telling you that you need to start preparing for the real world.

To dream that you have to repeat high school, suggests that you are doubting your accomplishments and the goals that you have already completed. You feel that you may not be measuring up to the expectation of others. The dream may occur because some recent situation may have awakened old anxieties and insecurities.

*Please See Also School.

Highlighter

To see a highlighter marker in your dream, represents enlightenment. There is something that you need to pay closer attention to. Consider what you are highlighting and the significance of the message.

Hijack

To dream that something has been hijacked, symbolizes your loss of control. The dream may be analogous to someone or something that has taken over an aspect of your life. In particular, to dream that an airplane is hijacked, signifies disturbing feelings and past emotions in your unconscious mind.

Hiking

To dream that you are hiking, represents progress and achievement. With perseverance and strong-will, you will make it far in life.

Hill

To dream that you are climbing a hill, signifies your struggles in achieving a goal. You need to focus your energies on the prize. To dream that you are standing on top of a hill, suggests that you have succeeded in your endeavors. You have the necessary resources to complete the task at hand.

Hippie

To see a hippie in your dream, represents excess and freedom of expression.

To dream that you are a hippie, suggests that you want to be different. You are rejecting some aspect of society.

Hippopotamus

To see a hippopotamus in your dream, symbolizes your aggressive nature and your hidden strengths. You have more influence and power than you realize. Alternatively, it indicates that you are being territorial. Perhaps someone is overstepping their boundaries.

To see a group of hippopotamuses in your dream, suggest that you need to escape from the daily grind and relax.

Hips

To notice your hips in your dream, represents your mobility adaptability to some situation. It relates to getting things done. The dream may also be a pun on being hip.

Hitchhiking

To dream that you are hitchhiking, suggests that you have not earned or deserved to be in this position you are at currently. The dream may also be a metaphor that you are getting a free ride. You are becoming too dependent on others.

To pick up a hitchhiker in your dream, indicates that you are taking on too many responsibilities. There is a fine line between helping others and letting them take advantage of you.

Hitler

To see Hitler in your dream, symbolizes oppression, fear, manipulation of power, and absolute control. The dream could be brought about by a situation where you are feeling helpless or by someone who is overly controlling or is making you feel less than human.

Hitman

To dream that you are a hitman or that you hire one, indicates that there is some aspect of yourself that you are desperately trying to rid yourself of.

Hive

Please See <u>Beehive</u>.

Hockey

To dream that you are playing or watching hockey, is analogous to how you are achieving and protecting of your goals. It also suggests that you may be dealt with a lot of hard blows in your life.

Hole

To see a hole in the ground, denotes hidden aspects of your activities. On the other hand, it may mean that you are feeling hollow or empty inside. This dream may be an awakening for you to get out and expose yourself to new interests and activities. Alternatively, the dream may be a pun on "wholeness' or completeness.

To dream that you fall into a hole, represents a pitfall in some waking situation. You feel you are stuck. Perhaps, you have dug yourself into a hole and cannot get out of it.

To dream that there is a hole in your clothing, indicates that there are some flaws in your thinking or thought process. You may need to undergo an image makeover.

Hollywood

To dream that you are in Hollywood, symbolizes fame and glamour. The dream may be telling you to be more realistic with your goals. You need to come down from you lofty ambitions or idealistic notions.

Holocaust

To dream about the Holocaust, indicates that you are being unjustly blamed for something. The dream may also be brought about by a movie or book related to the Holocaust. Perhaps, the disturbing events may have left a strong impression in your mind. Note that your own personal feelings about the Holocaust will overrule any other interpretation.

Home

To see your home in your dream, signifies security, basic needs, and values. You may be feeling at "home" or settled at your new job or environment. Alternatively, the dream represents your basic needs and priorities.

In particular, to see your childhood home, your hometown, or a home that you previously lived in, indicates your own desires for building a family and your family ideologies. It also reflects aspects of yourself that were prominent or developed during the time you lived in that home. You may experience some unfinished feelings that are being triggered by some waking situation. Alternatively, the dream may represent your outdated thinking.

To dream that you cannot find your way home, indicates that you have lost faith and belief in yourself. It may also signify a major transition in your life.

Homeless

To dream that you are homeless, indicates that you are feeling insecure. You are unsure of yourself and where you are headed.

Homosexual

If you are not homosexual in your waking life and dream that you are homosexual, represents a union with aspects of yourself. It is symbolic of self-love, self-acceptance, and compassion. If you are uncomfortable with homosexuality in your dream, then it suggests some fears or anxieties about your masculinity (if you are male) and femininity (if you are female). You may be experiencing some insecurity in your relations with the opposite sex.

To dream that the guy you like in real life is gay, represents your anxieties and fears that he won't like you back. By seeing him as gay, then it would be easier for you to dismiss your feelings for him because you have no chance with him.

On a side note, it is common for expectant fathers to have dreams of homosexual encounters.

If you are homosexual in your waking life, then the dream is simply a reflection of your own self.

Homework

To dream that you are doing homework, symbolizes the lessons that have learned or are learning. Pay attention to the assignment in your dream and figure out how it can be applied to your waking life. Alternatively, the dream represents your anxieties about your ability and performance. If you have a homework assignment that is due in real life, then the dream may just be your preoccupation and worry over the assignment.

Homicide

*Please See Murder.

Honey

To see honey in your dream, denotes that you need to be less meek and more honest in communicating with others. You need to assert yourself and make sure you are heard. Alternatively, seeing or eating honey in your dream represents gentleness, sweetness, compassion, wisdom, peace, longevity and joy. It is also symbolic of fertility and productivity. The dream may also be a pun on the "honey" in your life.

Honeymoon

To dream that you are on your honeymoon, indicates that you are expressing some fear in your sex life. You may also be expressing a desire for some new excitement in your relationship. Perhaps you are nervous about some new turn that the relationship is taking. Alternatively, the dream may represent your desires for a dream honeymoon. You are looking forward to a getaway.

Hood

To see a hood in your dream, signifies that you are hiding and cowering from a person or situation. You or someone may be deceitful about something. Consider also the saying, "having the hood pulled over your eyes".

Hookah

To see or smoke a hookah in your dream, represents ease and relaxation. Alternatively, it refers to the difficulties your are facing in your waking life. You may be bottling up your emotions.

Hooker

*Please See Prostitute.

Hooks

To see a hook in your dream, suggests that you are caught in some mischief and deceit. It also indicates your quest for material gains or feelings of deprivation. There is a force that is drawing you toward a certain direction, thinking or habit.

To dream that you are catching something with a hook, suggests that you need to acknowledge and incorporate some aspect or characteristic into your self-image. Alternatively, the dream refers to a sexual relationship. It may refer to your love or sexual relationship and issues of intimacy.

Hopscotch

To dream that you are playing hopscotch, represents your childish and/or immature behavior. Alternatively, it may indicate your tendency to jump from task to task or not being able to stay in one place.

Horizon

To see the horizon in your dream, symbolizes a new beginning or a somber conclusion. The horizon represents your goals and future plans. You are in a continual state of growth, rebirth, and regeneration.

Horn

To see or hear a horn in your dream, signifies your need to pay attention to your inner voices and intuition. Alternatively, you may be bragging and "blowing your own horn".

To see the horns of an animal in your dream, represent conflict and confrontation. You are at odds with someone. Alternatively, the dream also means that you have a hardened shell.

Horse

To see a horse in your dream, symbolizes strength, power, endurance, virility and sexual prowess. It also represents a strong, physical energy. You need to tame the wild forces within. The dream may also be a pun that you are "horsing around". Alternatively, to see a horse in your dream, indicate that you need to be less arrogant and "get off your high horse".

To see a black or dark horse in your dream, signifies mystery, wildness, and the unknown. You are taking a chance or a gamble at some unknown situation. It may even refer to occult forces. If the horse is white, then it signifies purity, prosperity and good fortunes. To dream that you are being chased by a white horse, may be a pun on chaste. Perhaps you are having difficulties dealing with issues of intimacy and sexuality.

To see a dead horse in your dream, indicates that something in your life that initially offered you strength is now gone. This may refer to a relationship or situation. Consider the phrase "beating a dead horse" to indicate that you may have maximized the usefulness of a certain circumstance.

To see a herd of wild horses in your dream, signifies a sense of freedom and lack of responsibilities and duties. Perhaps it may also indicate your uncontrolled emotions. If you are riding a wild horse, then it represents unrestrained sexual desires.

To dream that you are riding a horse, suggests that you are in a high position or position of power. Alternatively, it indicates that you will achieve success through underhanded means. You lack integrity. If you are riding a horse that is out of control, then it means that you are being carried away by your passions.

To see an armored or medieval horse in your dream, refers to your fierceness, aggression, power and/or rigidity. You may too confrontational. Alternatively, you may be trying to protect yourself from unconscious material or sexual desires that is emerging.

To dream that you are bathing a horse, represents a renewal of strength and vigor. You are experiencing a burst of energy in some aspect of your life.

Horseshoe

To see a horseshoe in your dream, signifies luck and success in your endeavors. It may also indicate a wedding in the near future. If the horseshoe is turned downward, then it has the opposite meaning and is considered unlucky. All the energy that you are putting into a project may not be worthwhile.

Hose

To see a hose in your dream, represents renewal, rejuvenation and cleansing. You need to heal those emotional wounds so that you can continue to grow as a person. Alternatively, a hose may be a metaphor for sex and sexual gratification. Or it may be a pun that you are "getting hosed" or blindsided in some situation.

Hospital

To see or dream that you are in a hospital, symbolizes your need to heal or improve your physical or mental health. You need to get back to the flow of everyday life. Alternatively, the dream suggests that you are giving up control of your own body. Perhaps you are afraid of losing control of your body.

Hostage

To dream that you are a hostage, indicates that you are feeling victimized or powerless. You feel limited in your choices or physically immobilized. Perhaps this dream is paralleling some situation or difficulty in your daily life or relationship. Alternatively, to dream that you are a hostage suggests that a part of yourself is not fully expressed.

Hot

To dream that you are hot, signifies passion and heated emotions. It may reflect a situation that is potentially dangerous or a relationship where you are getting burned. Alternatively, the dream may represent a person who is great looking or perhaps you are lusting after someone. On the other hand, you may be feeling beautiful.

Hot Air Balloon

To see or dream that you are in a hot air balloon, suggests that it is time to overcome your depression. The dream may be a metaphor indicating that you are losing your ground or your foothold on some situation/problem. Alternatively, it represents the process of individuation and your quest to fulfill some spiritual needs. Perhaps, you want to be elevated in someone's eyes.

Hotel

To see a hotel in your dream, signifies a new state of mind or a shift in personal identity. You are undergoing some sort of transition and need to move away from your old habits and old way of thinking. You need to temporarily escape from your daily life. Alternatively, the dream may imply a loss in your personal identity.

Hour

To dream about the hour, refers to a passage of time. The dream may serve to remind you of an appointment, deadline, or anniversary. Consider the significance of a particular number or any superstitions that may be associated with a particular hour. For example,12pm represents some confrontation or turning point.

To dream about happy hour, represents sensual enjoyment, stimulation, and relaxation. You are filled with inspirational power and enlightenment. Alternatively, it indicates avoidance in dealing with your problems and in facing your anxieties.

Hourglass

To see an hourglass in your dream, denotes that time is running out for you. This may be a deadline that you have to meet for school or work. Alternatively, an hourglass represents a situation that is being turned upside down.

House

To see a house in your dream, represents your own soul and self. Specific rooms in the house indicate a specific aspect of your psyche. In general, the attic represents your intellect, the basement represents the unconscious, etc. If the house is empty, then it indicates feelings of insecurity. If the house is shifting, then it suggests that you are going through some personal changes and changing your belief system. To dream that a house has no walls, represents a lack of privacy. You feel that everyone is looking over your shoulder or up in your business.

To dream that you are cleaning your house, signifies your need to clear out your thoughts and getting rid of old ways. You are seeking self-improvement.

If you live with others in your waking life, but dream that you are living alone, suggests that you need to take new steps toward independence. You need to accept responsibilities and be more self-reliant.

To see an old, run-down house in your dream, represents your old beliefs, attitudes and how you used to think or feel. A situation in your current life may be bringing about those same old attitudes and feelings. Alternatively, the old house may symbolize your need to update you mode of thinking. To dream that your house is damaged, indicates your waking concerns about the condition of your house.

To see a new house in your dream, indicates that you are entering into a new phase or new area in your life. You are becoming more emotionally mature. If you are locked out of the house, then it represents rejection and insecurity. You feel you are being left behind.

To dream that your house is broken into, suggests that you are feeling violated. It may refer to a particular relationship or current situation in your life. Alternatively, it indicates that some unconscious material is attempting to make itself known. There are some aspects of yourself that you have denied.

To dream that a house has disappeared, indicates that you are not feeling grounded. You feel uprooted by a particular circumstance or relationship in your life.

To dream that water is rising up in your house, suggests that you are becoming overwhelmed by your emotions.

Hugging

To dream that you are hugging someone, symbolizes your loving and caring nature. You are holding someone or something close to your heart. Alternatively, it may indicate your need to be more affectionate.

Hula Dancing

To hula dance in your dream, represents an appreciation and celebration of life. You are living life to the fullest.

To see hula dancing in your dream, symbolizes joy. Pay attention to the message that the dance is trying to convey.

Hula Hoop

To see a hula hoop or to hula hoop in your dream, indicates that some aspect of your life is taking you in circles. You are going nowhere.

Hummingbird

To see hummingbirds in your dream, suggest that seemingly small ideas and concepts can possess much potential and power. Alternatively, it symbolizes your flighty thoughts and frivolous ideas. The hummingbird may also be seen as a metaphor for your inability to commit to a relationship.

Humpty Dumpty

To see Humpty Dumpty in your dream, suggests that you need to exercise care in some fragile situation. Alternatively, it refers to some irreversible plan or action. You cannot go back to the past; you need to just accept the consequences of your actions.

Hunger

To dream that you are hungry, signifies a feeling of unfulfilment in some area of your life. You may be starving for love. recognition, power, sex, wealth, or fame. You are longing to achieve something that you have desired for awhile. Alternatively, the dream may simply be that you are really feeling hungry and it is being manifested in your dream.

Hunting

To dream that you are hunting, suggests that you are seeking or pursuing some inner desire, either emotional or physical. You may be "hunting" for a solution or for a sexual conquest.

To dream that you hunt and kill an animal, signifies that you are trying to repress or destroy an instinctive part of yourself.

To dream that you are being hunted, indicates that you are being overwhelmed by life's challenges.

Hurdle

To see hurdles in your dream, symbolize the barriers and obstacles that are in your way throughout your life. If you jump over the hurdles, then it indicates that you are goal-oriented and do not let anything get in your way of your success. If you knock over the hurdle, then it represents difficulties. You will need to work hard in order to achieve your goals.

Hurricane

To see a hurricane in your dream, indicates sudden, unexpected changes occurring in your life. You may be experiencing some destructive and powerful emotions.

To dream that you are swept up in a hurricane, suggests that both your mental and emotional forces are building up inside and making themselves known. You may be literally consumed by your emotions. Alternatively, the dream indicates that you are being pressured and pushed against your will toward something you do not want to do.

Hurry

To dream that you are in a hurry, suggests that may be unprepared for a situation. There is a lack in your planning of things. Alternatively, to dream that you are in a hurry means that you are feeling out of place. This dream may also be a literal reflection of your daily life where you feel that you are always in a rush. And that there is not enough time to do all the things you want to do. The dream may occur due to this type of stress.

Husband

To see your husband in your dream, signifies the waking relationship with your husband and the unconscious feelings you have towards him. The dream may be trying to focus on hidden elements that you are not addressing in your waking life.

To dream that you have a husband (but you do not in your waking life), symbolizes some sort of partnership and/or commitment. Often, your dream husband represents the qualities of your father in which you projected onto this figure or the masculine side of your own personality.

Hut

To see or live in a hut in your dream, represents the basic necessities and comforts. You need to simplify your life and get back to the bare basics. Accept what you already have and know that that is enough.

Hydroplane

To see a hydroplane in your dream, suggests that you will get through an emotional issue with relative ease.

Hyena

To see a hyena in your dream, indicates greed or uncleanness. It also suggests that you are overwhelmed with responsibilities. You feel that someone is relying on you too much. Alternatively, a hyena represents someone in your waking life who has a sense of humor.

Hypnotize

To dream that you are hypnotized, signifies your limitations. You are being influenced or swayed by others.

To dream that you fail to be hypnotized, indicates that trouble is looming over you. You are the only one who can confront the problem and rise above it.

I

To see the letter "I" in your dream, is on pun on me, myself and I. You need to focus on you. Or the dream may be an indication that you are being too selfish. Alternatively, the letter represents action and responsibility.

Ice

To see ice in your dream, suggests that you are lacking a flow of ideas and thoughts. You are not seeing any progress in your life. Alternatively, you may be feeling emotionally paralyzed or rigid. You need to let your feelings be known.

To dream that you are walking on ice, indicates that you are standing on shaky or instable ground. You need to proceed with caution in some matter or situation. Alternatively, the dream also suggests that you are taking risks that you shouldn't be taking.

To dream that you slip on ice, symbolizes your insecurities and self-esteem issues. There may also be an obstacle ahead for you.

To dream that you fall through ice, suggests that your emotions are threatening to come crashing through.

Ice Cream

To see or eat ice cream in your dream, denotes good luck, pleasure, success in love and satisfaction with your life. You need to savor the moment and enjoy it. Alternatively, the dream may suggest that you need to cool off and not let your temper get out of hand. On the other hand, the ice cream may be a pun on "I scream". Perhaps there is something that you need to let out.

To dream that you are eating bad or sour ice cream, signifies sorrow, disillusionment, or betrayal.

To see ice cream melt in your dream, symbolizes failure to realize your hopes and desires.

Iceberg

To see an iceberg in your dream, suggests that you are not utilizing your fullest potential and strengths. Or you are trying to hide under a facade. Alternatively, the dream means that you are not looking deep enough into some decision or problem. You need to look beyond the surface and the obvious.

Icicles

To see icicles in your dream, indicate a problem or concern that has been lingering over you. If the icicles are melting in your dream, then it indicate that the tough times are almost over. You will overcome your problems.

To see icicles forming in your dream, symbolize difficulties in your life. You feel unsupported by those around you.

Icing

To put icing on a cake or pastry, indicates that you are behaving superficially. Something may look good on the exterior, but prove empty or unsubstantial on the inside. In other words, looks can be deceiving. Alternatively, the dream represents the finishing touches in your life that brings about fulfillment and completion.

To see or eat icing in your dream, suggests that what may seem good in the beginning, will ultimately be unsatisfying and unfulfilling.

Identification

To see your I.D. in your dream, signifies your own self-confidence. To dream that you lose your I.D., denotes confusion about your own self-identity and your sense of individuality.

Igloo

To see or live in an igloo in your dream, symbolizes someone who appears cold and frigid on the outside, but is really a warm and caring person on the inside. Alternatively, the igloo represents the feminine and her hard cold barrier that sometimes need to be broken down.

Iguana

To see an iguana in your dream, represents harshness, cold-heartedness or fierceness. You approach situations or problems with both hostility and unstoppable determination. The iguana may also remind you of someone or some situation in your waking life that you find frightening yet awe inspiring.

Imposter

To dream that you have an imposter, suggests that you are trying to be someone you are not. The dream may be pointing out qualities that are uncharacteristic of your personality.

Impotence

To dream that you are impotent, signifies a fear of losing power. Maybe you are afraid that you won't measure up to a particular person or task in your life. A more direct interpretation suggests that you may be having problems with sex in your waking life.

Inauguration

To dream of an inauguration, signifies personal growth or a rise in your current status. You are being recognized for your achievements.

Incense

To dream that you are burning incense, indicates spiritual learning. It represents a high level of awareness.

Incubator

To see an incubator in your dream, suggests that you need some stability and calmness in your life. Alternatively, it is symbolic of fresh and new ideas, growth, and development of the Self.

To dream that you are in an incubator, indicates that you have been acting prematurely. It may also suggest that you are trying to escape from the burdens and responsibilities of your waking life.

Indigo

To see indigo in your dream, suggests that you are taking advantage of others. The color indigo implies spirituality and divine protection. It may also mean deceit.

Infertile

To dream that you are infertile, represents a lack of creativity. Something in your waking life is not working out the way you want it to. The dream may also reflect your own state of infertility and the struggles to have a baby.

Infinity

To see the infinity symbol in your dream, represents time and longevity. Alternatively, it symbolizes wealth or the number 8.

Inflate

To dream that you are inflating something, represents intellect, knowledge and a higher power. Alternatively, it may symbolize your inflated ego or inflated sense of self.

Initials

To see initials in your dream, may be a pun on a phrase or a metaphor. For example, the initials T.C. may be a pun on "teasing". Or the initials J.J., may be symbolic of double hooks. As a more direct interpretation, seeing initials represent someone in your waking life who shares that same initial.

Injection

To dream that you are being injected for medical reasons, indicates that you need to develop yourself on a mental and spiritual level. You are looking for an emotional uplift or need some time to heal. Alternatively, the dream may be a metaphor that you need to "inject" more energy into your walking life.

To dream that someone is forcibly injecting you, represents your negative attitudes about a particular situation/person. It also indicates the influence of peer pressure working against you. You are recognizing that someone is forcing their negative and unwelcome views/values on you.

Inner Tube

To see an inner tube in your dream, represents the Self. You are not feeling emotionally whole.

To dream that you are inner tubing, suggests that you are on experiencing emotional ups and downs.

Insanity

To dream that you or someone is insane, represents your retreat from reality. Alternatively, the dream suggests that some waking aspects of your life is out of control. You have difficulties telling what is right and wrong.

Insect

To see insects in your dream, signify minor obstacles that you must overcome. There are small problems and annoyances that need to be dealt with. You feel that you are under attack. Or something or someone may be "bugging" or pestering you. Alternatively, insects are symbolic of precision, alertness, and sensitivity. You may need to organize your thoughts and sort out your values. Sometimes they are seen as divine messengers.

Inside

To dream that you are inside, suggests that you need to take time for some self introspection. The dream may be a metaphor that you need to look within yourself. It is what is in the inside that matters. Alternatively, dreaming that you are inside indicates that there are some family or domestic issues that you need to deal with.

Inside Out

To dream that your clothes are worn inside out, represents your non-conformist attitude. You like to go against what everybody else says or does.

To turn your clothes inside out in your dream, suggests that you are trying to protect yourself against something. You don't want to get hurt.

Instant Message

To dream that you receive an instant message, signifies an urgent message from your unconscious. It implies self-confidence.

To dream that you are sending an instant message, represents your connection to others and your network of friendships.
Alternatively, the dream may also be a pun on "I am" and thus symbolize the act of "being".

Instructions

To follow or read instructions in your dream, suggests that you are seeking some advice on what you should do next. Consider what the instructions are for and how it relates to a waking life issue. For example, to read instructions on how to assemble a table, indicates that you are trying to be more sociable and open. To read instructions on how to operate an electronic item, means you need to learn to make your life less complicated.

Instruments

To see musical instruments in your dream, indicate the expectation of fun and pleasures. You are focused on enjoying life and all that it has to offer. The dream also represents your talents and your ability to communicate with others. Certain musical instruments are symbolic of sexual organs and thus point to your sexuality. If you play a musical instrument in your waking life, then the dream may serve as a rehearsal to improve your technique.

To see surgical or medical instruments in your dream, mean that you need to carefully plan out your next move. You need to act with deliberate action and precision.

Insult

To dream that you insult someone, indicates that you are feeling insecure about a waking relationship or situation. Alternatively, the dream suggests that you are trying to hide your true feelings. You are expressing your anger towards someone within the confines of your dream. You need to confront this person in real life.

To dream that you have been insulted, suggests that you are suffering from low self esteem.

Internet

To dream of the internet, signifies your need to connect and communicate with a larger network of people. The dream may be highlighting the importance of networking. Consider the types or names of the websites you were looking at for additional significance.

Interrogation

To dream that you are being interrogated, indicates that something or someone in your waking life is trying to squeeze every bit of energy or information out of you. You are feeling stressed or burdened.

Intersection

To dream that you are at an intersection, represents a decision or choice that you need to make in order to progress forward.

Interview

To dream that you are at an interview, denotes your anxiety over being judged by others. You may be experiencing some dissatisfaction with some aspect of yourself.

Intestines

To see intestines in your dream, signify compassion. The image is analogous to the twist and turns of life. The dream may also be a metaphor for courage and your gutsiness.

Intravenous Drip

To see or have an intravenous drip in your dream, represents a time for healing. Alternatively, it denotes an urgent message that needs to be delivered.

Invincible

To dream that you are invincible, symbolizes power and confidence. Such dreams also forewarns that you may be too overly confident.

Invisible

To dream that you are invisible, signifies feelings of not being noticed or recognized for what is important to you. You feel you are being overlooked. Alternatively, the dream indicates that you are trying to withdraw from the realities of life.

IQ Test

To see or dream that you are taking an IQ test, signifies feelings of insecurities and concerns about your performance in a waking area of your life. You feel that you are not measuring up.

Iron

To see iron metal in your dream, symbolizes harshness, anger, aggression, ruthlessness, and conflict. On a positive note, it may signify strength, endurance, and willpower.

To see red, hot iron in your dream, represents action. Perhaps the dream is telling you to "strike while the iron is hot". You need to take advantage of certain opportunities while it is still available.

To see old, rusty iron in your dream, signifies poverty and disappointment.

Ironing

To dream that you are ironing, signifies domestic comfort and orderliness. Alternatively, the dream represents the monotony of your daily routine. You may be bored and are looking for some excitement to your life. The dream may also be a pun that you need to "iron the wrinkles" out of your life.

To dream that you burn your hands while ironing, signify loss of tranquility, illness, or jealousy. Alternatively, the dream may suggest that you need to stop interfering into other people's business.

Island

To see or dream that you are on an island, signifies ease, relaxation and comfort. The dream is telling you that you need a vacation and escape the stresses in your life. It is time for some solitude.

To dream that you are stranded on an island, suggests that you need to get away from the demands of your daily life. Or perhaps you are running away from a situation instead of trying to confront it. Alternatively, the dream means that you feel cut off from society. You are in a rut and do not know what to do with your life.

Ivory

To see ivory in your dream, symbolizes purity, strength, and endurance. The color ivory, signifies your superiority over others. Alternatively, ivory symbolizes tainted purity. Something or someone is not as perfect as you had thought.

Ivy

To see ivy in your dream, symbolizes longevity and immortality. It may be a metaphor for an ivy-league college. Alternatively, the ivy represents your close-knit relationships and the security and comfort they provide. However, it can also lead to clinginess and dependency issues.

To see withered ivy in your dream, denotes broken engagements and sadness.

J

To see the letter "J" in your dream, means that there is something that you need to hold on to and grasp. Alternatively, the dream may be a pun on someone named "Jay" or whose initial starts with J.

Jack

To see or use a jack in your dream, suggests that you are looking for balance in your life. The dream may also symbolize a person who is named "Jack" in your life.

Jack In The Box

To see or play with a jack in the box toy in your dream, signifies a pleasant surprise. Alternatively, the dream may mean that you are all wound up about something that is weighing in your mind.

Jack O' Lantern

To see a Jack O' Lantern in your dream, represents a force or spirit that is protecting over you.

To carve a Jack O' Lantern in your dream, suggests that you are trying to put on a tough or mean face. It refers to a superficial facade.

Jackal

To see a jackal in your dream, refers to manipulation. You have a tendency to feed off of others.

Jacket

To see or wear a jacket in your dream, represents the image that you want to present and project to the outside world. Alternatively, it symbolizes your protective and defensive persona. You tend to distant your feelings and as a result, you may isolate yourself. Consider also the color, appearance, and type of jacket for additional significance.

Jackhammer

To see a jackhammer in your dream, suggests that you need to make some drastic changes in your life. Break away from your old outdated attitudes and habits.

Jade

To see jade in your dream, indicates growth, healing power, purity, harmony, luck, immortality, and truth. It refers to the shaping and development of your personality.

Jaguar

To see a jaguar in your dream, represents speed, agility, and power.

Jail

To dream that you are in jail, suggests that you are feeling restrained or censored in your work environment, relationship or situation in your life. You are feeling confined and suffocated. Alternatively, it represents self-punishment and guilt. You are involved in some wrongdoing.

Jam

To dream that you are eating jam, signifies pleasant surprises, sweet things and new discoveries. Alternatively, the dream may also be a pun that "caught in a jam". Are you in trouble or in a sticky situation?

To dream that you are making jam, refers to a happy home life.

To dream that you are spreading jam, indicates that you may be spreading yourself too thin. You have too many responsibilities and commitments. You need to learn to say no.

January

To dream of the month of January, signifies loss of love and broken companionship.

Jar

To see a jar in your dream, symbolizes the feminine womb. You are seeking protection. The dream may also be a pun on feeling "jarred" or shaken up by something or someone.

Jaw

To see the jaws of an animal in your dream, indicate a misunderstanding. It may also mean that you are rushing into things. Alternatively, the dream suggests that someone or some situation is taking a large bite of your time, energy or some aspect of yourself.

To see your own jaw in your dream, represents your stubbornness, determination and forcefulness. You may need to have more willpower and fortitude in some situation. To dream that your jaws are tight, indicates unexpressed angers and other powerful feelings which you are holding back.

To dream that you break or dislocate your jaw, suggests that you are compromising your own beliefs and principles.

Jawbreaker

To see or eat a jawbreaker in your dream, indicates that a situation may look tempting and inviting, but it is in actuality very difficult to handle and control.

Jealousy

To dream that you are jealous of another person, signifies that such feelings may be carried over from your waking life. The dream may reveal your unconscious feelings of jealousy toward that particular person. Alternatively, to dream of jealousy represents your vulnerability and your fear of intimacy. You need to work on self-love and on acknowledging your self-worth.

Jeans

Wearing jeans in your dream may simply be a reflection of your waking Self and bear no additional significance. However, if there is a particular focus to the jeans, then the dream means that you need to take a more relaxed approach to some situation. If you are wearing or buying designer jeans in your dream, then it indicates that you have a relaxed attitude about money and other financial matters.

To dream that your jeans are too tight, suggests that your ideals are set too high. Alternatively, the dream means that you are feeling restrained in some relationship or situation. You are lacking freedom.

To see ripped jeans in your dream, implies that you are being overly lackadaisical about a situation or problem. The dream also denotes that you are acting inappropriately in some situation.

To dream that you are trying on jeans, indicates that you are trying hard to fit in with others.

Jedi

To dream that you are a Jedi, indicates that you are in tune with your spiritual powers. You need to believe in mind over matter. Or you need to trust in your own metal powers.

To see a Jedi in your dream, symbolizes the challenges in your life and the difficult decisions you are confronted with. Alternatively, it represents your quest for order and peace.

Jeep

To see a jeep in your dream, suggests that you need to adopt a more active lifestyle. You need to get out and start doing! Alternatively, the dream may be a pun on "jeepin", which is slang for having sex in the car. Perhaps you need to add some excitement or non-conventionality to your sex life.

Jellybean

To see or eat jellybeans in your dream, signify light heartedness, positive energy and joy. You are feeling content and relaxed.

Jellyfish

To see a jellyfish in your dream, represents painful memories that is emerging from your unconscious. There may be hidden hostility or aggression in some aspect of your waking relationship or situation. Alternatively, a jellyfish indicates feelings of inadequacy, uncertainty and a lack of self-esteem. Perhaps there is some situation in which you are unable to assert yourself.

Jesus

To see Jesus in your dream, foretells that your greatest desires and goals will be realized. This dream serves to console and strengthen you in your times of adversity, hardship and struggle. You will rise above a difficult situation or circumstance and become victorious.

To dream that Jesus speaks to you or that you are praying with Him, signifies that you will be blessed with true peace of mind, joy and contentment.

Jet

To see a jet flying overhead in your dream, signifies speed, pride or power.

To see a jet stone in your dream, signifies a period of mourning and sadness.

Jewelry

To see jewelry in your dream, signifies status and your own sense of self worth and personal value. It is also symbolic of knowledge, identity, or whatever qualities you hold precious in your life. Jewelry highlights the importance of spiritual and psychological riches. If you dream of a specific piece of jewelry that you own, then it symbolizes aspects of a waking relationship.

To dream that you receive jewelry as a gift, indicates that you need to acknowledge and incorporate those corresponding qualities within your own self. Consider the type of jewelry and what it is made of.

To see broken jewelry in your dream, signifies disappointments in achieving your goals and attaining your highest desires.

To dream that you are wearing too much jewelry, means that you are trying to hard to impress others.

Job

To dream that you are looking for a job, suggests that you are feeling unfulfilled and frustrated in a current phase of your life. If you are applying for several jobs in your dream, then it suggests that you need a clear direction and focused goal.

To dream about your current job, suggests that you need to work harder or be more effective at work. There may be something or some task that must be done at once. Or the dream may mean you are overworked or preoccupied with work. You need to make time for leisure and relaxation.

To dream that you lose your job, represents instability and insecurity in your waking life.

Jockey

To see or dream that you are a jockey, suggests that you are in an elevated position. You are showing confidence in your ability.

Joke

To dream that you are telling a joke, denotes that you are not being taken seriously and as a result you are feeling frustrated. On the other hand, you may not be the one who is taking an issue seriously.

To hear a joke in your dream, signifies that you are doing something that is either pointless or ridiculous. The dream may serve to alleviate some tension that has been weighing on you.

Joker

To see the joker card in your dream, indicates endless possibilities. You can be anything you want if you set your mind to it.

Jousting

To joust in your dream, signifies your determination and drive to push forward in any circumstance.. Alternatively, jousting refers to some sexual conquest. It may be a metaphor for sex.

To watch a jousting match in your dream, indicates that you need to be more direct about a problem or situation that you are trying to deal with.

Judge

To see a judge in your dream, denotes feelings of guilt. You are afraid of getting caught. Your dream may be helping and guiding you toward making better judgments. Alternatively, a judge indicates your insecurities and concerns of being judged or criticized for your actions. On a more direct note, your dream may indicate that waking disputes be resolved through some legal proceedings.

Juggling

To dream that you are juggling, indicates that you are trying to do too much at one time. You are feeling overwhelmed, especially if you fail to keep all the balls in the air. Alternatively, the dream represents your ability to balance aspects of your life with success.

Juice

To drink juice in your dream, represents the gift of life and vitality.

July

To dream of the month of July, signifies hope, knowledge or productivity.

Jumping

To dream that you are jumping, indicates that you need to take a risk and go for it. You will overcome your obstacles and find progress toward your goals. Consider the metaphors "jumping for joy" to mean thrill and excitement or "jumping the gun" to mean impatience or impulsiveness. The way you feel in the dream will provide additional significance and meaning to your dream.

To dream that you fail to jump or are afraid to jump, indicates that you fear uncertainty. You do not like change.

Jumping Jacks

To dream that you are doing jumping jacks, signifies your need for more balance in your life. You need to do more methodical in how you pursue your goals.

Jump Rope

To dream that you are jumping rope, represents your ability to coordinate your actions and execute your plans.

June

To dream of the month of June, signifies gains and progress in your endeavors.

Jungle

To dream that you are in a jungle, signifies aspects of yourself and your personality that may be inhibited. You may be experiencing some chaos and unpredictable circumstances in your waking life. Consider the phrase "it's a jungle out there!"

If you are lost or trapped in a jungle, then it indicates that your negative feelings are hindering your progress. You need to come to terms with aspects of your unconscious.

Jupiter

To see Jupiter in your dream, symbolizes creativity, energy, success, optimism, generosity, pleasure and extravagance. The dream may indicate your need to exhibit some of these qualities in your waking life. Alternatively, seeing Jupiter in your dream, indicates your need to expand your knowledge and explore your limits.

Jury

To see a jury in your dream, suggests that you are placed under scrutiny by others. You feel that others are judging you and your actions. Alternatively, the dream indicates that you are too overly concerned with what others think about you.

To dream that you are part of a jury, indicates your tendency to pass judgment on others. Perhaps you are being to judgmental.

K

To see the letter "K" in your dream, implies that something is "okay". Alternatively, the dream may be a pun on someone named "Kay" or whose initial starts with K.

Kaleidoscope

To see a kaleidoscope in your dream, symbolizes the different fragments and facets that make up character. Various aspects of your life are coming together. Alternatively a kaleidoscope foretells of difficulties in achieving your goals and choosing your path in life.

Kangaroo

To see a kangaroo in your dream, refers to maternal and paternal protection. You may be expressing your nurturing and mothering nature. Perhaps, you are being too overly protective. Alternatively, a kangaroo symbolizes aggression. If the kangaroo is hopping, then the dream is analogous to how you jump from one thing to another. You lack the ability to stick to one thing.

To dream that a kangaroo attacks you, indicates that your reputation is being called into question.

Karaoke

To dream that you are taking part in karaoke, suggests that you are too overly confident in your abilities. Alternatively, you may not be utilizing your talents to its fullest potential.

Karate

To dream that you are doing karate, suggests that you need to direct your energy and concentrate them toward your goals.

Keg

To see a keg in your dream, symbolizes your struggles against adversity. If the keg is full, then it suggests that you need to carry on the same course. If the keg is empty, then it indicates that you need to deviate from your plans. Alternatively, the dream indicates that you need to conserve your energy.

Ketchup

To see or eat ketchup in your dream, represents simplicity, youth, and happiness. Alternatively, the dream may be a pun on your need to "catch up" on something.

Key

To see a key in your dream, symbolizes opportunities, access, control, secrets, freedom, knowledge or responsibilities. You may be locking away your own inner feelings and emotions. Or you are unlocking the answer to some problem. In particular, a ring of keys, represents status, authority, and power. It also highlights your adaptability to a situation. If the key is gold, then it suggests that influence, power and wealth will give you access to almost anything you want.

Alternatively, keys have sexual connotations. They can represent intercourse, impotence, infidelity, etc. depending on the condition and usage of the key.

To dream that you lose your keys, signify fears of losing control of yourself or losing your position or status in life. It may also indicate unexpected changes, frustrations, and unpleasant adventures. The dream could be analogous to lost or missed opportunities. If you give your key away, then it suggests that you have given up control of some situation or responsibility.

To dream that you find a key, indicates that you have found a solution to a problem.

To see broken keys in your dream, represent a lost in status. You are denied access to a place where you were previously allowed. If the key is rusty, then it symbolizes a talent or skill that you have neglected.

To hear the sound of keys rattling, indicate that you have the right attitude toward life. You are heading in the right direction and asking all the right questions in the process. It is also a sign of decisive action.

Keyboard

To see a computer keyboard in your dream, indicates that there is a message that you need to get out. The keyboard also symbolizes something that you have to get done.

To see or play a musical keyboard in your dream, represents harmony. Your life is well balanced.

Kick

To dream that you are kicking someone, represents suppressed aggression that you are unable to express in your waking life.

To dream that you are being kicked, indicates that you feel victimized or taken advantage of. The dream may be telling you to stop feeling sorry for yourself. Alternatively, being kicked is a way for your unconscious to push you ahead and motivate you to continue on toward your goals. Sometimes you need a kick. You need to be more aggressive.

Kidnapper

To dream that you are being kidnapped, denotes feelings of being trapped and restricted. Someone or some situation may be diverting your concentration and your attention away from your goals.

To dream that someone has been kidnapped, indicates that you are not letting aspects and characteristics of that person be expressed within you. You are trying to contain and/or suppress those qualities of the kidnapped person.

To dream that you are a kidnapper, signifies that you are holding on to something that you need to let go. You may be forcing your views and opinions on others.

Killing

To dream that you kill someone, indicates that you are on the verge of losing your temper and self-control. Consider the person you have killed and ask yourself if you feel any rage towards him or her in your waking life. Your dream may be expressing some hidden anger. Alternatively, you may be trying to kill an aspect of yourself that is represented by the person killed. Identify the characteristics of this person and ask yourself which of these qualities you are trying to put an end to.

To dream that you have been killed, suggests that your actions are disconnected from your emotions and conscience. The dream refers to drastic changes that you are trying to make. There is a characteristic that you want to get rid of or a habit that you want to end within yourself. Killing represents the killing off of the old parts and old habits. Alternatively, the dream represents feelings of being let down or betrayed by someone in your waking life. You are feeling overwhelmed, shocked and disappointed.

*Please See Also <u>Murder</u>.

Killer Whale

To see a killer whale in your dream, indicates that you need to be more social or more vocal about something. Step up and speak up. Alternatively, the dream symbolizes spiritual guidance. You are ready to explore your emotions, but you need to make the connection between the conscious and unconscious aspects of yourself.

Kilt

To see or wear a kilt in your dream, signifies kinship, camaraderie and masculinity. You are expressing a desire to belong. Consider the color and the pattern of the kilt for additional significance.

King

To see a king in your dream, indicates that success and prestige are within reach. You will rise above your problems and adversities. The king is symbolic of power and control. Alternatively, the king symbolizes your father or some father figure. You are looking for support.

To dream that you are the king, represents your masculine power. Alternatively, it indicates that you have attained a high level of authority and power. Perhaps you are becoming too domineering or overly confident.

Kiss

To dream of a kiss, denotes love, affection, tranquility, harmony, and contentment. To see others kissing in your dream, suggests that you are too involved in someone else's personal lives and relationship. You need to give them some space. If the dream ends just about as you are about to kiss someone, then it indicates that you are unsure of how he or she really feels about you. You are looking for some sort of relationship with this person but you are not sure about how to go about achieving it. If you are heterosexual and you dream that you are kissing someone of the same sex, then it represents self-acceptance. You are acknowledging the feminine or masculine side.

To dream that you are kissing someone's hand, signifies respect. If you are kissing someone's foot, then denotes respect and humility.

To dream that you are kissing someone else's boyfriend or girlfriend, indicates your wish to be in a relationship and to experience the energy of love. Perhaps you are somewhat jealous. You may be sexually acting out and desire to awaken your passion. Alternatively, the dream indicates a lack of integrity on your part.

If you are kissing a close friend, then it represents your respect and adoration for your friend. You are seeking some intimate closeness that is lacking in some waking relationship. It may or may not signify a romantic interest for him or her.

If you dream that you are kissing a stranger, then it represents acknowledgement and acceptance of the repressed aspect of yourself. If you are kissed by a stranger, then your dream is one of self-discovery. You need to get more acquainted with some aspect of yourself.

To dream of kissing an enemy, signifies betrayal, hostility, or reconciliation with an angry friend. Consider also the saying "this kiss of death".

Kitchen

To see a kitchen in your dream, signifies your need for warmth, spiritual nourishment and healing.

It may also be symbolic of the nurturing mother or the way that you are for your loved ones. Alternatively the kitchen, represents a transformation. Or perhaps the dream could be telling you that if "you can't stand the heat, then you need to get out of the kitchen". You need to abort your plans.

Kite

To dream that you are flying a kite, suggests that even though you have high ambitions and goals, you still remain well-grounded. Persistence will pay off in the end no matter how difficult your current task may be. Alternatively, the dream implies that some choice or gift comes with strings attached. There is a price you will need to pay. Or it may suggest that someone is pulling the strings. You are not really in control of the direction that your life is taking.

To see a kite in your dream, symbolizes your spiritual or childlike awareness. Consider the design, shape and color of the kite for additional significance.

Kiwi

To see or eat a kiwi fruit in your dream, suggests a need to be reenergized or revitalized. You are looking for that little bit of strength in order to move forward in a situation.

To see a kiwi bird in your dream, indicates that there is a situation that you are trying to avoid or hide from.

Knee

To dream of your knees, symbolize a level of support you may be receiving. You are feeling very emotional. Feelings of inadequacy and issues of power/control also come into play. Perhaps, you are taking on more than you can handle.

Kneel

To dream that you are kneeling, represents your humbleness. It also indicates that you are open to the influences of others.

Knife

To dream that you are carrying a knife, signifies anger, aggression and/or separation. There may be something in your life that you need to cut out and get rid of. Perhaps you need to cut ties or sever some relationship. Be more divisive. Alternatively, a knife refers to some sexual tension or sexual confrontation.

If the knife is dull, then it denotes that your hard work will result in little or no gain.

To dream that you are wounded by a knife, is symbolic of masculine or animalistic aggression.

To see an electric knife in your dream, indicates your power to get down to the truth of a situation quickly.

Knight

To see a knight in your dream, signifies honor, protection and security. The knight can be seen as a savior or someone who sweeps you off your feet, as in the "knight in shining armor".

To dream that you are knighted, indicates that you are being recognized for your good character. You are being entrusted with power and authority.

Knocker

To see or use a knocker in your dream, symbolizes opportunities and welcomed expectations. You are seeking for assistance and spiritual guidance. On a negative note, to see a knocker in your dream, signifies repressed thoughts, death, and dreaded expectations. It is a bad omen.

Consider also a knocker as a sexual innuendo referring to a woman's breasts.

Knocking

To hear knocking in your dreams, suggests that your unconscious is trying to attract your attention to some aspect of yourself or to some waking situation. A new opportunity may be presented to you. Alternatively, the dream may be a pun that you are "knocking" on or insulting something or someone. Or perhaps there is a habit or behavior that you to stop or "knock it off".

Knots

To see knots in your dream, signify your worries over minor problems and small matters. You may be trying to find a resolution to a situation. It also denotes constraints and restrictions in your thoughts, feelings and actions.

To dream that you are tying a knot, symbolizes your independent and unyielding nature. You have everything under control. It may also mean a union of two people or a commitment to a relationship as suggested by the coming phrase "tying the knot".

Koala

To see a koala in your dream, represents your link the physical world, the unconscious, and the spiritual realm. The koala also symbolizes security, nurturance, protection, and/or feminine qualities. You may be expressing a desire to regress back into infantile dependence and escape from your daily responsibilities/problems.

L

To see the letter "L" in your dream, is symbolic of loser. Alternatively, the dream may also signify your fear of the "l-word". You cannot even bring your dreaming mind to express love.

Labor

To dream that you are laboring, suggests that your goals will take a lot of hard work to accomplish.

If you are a woman and dream that you are in labor, indicates your desire to be pregnant and to start a family. To experience or feel labor pains or Braxton Hicks contractions in your dream, indicate the anticipation of hard work ahead. If you are actually pregnant, then the dream serves as a rehearsal for the actual birth. The dream is trying to prepare you for labor and proper breathing.

Laboratory

To dream that you are in a laboratory, suggests that you are experimenting with your inner feelings, beliefs, or fears. You are testing yourself or some relationship. Alternatively, being in a laboratory means you are going through some sort of transformation.

Lace

To see lace in your dream, points to your sensuality and femininity. Alternatively, it denotes tradition and old fashioned ideals. Perhaps you are being overly practical in some area of your life.

Ladder

To dream that you are climbing up a ladder, suggests that you have reached a new level of achievement. It is symbolic of prosperity, hard work and your efforts. Consider also the phrase of "climbing the social ladder" in which you have achieved a promotion, a higher status, more power, or an important goal. Alternatively, it indicates meditation and prayer. You are setting forth on a spiritual path and higher awareness. Each rung of the ladder is symbolic of a stage in your spiritual awareness. The dream may also highlight how you are looking things from a different perspective.

To dream that you are climbing down a ladder, suggests that you are escaping from your spiritual responsibilities. It is an indication of future disappointments.

To dream that you are walking under a ladder, signifies bad luck. Perhaps you are having regrets over a decision you made.

To dream that someone is holding a ladder for you, indicates that you will find success if you have the support of others. You will rise to a level of prominence.

To dream that you fall from a ladder, denotes the hardships, risks or failures you are faced with in your endeavors.

To see a broken ladder in your dream, indicates consistent failures in your undertakings. You may feel that you are being handicapped in pursuing your goals.

To dream that you escape by means of a ladder, signifies that you will be successful after much struggle and obstacles.

Ladybug

To see a ladybug in your dream, symbolizes beauty, and good luck. The dream may be a pun on something that is bugging your or a lady in your life.

Lake

To see a lake in your dream, signifies your emotional state of mind. You feel restricted and that you can't express your emotions freely. Alternatively, the lake may provide you with solace, security, and peace of mind. If the lake is clear and calm, then it symbolizes your inner peace. If the lake is disturbed, then you may be going through some emotional turmoil.

Lamb

To see a lamb in your dream, symbolizes deception. The lamb is also representative of something vulnerable, pure and innocent. Consider the metaphor "as gentle as a lamb".

To dream that you are holding a lamb in your arms, refers to the sacrifices in your life.

Lamp

To see a lamp in your dream, symbolizes guidance, hope, inspiration, enlightenment and reassurance. If the lamp is dimly lit or unlit, then it suggests that you are feeling overwhelmed by emotional issues. You have lost your ability to find your own way or see things clearly.

To see a broken lamp in your dream, suggests that you are shutting out those who are trying to help you. It is also symbolic of disappointments, misfortune and bad luck.

Landscape

To dream of various landscapes in your dream, represent where you are in your life or in your relationships. How do you see yourself with respect to the rest of the world and those around you? Consider what is going on in the landscape and how it may parallel your own waking life. In particular, a barren or dry landscape depicts dissatisfaction in your love life. According to Freud, the dream landscape symbolizes the human body. A landscape with gentle contours symbolize the female body, while a rocky landscape represents the male body. Also consider the feelings that the landscape invokes.

To dream of ever changing landscapes, indicates psychological transitions or emotional progress. It represents the various stages in your life. Alternatively, it may be offering you various viewpoints in looking at the same idea or situation. Something may be slipping away from your grasp. Look at the symbolism of key elements in the landscape.

Landslide

To see a landslide in your dream, represents emotions that you have been holding back for a long time. You are on the verge of emotional overload. Your emotions are erupting in an unexpected or violent way. The dream may also symbolize the stresses in your life and all the responsibilities that rest on your shoulders.

Language

To dream that you are studying a language, suggests that you are having difficulties expressing your thoughts. You are confronted with an unfamiliar problem that you do not know how to approach and resolve.

To hear foul or vulgar language in your dream, signifies an embarrassing situation.

To hear or speak a foreign language in your dream, indicates a message from your unconscious that you do not yet understand.

Lap Dance

To give or perform a lap dance in your dream, suggests that you may be repressing your sexual desires. Perhaps you are feeling inhibited in discussing your sexual pleasures.

To see or receive a lap dance in your dream, indicates your need for a little more excitement in your sex life. Or you are looking for some intimacy.

Large

Please See Big.

Laryngitis

To dream that you have laryngitis, indicates a loss of identity and a lack of personal power. You are unable to speak up and stand up for yourself. Alternatively, the dream points to your inability to convey a certain message. You are not sure how to put into words what you want to say to somebody.

Laser

To see a laser in your dream, symbolizes clarity and truth. You are seeing and understanding things much more clearly. Alternatively, it suggests that you need to focus your attention and concentrate on one task at a time.

Late

To dream that you are late, signifies your fear of change and your ambivalence about seizing an opportunity. You may feel unready, unworthy, or unsupported in your current circumstances. Additionally, you may be overwhelmed or conflicted with decisions about your future. Time is running out and you no longer have time to accomplish all the things you want. Alternatively, being late in your dream could be telling you that it is better late than never.

Laughing

To hear laughing or dream that you are laughing, suggests that you need to lighten up and let go of your problems. Don't put so much pressure on yourself. Laughing is also a sign of joyous release and pleasure. If you are being laughed at, then it indicates your insecurities and fears of not being accepted.

To hear evil, demonic laughing in your dream, represents feelings of humiliation and/or helplessness. You feel that someone is working against you.

Lava

To see lava in your dream, signifies violent anger which you have kept inside for a period of time.

Lava Lamp

To see a lava lamp in your dream, represents slow, fluid motion. Something in your waking life is moving in a similar fashion as the lava lamp. Perhaps, you are taking your time to do something and making sure it is thorough. Consider the color of the lava lamp for clues.

Law

To dream that you are referring to the law, suggests that you need to show more restraint in certain areas of your life.

To dream that you are studying law, denotes success in your endeavors and projects.

Lawn Mower

To see a lawn mower in your dream, suggests that you need to channel your negative thinking into positive energy. You also need to keep your temper and attitude under control. Alternatively, the dream points to your need to keep up your appearances.

Lawyer

To see or dream that you are a lawyer, means that help is available to you if you ask. You need to put aside your pride and look upon others for their assistance. On a more direct level, the dream indicates that you are concerned or preoccupied with some legal issue in your waking life.

Lazy

To dream that you are feeling lazy, means that you are feeling emotionally drained; you need to take a break from life. The dream may be an actual reflection of your waking state.

To dream that others are lazy, indicates feelings of resentment. You feel that you are doing the work, while others are not pulling their own weight.

Leak

To see a leak in your dream, symbolizes loss, disappointments, frustrations and distress. You are wasting your energy on fruitless endeavors. Alternatively, the dream indicates some repressed feelings emerging from your unconscious or from your past. Metaphorically, the dream may suggest that some secret information has "leaked" out.

Leash

To dream that you are holding a leash, indicates a need for more control in your life. You need to take the lead in some projection or situation.

To dream that you are wearing a leash, suggests that you need to show more restraint with regards to your sexual urges and desires. Alternatively, the dream indicates that you are too easily led or too easily influenced. You are letting other people control you and take you in a direction that you do not really want to go.

To dream that the leash is broken or that your pet has broken free from the leash, implies that you have successfully broken away from somebody's control and influence.

Leather

To see or wear leather in your dream, represents toughness and ruggedness. It may imply your thick-skinned nature. Or perhaps you are seeking protection from the elements. Alternatively, the dream refers to your instinctual and animalistic nature. It may also have sexual connotations.

Leaves

To see leaves in your dream, signify new found happiness and improvements in various aspects of your life. It is symbolic of fertility, growth and openness. Alternatively, leaves represent a passage of time. Depending on the color and type of leaf, the dream could be highlighting a certain period of time. The leaves may also be a metaphor to "leave" you alone.

To see brown or withered leaves in your dream, signifies fallen hopes, despair, sadness and loss. If you are sweeping or raking leaves, then it represents the end of a project, relationship or situation. It also signifies experience.

Leeches

To see or be bitten by leeches in your dream, refer to something in your life that is draining the energy and vigor out of you. The dream may refer to people, habits, or negative emotions that are sucking you out of your vitality.

Alternatively, if your body is covered in leeches, then you are feeling disgusted by your own body or repulsed by something you have done.

Left

To dream of the direction left, symbolizes the unconscious and your repressed thoughts/emotions. It is an indication of passivity.

To dream that you are left behind, represents feelings of rejection or not fitting into a group. It may also highlight fears of not being able to keep up. You are questioning your abilities. The dream may be telling you that you are not utilizing your full potential. If you left something or someone behind, then it indicates that you are ready to let go of the past or move forward.

Legs

To see your legs in your dream, indicate that you have regained confidence to stand up and take control again. It also implies progress and your ability to navigate through life. If your legs are weak, then you may be feeling emotionally vulnerable. If you dream that you are crossing your legs, then it implies defensiveness or your close minded attitude.

To see someone else's legs in your dream, represent your admiration for that person. You need to adopt some of the ways that this person does things.

To dream that your leg is wounded or crippled, signifies a lack of balance, autonomy, or independence in your life. You may be unable or unwilling to stand up for yourself. Perhaps you are lacking courage and refuse to make a stand.

If you are a woman and dream that your legs are hairy, then it suggests that you are domineering or that you dominate in the relationship.

To dream that one of your leg is shorter than the other, suggests that there is some imbalance in some aspect of your life. You are placing more emphasis and weight on one thing, while ignoring other important aspects that need attention as well.

To dream that you have three or more legs, denotes that you are undertaking too many projects. You are taking on more things that you can handle. Some of these projects will prove counterproductive.

To dream that you have a stick leg or a wooden leg, suggests that balance has been restored in your once chaotic or hectic life. You are able to stand up again with the help and support of others. Alternatively, the dream may be telling you to slow down.

Lei

To dream that someone is giving you a lei, signifies a welcoming, acceptance, and acknowledgement. The dream may also be a pun on "getting laid".

Lemons

To see a lemon in your dream, indicates something that is inferior in quality. Perhaps a situation or relationship has turned sour.

To eat or suck on a lemon in your dream, refers to your need for cleansing or healing.

To dream that you are squeezing a lemon, suggests that you need to be more economical.

Leo

To dream that someone is a Leo, symbolizes someone who is creative, generous, playful and authoritative. Perhaps you need to incorporate these aspects into your own character. In addition, you tend to be drawn to drama and like to be the center of attention. You also have a sunny disposition and great leadership ability. Alternatively, it relates to issues of the heart. The dream may also be a pun on someone named Leo in your waking life.

Leopard

To see a wild leopard in your dream, suggests that you will eventually overcome your difficulties through persistence. If the leopard is in a cage, then it suggests that you will overcome any obstacles with relative ease. Alternatively, dreaming of a leopard, means that you are who you are, just like a leopard can't change its spots.

To dream that you kill a leopard, refers to success in your projects.

To dream that a leopard is attacking you, indicates that you are overly confident in your future success. You do not realize the difficult struggles and challenges that you will have to endure.

Leprechaun

To see a leprechaun in your dream, suggests that through perseverance and dedication, you will reap the benefits and rewards of your hard work. Alternatively, the dream means that you are trying to take the quick and easy path to success.

To dream that you are a leprechaun, refers to the mischievous aspect of your personality.

Lesbian

If you are not a lesbian in your waking life, but dream that you are a lesbian, then it signifies a union with aspects of yourself. It is symbolic of self-love, self-acceptance, and passion. You are comfortable with your sexuality and femininity. If, in your dream you abhor the notion of lesbianism, then it represents your fears and rejection of aspects of your own sexuality.

If you are a lesbian in your waking life, then the dream is simply a reflection of your own self.

Letter

To dream that you receive a letter, signifies a new opportunity or challenge. Alternatively, the letter represents a message from your unconscious. The contents of the letter may offer you some guidance in a current situation. Consider also how the letter may be a pun on "let her".

To tear up a letter in your dream, symbolizes past mistakes and regrets in your life.

To see an unopened letter in your dream, means that you are intentionally ignoring some information. You are refusing to accept the facts about a situation.

Lettuce

To see lettuce growing in your dream, represents abundance. It points you back to a simpler time.

To dream that you are eating lettuce, signifies your need for spiritual nourishment. It may also mean that you are lacking in a particular nutrient. You need to eat a more well balanced diet. The dream may also be a pun on "let us". Is there some situation where you are seeking approval or permission?

Leveler

To see or use a leveler in your dream, symbolizes balance and harmony. Everything is in alignment. The dream may also suggest that you need to look at things from a different level in order to gain a new perspective.

Liar

To dream that someone is calling you a liar, denotes that you will be irked by some deceitful person.

To dream that you are lying, suggests that you are trying to deceive yourself into believing in something that goes against your natural instincts or long held values. Ask yourself what you are hiding from yourself or from others.

To dream that someone is a liar, indicates your growing distrust for that person. You may have lost your faith in that individual. Alternatively, it suggests that you are no longer as confident.

Libra

To dream that someone is a Libra, indicates fairness, harmony and cooperation. You are trying to restore order to your waking life.

Library

To dream that you are in a library, signifies your search for knowledge and your hunger for ideas. You may be trying to seek out new meanings to life. You need to study and evaluate your situation before taking action. If the library is disorganized, then it suggests that too much information is coming at you at the same time. You are having difficulty sorting it all out.

To dream that you cannot find a book in the library or that the book you are looking for is already checked out, suggests that a certain aspect of your self is lacking enrichment or is under developed.

To see a library in your dream, symbolizes the knowledge you have accumulated over the years.

Lice

To see lice in your dream, signify frustrations, distress and feelings of guilt. You may be feeling emotionally or physically unclean. Alternatively, the lice represents a person, situation, or relationship that you want to distance yourself from. You may be feeling used or taken advantage of.

Lick

To dream that you are licking something, signifies your need to be more cautious before proceeding on to new situations or adventures. You need to be more careful and methodical in your endeavors. Alternatively, it may also represent satisfaction in some minor matters.

To dream that you are licked by an animal, means that you will be called upon for advice.

Lie Detector

To see a lie detector in your dream, represents your lack of confidence. You are experiencing a loss of faith in others.

To dream that you are taking a lie detector test, suggests that it is time to face the facts. Stop being in denial.

Lifeguard

To see or dream that you are a lifeguard, means that you are keeping your emotions well guarded. Perhaps you are seeking some guidance and support while you carefully explore aspects of your unconscious.

Lift

To dream that you are being lifted, represents that you are rising above some unpleasant situation or issue.

*Please See Also <u>Elevator.</u>

Light

To see light in your dream, represents illumination, clarity, guidance, plain understanding, and insight. Light is being shed on a once cloudy situation or problem. You have found the truth to a situation or an answer to a problem. Also consider the color of the light for additional significance.

If the light is particularly bright, then it indicates that you need to move toward a higher level of awareness and feeling. Bright light dreams are sometimes common for those who are near death.

To see soft or shadowy lighting in your dreams, indicates feelings and thoughts from the primal aspects and less developed parts of your unconscious.

To dream that you cannot turn on the light, indicates a lack of insight and perspective on a situation.

Light Bulb

To see a light bulb in your dream, suggests that you are ready to accept and/or face reality. It refers to your consciousness. The dream also symbolizes spiritual enlightenment, hope, new ideas and visions. You are approaching a situation from a new direction.

To see a burned out light bulb in your dream, indicates that you are feeling ineffective. You feel that you are out of ideas or that you have nothing to offer.

Lighter

To see or use a lighter in your dream, represents a spark of some new idea.

Lighthouse

To see a lighthouse in your dream, indicates that you are seeking guidance during a difficult and tumultuous time.

Lightning

To see lightning in your dream, signifies sudden awareness, insight, spiritual revelation, truth and purification. Alternatively, lightning implies a shocking turn of events. There are many forces governing your life that may be beyond your control and even destructive.

To dream that you are struck by lightning, symbolizes irreversible changes occurring in your life. You are undergoing a permanent transformation.

Lily

To see lilies in your dream, symbolize tranquility, spirituality, faith, peace, purity, joy and bliss. It is also connected mourning.

Limousine

To see a limousine in your dream, indicates that you have an exaggerated sense of self-worth and self-importance. You may also feel the need to show off and impress others. Furthermore, if the limousine is black, then it suggests that your are unwilling to make any changes or yield to others. Alternatively, it may symbolize prestige, wealth, and power.

Limping

To dream that you are limping, refers to a lack of balance in some relationship in your life. You feel that the relationship is one-sided. Perhaps you feel that you are giving more than you are getting back or vice-versa.

To see an animal limping in your dream, indicates that you have suffered a setback to your personal freedom.

Line

To see a line in your dream, symbolizes duality, limits, boundaries and rules. It also relates to movement or non-movement. To dream that you are crossing a line, suggests that you are overstepping your boundaries or that you are moving beyond the limits in some area of your life.

To see a line of people or objects, indicates that you need to be more aware of some situation or relationship.

To dream that you are standing in line, represents your need for patience. You need to learn to wait for something and not always have it right away.

Lingerie

To dream that you are wearing lingerie, represents your sexual identity, body image and your self-esteem. You may finally be recognizing and acknowledging an aspect of yourself that was not previously expressed.

To dream that you are buying or shopping for lingerie, indicates that you are compensating for your inner feelings of emptiness. You may be trying to fulfill some sexual/emotional need. Alternatively, the dream means that you are looking to change your image and attitude. You may feel one way on the inside, but behave another way on the outside.

*Please See Also <u>Underwear</u>.

Lion

To see a lion in your dream, symbolizes great strength, courage, aggression and power. You will overcome some of your emotional difficulties. As king of the jungle, the lion also represents dignity, royalty, leadership, pride and domination. You have much influence over others. You also need to exercise some restraint in your own personal and social life.

To dream that you are attacked by a lion, suggests that a force may be driving you to self-destruction. You need overcome these challenges and obstacles.

To see a black lion in your dream, represents a negative force. You are using your position of power for evil.

Lip Synching

To dream that you are lip synching, indicates that someone else is speaking on your behalf. You need to learn to speak up for yourself and assert your opinions. Alternatively, the dream suggests that you lack your own identity. You are trying to live up to the expectations of others.

Liposuction

To dream that you have liposuction, represents your preoccupation with your physical shape and appearance. Alternatively, it suggests that you are taking drastic measures to rid yourself of all the responsibilities and things that are weighing you down. The dream may also refer to your anxiety about an actual liposuction that you are having.

Lips

To see lips in your dream, signify sensuality, sex, love, and romance, especially if they were pursed. Lips are a means of communication as reflected in the familiar phrase "read my lips".

To dream that you or someone has blue lips, indicate illness or possible problems with your blood circulation.

To dream that you or someone has black lips, suggests that you are refusing to say anything about a particular situation. You are remaining completely silence.

Lipstick

To buy, see, or wear lipstick in your dream, suggests that you are not entirely truthful about something. The dream seeks to draw attention to your lips. Perhaps you need to be careful about what you or someone else is saying. Alternatively, it signifies sexuality and sensuality, especially if the color is red.

Little

*Please See Small.

Liver

To see yours or someone else's liver in your dream, suggests the possibility of a physical disorder. The dream forewarns that you need to reduce your alcohol consumption. You need to reevaluate your physical health and perhaps even go get a doctor's physical. Alternatively, it indicates that someone in your life does not have your best interest at heart. You are being belittled.

Living Room

To dream that you are in the living room, represents the image that you portray to others and the way which you go about your life. It is representative of your basic beliefs about yourself and who you are. Alternatively, the living room is indicative of your freedom and space. The living room is a symbolic boundary between your personal self and your public self. Objects that do not belong in the living room denote the various aspects of your life that are invading your personal space.

Lizard

To see a lizard in your dream, signifies your primal instincts and reactions toward sex, food, etc. and your anxieties toward these feelings. The lizard may also be representative of a person who you view as cold-blooded, fearful, or thick-skinned. On a more positive note, the lizard also symbolizes emerging creativity, renewal, and revitalization. It may suggest that you are well-grounded.

Loaf

*Please See Bread.

Lobotomy

To see or dream that you have a lobotomy, indicates that you are either trying to get to your subconscious and access its insights or you are trying to suppress it and erase it from your consciousness. Alternatively, the dream means that you are under tremendous mental stress.

Lobster

To see a lobster in your dream, represents strength and persistence. You will hold your own ground and overcome minor difficulties and problems.

To dream that you are eating lobster, indicates that you will regain your confidence.

Loch Ness Monster

To see a Loch Ness Monster in your dream, symbolizes disappointments or misunderstanding in some situation or relationship. You may have unrealistic goals and setting yourself up for failure.

Lock

To see a lock in your dream, signifies your inability to get what you want. You are being kept out of some activity or situation. Perhaps an aspect of yourself is locked up inside and it needs to be expressed.

To dream that a lock is accidentally shut around your wrist, suggests that you are debating on whether to be more open about your feelings or keep them to yourself. You feel that you are taking a major risk in letting your feelings known.

Locker

To see or use a locker in your dream, signifies aspects of yourself which you have kept hidden inside. Consider what items and belongings are in the locker. In particular, to dream of a school locker, denotes hidden feelings, knowledge, and attitudes that you need to learn and/or acknowledge.

To dream that you cannot open a locker or that your forgot the combination, suggests that you are unsure of where you stand in a particular situation. You feel you have lost some aspect of yourself. In other words, you are on shaky ground. If you cannot find your locker, then it symbolizes your insecurities about your role or position in a situation.

To dream that someone else is using your locker, suggests that someone can see right through you and your facade. You feel that this person has access to your hidden Self.

Locket

To see or wear a locket in your dream, signifies a long lasting relationship. The dream may also be a pun on "lock it". Perhaps there is something that you need to keep safe. Consider the shape of the locket and what is inside it.

Logger

Please See Lumberjack.

Log

To see a log in your dream, represents a significant and meaningful aspect of yourself. It may reflect some unconscious idea. Alternatively, a log signifies a transformation. You are headed toward a new direction in your life. The dream may also be metaphor that you are being a "log" or lazy. You need to get up and take action.

To dream that you are sitting on a log, indicates personal satisfaction and joy in you life.

To see a log floating in water, represents new opportunities. You may be overlooking something important.

Loincloth

To wear a loincloth in your dream, represents raw male sexuality.

Lollipop

To see or lick a lollipop in your dream, indicates surprises, new experiences and adventures. It also represents indulgence, sensuality and the pleasant aspects of your life. Alternatively, the lollipop may be a pun for "sucker" and thus suggests that you need to proceed with caution in some relationship or situation. Someone may be taking advantage of you.

Loneliness

Please See Alone.

Lose

To dream that you lose something, indicates that you may really have misplaced something that you had not realized yet. It may also be a signal for you to clean out and reorganize your life. Perhaps you are overwhelmed and distracted with the hustle and bustle of day-to-day life. Alternatively, losing something often coincides with a significant life change or waking issue.

On a symbolic note, losing things in your dream suggests lost opportunities, past relationships or forgotten aspects of yourself. Your personal associations to the thing you lose will clue you into the emotional meaning and interpretation of your dream.

Lost

To dream that you are lost, suggests that you have lost your direction in life or that you have lost sight of your goals. You may be feeling worried and insecure about the path you are taking in life. If you try to call for help, then it means that you are trying to reach out for support. You are looking for someone to lean on. Alternatively, being lost means that you are still adjusting to a new situation in which the rules and conditions are ever changing.

To dream that someone else is lost, represents some unresolved issues or feelings pertaining to the person that is lost. Consider what aspect of that person you may have lost within your own self. Perhaps you need to recapture and re-acknowledge those aspects.

Lottery

To dream of playing the lottery, suggests that you are relying too much on fate instead of taking responsibility for your own actions or decisions. You need to reconsider some issue or situation before committing to it.

To dream that you win the lottery, represents your inner desires to live without having to worry about financial and material troubles. Alternatively, the dream may be a metaphor that your number has come up and thus imply trouble coming your way.

Love

To dream of love or being in love, suggests intense feelings carried over from a waking relationship. It refers to your contentment with what you already have and where you are in life. On the other hand, the dream may be compensatory and implies that you may not be getting enough love in your life. We naturally long for the sense to belong and to be accepted.

To see a couple in love or expressing love to each other, indicates success ahead for you.

To dream that your friend is in love with you, may be one of wish fulfillment. Perhaps you have developed feelings for your friend and are wondering how he or she feels. Your preoccupation has found its way into your dreaming mind. On the other hand, the dream may suggests that you have accepted certain qualities of your friend and incorporated it into your own character.

To dream that you are making love in public or in different places, relates to some overt sexual issue or need. Your dream may be telling you that you need to express yourself more openly. Alternatively, it represents your perceptions about your own sexuality in the context of social norms. You may be questioning your feelings about sex, marriage, love, and gender roles.

Luggage

To see or carry luggage in your dream, symbolizes the many desires, worries, responsibilities or needs that you are carrying with you and weighing you down. The size or weight of the luggage parallels the demands you are facing. You need to reduce your desires and problems in order to alleviate the pressure you are putting on yourself. Perhaps you feel that you are being held back by past emotions or issues. Alternatively, luggage symbolizes your identity and sense of security.

To dream that you lose your luggage, represents a lost in your identity. Consider how you feel when you discovered that your luggage is lost. If it is a positive reaction, then it signifies an opportunity for you to start fresh. If your reaction is negative, then it suggest that you are feeling lost.

Lunch

To see or eat lunch in your dream, indicates that you are lacking spiritual enrichment and enlightenment in some area of your life.

Lungs

To see lungs in your dream, symbolize insight, creativity, and inspiration. Alternatively, lungs may indicate a stressful situation and refer to a relationship/situation in which you feel suffocated. You need to take a deep breath and face up to the challenge.

Lyre

To see a lyre in your dream, represents joy, calmness and harmony. The symbol may also be a pun on "liar".

M

To see the letter "M" in your dream, suggests that there is something that you are keeping silent about. Perhaps you have been sworn to secrecy. Alternatively, the dream may imply "Mmmmm". Your unconscious mind is hungering for knowledge or information. As a Roman Numeral, it could represent the number 1000.

Mace

To see or use mace in your dream, represents your quest for objectivity over subjectivity. You do not let your emotions rule your actions.

Machinery

To see machinery in your dream, suggests that you are too mechanical - going about your way without much thought and making decisions without thinking it through. You need to get out of your boring pattern. Alternatively, the machinery symbolizes your mind or your body. Examine how the machinery is running and its condition and function. If the machinery is in need of repair, then it suggests that you may need to repair aspects of your self-image or a relationship. If the machine is rusty, then it signifies an outdated way of doing something.

Mafia

To dream that you are a member of a mafia, suggests that you are allowing others to manipulate you. Or you are using your power against others.

To dream that you come in contact with the mafia, indicates that you are experiencing some inner conflict and turmoil.

Magenta

Magenta represents kindness and compassion. You are ready to come out of some dark time.

Maggot

To see maggots in your dream, represent your anxieties about death. It may also be indicative of some issue or problem that you have been rejecting and it is now "eating away" at you. You need to confront it for it is destroying your sense of harmony and balance.

In particular, to dream that you are stepping on maggots, indicate guilt and impurity. You are trying to repress your immoral thoughts or behavior. On a positive note, this dream symbolizes your resilience, persistence, and your ability to bounce back from adversity.

Magic

To perform or dream of magic, suggests that you need to look at things from a different view or approach your problems from a new angle in order to successfully move forward. Alternatively, magic symbolizes creativity and wonder. Perhaps someone or something has caused you to be in awe. The dream may also be a metaphor that you or someone is "up to some trick".

To dream of black magic, implies that you have obtained your wishes and wants through underhanded tricks. It also symbolizes deception, evil and treachery.

Magic Carpet

To dream that you are riding a magic carpet, indicates that you are overcoming your obstacles and physical limitations.

Magnet

To see a magnet in your dream, symbolizes negative forces that are drawing you towards a path of dishonor and ruin. Alternatively, the dream signifies personal empowerment. Some force is bonding or uniting your relationships together. The dream may also be a metaphor for your magnetic personality.

Magnifying Glass

To see or use a magnifying glass in your dream, indicates that something in your life needs to be examined and looked at more closely.

Magnolia

To see magnolias in your dream, symbolize beauty, grace and elegance.

Maid

To see or have a maid in your dream, suggests that you are depending too much on others for their help. You need to be more independent and look after your own self.

To dream that you are a maid, indicates that you need to clear up the clutter in your life. Metaphorically, the dream suggests that you need to nurture yourself and cleanse your emotions.

Mail

To dream that receive mail, indicates that you need to communicate or re-establish contact with someone from your present or past. It may also represent messages from your unconscious or intuition. The mail may also be a pun on a "male" in your life.

To dream that mail is lost, suggests that you are feeling isolated of left out in some waking situation.

If you receive mail from someone you don't know, then it symbolizes a message from your unconscious.

Mailman

To see a mailman in your dream, symbolizes your communications with others. You need to get the word out about something. If the mailman does not have any mail for you, then it signifies disappointments in some aspect of your life.

If you are not a mailman in real life, but dream that you are one, then it suggests that a message is being channeled to you from your unconscious. Pay close attention to the message of this dream. Alternatively, it may mean that you have been entrusted with a special message or secret.

Makeup

To dream that you are applying makeup, suggests that you are trying to cover up or conceal an aspect of yourself. Alternatively, it indicates that you are putting on your best face forward. You are trying to enhance your self-image and increase your sense of self-confidence. The dream may also be a metaphor that you need to "make up" with someone. It is time to forgive and forget.

To dream that you are wearing too much makeup, indicates that you are putting too much emphasis on beauty and outside appearances rather than what is inside.

Making Out

To dream that you are making out with someone, suggests that you have an unconscious desire to pursue a relationship, but fear that it will jeopardize the friendship. If you don't like this person in this way, then the dream suggests that you need to acknowledge and incorporate aspects of this person into your own character. Consider specific traits that this person possess.

Mall

To dream that you are at the mall, represents your attempts in making a favorable impression on someone. You are trying to establish your identity and sense of self. The mall is also symbolic of materialism and the need to keep up with the trends, fads, and/or the latest technology.

Man

To see a man in your dream, denotes the aspect of yourself that is assertive, rational, aggressive, and/or competitive. Perhaps you need to incorporate these aspects into your own character. If the man is known to you, then the dream may reflect you feelings and concerns you have about him.

If you are a woman and dream that you are in the arms of a man, then it suggests that you are accepting and welcoming your stronger assertive personality. It may also highlight your desires to be in a relationship and your image of the ideal man.

To see an old man in your dream, represents wisdom or forgiveness. The old man may be a archetypal figure who is offering guidance to some daily problem.

Mango

To see or eat a mango in your dream, symbolizes fertility, sexual desires, and lust. Alternatively, the mango may also be a pun to mean "man go" in reference to a relationship in which you should let go and move on.

Mansion

To see a mansion in your dream, symbolizes your greatest potential and growth. You may feel that your current situation or relationship is in a rut.

Manslaughter

Please See Murder.

Manta Ray

To see a manta ray in your dream, signifies emotional freedom. You are navigating through your emotions with ease.

To dream that you or someone is attacked by a school of manta rays, indicates that emotions that have been suppressed into your unconscious are becoming too overwhelming to keep inside any longer.

Manure

To see manure in your dream, suggests that you are learning from past experiences. You are drawing from those experiences and putting it to use in your current situation. Alternatively, the dream may symbolize fertility.

Map

To see or study a map in your dream, suggests that your current life path will lead to fulfillment of your needs and realization of your goals. It also indicates that you are set on the path to self knowledge and self discovery. If you have difficulties understanding or reading the map, then it means that you are feeling lost. You are literally still trying to find yourself and figure out where you want to go in life.

Marathon

To dream that you are running in a marathon, represents life's journey and how you are performing or feeling. It is symbolic of your endurance and willpower. Consider how you feel about the marathon and how you are approaching it.

Marble

To see marbles in your dream, symbolize your perceptiveness, insightfulness and observation. If you are polishing a marble, then it represents your enduring efforts and perseverance.

March

To dream of the month of March, signifies disappointments. It also heralds the coming of spring and thus indicates new beginnings. The dream may also be a metaphor to "march" on, especially during difficult times.

Marching

To dream that you are marching to the beat of music, signifies teamwork, conformity, and structure. Perhaps the dream serves as a calling as a soldier or as a public officer.

To see people marching in your dream, denotes your desires in wanting to associate with people in public positions.

Marijuana

To dream that you are using marijuana, signifies illicit activity or ill health. If someone else is using marijuana or trying to get your to use it, then it indicates negative peer pressure. You are on the verge of losing control. Perhaps you feel that your identity and sense of self is being compromised or disrespected.

To see or smell marijuana in your dream, suggests that you are experiencing an expanded sense of awareness and consciousness. You need to take advantage and draw insight from this new consciousness. The dream may also mean that you need to look on your inner strength for stimulation instead of relying on outside forces.

Marilyn Monroe

To see Marilyn Monroe in your dream, indicates that you need to be more open and expressive with your sexuality. In particular, if you are wearing Marilyn Monroe's clothes, then it means that you need to be more in touch with your femininity.

Markers

To see or use markers in your dream, represent your creativity. Perhaps you need to introduce some liveliness in your life. Consider the significance of the marker color. Alternatively, the dream may be telling you that there is something you need to "mark" down or remember.

Market

To dream that you are in a market, represents some emotional or physical need that you are currently lacking in your life. You may be in need of nurturance and some fulfillment. Consider the specific items that you are shopping for. Alternatively, the market signifies frugality.

To see an barren market in your dream, signifies depression and gloominess. There is a void in your life. If the market is large or well-stocked, then it means possibilities and choices.

*Please Also See <u>Store</u>.

Marriage

To dream of a marriage, signifies commitment, harmony or transitions. You are undergoing an important developmental phase in your life. The dream may also represent the unification of formerly separate or opposite aspects of yourself. In particular, it is the union of masculine or feminine aspects of yourself. Consider the qualities and characteristics of the person that you are marrying. These are the qualities that you need to look at incorporating within yourself.

To dream of a proposal of marriage, suggests that some situation will take a turn for the worse.

To dream that you are getting married to your ex, suggests that you have accepted aspects of that relationship and learned from those past mistakes. Alternatively, it means that a current relationship shares some commonality with your previous relationship with your ex. However, since you are aware of the similarities, you know not make those same mistakes.

To dream that you are in an arranged marriage, suggests that you are feeling forced to do something you do not want to do. You feel that you have no voice or no choice in a situation. Consider how a waking situation may be making you feel voiceless.

*Please See Also Wedding.

Mars

To see Mars in your dream, symbolizes energy, drive, passion, fearlessness and ambition. It also represents war, violence and masculine power.

Marshmallows

To see or eat marshmallows in your dream, represent timidity and lack of self-confidence. You need to learn to be more assertive and stand up for yourself.

To dream that you are roasting marshmallows, indicate growth and motivation.

Mask

To dream that you are wearing a mask, suggests that you are trying to be someone you are not. You are trying to hide your true feelings and only reveal half truths. If you have trouble taking off your mask, then it suggests that your true self is lost or blurred. Alternatively, wearing a mask signifies temporary trouble due to some misunderstanding of your action and conduct.

To see someone wearing a mask in your dream, denotes that you are struggling against deceit, falsehood, and jealousy. If someone removes their mask, then it symbolizes failure in gaining the admiration and/or respect of someone sought for.

Massage

To dream that you are getting a massage, suggests that you are lacking sensual or sexual stimulation in your waking life. You need to be more in touch with your sensuality. Perhaps you need to take better care of your body. The dream also represents nurturance, ease and comfort. Alternatively, getting a massage suggests that you need to let go and stop being so defensive.

Masturbation

To dream that you are masturbating, represents your unacknowledged and unexpressed sexual needs/desires. It may also indicate you need to take care of yourself in sensual or emotional ways which are not necessarily sexual. Or perhaps, you may need to put forth a little more effort toward some relationship.

To see others masturbating in your dreams, denotes your anxieties and concerns about your inhibitions. It may also be a reflection that something in your waking life is not as satisfying as it could be. Keep in mind that this dream may not necessarily represent sexual inhibitions or satisfaction, but may be analogous to some situation or relationship.

Mat

To see a mat in your dream, suggests that you feel others are walking all over you. You feel being taken advantage of. Alternatively, the dream may be a pun on someone who is named Matt in your life.

Matador

To see or dream that you are a matador, suggests that you need to challenge yourself and prepare for the obstacles ahead. Work on your bravery.

Matches

To see or strike a match in your dream, suggests that there is something that you need to ignite and rekindle in your life. The dream maybe a pun on something or someone who is your match.

Mathematics

To dream about mathematics, indicate that you are evaluating a situation in your waking life where you need to be more rational in your thinking. Try not to act on your emotions.

To dream that you are unable to solve a mathematical problem or equation, parallels a waking problem where you may be confused about. The dream may offer a hint toward a new approach to this waking problem. Something does not add up in your life.

Maxi Pad

To see a maxi pad in your dream, indicates that you need to release some pent up anger or tension. It may also mean that some creative energy is being released or recognized. If you see Always Maxi Pads in your dream, then the dream may be telling you "always" is the answer to some question or comment.

May

To dream of the month of May, signifies prosperity and times of pleasure. The dream may also be a metaphor for "may I?" Perhaps you are seeking permission for something.

Maze

To dream that you are in a maze, denotes that you need to deal with a waking task on a more direct level. You are making the situation harder than it really is. Alternatively, the maze symbolizes life's twists and turns. It represents indecision, confusion, missteps, feeling lost or being misled.

McDonalds

To see or dream that you are at McDonalds, signifies happiness and a worry-free attitude. The dream also suggests that you are living large. Perhaps the dream is telling you to expand your thinking or horizons. Supersize it! Alternatively, the dream may just mean you are hungry.

Measles

To dream that you have measles, indicate that your problems and worrying are affecting your educational or professional pursuits.

To see others with measles in your dream, denotes that the problems of others are becoming your own problems. It is giving you much stress and worry.

Measurement

To see or dream about your measurements, indicate that you are setting standards for yourself or of what you think others expect of you. How are you measuring up? Perhaps you need to stop comparing yourself to others.

Measuring Tape

To see or use a measuring tape in your dream, suggests that you are comparing yourself to others. The dream may be a metaphor on how you "measure up" to others. Or you are taking certain measures in order to accomplish something. Perhaps you are experiencing some self-doubt or that you are not good enough.

Meat

To see raw meat in your dream, represents obstacles and discouragements that you will come across as you move toward achieving your goals. Alternatively, it may reflect your untamed, animalistic nature and raw emotions.

To eat or cook meat in your dream, suggests that you are getting to the heart of the matter. You are recognizing and utilizing your instinctual energies. Alternatively, you are seeing others achieve what you are still striving for.

To see rotten meat in your dream, refers to a degradation of your physical and psychological being. The dream may be a metaphor for some health problems.

Mechanic

To see a mechanic in your dream, suggests that you need to work on healing your past hurts and trauma.

Mechanical Bull

To see or ride a mechanical bull in your dream, is analogous to your sex life. Perhaps it has become routine or devoid of emotion and passion.

Medal

To see a medal in your dream, signifies a reward or an acknowledgement of your hard work. You are being recognized for your abilities and talents.

Media

*Please See <u>Press.</u>

Medicine

To dream that you are taking medicine, represents a period of emotional and/or spiritual healing. It also indicates that the troubles you are experiencing are only temporary. Things will work out in the long run.

To dream that you are giving medicine to someone, indicates that you are trying to take advantage of a situation or of someone. If you are given the wrong medication, then you are being manipulated. Someone is trying to take advantage of you.

Medusa

To see Medusa in your dream, signifies cunningness and terror. Alternatively, the dream may imply that you are draining all the energy out of others. You are burdening others with your problems and putting a strain on the relationship.

Meeting

To dream that you are in a meeting, suggests that you need to redirect your energies toward a more productive endeavor. Alternatively, the dream means that you are learning to accept various aspects of yourself and integrating them into your personality.

To dream that you are late or miss a meeting, signifies anxieties that you are not measuring when it comes to achieving your goals. You may unprepared in some situation or challenge in your waking life.

Megaphone

To dream that you are using a megaphone, indicates that you need to be more vocal and expressive about your feelings. Speak up and express yourself. Perhaps you feel that you are being overlooked and feel that your voice is not being heard.

Melon

To see or eat a melon in your dream, indicates that you need to relax and take it easy. Alternatively, the dream signifies fertility, sensuality, gluttony or vitality. Melons may also be a metaphor for breasts.

Melting

To see melting ice or snow, signifies that you are letting go or releasing negative and cold emotions that you have been holding onto. You are warming up to a situation.

Menopause

To dream about menopause, suggests that you are smothering the people around you. You need to be less codependent.

Menorah

To see a Menorah in your dream, represents the seven days of the week. It is also symbolic of the sun, the moon, and the five main planets. Alternatively, it symbolizes beauty, strength, and wisdom. This dream imagery may also be a reflection of your religious faith.

Menstruation

To dream of menstruation, indicates that you are releasing your pent-up tension and worry. It signals an end to the difficult times and the beginning of relaxation. Some creative energy is being released or recognized. Alternatively, the dream means that you are denying your feminine side.

For women in particular, dreaming of their menstrual cycle when it is not time yet, may indicate your anxiety about your cycle. It may sometimes signal an early or unexpected period. Studies have also shown that more vivid dreams seem to coincide with a woman's menstrual cycle. Dreams about being pregnant, giving birth, or motherhood occur more often while a woman is ovulating.

Mentally Challenged

To dream that you are mentally challenged, indicates that you are experiencing feelings of self-doubt. You are afraid of being left out or left behind.

To see a mentally challenged person in your dream, suggests that someone around you is feeling ignored or overlooked. Perhaps you have failed to listen to what they have to say and as a result are alienating them.

Mentor

*Please See _Teacher._

Meow

To hear meowing in your dream, signifies neediness. You are seeking attention.

Menu

To see a menu in your dream, indicates that you are seeking some spiritual or emotional nourishment. Consider the type of items that were on the menu and the costs to determine how much value you are placing on each item.

Mercedes Benz

To see Mercedes Benz in your dream, symbolizes status, wealth, luxury and prestige. The dream could also be a metaphor for someone who is named Mercedes.

Mercury

To see mercury in your dream, represents quick movement. You need to speak up first and think it through later. Trust your intuition.

To see the planet Mercury in your dream, symbolizes alertness, awareness, open communication, reason, and versatility. The dream may indicate your need to exhibit some of these qualities in your waking life. You are exhibiting efficiency in your work.

Mermaid

To see a mermaid in your dream, signifies the female aspect of yourself that is mysterious, vulnerable and secretive. It may also show a fear of sex. In particular, for a man to dream of a mermaid, it indicates that he is having fears of being drowned by the feminine aspect of his psyche. For a woman, it suggests doubts over her femininity.

Merry-Go-Round

To dream that you are on a merry-go-round, indicates a fear of reliving your childhood. You feel that you are going nowhere or in a state of stagnation. Or you may be expressing some anxiety about your transition into adulthood. Alternatively, it suggests that you are in the beginning stages of romantic love.

To see a merry-go-round in your dream, represents childish joy.

Mess Hall

To dream that you are in a mess hall, suggests that have a disciplined view toward food. Perhaps you are on a diet.

Alternatively, there are some issues or feelings that are eating up inside you.

Metal Detector

To see or use a metal detector in your dream, indicates that you are in search of your inner strength or are trying to connect with your unconscious. Alternatively, the dream suggests that you are looking for that hidden talent and potential within yourself. You want to recapture something that you have lost, but once valued or cherished.

Meteor

To see a meteor in your dream, suggests that you will experience success in a project. You are on your way toward realizing your goals and desires. Alternatively, the meteor refers to wishful thinking and idealistic thoughts.

To see a meteor shower in your dream, signifies romantic thoughts and idealistic notions.

Mickey Mouse

To see Mickey Mouse in your dream, signifies the magic and joy of childhood. It is time to go back to a period where you can be more carefree.

Microphone

To see a microphone in your dream, suggests that you need to be more assertive and forceful. You need to voice your opinions more strongly and make your views known. The microphone may also be a pun on someone in your life who is named "Mike".

Microscope

To see a microscope in your dream, suggests that you need to take a closer look at some situation. Something that may seemingly be insignificant may actually be causing much troubles or hindrances.

Microwave

To see a microwave in your dream, represents your quick thinking and quick-action. You need to consider new and better way of doing things.

Midget

To see a midget in your dream, suggests that you are feeling small and insignificant. Do you feel helpless in some situation or have a deflated sense of self-worth?

Midnight

To dream that it is midnight, indicates that you need to face reality.

Mildew

To see mildew in your dream, symbolizes neglected feelings and emotions that you are unwilling to confront. It is time to bring those feelings to the surface and work through them.

Military

To see the military in your dream, signifies rigid authority and emotional repression. Perhaps you need to be more disciplined.

If you have served with the military, then this dream may represent your actual life experiences and memories.

Milk

To see milk in your dream, symbolizes maternal instincts and motherly love. It also denotes human kindness, wholesomeness, and compassion. Alternatively, the dream may be a metaphor that someone is "milking" you, either emotionally or financially.

To dream that you are drinking milk, signifies domestic bliss and inner nourishment. It may also imply that you need to strengthen your ties and relationships with others. If the milk is sour, impure or bad tasting, then it suggests that you need to hold back your support. If the milk is hot, then it represents comfort and calmness.

To spill milk in your dream, symbolizes a loss of faith, opportunity, and trust.

To dream that you are bathing in milk, indicates that you are surrounded by strong relationships and solid friendships. Alternatively, the dream suggests that you are in need of some relaxation.

To dream that you are choking on milk, indicates that you are being overprotected. You may be feeling smothered in some relationship.

Milking

To dream that you are milking a cow, signifies that great opportunities are being put before you, but still out of your reach. Through perseverance, you will win out in the end. Alternatively, the dream could also be a metaphor for "being milked" or used.

Millipede

To see a millipede in your dream, indicates that you are letting fears prevent you from achieving your goals. You are experiencing a major setback in life. Alternatively, the dream is symbolic of harmony and cooperation. You are a team player and work well with others.

Mime

To see or dream that you are a mime, suggests that you are having difficulties verbally communicating your thoughts and feelings across. Others around you may not understand your erratic behavior. You are trying to make light of how you really feel. Alternatively, the dream indicates that you need to think carefully before speaking. The dream may be depicting how you saying one thing, but you actually mean something else. Your actions are speaking louder than your words.

Mimic

To dream that you are mimicking someone, indicates that you are lacking your own identity. Alternatively, the dream means that you are trying too hard to live up to the expectations of others. You are being someone who you are not.

Mine

To dream that you are in a mine, suggests that you are getting to the core of an issue or condition. Alternatively, it indicates that something from your unconscious is coming to the surface. The dream may also be a metaphor to claim what is "mine".

Miniatures

To see miniatures in your dream, indicate that you are feeling larger than life. You are experiencing new found confidence and self esteem. Consider what is being miniaturized. If it is someone you know who is miniaturized, then it means that you lack respect for them. You do not think much of this person. If you are the one that appears as a miniature, then it suggests that you are feeling unworthy, helpless, insignificant or overshadowed.

Minister

To see or dream that you are a minister, suggest that you need to be more compassionate and understanding in some situation or relationship. Alternatively, the dream indicates that you have overstep your boundaries and into another's rights. If the dream has negative overtones, then the minister may be a symbol of repressed thoughts and feelings.

Mint

To smell or taste mint in you dream, suggests that there is a calming influence in your life. You may be too overexcited or hyperactive and need to relax. Alternatively, the dream refers to a situation or relationship that you need to soothe over. Perhaps it is time to make amends.

To eat a breath mint in your dream, indicates that you are trying to phrase your thoughts in a way that is going to be presentable or more palatable. Alternatively, a breath mint may mean that you have said something that has offended someone.

Mirage

To see a mirage in your dream, represents your disillusionment. What you think is true about others may turn out to be the contrary.

Mirror

To dream of your own reflection in the mirror, suggests that you are pondering thoughts about your inner self. The reflection in the mirror is how you perceive yourself or how you want others to see you. You may be contemplating on strengthening and changing aspects of your character.

To dream that you are looking through a two-way mirror, indicates that you are coming face to face with some inner or worldly issue. What you see is related to your persona and unconscious. Seeing images through the mirror may be a safe way for you to consider and/or confront material from your unconscious. Mirrors symbolize the imagination and the link between the conscious and unconscious.

If you are being watched through a two-way mirror, then it suggests that you feel you are being scrutinized and criticized. Alternatively, the dream means that you are unwilling to acknowledge your unconscious emotions.

To break a mirror in your dream, suggests that you are breaking an old image of yourself. You may be putting an end to an old habit. Breaking a mirror is also an old symbol for seven years of bad luck.

To see a cracked or broken mirror in your dream. represents a poor or distorted self-image. Alternatively, it means that you have put an end to your old habits and ways.

To see a fogged mirror in your dream, signifies a hazy concept of who you are and confusion in your life goals. You are lacking clarity and purpose and questioning your self-identity.

Miscarriage

To dream that you have a miscarriage, suggests that some idea or plan did not go as expected. The dream may also serve as a warning against your continued course of action. You need to alter your path or risk losing something of significance and value to you. Alternatively, the dream indicates that you have been wronged in some way.

If you are currently pregnant, then dreams of miscarriages are common in the second trimester of pregnancy.

Missile

To see or be attacked by a missile in your dream, represents feelings of helplessness and forces beyond your control. Alternatively, a missile may indicate insecurities about sex.

Mistletoe

To see mistletoe in your dream, symbolizes joyous occasions and happiness. Alternatively, the dream suggests that you need to let go of your inhibitions. Perhaps you are attracted to someone around you and it is time to act on it.

Mistress

To dream that you (or your mate) have a mistress, refers to your unconscious desire to end your current relationship. You are trying to sabotage your relationship in some way. Alternatively, the dream indicates that you are feeling neglected in the relationship. Perhaps you feel that you are not measuring up to the expectations of others, especially to your mate.

To dream that you are a mistress, indicates your desires for the finer things in life.

To see a mistress in your dream, suggests that you or someone is being lured or tempted into some negative activity.

Mixer

To see or use a mixer in your dream, suggests that you are getting "mixed" up about something. Perhaps you are experiencing mixed feelings about something or someone.

Moat

To see a moat in your dream, suggests that you have put up an emotional wall around you. You are shutting others out and blocking out some hurt.

Mockingbird

To see or hear a mockingbird in your dream, represents cockiness, cleverness, or independence. Alternatively, the dream indicates that you are taking credit for the work of others. You also have a tendency to get what you want.

Model

To see or dream that you are a fashion model, represents an image that you want to portray. You are trying to be someone or something that you are not. Alternatively, it symbolizes your idea of beauty. You are striving for something that you cannot attain.

To see or build a model vehicle in your dream, indicates that you are going through a new developmental phase in your life. You are laying out a plan.

Modem

To see or use a modem in your dream, represents communication. You need to better convey your feelings to others.

Moisturizer

To use or apply moisturizer in your dream, represents renewal. You have a fresh outlook in life. .

Mohawk

If you don't have a Mohawk in real life, but dream that you or someone has a Mohawk, then it represents non-conventional thinking. You need to start thinking outside the box and reshape the way you see things. Note that your personal associations with Mohawks will play dominantly in the meaning of this dream.

Molasses

To see or eat molasses in your dream, signifies a happy home life and good hospitality. Alternatively, the dream may be a metaphor for some situation or something that is moving slowly.

Mold

To see mold in your dream, indicates that something in your life has been ignored or is no longer of any use. It may also represent transformation and new growth.

To see a broken mold in your dream, suggests that you need to break away from your old habits and explore new ideas. You are lacking creativity and are too rigid in your thinking.

Moles

To see a mole in your dream, represents destruction and unforeseen danger. You are secretly plotting against others or someone else is working against you. Someone around you has their own hidden agenda. Alternatively, a mole is symbolic of your unconscious drives. You need to delve deeper and uncover what is going on.

To dream that you have a mole on your face or body, suggests that something is interfering with your personal esteem. You are unable to gain the esteem of others.

Monday

To dream of Monday, signifies the start of some project or task. You are ready to face your problems head on.

Money

To see or win money in your dream, indicates that success and prosperity is within your reach. Money represents confidence, self-worth, success, or values. You have much belief in
yourself. Alternatively, dreaming about money, refers to your attitudes about love and matters of the heart. It is a common symbol for sexuality and power. In particular, finding money indicates your quest for love or for power.

To dream that you lose money, suggests that you are lacking ambition, power and self-esteem. You are experiencing unhappiness and setbacks in your waking life. You may also be feeling weak, vulnerable, and out of control in your waking life.

To give or spend money in your dream, is analogous to giving love. You are looking for love. To see others giving money away, suggests that you are feeling ignored, overlooked or neglected. Someone is not paying enough attention and showing enough affection toward you. If you are hogging or hoarding money, then it denotes insecurity or selfishness.

To dream that you have no money, indicates a fear of losing your place in the world. You are lacking the abilities needed to achieve some desired goal. If you are borrowing money in your dream, then it suggests that you are overextending your resources. You are spreading yourself too thin.

To dream that you steal money, forewarns that you are in danger. You need to be more cautious. On a positive note, the dream indicates that you are finally going after what you want in life. Alternatively, stealing money means that you are lacking love. You are desperate to be accepted.

Monk

To see a monk in your dream, signifies devotion, faith, and spiritual enlightenment.

To dream that you are a monk, symbolizes the introspective aspect of yourself. You need to emotionally withdraw yourself from a situation in order to regain some control, structure, and order.

Monkey

To see a monkey in your dream, symbolizes deceit, insight and intuition. Those around you are working to advance their own interest. Alternatively, monkeys indicate an immature attitude, a playful nature and the mischievous side of your personality.

To see a monkey hanging or swinging from a tree, suggests that you are feeling troubled by some issue.

To dream that you are feeding a monkey, means betrayal by someone whom you thought cared about your interests.

Also consider the significance of the Three Mystic Monkeys who cover their eyes, ears and mouth to mean that they see no evil, hear no evil and speak no evil.

Monkey Bars

To see or play on the monkey bars in your dream, denotes the carefree nature of childhood. Alternatively, it represents your strength, competence, determination and ability to achieve your goals. Don't give up.

Monster

To dream that you are chased or followed by a monster, represents aspects of yourself that you find repulsive and ugly. You may possess some fears or some repressed emotions. Try to confront the monster in your dream and figure out who or what aspect of yourself the monster represents.

To dream that you kill a monster, means that you will successfully overcome your rivals and advance to a higher position.

Moon

To see the moon in your dream, represents some hidden, mysterious aspect of yourself. It is often associated with the feminine mystique and intuition. Alternatively, the moon signifies your changing moods.

To see the eclipse of the moon in your dream, signifies that your feminine side is being overshadowed. Or it may mean that some hidden aspect of yourself is coming to the surface.

To see the crescent moon in your dream, indicates cyclic changes, renewal, and movement. You are progressing smoothly toward your life path. A full moon signifies completion and wholeness, while a new moon symbolizes new beginnings.

Moose

To see a moose in your dream, represents long life and longevity. It may refer to the elders around you. Alternatively, a moose indicates that you can be both powerful and gentle. You exert your power only when it is necessary.

Mop

To dream that you are mopping, suggests that you are ready to let go something. It is time to release your emotions and express it in a productive way.

To see a mop in your dream, symbolizes domesticity and the monotony of your daily routine. Perhaps you are searching for a little more variety or excitement. Alternatively, the dream expresses your desires to want things to be neat and clean. You realize that it takes work to maintain and keep a household together.

Morning

To dream that it is morning, suggests that fortune and pleasure are within near reach. It also denotes new beginnings, renewal, an awakening or starting over. Alternatively, the dream may also be a pun on "mourning". Are you grieving over something or someone? In particular, if the morning is cloudy, then it signifies an important situation that will burden you for a while.

Morph

To dream that you or someone is morphing into another person, suggests that you need to incorporate aspects of this other person into your own character. You are in need of a major change in your life. Alternatively, you need to learn to see things from someone else's perspective and expand your awareness.

To dream that you are morphing into an animal, suggests that you need to express yourself more freely and without restraint.

To dream that something is morphing into something else that morphs into something else, represents your indecision or your ever changing attitudes toward some situation or issue. It also means that you are looking at something from a new angle or different perspective. Consider the significance of each morphed object.

Morse Code

To use or hear Morse code in your dream, suggests that you are lacking communication skills. You need to express your feelings and emote. Alternatively, the dream indicates that you need to be more direct some matter. Get to the point.

Mortuary

To see or dream that you are in a mortuary, suggests that you are hindering your own self-growth by not utilizing your abilities and talents. Alternatively, it represents aspects of yourself that you need to discard and get rid of.

Mosaic

To see a mosaic in your dream, represents the various aspects and components that make up life as a whole. You need to consider things from a wider perspective. Things may look insignificant and meaningless up close, but you need to stand back and consider the overall picture.

Mosquito

To see mosquitoes in your dream, suggest that some situation or someone has been draining you of your energy and resources. Alternatively, mosquitoes indicate that your resistance to attacks will be in vain.

To dream that you are killing mosquitoes, denote that you will eventually overcome your obstacles. Happiness and fortune will be in your grasp.

Moss

To see moss growing in your dream, indicates an extremely slow progress in some project or relationship. You need to be more patient.

Moth

To see a moth in your dream, indicates that some unseen irritation may not surface until it is too late. It is important to pay attention to the minor details and not to overlook certain things. Alternatively, the moth symbolizes your weaknesses, character flaws or fragileness.

Mother

To see your mother in your dream, represents the nurturing aspect of your own character. Mothers offer shelter, comfort, life, guidance and protection. Some people may have problems freeing themselves from their mothers and are thus seeking their own individuality and development.

To dream that you are having a conversation with your mother, denotes a matter that has preoccupied your mind and you are not sure how to deal with it in your waking life. It indicates unresolved problems that need to be worked out with your mother.

To hear your mother call you in our dream, suggests that you have been negligent in your duties and responsibilities. You are pursuing down the wrong path.

Mother-In-Law

To see your mother-in-law in your dream, indicates an amicable resolution to some matter.

Motorcycle

To see or ride a motorcycle in your dream, symbolizes your desire for freedom and need for adventure. You may be trying to escape from some situation or some other responsibility in your waking life. Alternatively, a motorcycle is symbolic of raw sexuality. Perhaps you are moving too fast.

Mount Fuji

To see Mount Fuji in your dream, represents an aspect of your life that may be deceivingly calm. It is a place where heaven and earth and fire comes together. Consider an aspect of your life where you are struggling with your spirituality, your practicality and your passions.

Mountains

To see mountains in your dream, signify many major obstacles and challenges that you have to overcome. If you are on top of the mountain, then it indicates that you have achieved and realized your goals. You have recognized your full potential. Alternatively, mountains denote a higher realm of consciousness, knowledge, and spiritual truth.

To dream that you are climbing a mountain, signifies your determination and ambition.

To dream that you fall off a mountain, refers to your rush to succeed without thoroughly thinking about your path to success. Perhaps you are being pushed upward into a direction that you do not want to go or that you are not ready for. Falling off a mountain also means that you have a tendency to give up too easily or escape from demanding situations. You take the easy way out.

Mouse

To see a mouse in your dream, indicates fear, meekness, insignificance and a lack of assertiveness. You are experiencing feelings of inadequacy and fears that you are not measuring up. The dream may be telling you that you are spending too much time hiding in the shadows of someone else. Alternatively, a mouse symbolizes minor irritations and annoyances. Perhaps you are letting petty problems or insignificant issues eat away at you. The dream may also be a pun on a computer mouse and your connection to work or to the virtual world.

To dream that you kill or trap a mouse, suggests that others are making a big deal out of certain minor issues in your life.

To dream that you or someone is eating a mouse, indicates that there is something nagging at your conscience. You need to get it off your chest.

To dream that a mouse is being chased, suggests that you are not standing up for yourself. You are letting others push you around.

Mouse Trap

To see a mouse trap in your dream, suggests that you need to be more cautious. Be leery of people who want to help you. Alternatively, a mouse trap symbolizes ingenuity, insight, and creativity. You need to look at a better way of doing something.

To dream that you are setting a mouse trap, indicates that you will outwit your opponents.

To dream that you catch a mouse in a mouse trap, suggests that you are being taken advantage of.

Mouth

To see a mouth in your dream, signifies your need to express yourself or talk about an issue that's bothering you. Alternatively, the dream suggests that you have said too much and you need to keep your mouth shut.

Mouthwash

To see or use mouthwash in your dream, indicates that you need to literally wash your mouth as a result of something you said. You need to think first before saying something you might regret.

Movie

To dream that you are watching a movie, suggests that you are watching life pass you by. Perhaps you are living vicariously through the actions of others. Consider also how the movie parallels to situations in your waking life. Observe how the characters relate to you and how they may represent an aspect of yourself.

To dream that you are playing a role in the movie, foretells that something from your unconscious is about to emerge or be revealed. It may also represent memories of images from your past. Alternatively, the dream may be pointing you toward a new role that you might be undertaking. Your unconscious is psychologically preparing you for this new role.

To dream that the movie screen is blank, suggests that you are feeling excluded in some situation. You feel lonely and sad.

Moving

To dream that you are moving away, signifies your desire or need for change. It may also mean an end to a situation or relationship; you are moving on. Alternatively, it indicates your determination and issues regarding dependence and independence.

MTV

To dream that you are watching MTV, suggests that you are watching too much MTV. It is effecting your thinking and clouding your judgment. Consider what show you are watching and how it parallels a certain aspect of your waking life.

Mud

To see mud in your dream, suggests that you are involved in a messy and sticky situation. It also suggests that some spiritual cleansing is needed.

To dream that you are walking in mud, suggests that you are feeling weighed down by a situation, problem, or relationship. You are feeling frustrated.

To dream that mud has gotten on your clothing, means that your reputation is being attacked and called into question. Consider the term "mud-slinging" to refer to some politicians.

Mug

To see or use a mug in your dream, represents love, nurturance and the womb. The mug also signifies rejuvenation and healing. Alternatively, it indicates a transcendence into a realm of higher consciousness. The mug may also be a pun on your face or that you are "mugging" for attention.

To see or use an insulated mug in your dream, suggests that you are trying to keep a certain feeling or hope alive. You want to keep an idea "hot" or a project on track. Negatively, the dream means that you may be trying to hold onto something too long and it may be time to let go.

Mugshot

To see or dream that you are taking a mugshot, indicates that you need to face up to your responsibilities and acknowledge the mistakes you have made.

Mummy

To see a mummy in your dream, suggests that you are feeling trapped in a situation. You feel that you are not being heard.

Murder

To dream that you have committed a murder, indicates that you are putting an end to an old habit and a former way of thinking. This could also refer to an end to an addiction. Alternatively, the dream indicates that you have some repressed aggression or rage at yourself or at someone. Note also that dreams of murder occur frequently during periods of depression.

To dream that you witness a murder, indicates deep-seated anger towards somebody. Consider how the victim represents aspects of yourself that you want to destroy or eliminate.

To dream that you are murdered, suggests that some important and significant relationship has been severed. You are trying to disconnect yourself from your emotions. The dream may also be about your unused talents.

*Please Also See Killing.

Muscle

To see muscles in your dream, symbolize power, strength, and flexibility. You need to develop these qualities within yourself in order to become a more stronger and confident person.

Museum

To see a museum in your dream, indicates that your non-traditional path to success will make you stand out from the rest. Sometimes you need to take a risk. Alternatively, the museum represents your own personal history. You can learn a lot from your past and your heritage. Consider what you have gained from these experiences and apply them to your current circumstances.

To dream that you are in a museum, represents the things you value in life. Objects in the museum symbolizes memories and talents.

Mushroom

To see mushrooms in your dream, signify unhealthy pleasures and unwise decisions in your waking life. Things that come too quickly have a tendency to disappear just as quick. Learn to appreciate the things you have.

To dream that you are eating mushrooms, represent your leadership ability. You hold a lot of strength and power.

Music

To hear harmonious and soothing music in your dream, signifies prosperity and pleasure. You are expressing your emotions in a positive way. Music serves to heal the soul.

To hear discordant or out of tune music in your dream, signifies unhappiness, lack of harmony, and troubles in your relationship or domestic life.

Musical Chairs

To dream that you are playing musical chairs, signifies instability in some area of your life. You are feeling uneasy about your position or about some decision you made.

Mussels

To see mussels in your dream, indicate that you are closing yourself off and isolating yourself from others. Ask yourself why you are shutting others out. The dream may also be a pun on "muscles".

Mustache

To dream that you have a mustache when you don't really have one, signifies that you are hiding an aspect of yourself. You are putting on a disguise or showing a different aspect of your personality.

To dream that you shave off your mustache, denotes that you are revealing your true self. You no longer have to hide under some disguise or some shield. Alternatively, the dream means that you are trying to reestablish your reputation, by renouncing your previous activities.

If you are a woman and dream that you have a mustache, then it indicates that you are expressing your power through your words and your verbal expression.

Mute

To dream that you are mute, indicates that you are afraid to say something for fear of being criticized or judged. There may also be a situation in your waking life that has left you speechless.

Mutilate

To dream that you are being mutilated, indicates that there is a waking situation that you need to be careful about. You may be putting yourself in some sort of danger, either physical or mental. If you are mutilating yourself, then it means that you are seeking attention. You are expressing a desperate cry for help. Or you are trying to disconnect yourself from the unbearable pain you are experiencing in an aspect of your life.

To dream that someone or something is mutilated, indicates that your integrity is put into question.

N

To see the letter "N" in your dream, implies the end of some habit, journey, relationship or condition.

Nail Polish

To polish your nails in your dream, suggests that you need to put more focus onto what you are doing and what you are trying to accomplish.

To dream that you are changing your nail polish color, represents your creativeness or emotional nature.

Look up the color of the nail polish for additional significance. In particular, to see blue, green black, purple or other non-traditional nail polish color in your dream, represents your free spirit. You like to express yourself in unique ways. If you see clear nail polish in your dream, then it signifies your objectiveness in a situation.

Nails

To hammer nails in your dream, represent your tenacity and ability to drive a hard bargain. Also consider the pun, "getting nailed" which refers to a sexual innuendo or which means getting caught with something. Alternatively, the dream may also point to another popular phrase "hitting the nail on the head", which suggests that you have fully resolved a situation.

To see nails in your dream, symbolize long and hard work for little compensation and pay. It may also be analogous to some rugged or tough force.

To dream that you hurt yourself with a nail, suggests that you need to be careful with what you say.

*Please See Also *Fingernails.*

Naked

To dream that you are naked, denotes fear of being found out and exposed over your activities. You feel that you are being misjudged.

To dream that you suddenly discover your nudity and are trying to cover up, signifies your vulnerability to a situation.

To see a naked person in your dream and you are disgusted by it, represents some anxiety about discovering the naked truth about that person or situation. It may also foretell of an illicit love affair, a loss of prestige or some scandalous activity. On the other hand, if you are accepting of someone else's nudity, then it implies that you can see right through them and their intentions. Or perhaps, you are completely accepting them for who they are. If you do not care about someone else's nudity, then it suggests that you need to learn not to be afraid of rejection.

Name

To dream that you forget your name or someone else's name, suggests that you are feeling overwhelmed and burdened. It may also indicate that you have forgotten your true self or your family roots.

To hear your name being called, indicates that you are in touch and in tune with your spirituality. You need to be more aware of your own uniqueness and your individuality.

To see a familiar name written in your dream, symbolizes the way you feel about that person. Your intuition about them may turn out to be true.

To dream that you changed your name or are referred to by a different name, suggests that you are undergoing some major transformation or metamorphosis in your waking life. You are experiencing a reawakening.

Navel

To see your navel in your dream, represents your being and self. The dream may indicate that you need to find your center and middle ground. Alternatively, to dream of your navel signifies the bonding to their mother.

To dream that you or someone has a navel piercing, denotes your deep connection with your mother. Perhaps the dream is telling you to reconnect with your mother or that you need to be in touch with your maternal instincts.

Neck

To see your neck in your dream, signifies the relationship between the mind/mental and the body/physical. It represents willpower, self-restriction and your need to control your feelings and keep them in check. Consider the familiar phrase, "don't stick your neck out" which serves as a warning against a situation.

To dream that your neck is injured or sore, indicates a separation between your heart and mind. There is a literal disconnect between how you feel and what you think. You are feeling conflicted. Alternatively, the dream represents something or someone, who is literally a pain in the neck.

If you dream that your neck is thick or swollen, then it represents your quick temperedness.

Necklace

To see or wear a necklace in your dream, represents unsatisfied desires. It also highlights your intellect and your desire to have more influence and power over others. If the necklace is broken or lost, then it indicates that your rational thinking is in accordance with your emotional thinking. You need to act on your gut instinct about some situation or relationship.

Needle

To see or use a needle in your dream, indicates that you need to mend some relationship or situation that has gotten out of hand. A needle is also symbolic of some emotional or physical pain. Alternatively, the dream is a metaphor for male sexuality or a sexual act. In particular, to see knitting needles in your dream, suggest that you are manipulating a situation in order to get a desired outcome.

To dream that someone is using a needle, suggests that you need to incorporate and join together various aspects of your consciousness.

To look for a needle in your dream, symbolizes useless worries over small, trivial matters. Consider the phrase of looking for a needle in a haystack to represent our fruitless pursuits.

To dream that you are threading a needle, represents unfinished issues that you need to tend to and perhaps even repair. Alternatively, the dream may have sexual connotations.

Negatives

To see picture negatives in your dream, represent a relationship or situation that is developing. The dream may be a pun on some "negative" person or force in your life. Consider also what is being depicted in the negative.

Neon Light

To see neon lights in your dream, symbolize your aspirations and desires for recognition or fame, particularly if it is your name in neon. Also consider what is written in neon. There is an important message that your unconscious is trying to convey.

Neptune

To see the planet Neptune in your dream, represents inspiration, imagination, and devotion. You may need to show some more compassion and understanding.

To see the Neptune god in your dream, indicates some supercharged emotion that you need to address in your waking life. You need to control your temper.

Nervous Breakdown

To dream that you or someone has a nervous breakdown, suggests that you have lost your frame of reference in a relationship or situation. You are seeking more clarity and insight. The dream also indicates that you are having difficulties trusting your own judgment and decisions. You are feeling insecure.

Nest

To see a nest in your dream, signifies comfort, safety, homeliness, protection, or new opportunities. Consider the condition of the nest and how it parallels your waking home situation and home life. Alternatively, the nest also means emotional dependency.

If the nest is full of eggs, then it symbolizes your financial future and financial security. The dream could thus be a pun on "nest egg". If the eggs in the nest are broken or bad, then it symbolizes disappointments and failures. You are being pulled into someone else's problems or arguments.

Net

To see a net in your dream, suggests that you are caught in a complicated life situation. You feel trapped. Alternatively, the dream means that you need to expand your reach. it is time to "cast those nets" and see what comes back. The net may thus be a metaphor for your network of connections or the internet.

Nettles

To see nettles in your dream, represents a difficult situation that you need to avoid. You may be experiencing difficulty in expressing yourself. Perhaps you are in the middle of a "stingy" situation.

New Year

To dream of the New Year, signifies prosperity, hope, new beginnings and an opportunity to make a fresh start. It also represents the start of some new project or a fresh outlook in life. On a spiritual level, the New Year represents enlightenment or new found understanding.

New York

If you do not live in New York, but dream that you are in New York, then it symbolizes your fast paced lifestyle. Perhaps things are moving too fast and you are unable to keep up with the demands of everyday life. Alternatively, the dream represents your desires for more excitement in your life. Or you are striving for success in your professional career. Known as "the big apple, dreaming of New York City could mean that you need to eat a more healthy diet.

Newborn

*Please See Baby.

News

To watch or listen to the news in your dream, signifies an important message from your unconscious. Alternatively, the dream may mean that you need to be more objective in a situation.

To hear good news in your dream, is a dream of the contrary and represents a negative turn in events. If you hear bad news in your dream, then a situation is not as bad as you had anticipated.

Newspaper

To see or read a newspaper in your dream, signifies that new light and insight is being shed on a waking problem that is nagging on your mind. You are seeking knowledge and answers to a problem. Pay attention to the dream as it may offer a solution. Alternatively, reading the newspaper implies that you need to be more vocal. You need to express yourself. It is time to make the headlines.

To dream that you are unable to read the newspaper, indicates that your reputation is being called into question. There is some uncertainty in a situation that you are pursuing.

To dream that you are selling newspapers, suggest that you are trying to inform and alert others to some important information. Perhaps you have a significant announcement to make.

Nickel

To see a nickel in your dream, symbolizes the number 5 and thus means a change in your path or course of action. Or it may also indicate your persuasiveness and spontaneity. Alternatively, the dream refers to money issues. You need to do some serious saving! Also consider the phrase to "nickel and dime", which implies that you are being too petty over minor issues. At the same time, little things can add up to be a major issue later if not addressed immediately.

Night

To have a dream that takes place at night, represents some major setbacks and obstacles in achieving your goals. You are being faced with an issue that is not so clear cut. Perhaps, you should put the issues aside so you can clear your head and come back to it later. Alternatively, night may be synonymous with death, rebirth, reflection, and new beginnings.

Nike

To see the Nike logo in your dream, is telling you to "just do it". You need to stop sitting around and start moving more quickly. Alternatively, the dream symbolizes speed, agility and athleticism.

Nine

Nine denotes completion, closure, rebirth, inspiration, and reformation. You are on a productive path, seeking to improve the world. The number nine also symbolizes longevity.

911

The appearance of this number in your dream, symbolizes an emergency. You need not be afraid to ask for help. There is an important lesson to be learned from in your dream.

Nineteen

Nineteen indicates independence and the overcoming of personal struggles. You will find that you often have to stand up for yourself. This number also suggests your stubbornness and you hesitance in accepting help from others.

Ninja

To see a ninja in your dream, symbolizes a someone in your life whose intentions are unclear. You may feel threatened by this person's abilities or suspicious of their motivations.

To dream that you are a ninja, indicates passive aggressive behavior. You are trying to be defiant without appearing confrontational.

No

To dream that you are saying no, suggests that you are standing up for what believe even though you are going against the majority. You are putting yourself first and making decisions for yourself, not for others.

Noise

To hear or make a strange noise in your dream, signifies the unexpected and the unknown. You may be expressing some fear or confusion about a situation in your waking life. The noise in your dream may serve as a way to attract your attention to that issue. Alternatively, a noise represents a breakthrough into your personal struggles. Perhaps you need to be more vocal and be heard. Or perhaps you need to break through a barrier that has been holding you back.

Noodles

To see noodles in your dream, symbolize longevity and abundance. Alternatively, the dream indicates that you are looking for some sort of nourishment. The dream may also be a pun that you need to "use your noodle". In other words, there is something that you need to think long and hard about.

Noose

To see a noose in your dream, represents your lack of independence. You feel restricted and restrained from being able to express yourself.

To dream that a noose is around someone's neck, signifies repressed anger and rage at that person or towards a particular condition.

North

To dream of the direction north, symbolizes reality. It also indicates that you are making progress and moving forward in life.

North Pole

To dream that you are at the north pole, signifies completion and an ending to some journey, situation, or relationship. You have successfully completed your transformation.

Nose

To see your own nose in your dream, signifies a conscious effort to achieve whatever endeavor you chose to undertake. The nose represents energy, intuition, and wisdom. The dream may suggest your need to learn more about a situation at hand. Alternatively, the nose symbolizes curiosity, as in being nosy. Perhaps you are interfering into situations and things that are none of your business. If you dream that your nose is growing, then it suggests that you or someone is lying and being dishonest.

To dream that hair is growing on your nose, signifies your strong will and solid character.

To dream that a bug or insect is coming out of your nose, indicates that you are being nosy to the point where it is "bugging" and bothering others. You need to learn to when to get out of people's business and respect their privacy.

To dream that you have a bloody nose, means that your character is under attack. If your nose is stuffed up, then it suggests that you unable to freely and fully express yourself.

Notes

To read or write a note in your dream, suggests that there is an important message that you need to convey. There is something that you need to let others know.

To dream that you are passing notes, symbolize your pursuit for knowledge and information.

To see musical notes in your dream, represent harmony or disharmony in your waking life, depending on whether the musical note was a sharp note or flat note.

November

To dream of the month of November, indicates your indifference to a situation or problem.

Nude

*Please See <u>Naked.</u>

Nuclear Bomb

To dream of a nuclear bomb, suggests feelings of helplessness and loss of control. You are experiencing some strong hostility and rage, where it is nearly destructive. Important changes are about to occur. You may also be expressing a desire to wipe out some aspect of yourself. Alternatively, the nuclear bomb serves as an indication that something crucial and precious to you has ended.

Numbers

To see numbers in your dream, symbolize material gains and possessions. You are keeping close track of things. Alternatively, numbers indicate that you are being over analytical or rational. Or that you need to evaluate a situation more thoroughly. Numbers also carry much personal significance. They may represent a special date, address, age, lucky number or something meaningful and significant to only you.

To hear numbers in your dream, mean that you need to pace yourself in some situation. Or perhaps you need to calm down and take things a little slowly.

Look up the specific number for additional significance.

Nun

To see a nun in your dream, signifies purity, chastity and obedience. It also indicates that you need to live up to the vows and promises you have made. Alternatively, material fortune and gain may be interfering with your spirituality. Consider also the pun of being "none" or "nothing".

If you are a woman and dream that you are a nun, then it indicates unhappiness with your current situation and environment. You are looking for an escape. Alternatively, the dream suggests that you are looking for a sense of security or calmness in your life.

Nurse

To dream that you are a nurse, suggests that you need to show more compassion in a situation.

To see a nurse in your dream, means that you need to take time out in order to heal, mentally, physically and spiritually.

Nursery

To see a baby's nursery in your dream, symbolizes your maternal instinct. The dream may suggest that you are expecting a new addition to your family. Alternatively, a nursery indicates that you are regressing back to your childhood. Perhaps you are wanting to go back to a simpler time where you were cared for and did not have to worry about anything.

To dream that you are in a plant nursery, represents spiritual development, potential, growth and transformation. You need to nurture the changes in your life.

Nutcracker

To see a nutcracker in your dream, represents power, strength and stamina. You can achieve anything you want if you set your mind to it. Alternatively, the dream may be a pun on a powerful or tough woman.

Nuts

To see nuts in your dream, represent craziness or confusion. It may also refer to someone who is "nuts" or someone who is driving you crazy. Alternatively, the dream is telling you that you are approaching a waking situation all wrong and need to look at it from a different perspective. Also consider nuts as a pun on "testicles" and thus allude to some sexual innuendo.

To dream that you are eating nuts, signify prosperity and attainment of your desires. You are trying to get to the core of a matter or situation.

Nylons

*Please See <u>Pantyhose.</u>

O

To see the letter "O" in your dream, signifies an exclamation of surprise as in "oh!". Alternatively, the letter O, implies that you need to open wide. Perhaps there is something that you need to open up about and vocalize. It may refer to a sexual innuendo as in "the big O" or orgasm. This letter may also share the same significance as the number zero or a circle.

Oak Tree

To see an oak tree in your dream, symbolizes longevity, stability, strength, tolerance, wisdom, and prosperity. You have built a solid foundation for success in some endeavor.

If there are acorns on the tree, then the symbol refers to your climb up the social ladder and rise in status.

Oars

To see or use oars in your dream, signify control over your emotions. You are able to navigate through life based on the lessons and skills you have learned. If you are rowing energetically, then it suggests that you need to approach some situation with more aggression and determination.

To dream that you are paddling with one oar, indicates that you are going around in circles and headed nowhere. You need help in some situation or matter. Alternatively, it suggests that you are missing a partner in life. If you lose an oar, then it suggests that you have lost your groove or have taken something for granted.

Oasis

To see an oasis in your dream, refers to your need for a vacation. You need to allocate time for pleasure leisurely pursuits.

To dream that you are searching for an oasis, symbolizes inner fears, insecurities, and overwhelming circumstances. You are looking for emotional support.

Observatory

To see an observatory in your dream, signifies your high goals and aspirations. The dream may be telling you that you need to acknowledge your spirituality.

Observe

*Please See Watching.

Obstacle

To see or experience obstacles in your dream, represent things in your life that you need to overcome. The dream is offering you a solution on how to approach and tackle a problem in your waking life. You may have some self-doubt in your abilities and in coming to a decision.

Obstacle Courses

To dream that you are going through an obstacle course, symbolizes the hardships and difficulties that you are experiencing in your waking life. It represents the things that you must overcome in order to reach your goals. The elements in the obstacle course is analogous to the barriers and problems in your life.

Ocean

*Please See Sea or Water.

Octagon

To see an octagon in your dream, indicates a spiritual reawakening, eternal life or resurrection.

October

To dream of the month of October, signifies gratifying success in your endeavors.

Octopus

To see an octopus in your dream, means that you are entangled in some difficult matter. Your judgment is being clouded. Alternatively, the octopus indicates that you are overly possessive and maybe too clingy in a relationship.

Office

To dream of your work office, indicates that you cannot seem to leave your work at the office. You are overworked or have too much on your mind. Alternatively, an office symbolizes practicality, status, accomplishments and your place in the world. If the office in your dream is unfamiliar or strange, then it suggests that you are comparing yourself to someone else. You are measuring yourself against other's standards.

To dream that you hold public office, represents your acceptance for the consequences of your actions. You are taking responsibility for what you do.

Oil

To see oil in your dream, represents your desires to have things run more smoothly. Perhaps you need to put a little oil in something to get things moving. Alternatively, you may need to show more love and compassion in your life. Metaphorically, dreaming of oil may refer to someone who is slick or smooth.

To see baby oil in your dream, indicates that you need to soothe the child within you. It is okay to let loose once in a while.

To see crude oil in your dream, signifies great wealth and riches. Alternatively, the dream refers to over- consumption. You need to conserve and be more environmentally conscious.

To see massaging oils in your dream, symbolize your sensual side. Perhaps you need to express your sensuality more.

Oil Spill

To see an oil spill in your dream, suggests that you are in emotional turmoil. You are experiencing problems and distress in your personal relationships.

Old

To see something old in your dream, suggests that there is something in your life that you need to replace or get rid of. Alternatively, the dream means that there may be something in the past that you need to incorporate into your current life.

Olives

To see or eat olives in your dream, symbolize healing and immortality.

To see an olive tree or branch, signifies reconciliation, peace, and hope.

To see or wear a crown of olive leaves, indicates that you will overcome your obstacles and find a resolution to a conflict. A burden will be lifted off you and you will come out victorious.

Olympics

To dream that you are competing in the Olympics, symbolizes the spirit of competition. You need to go after what you want. Alternatively, the Olympics represent unity. It may be telling you that despite our differences and disagreements, we can all still come together. You need to apply this ideology to some aspect of your waking life. A more direct interpretation may represent your aspirations of being an Olympian athlete.

Omelet

To see or eat an omelet in your dream, indicates a bright start to your day. The dream is telling you that you are headed in the right direction. Also consider the phrase "you can't make an omelet without breaking eggs". Perhaps the dream is trying to tell you that there are certain sacrifices that you need to make in order to achieve your goal.

One

One stands for individuality, autonomy, leadership, originality, confidence and the ego. To be number one means that you are a winner and the best. Alternatively, one signifies solitude or loneliness. It also stands for a higher spiritual force.

Onions

To see or eat onions in your dream, represent the multitude of layers that you need to get through in order to unveil what is really underneath. You need to dig a little deeper into a situation or problem. The dream may be a metaphor for some revelation.

To dream that an onion is making you cry, indicates that you are not being genuine. It symbolizes phoniness, fakeness and deceit.

Onyx

To see onyx in your dream, represents self- confidence, spiritual and mental balance and peace of mind. Alternatively, an onyx signifies some unknown or unacknowledged power.

Opera

To watch an opera in your dream, represents your quest for the grander things in life. The dream may also be trying to tell you that you are being overly dramatic in some waking situation.

Oral Sex

To dream that you are giving or receiving oral sex, signifies your willingness to give or receive pleasure/joy. It is symbolic of your creative energy and reaffirms that you are headed in the right direction in life. The dream may also be a pun on "talking about sex." Perhaps, you need to communicate with your mate about your sexual needs and desires. Or you are acting out your sexual wishes.

To dream that you are performing oral sex on yourself, represents your need for self-gratification.

Orange

Orange denotes hope, friendliness, courtesy, generosity, liveliness, sociability, and an out-going nature. It also represents a stimulation of the senses. You feel alive! You may want to expand your horizons and look into new interests.

Oranges

To see an orange tree in your dream, signifies health and prosperity.

To dream that you are eating oranges, indicate satisfaction with your life and where you are at. You are in a good place. Alternatively, it means that you need to be reenergized.

Orchids

To see orchids in your dream, symbolize gentleness, romance, beauty, lust and sensuality. There is a situation or relationship that requires special attention and care. Alternatively, the orchid serves as a reminder that you are surrounded by wealth and riches.

Organ

To hear or play an organ in your dream, represents your spiritual connection and religious views. The dream may also be a metaphor to represent the penis.

To dream of your internal organ, indicates concerns about your health. Consider the specific organ for additional significance.

Orgasm

To dream that you are having an orgasm, represents an exciting end to something. What have you just completed in your life? Alternatively, the dream means that you are not getting enough sex. You need to relieve some of your sexual tensions.

To dream that you do not achieve orgasm, signifies some frustration in your life. Something is leaving you unfulfilled and unsatisfied. Note that the frustration may not necessarily be sexually related.

Orgy

To see an orgy in your dream, signifies repressed desires of your own sexuality and passion. Perhaps you are too conservative in your sex life and need to experiment. It may also mean that there is some sort of confusion in how and where you distribute your energies. You may be going into too many directions and as a result, are spread too thin.

Origami

To fold or make origami in your dream, represents your creativity. You need to learn to express yourself through paper and your imagination. In other words, you should write more. Consider also what you are making in origami and look up the significance of that object.

Orphan

To see an orphan in your dream, signifies fears of abandonment. You feel lonely and rejected.

To dream that you are an orphan, suggests that you need to learn to be more independent and self-sufficient. Alternatively, the dream may be telling you that you have a lot of love to offer others. Don't sell yourself short.

Ostrich

To see an ostrich in your dream, suggests that you are not facing reality. You are in denial about something and living in a world of your own. Perhaps, there is a situation that you are unwilling to accept. Alternatively, the ostrich can symbolize truth and justice.

To see an ostrich egg in your dream, symbolizes rebirth.

Ouija Board

To see an Ouija board in your dream, indicates that some relationship or situation is falling apart. Nothing is going according to planned. Alternatively, it suggests that you are ready to take certain risks in order to move ahead. The dream may also be a way of connecting with your unconscious. Consider the message that the Ouija board is telling you.

To dream that the Oiuja board fails to function, indicates that your pursuit for pleasure will cause your demise and downfall. Alternatively, the dream implies that you are inviting negativity into your life.

Outhouse

To see an outhouse in your dream, suggests that you need to be more open with your feelings. You are holding something back, especially when it comes to your emotions.

Outlet

To see an outlet in your dream, represents your potential and untapped energies. The dream symbol may also be a metaphor for something shocking. Or perhaps you are looking for an "outlet" to express your raw emotions.

Outside

To dream that you are outside, represents freedom, openness and opportunities. You are able to spread out and enjoy. Alternatively, the dream signifies your need to be more expressive. It is telling you that you need to stop closing yourself off.

Oval

To see an oval in your dream, represents the vagina, womb and feminine qualities. The oval shape is also symbolic of your aura and your spiritual energy.

Oven

To see a hot oven in your dream, indicates passion, loyalty, warmth, devotion, togetherness and unselfishness. You are surrounded by friends and family. Alternatively, an oven symbolizes the womb. You are either in anticipation or in fear of having children. Consider the phrase " a bun in the oven" to indicate a pregnancy.

Overdose

To dream that you or someone overdoses, suggests that you do not know your limits. You may be pushing yourself too hard. Alternatively, the dream means that you are on a self-destructive path. You need to make some significant changes to your life.

Ovulation

*Please See <u>Menstruation.</u>

Owl

To see an owl in your dream, symbolizes wisdom, insight, magic, expanded awareness and virtue. You are highly connected to your intuitive senses and psychic power. The owl is also synonymous with death, darkness and the unconscious. The appearance of an owl may be telling you to let go of the past or certain negative behaviors.

To hear the hoot of an owl in your dream, denotes disappointments and death. Your unconscious mind may be trying to get your attention.

To see a dead owl in your dream, signifies some illness or death. Death in this sense may be a symbolic death, as in an important transition in life or the end of a negative habit.

Ox

To see an ox in your dream, represents the balance between the masculine power and the feminine mystique. You are well in tune with the opposite sex. Alternatively, an ox symbolizes hard work, strength, and reliability. Consider also the familiar metaphor, "as stubborn as an ox".

Oysters

To dream that you are eating oysters, indicate sexual urges and gratification.

To see oysters in your dream, symbolize beauty, humility, wealth, and wisdom. Alternatively, oysters indicate that you are closing yourself off and shutting others out. Or perhaps, the dream is telling you that "the world is your oyster". You need to go out and go after what you want and achieve your heart's desires. Experience life.

To see oyster shells in your dream, signify financial frustrations.

P

To see the letter "P" in your dream, is a pun on "pee" or urine. You need to better express your emotions.

Pacifier

To see a pacifier in your dream, represents emotional nurturance. You are expressing a desire to escape from your daily responsibilities and demands.

To dream that you are sucking on a pacifier, implies that you are trying to "suck up to" someone in your waking life. It may also denote your immature attitude.

Packing

To dream that you are packing, signifies big changes ahead for you. You are putting past issues to test or past relationships behind you. Alternatively, it represents the burdens that you carry.

To dream that you are packing, unpacking and packing and unpacking again, represents chaos in your life. You are feeling overwhelmed with the various things you are juggling in your life. You are carrying around too many burdens and need to let go. Consider what unfinished business you have to tend to. Try to resolve these issues so they can finally be put to rest.

Pageant

To watch or dream that you are in a beauty pageant, refers to your own insecurities about your appearances. You are constantly comparing yourself to others and how you measure up to them. You may also be subscribing to society's unattainable standards of beauty.

Pager

To see a pager in your dream, suggests that someone is trying hard to communicate their thoughts to you. Someone is trying to get through to you one way or another. On the other hand, you may feel that someone is pushing their beliefs and ideas onto you.

Pail

To see or carry a pail in your dream, indicates an improvement in your current situation. If the pail is filled, then it signifies abundance, love and wealth. If the pail is empty, then it means that you will overcome some loss or conflict. The dream may also be a pun on "pale."

Pain

To dream that you are in pain, suggests that you are being too hard on yourself, especially if a situation was out of your control. The dream may also be a true reflection of actual pain that exists somewhere in your body. Dreams can reveal and warn about health problems. Consider where the pain is for additional significance. If the pain is in your neck, then the dream may be a metaphor that you are literally being a "pain in the neck".

To dream that you are inflicting pain to yourself, indicates that you are experiencing some overwhelming turmoil or problems in your waking life. You are trying to disconnect yourself from your reality by focusing on the pain that you inflicted to yourself.

Paint

To see paint in your dream, symbolizes expression of your inner emotions. Consider the color of the paint and how the color makes you feel. It is this feeling that you need to express more in your waking life.

To mix paint in your dream, suggests that you are incorporating a little variety in your life.

Paintball

To dream that you are playing paintball, represents your competitive, but fun side. You have a chance to accomplish something great in an area of your life. However, you need to proceed carefully to avoid being ambushed or blindsided, especially by malicious coworkers, friends or enemies. If you are hit by a paintball, then it symbolizes a minor setback. Also consider the color of the paint for clues on your emotions.

To dream of stalking someone in paintball, signifies your eagerness to tackle a challenge.

If you are being stalked in paintball, then it symbolizes hidden dangers.

Painting

To dream that you are painting your house, indicates that you will experience success in a new project. You may even be promoted to a coveted position. You may be expressing your creativity. Alternatively, the dream indicates that you are covering up something. If someone else is painting your house, then it suggests that someone close to you is hiding something from you. Also consider the color of the paint to determine any additional significance. For example, red colored paint may imply painting the town red and releasing pent up excitement.

To dream that paint has gotten on your clothes, signifies that you are too easily offended by criticism about you.

To see a painting in your dream, represents creativity and your need for self-expression. The painting is symbolic of your intuition and inner realizations.

To dream that you are painting a picture, indicates that you need to express your creative side more.

Pajamas

To see or wear pajamas in your dream, suggests that you need to relax and get some rest. In particular, if you dream that you are wearing pajamas in public, then it means that you are unaware of something important that may be right in front of you. You are drifting through life without fully paying attention to what is going on around you.

Palm Reading

To dream that you are having your palms read, represent your life goals and ambition. The dream shows how you want to live your life and where you want to be headed.

Palm Tree

To see a palm tree in your dream, represents tranquility, high aspirations, fame, victory, hopes, and longevity. It also symbolizes paradise and leisure. Perhaps you need to take time for a vacation and relaxation.

Pan

To see a pan in your dream, refers to your attitude and your stance on a particular situation. It may also represent criticism and anger. If the pan is made of glass, then it means that you being conscious and aware about a particular situation. You are also opening yourself up to criticism. As a receptacle, it symbolizes the womb.

To see a frying pan in your dream, represents completeness in love. Alternatively, it suggests that you need to start accepting the consequences of your actions. You may have found yourself in an inescapable situation.

Panda

To see a panda in your dream, suggests that you are having difficulties coming to a compromise in a waking situation. You need to find a middle ground so that all parties involved will be satisfied. Alternatively, a panda is symbolic of your own childlike qualities or something that is cuddly.

Pansy

To see a pansy in your dream, symbolizes undying and never ending love. It may also mean thoughtfulness, remembrance and nobility of the mind. Alternatively, it suggests that you are being too gullible. Or that you are not standing up for yourself.

Panther

To see a panther in your dream, signifies lurking danger and enemies working to do you harm. It represents darkness, death, and rebirth. On a more positive note, panthers signify power, beauty and/or grace. Consider the feel of your dream to determine which meaning applies.

Pants

To see or wear pants in your dream, suggest that you are questioning your role in some situation. Consider the material and color of the pants for additional interpretation. Alternatively, the dream may be hinting at some sexual matter.

To dream that you are wearing velvet pants, signifies your sensual side.

Pantyhose

To see or wear a pantyhose in your dream, represents alluring sexuality. Consider the color of the pantyhose. If it is nude or beige color, then it signifies your discreteness. If it is black, then it symbolizes your hidden sexuality waiting to be expressed. If it is red, then it represents overt sexuality. If the pantyhose is torn or have a run, then it indicates lacking self esteem and reduced self confidence.

Papaya

To see or eat papaya in your dream, indicates a healthy sex drive.

Paper

To see blank white paper in your dream, signifies your desire to make a fresh start in your life. You need to express yourself through writing or art. Alternatively, blank paper indicates that you need to work on being more communicative.

To see a stack of papers in your dream, denotes overwhelming responsibilities and stress that you are having to cope with. You are not effectively dealing with the issues at hand.

Paperclip

To see or use a paper clip in your dream, indicates that you are trying to hold together a relationship. Alternatively, a paperclip means that you need to organize certain aspects of your life.

Paparazzi

To dream that you are being chased or stalked by the paparazzi, indicates that your privacy is being violated. You feel that your own identity is lost. Alternatively, the dream represents your aspirations for fame.

To dream that you are a paparazzo, suggests that you chasing and seeking fame.

To see the paparazzi in your dream, represents your need to focus in on a particular situation. You are trying to capture some idea or concept.

Parachute

To dream that you are in a parachute, represents a protective force over you. You have a sense of security. Alternatively, the dream implies that it is time to bail out of a situation or abandon an old idea or habit.

To dream that you have difficulties with a parachute or that the parachute does not open, suggests that you are let down by someone you relied on and trusted. You feel abandoned.

Parade

To dream that you are watching a parade, indicates that you are being sidetracked or distracted from achieving your goals. You may even be purposely preventing yourself from pursuing your goals and desires because you fear that you will fail. Alternatively, the parade symbolizes cycles, passage of time, or a special event in your life. Consider also the symbolism of whatever figures/animals/floats are in the parade. They may reflect a need for you to incorporate these attributes into your own character.

To dream that you are in a parade, indicates that you are going along with the masses and with what everybody else wants. Alternatively, the dream indicates that you have a set path in life and know which direction you want to go.

Paralyzed

To dream that you are paralyzed, reflects the current state of your body while you are dreaming. During the REM state of sleep, your body is really immobile and paralyzed. People report that they cannot run or hit, despite how hard they try.

Symbolically, dreaming that you are paralyzed means you are feeling helpless or pinned down in some aspects or circumstances of your waking life. You may feel unable to deal with a situation or change anything. Alternatively, the dream suggests that you are feeling emotionally paralyzed. You have difficulties expressing your feelings.

Parasite

To see a parasite in your dream, suggests that you are feeling physically drained. You are becoming too dependent on others and experiencing a significant lost of vitality. Alternatively, a parasite refers to your tendency of taking without giving back.

Parents

To see your parents in your dream, symbolize both power, shelter, and love. You may be expressing your concerns and worries about your own parents. Alternatively, it represents the merging of the female and male aspects of your character.

To dream about the death of your parents, indicates that you are undergoing a significant change in your waking life. Your relationship with your parents has evolved into a new realm.

*See _Father_ and _Mother_.

Park

To dream that you are at a park, represents a temporary escape from reality. It indicates renewal, meditation, and spirituality. You may be undergoing a readjustment period after experiencing some serious personal conflict or an end to a passionate affair.

To dream that you are lost in a park, indicates your struggles with your career, relationship, or other problem. You may feel alienated by society.

To dream that you are parking your car, represents your desire to settle down. Alternatively, it means that you feel accomplished in your goals and satisfied with your life. If you have difficulty parking the car, then it means that you are in some sort of a rut. You are feeling restless. Perhaps you wished you had taken a different path in your life.

To dream that you parked your car in a non-parking zone, suggests that you are poking your head in places where you do not belong. If you forgot where you parked, then it indicates that you have lost your direction in life. You are going off track.

Parking Lot

To dream that you are in parking lot, suggests that you need to slow down and take time from your daily activities.

To dream that you cannot find a parking space, indicates your inability to find your place in life. You may still be searching for your niche. Alternatively, the dream may reflect your busy life and the lack of time you have.

Parking Ticket

To dream that you are getting a parking ticket, suggests that you are feeling lost and not knowing what you want to do with your life. You feel that you are being judged and criticized for the path you want to take. The dream may also be analogous to your lack of accomplishments or to the setbacks in your life.

Parkour

To dream that you are performing a parkour move, indicates that you are not letting any obstacles stand in your way of your goals. Alternatively, the dream means that you are in tune with your surroundings and environment. You are able to adapt to any situation.

To see someone performing parkour in your dream, suggests that you need to be more flexible and efficient with how your manage your time.

Parrot

To see a parrot in your dream, represents some message or gossip that is being conveyed to you. You need to think twice about repeating or sharing certain information. Alternatively, the parrot can denote a person in your waking life who is eccentric or obnoxious. It may also mean that you or someone is being repetitive or even mocking you.

Party

To dream that you are at a party, suggests that you need to get out more and enjoy yourself. If the party is a bad one, then it indicates that you are unsure of your social skills. If you dream that you are at your own birthday party, then it represents appreciation of the life you have.

Passport

To see a passport in your dream, represents your identity and your ability to traverse through various situations. You are experiencing new found freedom to do what you want and go where you want. You may be going through a period of self-discovery.

To dream that you lose your passport, indicates that you are trying to find yourself and get a sense of who you are. Alternatively, the dream means that opportunities are closing off to you.

To dream that your passport is getting stamped, represents approval. You are given the green light to go ahead with a new project or journey.

Password

To see a password in your dream, represents access and control. You hold the key to unlocking your inner feelings and emotions. Analyze the letters and/or numbers within the password for additional significance. It could be a hidden message.

To dream that you forget your password, indicates a loss of control in some aspect of your waking life.

Past

To dream of the past, suggests that a current waking situation is paralleling a past situation. You need to learn from the past and not make the same mistake again. Alternatively, the dream may represent unresolved issues from the past. Or that you need to stop living in the past and look forward toward the future.

Pasta

To make or eat pasta in your dream, represents your need for energy. Also consider the shape of the pasta and how it relates to a waking situation. Penne signifies your narrow perspective. Spaghetti noodles symbolize an entangling situation. Elbow shaped pasta represents your need to focus on yourself more. And corkscrew pasta means that some aspect of your life is out of control.

Pastel

To dream of pastel colors, indicate that you are not fully recognizing and dealing with some part of your emotions. There is some ambiguity in your life.

Patient

To dream that you are a patient, suggests that you are going through a healing process. Alternatively, this dream may be a pun on your need for patience. Remember that good things come to those who wait.

Pawnshop

To see or be in a pawnshop in your dream, suggests that you are depleting your resources, either physically, spiritually or emotionally. You need to be more careful with how you are allocating these resources or risk spreading yourself too thin and ending up with nothing. Alternatively, the dream indicates that you are not really dealing with your problems in the best of way.

Paycheck

To see your paycheck in your dream, symbolizes the results of your hard work and the fruits of your labor. It is an indication of your level of confidence and strength. The dream also serves as encouragement and motivation for you to continue working hard. You will be rewarded for your efforts. Consider the amount on the check. If it is higher than expected, then it means that you are being well rewarded. If it is lower than expected, then you are being undervalued. It may also refer to money worries and your concerns about making ends meet. Perhaps you are lacking confidence and suffering from low self-esteem. You are unsure about your work performance.

PE

To dream that you are in PE class, indicates that you need to lay a better foundation for a healthier lifestyle. Your own personal experiences in PE class will play significantly in the interpretation of the dream. Something in your waking life maybe causing you to flashback to your experiences in PE. Alternatively, the dream suggests that you need to be more of a team player. Learn to work together.

Peach

To see a peach in your dream, represents pleasure and joy. You take pleasure in the simple things in life. The dream may also imply that something in your life is just "peachy" and going well. Alternatively, a peach may be indicative of virginity, lust and sensuality. Consider how it may be a metaphor for your sweetheart or loved one.

Peach is the color of innocent love intermixed with wisdom. It also implies your caring nature and how you tend to the needs of others. Alternatively, the dream may imply that things are "peachy" for you.

Peacock

To see a peacock in your dream, represents spring, birth, new growth, longevity, and love. It is a good omen, signaling prestige, success and contentment in your relationship or career. Alternatively, the peacock signifies pride, confidence and vanity. You may be showing off too much or are overly arrogant with your success and achievements. A peacock may also suggest that many eyes are watching you.

Peanut Butter

To see or eat peanut butter in your dream, suggests that you are having difficulties communicating your thoughts and ideas. It may also indicate a misunderstanding; your words are coming out all wrong.

Peanuts

To see or eat peanuts in your dream, symbolize the need to get to the truth or core of something. You may also need to start pushing yourself and utilizing your full potential. The peanuts in your dream may be a metaphor for money and what little you have of it. Are you experiencing financial difficulties?

Pear

To see a pear in your dream, symbolizes the womb and fertility. Thus, it may refer to some female in your life. It is also often associated with the Virgin Mary. The dream may also be a pun on a "pair" of something.

To see a pear tree in your dream, represents new opportunities.

Pearl

To see pearls in your dream, symbolize the human soul, inner beauty, perfection, purity and chastity. Alternatively, it represents tears and sadness.

To see a string of pearls in your dream, represents conformity and sameness.

To see a black pearl in your dream, denotes bad luck. There is a flaw in your thinking.

Peas

To see peas in your dream, symbolize some minor problems and annoyances that are continually bothering you.

Pedicure

To dream that you are getting a pedicure, indicates that you are moving in the right direction. You are progressing through life with great confidence, poise and integrity. Perhaps you are also seeking for some recognition for your progress. Alternatively, the dream represents your need to be pampered. You need to kick off your shoes, sit back and relax.

Pee

Please See Urination.

Pelican

To see a pelican in your dream, represents nurturance, sacrifice, and charity. It indicates your selflessness and how you put others first before yourself. You are always caring for others.

Pen

To see a pen in your dream, signifies self-expression and communication. Consider also the phrase of how the pen is mightier than the sword.

Pencil

To see a pencil in your dream, indicates that you are making a temporary impact in a situation. It may also suggest that a relationship will not last long.

To dream that you are sharpening a pencil, suggests that you need to be more flexible in your way of thinking. Listen to what others have to say; don't be so quick to reject their views and opinions. Alternatively, to sharpen a pencil means that you need to make your best offer in some business deal. Perhaps the dream is trying to offer you some professional advice on how to close a deal.

Pendulum

To see the back and forth swinging of a pendulum, suggests that you are experiencing some difficulties or confusion in making an important choice in your life. You are afraid of change. People around you are anxiously awaiting your decision.

Penguin

To see a penguin in your dream, signifies that your problems are not as serious as you may think. It serves as a reminder for you to keep your cool and remain level-headed. Alternatively, seeing a penguin in your dream suggests that you are being weighed down by your emotions or by a negative situation. You need to find some balance and inner harmony.

Penis

To see a penis in your dream, signifies sexual energy, power, aggression, and fertility. To see an exceptionally large penis, suggests doubts and anxieties about your sexual drive and libido.

Penny

To see a penny in your dream, indicates your fears of poverty or financial loss. Alternatively, the dream is often connected with your talents, energies, and perseverance. Do not underestimate your ability. If the penny is shiny, then it signifies luck.

To find a penny in your dream, suggests that you are discovering your hidden talents and are ready to unleash your potential. Consider the common phrase "a penny saved is a penny earned" and how the dream may be telling you to save money.

Pentagram

To see a pentagram in your dream, represents humanity and protection.

The five points of the pentagram symbolize the connection of your spirit to the earth, air, fire, and water. These elements contribute to various aspect of your well-being. It signifies protection.

To see an inverted pentagram (where the point is facing downward), signifies conflict, negativity and aggression. It is often associated with Satanism and evil. Are you feeling guilty about something? Alternatively, it represents the physical world and your preoccupation with materialistic gains.

People

To see people you know in your dream, signifies qualities and feelings of them that you desire for yourself. If these people are from your past, then the dream refers to your shadow and other unacknowledged aspects of yourself. It may represent a waking situation that is bringing out similar feelings from your past relationships.

To see people you don't know in your dream, denotes hidden aspects of yourself that you need to confront or acknowledge.

Perfume

To dream that you are spraying or wearing perfume, suggests that you are seeking for more pleasure in your life. It is also symbolic of your sexuality, sensuality, and indulgence.

To smell perfume in your dream, represents memories and nostalgia. You are reminiscing about the past.

Perm

To dream that that you are getting a perm, signifies a change in your outlook and way of thinking. You need to start to look at things from another point of view. Alternatively, the dream may be a metaphor for some "permanent" change in your life. .

Persimmon

To see or eat a persimmon in your dream, symbolizes joy, glory and victory.

Person

*Please refer to the type of person, i.e. boy, girl, ex, mother, etc.

Pet Food

To see or buy pet food in your dream, represents the development of some skill. Remember that it takes time and effort to hone and improve your skill. If you are feeding pet food to a pet in your dream, then it refers to disloyalty in some area of your life.

To eat pet food in your dream, suggests that you need to address some animalistic or primitive thoughts.

Peter Pan

To see Peter Pan in your dream, represents your desires to escape from your daily burdens. You want to retreat back to a time where you were free of any responsibilities, deadlines, or problems. Alternatively, the dream may be a variation of a flying dream. Perhaps, you need to look at things from a different perspective.

Pets

To see a pet in your dream, represents civilized instincts. You are keeping your temper in line. Alternatively, seeing a pet indicates a need for love and acceptance. Perhaps, you are lacking attention from others and are feeling neglected. The pet may also be a pun for "petting" as in some sexual behavior.

To dream of a dead pet, suggests that something that you had thought was left in the past is coming back to haunt you. Similarly to seeing your childhood home, a past pet serves the same function as trying to bring you back into that particular time period. A situation in your waking life may parallel a situation from your past and the dream is providing a means of resolving it.

Phone

Please See Telephone.

Phone Number

To see a phone number in your dream, suggests that you need to make contact with someone and reach out for help.

To dream that you cannot remember or find a phone number, means that you need to start being more independent and responsible.

To dream that you cannot dial a phone number correctly, suggests that you are having difficulties in getting through to someone in your waking life. Consider whose phone number you are trying to dial. Perhaps he or she is not taking your advice or listening to what you have to say. The message is not getting through.

To dream that you are giving someone your telephone number, means that you need to take the initiative and reach out to others. You need to make the first move.

Photo Album

To dream that you are looking through a photo album, suggests that you are unwilling to let go of your memories and the past. You are idealizing about the past.

Piano

To dream that you are playing a piano, indicates a quest for harmony in your life. Consider where the piano is placed as a clue as to what aspect of your life needs accordance.

To dream that you hear the sound of a piano, suggests harmony in your life. You are pleased with the way your life is going.

To dream that the piano needs to be tuned, indicates some aspect of your life is in discord. You need to devote more time to a relationship, family duties, project, or other situation.

Pickle

To see or eat a pickle in your dream, signifies some anxiety and fear of coming trouble. Alternatively, a pickle may be seen as a symbol for the penis. Sexual messages from the unconscious are usually disguised in symbols.

Pick-up Truck

To see a pick-up truck in your dream, represents hard work. You need to return to the basics. Alternatively, the dream may be a metaphor for something that you need to "pick up".

Pickpocket

To dream that someone picks your pocket, suggests that you are reluctant in sharing your ideas with others for fear that they will get the credit.

To dream that you are a pickpocket, indicates that you are willing to go to any lengths in order to get the information you need.

Picnic

To dream that you are at a picnic, signifies a joyful and tranquil domestic life. You prefer the simpler things in life.

To see a picnic basket in your dream, indicates an opportunity to share your ideas and opinions with others. You are receptive to different viewpoints.

Picture

To see a picture in your dream, symbolizes a mental imprint that remains persistent in your mind. Your actions are irreversible. There is no turning back in what you do. Also consider the pun on "picture this" or "seeing the big picture" in a situation. In particular, if the picture is in black and white picture, then it indicates that you need to consider opposing viewpoints. Alternatively, it may mean that you need to add more color and pizzazz to your life.

To dream that you are hanging a picture, represents acceptance the image that is depicted in the picture. You have come to an understanding or compromise regarding the situation.

To dream that you are taking a picture, suggests that you need to focus more attention to some situation or relationship. Perhaps, you feel that you need to recapture some past moments in a relationship. Alternatively, taking a picture refers to your desires to hold onto a certain moment in your life.

To see a blurry picture in your dream, suggests that your memory of the depicted event, incident, or people, is fading. Perhaps you need to let go of the past and stop holding on to what was and concentrate on what is. On the other hand, you are attempting to disguise a situation and refusing to see it as it really is. You need to learn acceptance.

Pie

To see a pie in your dream, symbolizes the rewards of your hard work. Perhaps you are reaching beyond your abilities. Alternatively, the pie may also have the same meaning as a circle. Or the pie indicates sharing and getting your fair share, as in your "piece of the pie".

Piercing

To dream that you are getting your tongue or lip pierced, refers to regret over some stinging remarks and hurtful words that you said.

To dream that you or someone is getting their eyebrow pierced, may be a metaphor for your "piercing eyes". Alternatively, the dream is drawing your attention to something disturbing or significant that you saw. Perhaps you saw something you that shouldn't have.

To dream that you or someone has a navel piercing, denotes your deep connection with your mother. Perhaps the dream is telling you to reconnect with your mother. Or that you need to be more in tune with your maternal instincts.

To dream that you are getting your ears pierced, represents some stinging remarks or insults.

Less symbolically, dreams of getting pierced, may just be your waking desire or anxiety on getting pierced.

Pig

To see a pig in your dream, symbolizes dirtiness, greediness, stubbornness or selfishness. Alternatively, the pig may represent gluttony, opulence and overindulgence. Perhaps it refers to someone who is dirty or someone who is chauvinistic.

If you like pigs and think that pigs are cute, then your dream about a fat dirty pig represents your misconceptions about certain things. What you believe and what is reality may be two different things. This pig may be analogous to a relationship or a man in your life. You think that the pig will be a certain way, but in actuality reality is not at all what you had imagined.

Pigeon

To see a pigeon in your dream, suggests that you are taking the blame for the actions of others. Pigeons also represent gossip or news. Perhaps the pigeon refers to a message from your unconscious. Alternatively, the dream may be expressing a desire to return home.

Piggyback

To dream that you are giving someone a piggyback ride, symbolizes your supportive role. You literally feel that you are carrying the weight of others. Perhaps you are feeling overwhelmed of being the responsible or dependent one.

To dream that you are riding piggyback on someone, represents your lack of power or control in a situation. You are just going along with whatever decisions are being made. Alternatively, being on piggyback points to issues of codependency.

Pillow

To see a pillow in your dream, represents comfort. relaxation, ease, and/or luxury. You need to take it easy on yourself. Alternatively, the dream indicates laziness.

To dream that you are lying on a pillow, suggests that you are in need of some mental support. Perhaps there is a situation or matter that you need to "cushion" and soften the blow.

To dream that your pillow is gone, indicates that you are in self-denial.

Pilot

To dream that you are a pilot, indicates that you are in complete control of your destination in life. You are confident and self-assured in your decisions and accomplishments.

Pimples

To dream that you have a pimple, relates to issues about your self-esteem and self-image. You are feeling awkward or out of place in some situation or relationship.

To dream that you are popping a pimple, indicates that some negative emotion needs to be expressed and acknowledge. These emotions that you are holding back are on the verge of erupting.

Pin

To dream that you are pricked by a pin, signifies a sticky situation or relationship that is falling apart or that is unstable. You may be feeling anxious or feeling the need to hold together a particular relationship. Consider the pun of someone who may be a "prick".

Alternatively, to see pins in your dream refer to feeling of being trapped or immobilized, as exemplified by the phrase "being pinned down".

Piñata

To see a piñata in your dream, symbolizes joy, celebration and festivities. If you smashed open the piñata, then it suggests that you will be well rewarded for your tenacity, drive and hard work. If you are unable to hit the piñata, then it indicates that you are experiencing difficulties toward success, even though it may be seemingly within reach. Perhaps you have a self-defeatist attitude. You need to believe in yourself and in your abilities.

To dream that insects are inside the piñata, indicates that you have been mislead. Perhaps someone in your life has not delivered on their promise. The dream could also be telling you that some offer may be too good to be true. Don't take it!

Pinball

To see a pinball machine or dream that you are playing pinball, suggests that with patience, control, and precision, you will succeed in your goals. Something that may look risky or challenging at first can be tackled if you break it down.

Pink

Pink represents love, joy, sweetness, happiness, affection and kindness. Being in love or healing through love is also implied with this color. Alternatively, the color implies immaturity or weakness, especially when it comes to love. Consider also the notion of getting "pink slipped". Pink is also the color for Breast Cancer Awareness.

If you dislike the color pink, then it may stem from issues of dependency or problems with your parents.

Pinwheel

To see or play with a pinwheel in your dream, suggests that you will succeed on your own power and your creative energy. Alternatively, a pinwheel symbolizes childhood and your carefree nature. Consider the color(s) of the pinwheel.

Pinch

To dream that someone is pinching you, suggests that you need a reality check. Perhaps your goals or ideals are too lofty. Alternatively, the dream indicates that things are going smoothly for you. You may even feel that something is too good to be true.

Pineapple

To see a pineapple in your dream, represents self-confidence, ambition and success. You are self-assured in what you do. Alternatively, the pineapples symbolize hospitality. Or perhaps you need to relax or take a vacation.

To eat a pineapple, indicates sexual problems and issues of losing control.

Pinecone

To see a pinecone in your dream, symbolizes wealth and good fortune. Alternatively, a pinecone represents life and fertility. The dream could also be a pun on "pining" for something or someone.

Pinocchio

To see Pinocchio in your dream, suggests that you or someone are not being truthful in some situation.

Pipe

To see a water pipe in your dream, indicates that you are open and receptive to new ideas. It may also represent your connections to those around you. You are able to steer something toward an direction.

To dream that you are inside a pipe, represents your narrow vision and your seemingly lack of options. Perhaps the dream is telling you to look at things from a different angle.

To dream that you are smoking a pipe, denotes knowledge or contemplation. Alternatively, it symbolizes comfort, relaxation, contentment and satisfaction with your waking life. If someone in your life smokes a pipe, then the dream symbol may serve as a reminder of him or her.

Pirate

To see a pirate in your dream, signifies that some person or situation is adding chaos to your emotional life. You feel that someone has violated your integrity or creativity. Alternatively, the pirate may symbolize freedom, risk, and adventure. You want to explore new adventures and take riskier ventures.

To dream that you are a pirate, suggests that you are taking advantage of others. The dream may be a metaphor that you are "pirating" something and taking something that does not rightfully belong to you.

Pisces

To dream that someone is a Pisces, indicates your sensitivity, imagination, compassion and sympathy for others. It suggests that you are ready to make certain sacrifices for what you believe in. Alternatively, the dream may reflect your inability to change who you are.

Piss

*Please See Urination.

Pizza

To see or eat pizza in your dream, represents abundance, choices, and variety. It may also indicate that you are lacking or feeling deprived of something. Alternatively, a pizza may have similar significance to a circle.

Planet

To see a planet in your dream, signifies creativity, exploration, and new adventures. You are trying to align yourself with untapped energies that you never knew you had. Alternatively, to dream of planets, suggests that you are trying to escape from your own waking reality. *Look up the specific planet for additional significance.*

Plank

To dream that you are walking the plank, suggests you are feeling emotionally vulnerable. You are plunging into new emotional territory.

To see a wooden plank, indicates something that is in need of repair or that you need to maximize your resources and make something out of seemingly nothing.

Plants

To see plants in your dream, indicate fertility, spiritual development, potential, and growth. Alternatively, the appearance of plants in your dream reflect your caring and loving nature. If you are estranged from your children, then the plants can be seen as representative for your children.

In particular, to see indoor plants in your dream, suggest that your growth is being hindered or slowed in some way. You are experiencing a lack of independence. Alternatively, the dream signifies your desire to be closer to nature.

To see droopy, withered or dead plants in your dream, suggest that you are at a standstill in your life. You are lacking initiative.

Plastic

To see plastic objects in your dream, suggests that you are being fake, artificial and/or insensitive in some way. You are not being genuine and true to yourself. Alternatively, it signifies flexibility in your way of thinking.

Platinum

To see platinum in your dream, symbolizes success, prosperity and wealth. Your achievements and accomplishments are attributed to your determination and drive. Do not ever believe that your goals are unattainable. Alternatively, the platinum represents coldness and toughness to your exterior persona.

Platypus

To see a platypus in your dream, refers to your tendency to wallow and dwell on your emotions. It may also suggest that your repressed thoughts and unconscious materials are slowly coming to the surface and making its presence known. Alternatively, a platypus is indicative of shyness and reservation, especially in social situations.

Play

To dream that you are playing, refers to your tendency to go against the norm and break the rules of convention. You are displaying unrestricted creativity. Alternatively, playing implies that you are all work and no play. You need to relax and let loose. On the other hand, the dream may also be saying that you are not taking things seriously enough. You need to face reality.

To dream that you are in a play, represents the roles you play in your life and the various acts and personas you put on. If you are watching the play, then it suggests that you need to draw from the inspiration of others.

Playpen

To see a playpen in your dream, suggests that you need to make time for leisure and
pleasure. Alternatively, the dream refers to your immature actions and behavior.

Pliers

To see a pair of pliers in your dream, suggests that you need to draw out all the details of a situation before you make a decision about it. Alternatively, the dream means that you need to rid yourself of something from your life.

Plug

To see a plug in your dream, represents power, potential and untapped energies. You need to draw from within in order to move forward. Alternatively, the dream may be a pun that you need to stay "plugged in" about some information or news. There is something that you need to be aware of.

Plum

To see or eat a plum in your dream, symbolizes youth and vitality. The plum may also represent you self-image and the way you feel about your body. Perhaps the dream is a pun on being "plump".

To see a plum tree in your dream, represents youth, vitality, and innocence. The dream also indicates that you will overcome some difficulties.

Plunger

To see a plunger in your dream, suggests that you need to force yourself to confront certain emotions. It is hindering your progress and preventing you from moving forward in your life.

Pluto

To see Pluto in your dream, symbolizes death and destruction. You are undergoing a rebirth an a transformation. Your hidden potential will also be unveiled.

Pocket

To see a pocket in your dream, represents your hidden talents and undeveloped abilities. You are not utilizing your strengths to the fullest potential. Did you find anything in the pocket? Consider the significance of what is inside the pocket. If the pocket is empty, then it symbolizes the womb and your desire to isolate yourself from others. Alternatively, a pocket symbolizes secrets. If there is a hole in the pocket, then it implies that your resources or abilities are being drained.

Pogo Stick

To see or play with a pogo stick in your dream, represents life's ups and downs. If you do not have control of your pogo stick, then it indicates that you are all over the place in your emotions and thinking. You need to focus and zero in on one issue at a time. Alternatively, being on a pogo stick may be analogous to sex.

Pointing

To dream that you are pointing at someone or something, indicates that you need to pay more attention to that particular person or object. The dream may be showing you the way to solving a problem in your waking life.

To dream someone is pointing at you, suggests feelings of self guilt or even shame. You are being accused of some wrongdoing.

Poison

To see poison in your dream, denotes that you need to get rid of something in your life that is causing you much sickness and distress. You need to cleanse and purge away the negativity in your life.

To dream that you ingest poison, indicates that you are introducing something into yourself that is harmful to your well-being. This may be feelings of bitterness, jealousy or other negative feelings that are consuming you.

Poker

To dream that you are playing poker, suggests that a situation in your waking life requires strategy and careful planning. You need to think things through before carrying out your actions. Alternatively, the dream may also be a pun on "poke her". Are you trying to get a girl's attention?

Pole Dancing

To dream that you are pole dancing, symbolizes your sexual expression. You need to be more open and expressive with your sexuality. The pole is a phallic symbol. Thus the dream may be analogous to some that you have wrapped around your finger.

Police

To see the police in your dream, symbolizes structure, rules, power, authority and control. You need to put an end to your reckless behavior or else the law will catch up to you. Alternatively, the dream refers to failure in honoring your obligation and commitments.

To dream that you are arrested by the police, suggests that you feel sexually or emotionally restrained because of guilt. The dream may also be a metaphor that you are feeling apprehensive about something.

To dream that you are a police officer, represents your own sense of morality and conscience. The dream may serve to guide you down a straight path. If you have recurring dreams that you are a police officer, then it may mean that your past actions are leaving you with guilt. Consider your behavior and actions as the cop. If your dream that you are in pursuit of a suspect, then it indicates that your naughty and devious side is in conflict with your moral standards.

To dream that you are having difficulties contacting the police, suggests that you have yet to acknowledge your own authoritativeness in a situation. You need to take control and be in command of the direction of your life.

To dream that you are pulled over by the police, suggests that you need to slow down and take things down a notch.

Pomegranate

To see a pomegranate in your dream, signifies fertility, good health, life and longevity. The allure and invitation of sex is also indicated. Alternatively, it represents blood.

Pompoms

To see pompoms in your dream, symbolize the spirit of competition. The dream is offering you motivation and encouragement to proceed with some endeavor. You need to forge ahead. Alternatively, to see pompoms waving in your dream, indicate that you are moving forward in the right direction. Keep doing what you're doing.

Pool

To see a pool of water in your dream, indicates that you need to acknowledge and understand your feelings. It is time to dive in and deal with those emotions. Alternatively, a pool indicates your desire to be cleansed. You need to wash away the past.

To dream that you are playing or shooting pool, represents your competitive nature. You need to learn to win or lose gracefully. Alternatively, shooting pool means that you need to concentrate harder on a problem in your waking life.

Pool Table

To see a pool table in your dream, suggests that you need to show more cooperation. Perhaps you need to "pool" your efforts together.

Poor

To dream that you are poor, refers to feelings of inadequacies. You are not utilizing your full potential or are underestimating your self-worth. Alternatively, to dream that you are poor symbolizes neglect of your sexual nature. You may be taking on too many responsibilities and working too hard that you are not catering to your sexual self.

Popcorn

To eat or make popcorn in your dream, suggests positive growth. You are full of ideas. Some important fact or truth is being made aware to you through the dream. If the popcorn is unpopped, then it symbolizes potential.

Pope

To see a pope in your dream, represents your spiritual guidance, beliefs, and spiritual self. The dream serves to be an inspiration. Alternatively, it may indicate your own self-righteousness, narrow-mindedness, and holier-than-thou attitudes.

Popeye

To see Popeye in your dream, indicates that you have overstepped your boundaries. Perhaps you are forcing your opinions or beliefs on others.

Popular

To dream that you are popular, signifies your desires to be liked and recognized. You want others to look up to you. Alternatively, the dream represents your insecurities. You are looking for some reaffirmation, encouragement and approval from others.

Porch

To dream of a porch, represents your personality, your social self, your facade and how you portray yourself to others. Consider the condition and size of the porch. In particular to dream of an enclosed porch, suggests of your tendency to distance yourself from others and your desires for privacy. If the porch is open, then it signifies your outgoing nature and welcoming attitude.

Porcupine

To see a porcupine in your dream, suggests that you need to look out for yourself and protect yourself from emotional or psychological harm. Trust and honesty are important qualities. Alternatively, a porcupine indicates that there is a situation which you need to approach with openness. Someone in your waking life may be on the defensive and are not be exposing their vulnerabilities.

Pork

To see or eat pork in your dream, signifies your desire for routine and normalcy. Alternatively, the dream may be a pun on overspending.

Pornography

To dream that you are watching pornography, indicates your issues with intimacy, power, control, and effectiveness. You may be having concerns about your own sexual performance. Alternatively, you are afraid of exposing some aspect of yourself.

To dream that you in a porno film, suggests your desire to be more sexually adventurous. It also implies lust and wish-fulfillment.

Posing

To dream that you are striking a pose, indicates that you are being someone you are not. You are trying to live up to the expectations of others. Perhaps, you are too idealistic. Alternatively, posing means that you are keeping your true self hidden. You are putting up a facade.

Possessed

To dream that you are possessed, represents your state of helplessness. You feel you are not in control of things.

Possum

To see a possum in your dream, indicates that something may not be what it appears to be. You need to dig deeper and look for the hidden meaning of some situation or circumstance.

Pot

To see a pot in your dream, represents your attitudes. The dream may be revealing hidden anger or frustration. You are up to something. Consider also how it may be a reference to marijuana and/or drug use.

To dream that the pot is boiling or bubbling over, suggests that you are filled with enthusiasm, excitement or ideas. Alternatively, a boiling pot indicates that you have more than you can handle. You are feeling overwhelmed with emotions.

Potato

To see potatoes in your dream, represent your earthiness and simplicity. Alternatively, the dream may be a metaphor that you are being a "couch potato". In other words, you are being lazy. Or seeing a potato in your dream may also be a metaphor that some issue is like a "hot potato". A situation is being passed around instead of properly dealt with; nobody wants to handle the issue.

To see or eat mashed potatoes in your dream, suggest that you are experiencing concerns over financial matters.

Potholes

To see a pothole in your dream, represents difficulties and setbacks in achieving your goals. You need to make some changes in how you approach your goals. The dream also indicates that things are not going smoothly for you in some aspect or situation in your waking life.

Power Lines

To see or become entangled in power lines, represents your struggle for power and empowerment. You are experiencing an obstacle toward your career goal or in your relationship.

Poverty

*Please See Poor.

Practice

To dream that you are practicing for a sport or musical instrument, suggests that you are visualizing success of your talent. Dreams can be used as a training ground. Alternatively, the dream signifies your commitment to success and to achieving your goals. It is offering you some encouragement. The dream is also telling you that "practice makes perfect." Don't give up.

Prank

To dream that someone is playing a prank on you, suggests that someone is undermining your ability. Your character is being called to question.

To dream that you are playing a prank on someone, indicates that you need to start taking things more seriously. Stop looking at things as a joke.

Praying

To dream that you are praying, signifies respect, sincerity and humility. You are looking for help from a higher source. You need to relinquish your worries and let go of your old problems. More directly, the dream means that you need to pray more. Alternatively, the dream may be a pun on "preying". Perhaps you are taking advantage of others or that someone is taking advantage of you.

Pregnant

To dream that you are pregnant, symbolizes an aspect of yourself or some aspect of your personal life that is growing and developing. You may not be ready to talk about it or act on it. Being pregnant in your dream may also represent the birth of a new idea, direction, project or goal. Alternatively, if you are trying to get pregnant, then the dream may be a wish fulfillment. If you are not trying to get pregnant, but dream that you are, then it symbolizes fear of new responsibilities.

To dream that you are pregnant with the baby dying inside of you, suggests that a project you had put a lot of effort into is falling apart and slowly deteriorating. Nothing is working out the way you had anticipated.

If you are really pregnant and have this dream, then it represents your anxieties about the pregnancy. If you are in your first trimester of pregnancy, then your dreams tend to be about tiny creatures, fuzzy animals, flowers, fruit and water. In the second trimester, dreams will reflect anxieties about being a good mother and concerns about possible complications with the birth. Dreams of giving birth to a non-human baby are also common during this period of the pregnancy. Finally, in the third trimester, dreams consists of your own mother. As your body changes and grows, dreams of whales, elephants and dinosaurs and other larger animals may also start appearing at this stage of pregnancy.

Please See Also Birth or Belly.

Pregnancy Test

To dream that you are taking a pregnancy test, indicates that you are entering a new phase in your life (a new job, relationship, etc.) You feel that you are being put to the test as to whether you are prepared or ready for these changes. Alternatively, this dream may be literal in meaning and address your anxieties/fears of getting pregnant.

Premonition

To dream of a premonition, signifies growth. Some relationship or situation is evolving or moving into a new phase.

President

To see the president of your country in your dream, symbolizes authority, power and control. Your own personal views and opinions of the president and their actions will also play strongly in the significance of this dream.

To dream that you are running for president, signifies your quest for power. You have set high goals for yourself. Alternatively, the dream indicates your belief that you can do a better job if you were in charge of things. You have a lot of confident in your abilities.

Pretzel

To see a pretzel in your dream, symbolizes devotion, spiritual beliefs and life's sweet rewards. You are embracing life and extending yourself to help others. Alternatively, a pretzel indicates that you are preoccupied with some complex issue and are not sure how to handle it.

Priest

To see a priest in your dream, represents your spiritual needs, sense of morality and religious beliefs. You are looking for guidance. It also symbolizes chastity and abstinence. Perhaps, you are feeling sexually repressed.

To see a dictatorial or condemning priest in your dream, signifies unyielding authority and over-protectiveness. You may feel that you are living under unreasonable rules.

Prime Minister

To see the prime minister of your country in your dream, symbolizes authority, power and control. Your own personal views and opinions of the prime minister and their actions will dominate in the meaning of the dream. Perhaps you are trying to incorporate a decision that the prime minister has made into your own life.

Prince

To dream that you are a prince, suggests that you are feeling important and needed. You may be admiring your own accomplishments.

To see a prince in your dream, signifies your association with honor and prestige. You will be recognized for some task. Alternatively, it indicates your desires for romance. Perhaps you are waiting for your Prince Charming.

Princess

To dream that you are a princess, indicates that you are realizing your full potential. However, there is still more growing that you need to do. It is also a symbol of youth and mental development. Alternatively, the dream may mean that that you are too demanding. Or that you are too use to getting your own way. Perhaps you are acting like a spoiled brat.

To see a princess in your dream, represents the object of your affections or desires.

If you are male and dream of a princess, then it represents your sister or an important female figure in your life. Perhaps you feel you feel that you have come to save the day. It also suggests your desires for the ideal woman.

Principal

To see the principal or dream that you are in the principal's office, indicates feelings of guilt. You are expressing some anxiety over your actions and the fear that you will be exposed. Alternatively, it represents inferiority or low self esteem.

Printer

To see a printer in your dream, suggests that you are trying to express a thought or idea in a way that others can understand.

To dream that the printer is not functioning, indicates your difficulties and frustrations in communicating your thoughts across.

Prison

To dream that you are in prison, indicates that you are being censored in some area of your life. You feel that your creativity is being limited and that you are not allowed to express yourself.

To see someone else in prison in your dream, signifies an aspect of yourself that you are unable to express freely.

To dream that you or someone is released from prison, means that you need to make some major changes in your waking life. Eventually, you will overcome your obstacles

Prisoner

*Please See <u>Convict</u>.

Privacy

To dream that you have no privacy, suggests that you are feeling exposed and unprotected. Perhaps there is something that are you trying to hide. To dream that you have privacy indicates that you are repressing your emotions and not allowing them to be fully expressed. You are worried that others will see the real you and criticize you.

Probation

To dream that you are on probation, suggests that you need to stop putting things off and start confronting the problem at hand. You have had enough time to reflect on your past mistakes. It is time to make amends.

Profanity

*Please See <u>Swearing</u>.

Prom

To dream that you are at a prom, signals an end to something and the beginning of something else. It refers to cycles and the passage of time. Alternatively, the dream may just be about your anticipation of your own upcoming prom in real life.

Proposal

To dream that you are being proposed to, indicates that you are merging a previously unknown aspect of yourself More directly, the dream may mean that you are thinking about marriage or some serious long-term commitment/project/situation. Are you thinking about proposing to someone? Your reaction to the proposal indicates your true feelings about marriage or commitment.

Prosthesis

To dream that you have a prosthesis, indicates that you are exploring a new perspective in life. You are reaching out in a different and profound way. Consider also where on the body the prosthesis is fitted as that body part may offer additional significance. If you have a prosthetic arm, then it means that you are exploring a completely new way of doing something. If you have a prosthetic leg, then it means that you are headed toward a new journey.

Prostitute

To dream that you are a prostitute, indicates your desires for more sexual freedom/expression and sexual power. You want to be less inhibited and explore other areas of sexuality. Perhaps your waking ideology about sex is too rigid. On a negative side, to dream that you are a prostitute suggests that you are harboring feelings of guilt toward a relationship. You are having difficulties integrating love and sexuality. Alternatively, the dream may be a metaphor suggesting that you are "prostituting" yourself in some situation, either emotionally or morally. Are you selling yourself in some way?

To see or dream that you are with a prostitute, suggests that you are feeling sexually deprived or needy. Alternatively, the dream is commenting on how you wished that sexual relationships were more simple and straightforward.

Protest

To dream that you are at a protest, indicates that you need to speak up for yourself and for your rights. Pay attention to the details of your dream as you may be ignoring or overlooking some important issue in your life. It is time to take action.

Psychic

To see a psychic in your dream, represents your desires to know the unknown. You are experiencing anxieties about the future and in achieving your goals. Additionally, you may feel a lack of control in the path that your life is taking.

To dream that you are psychic, represents your intuition and the sensitive side of your personality.

Public Speaking

To dream that you are speaking in public, indicates that you need to vocalize your feelings and thoughts. You need to communicate something important and/or urgent. Alternatively, the dream may highlight your fear and nervousness of speaking in public, especially if you have an upcoming speech to give. Consider the demeanor and behavior of the audience. Perhaps you are afraid of being scrutinized for your actions or being judged by others. It is also a form of an anxiety dream where you are feeling exposed or put on the spot.

To dream that there is no one listening to your speech, suggests that you are not being acknowledged for your work or achievement. Perhaps you are feeling ignored or neglected.

To hear someone speaking in public in your dream, suggests that your inner feelings are being made known to those around you. Consider what is said in the speech. If you hear a politician give a speech, then it represents egotism or deceit.

Pudding

To see or eat pudding in your dream, indicates that you are feeling slow and lethargic in your waking life. You need to be more active. Alternatively, the dream may be telling you that "the proof is in the pudding." You need to learn to question everything. Don't believe everything until you have seen it or experienced it yourself. .

Pulling

To dream that you are pulling something, refers to your burdens and struggles. You have difficulties accomplishing your tasks and goals. You need to unload and/or let go some of your responsibilities.
Perhaps it is a relationship that you need to let go of. Consider also what or who you are pulling.
Alternatively, the dream may be a pun on your "pull" or influence for some favor or decision.

Puke

Please See Vomiting.

Pumpkin

To see a pumpkin in your dream, implies your openness and your receptiveness to new ideas and experiences. A pumpkin is also symbolic of female sexuality. Alternatively, the dream may relate to the popular fairy tale of Cinderella where a carriage turns back into a pumpkin. In this regard, a pumpkin may represent some situation in which time is running out.

Punch

To dream that you are punching someone or something, represents hidden anger and aggression. It may also be a symbol of power and your ability to draw strength from within yourself.

To dream that you are unable to throw a punch, indicates that you are feeling helpless. You may have self-esteem and confidence issues. The dream may also be due to REM paralysis.

To dream that you are drinking punch, represents vitality and renewal.

Puppet

To see a puppet in your dream, suggests that you are easily swayed by others and are allowing them to control you. You feel you can not stand up for yourself.

Purple

Purple is indicative of devotion, healing abilities, loving, kindness, and compassion. It is also the color of royalty, high rank, justice, wealth and dignity.

Purr

To hear a purr in your dream, signifies satisfaction, contentment and comfort in your life. Things are going well for you. The dream may also be a pun on being "pure".

Purse

To see or carry a purse in your dream, represents secrets, desires and thoughts which are being closely held and guarded. It symbolizes your identity and sense of self. Consider also the condition of the purse for indications of your state of mind and feelings. Alternatively, a purse symbolizes the female genitalia and the womb.

To dream that you lost your purse, denotes loss of power and control. You may have lost touch with your real identity. If you find a purse, then it represents a renewed sense of self.

To see an empty purse, represents feelings of insecurity or vulnerability.

Push

To dream that you are pushing something, symbolizes energy, effort, encouragement and motivation. You have a new drive to succeed in life. Consider also how you or someone in your life may be a "pushover".

To dream that you are pushed or being pushed, suggests that you are being coerced into doing something. You are facing a lot of pressure. Alternatively, the dream implies that you do not have enough time to complete a task. You strive for perfection.

Putty

To dream that you are handling putty, represents some situation, person, or relationship that you are still molding and forming. Also consider the phrase "like putty in your hands" to mean how you or someone is being easily influenced.

Puzzle

To see or do a jigsaw puzzle in your dream, represents a mental challenge or problem that you need to solve in your waking life. If there are pieces missing in the puzzle, then it suggest that you do not have all the facts needed to make an informed decision.

To see or do a crossword puzzle in your dream, suggests that you are being faced with a mental challenge. The dream may be a pun on "cross words" directed at you or aimed toward someone.

Pyramid

To see a pyramid in your dream, symbolizes longevity and stability. You have built a solid foundation for success. Alternatively, the dream suggests that major changes will occur over a short period of time.

Q

To see the letter Q in your dream, is a pun on "cue". You are waiting for a sign to make the next move.

Quail

To see a quail in your dream, symbolizes lust, love and eroticism. The dream also suggest that you will overcome your obstacles and hardships. You will be victorious despite the negativity surrounding you in your life.

Quarantine

To dream that you are placed in quarantine, suggests that you need to distance yourself from others or from a situation. You need to alter your actions before you or someone gets hurt.

To dream that someone or something is in quarantine, indicates that someone is in desperate need of your help but is afraid to ask.

Quarter

To see a quarter in your dream, signifies incompleteness. You are not feeling whole.

Queen

To see a queen in your dream, symbolizes intuition, personal growth, power and influence. The queen is also a symbol for your mother.

For a woman to dream that she is a queen, indicates a desire for increased status and power. Alternatively, it may indicate that you need to listen to others. The queen may also be a metaphor for a homosexual man.

Queen of Hearts

To see the queen of hearts in your dream, represents your pompous and arrogant attitude.

Question

To question something in your dream, signifies self doubt. The ability to question things in your dream may also lead to higher knowledge and spiritual enlightenment.

To dream that someone is asking you a question, suggests that you have information or knowledge that needs to be shared.

Queue

Please See Line.

Quicksand

To dream that you are sinking in quicksand, indicates feelings of insecurity. You have misjudged the solid foundation that you are on. Perhaps you have mistakenly gotten too comfortable in some situation. You need to pay attention to what you are doing and where you are going. Alternatively, the dream is analogous to regressing into your unconscious.

Quiet

To dream that it is particularly quiet, indicates that you need to stop and reflect upon life. It is time for introspection and solace. You need some quiet time in order to restore some sanity and spiritual balance.

Quilts

To see a quilt in your dream, signifies harmony, protection, warmth, and pleasant and comfortable circumstances. The dream may be a metaphor for various components in your life that help to make up the overall scenario or big picture. Consider the color and pattern of the quilt for additional significance.

R

To see the letter "R" in your dream, suggests that you are in need of some "R & R" or some rest and relaxation.

Rabbit

To see a rabbit in your dream, signifies luck, magical power, and success. You have a positive outlook on life. Alternatively, rabbits symbolize abundance, warmth, fertility and sexual activity. Perhaps your sex life needs to be kept in check. The dream can also be associated with Easter time and your own personal memories of Easter.

In particular, to see a white rabbit in your dream, symbolizes faithfulness in love. The white rabbit also serves as a guide to steer you toward the right direction.

If the rabbit is hopping in your dream, then it indicates fertility. You will be surrounded by children. Alternatively, the dream may be analogous to your lack of commitment and how you jump from one thing or another.

Raccoon

To see a raccoon in your dream, signifies deceit and thievery. You are not being completely honest in some situation. Alternatively, the dream suggests that you are hiding something. You are keeping a secret.

Race

To dream that you are in a race, represents your competitive spirit and how you tend to measure yourself against others.
Alternatively, this dream may mean that you need to slow down and take a different course in life.

If you dream that you win a race, then it represents your full potential and your ability to achieve your goals. You are feeling empowered and able to overcome your obstacles and those who stand in your way. The dream gives you confidence and may be a "rehearsal" for your success.

If you dream you lose the race, then it indicates that you may be overextending yourself. You are setting your goals too high.

Radar

To see or use a radar in your dream, symbolizes your insight and intuition. The dream may be highlighting a message from your unconscious.

Radio

To dream that you are listening to the radio, symbolizes your awareness and intuition toward a particular situation. What you hear through the radio also represents messages from your unconscious. It is possible that it is some form of ESP or telepathic communication.

If you dream that the radio is turned off, then it indicates that you have the ability to help in some situation, but you are refusing to do so.

Radish

To see or plant radishes in your garden, signify abundance and prosperity.

To dream that you are eating a radish, refers to some indiscretion or thoughtlessness. Perhaps the dream may be a pun on something that is "rad-dish" or coolish.

Raft

To see a raft in your dream, indicates that you have not built a firm foundation for success. There is still much work ahead.

To dream that you are floating on a raft, suggests that you are drifting through life, not knowing where you are headed. You are confused about your purpose and direction in life.

To dream that you are white water rafting, means that you are experiencing some turbulent times.

Railroad

To see a railroad in your dream, indicates that you have laid out a set track toward achieving your goals. Your progress will be slow but steady. You are well disciplined and secure in your life. Alternatively, the dream indicates that you may be too linear and rigid in your thinking. Sometimes you need to go off track and explore other possibilities.

To see an obstruction on the railroad, refers to the obstacles standing in your way toward your goals. It may also mean that you have lost track of your goals.

To dream that you are walking alongside the railroad tracks, signify completion of your tasks.

To dream that you are crossing railroad tracks, indicate that you are going against the path that others have laid out for you. You are doing your own thing and not what others want or expect of you. Alternatively, the dream symbolizes a transitional phase. Consider the phrase of coming/being from "the wrong side of the tracks." Perhaps it signifies the progress you have made. Do not forget about your humble beginnings.

Rain

To see and hear rain falling, symbolizes forgiveness and grace. Falling rain is also a metaphor for tears, crying and sadness. Alternatively, rain symbolizes fertility and renewal. If you get wet from the rain, then it indicates cleaning from your troubles and problems.

To dream that you are watching the rain from a window, indicates that spiritual ideas and insights are being brought to your awareness. It may also symbolize fortune and love.

To hear rain tapping on the roof, denotes spiritual ideas coming to fruition in your mind.

Rainbow

To see a rainbow in your dream, represents hope, success and good fortune in the form of money, prestige, or fame. The rainbow is also seen as a bridge between your earthly, grounded self and the higher, spiritual self. It refers to joy and happiness in your relationship. Alternatively, the rainbow is a symbol for gay pride in the western culture.

To see an all white rainbow in your dream, signifies heightened spirituality and purity.

Raincoat

To dream that you are wearing a raincoat, suggests that you are shielding yourself from your emotions. You are not able to face the nastiness. Alternatively, wearing a raincoat in your dream refers to your pessimistic outlook and unpleasantness.

Raisins

To dream that you are eating raisins, represent some negative force that is working against you. The dream may also be a metaphor for something or someone who is old and shriveled.

Ram

To see a ram in your dream, signifies aggression, energy, and impulsiveness. You may be pursuing a decision that should be approached with more tact and consideration. A ram also symbolizes strong and powerful friends who will use their influence and authority to your advantage.

To dream that a ram is pursuing you, indicates some misfortune or unlucky threat. Perhaps, you feel that something is being "rammed" down your throat or that you feel that you are being rammed by a situation or decision.

Rapping

To hear or dream that you are rapping, suggests that you need to better verbalize your thoughts and feelings.

Rape

To dream that you have been raped, indicates vengeful or resentful feelings toward the opposite sex. You feel that you have been violated or that you have been taken advantage of. Something or someone is jeopardizing your self-esteem and emotional well-being. Things are being forced upon you. Dreams of rape are also common for those who were actually raped in their waking life.

To see a rape being committed in your dream, denotes sexual dysfunction or uncertainty.

Rash

To dream that you have a rash, indicates repressed anger, frustrations and annoyances. You may be holding in your anger and frustrations, instead of expressing it. Alternatively, the dream suggests that others are trying to put doubt in your head about some decision or choice that you are making. It may be a pun on a "rash" decision that you are making. You need to think twice before going through with your choice.

Rats

To see a rat in your dream, signifies feelings of doubts, greed, guilt, unworthiness and envy. You are keeping something to yourself that is eating you up inside. Or you have done something that you are not proud of. Alternatively, a rat denotes repulsion, decay, dirtiness, and even death. The dream may also be a pun on someone who is a rat. Are you feeling betrayed?

In particular, to see a black rat, represents deceit and covert activities. If you see a white rat in your dream, then it means that you will receive help from an unexpected source.

To dream that a rat is biting your feet, is analogous to the rat race that you are experiencing in your waking life.

Rattle

To see or play with a rattle in a dream, signifies joy, tranquility and contentment in the home.

To hear a rattle in your dream, represents some situation or issue that you need to tend to.

Raw

To eat something that is raw, signifies some unexplored or untried experiences. Perhaps you are feeling apprehensive and ill prepared about what is ahead for you. Alternatively, the dream may be a metaphor for your "raw" emotions.

Razor

To see a razor in your dream, suggests that there is a situation or problem that you need to smooth out.

To dream that you are sharpening a razor, indicates that you are ruthless and "cutthroat."

Real Estate

Please See Property.

Reality Show

To dream that you are in a reality show, suggests that you feel your life is under public scrutiny. You feel that someone is criticizing your decisions and actions. The dream may also be a pun that you are in need of a reality check.

Rear Ended

To dream that you have been rear ended, indicates that something from your past is still impacting your present situation. You need to learn from the past in order to move forward.

Rearview Mirror

To dream that you are looking through the rearview mirror, suggests that you are dwelling on the past too much. It may indicate regrets, past hurts or "what ifs". On the other hand, the dream may be telling you not to forget about the past and what you have left behind. You need to maintain a happy median between what is ahead for you in the future and what you left behind in the past.

Rebirth

To dream that you are born again, indicates that you need to deal with issues that you have been avoiding. You may have been given a second chance to regain what was previously thought to be lost. Alternatively, the dream means that you are starting or entering a new stage in your life. You are looking toward the future instead of dwelling on the past.

Some Christians are described as "born again". Thus the dream may also represent your renewed religious faith and commitment.

Recipe

To dream of a recipe, symbolizes your creativity, talents and enjoyment of life. You need to take advantage of life's pleasures. Consider what the recipe is for. Desserts suggest that you need to indulge in life and devote some time to leisure. A recipe for preparing meat represents your desires for physical/emotional satisfaction.

Record

To see or listen to a record in your dream, suggests that you need to consider both sides of a situation before making a decision. You need to be more in tune with your instincts. Maybe there is something that you need to say "on or off the record." Or the dream is telling you that you are going round and round in circles; you are not making any progress in life. Alternatively, a record represents a need for enjoyment and sensual pleasure.

To dream that the record is scratched, may be a pun on how you are "sounding like a broken record". Or the dream may literally mean "breaking a record".

Record Player

To see a record player in your dream, suggests that you are going around in circles over a problem or situation. In other words, you are going nowhere.

To dream that the record player is broken, indicates that you have broken free from a cycle or habit.

Rectangle

To see a rectangle in your dream, represents permanence, materialism and stability. Because of its four corners and four sides, it is also symbolic of the number 4.

Recurring Dream

To have recurring dreams, indicate unresolved issues, unhealthy behavior patterns, or unexpressed emotions in your waking life.

Red

Red is an indication of raw energy, force, vigor, intense passion, aggression, power, courage, impulsiveness and passion. The color red has deep emotional and spiritual connotations. Consider the phrase "seeing red" to denote anger. Alternatively, the color red in your dream indicates a lack of energy. You are feeling tired or lethargic.

Red is also the color of danger, violence, blood, shame, rejection, sexual impulses and urges. Perhaps you need to stop and think about your actions.

Red Carpet

To dream that you are walking on a red carpet, represents your desire to be admired and looked up to. You are seeking validation and acknowledgement for your achievements.

To see the red carpet in your dream, suggests that you are welcoming fun and festivities in your life. You are ready for a celebration.

Red Cross

To see the Red Cross in your dream, suggests that you are in need of spiritual healing. Don't be shy about asking for help when you need it. The Red Cross is also representative of humanitarian work.

Referee

To see a referee in your dream, signifies an inner battle between your own ideals and values and between the ideals and values of others. You are looking for a resolution to some conflict in your daily life.

Refrigerator

To see or open a refrigerator in your dream, represents your chilling personality and/or cold emotions. The dream may also be telling you that you need to put some goal, plan, or situation on hold. Alternatively, a refrigerator signifies that you have accomplished what you have been unconsciously seeking.

To dream that the refrigerator has broken down, suggests that you need to warm up to somebody or some situation. It is time to let go of those harsh, cold feelings.

Reincarnation

To dream that you have reincarnated into someone else, suggests that you are not being yourself. Perhaps you need to incorporate aspects of the dream person into your own character. Alternatively, reincarnating indicates that you are undergoing major changes in your life. If you reincarnated into an animal, then consider the qualities of the specific animal.

Reindeer

To see a reindeer in your dream, symbolizes the holidays, festivities, and the season of giving. Alternatively, a reindeer refers to your sense of loyalty.

Relationships

To dream about your waking relationships, indicate wish-fulfillment. Your dream relationship usually parallels your waking relationships in some way and may be highlighting something that you are doing wrong. In your dream state, you may be more incline to confront issues that you would normally ignore or are afraid of bringing up. Compare your dream relationship with your waking relationship.

To dream about a relationship with a stranger, represents the different sides of your personality. You may be trying to connect to unknown aspects of your unconscious.

Religion

To dream of your religion, represents your faithfulness and sense of spirituality. Perhaps your dream is telling you to be more religious or that you need to be more spiritual. Alternatively, the dream may be a metaphor for some behavior or habit which you are "religious" about.

To dream about a different religion from your own, suggests that you need to incorporate some key component of that religion in your own life. The dream may also mean that you need to be more accepting and tolerant of the differences in humanity. .

Remodeling

To dream that you are remodeling, indicates that you are reevaluating your values and making changes to your belief system. Alternatively, the dream means that you need a change in your life.

Remote Control

To see a remote control in your dream, refers to how your buttons are being pushed by someone. Perhaps a relationship or situation that is too controlling.

Report Card

To see a report card in your dream, symbolizes how you are performing in various aspects of your waking life. You may be questioning your job or your abilities. If you are still in school, then the dream may represent your anxieties about your grades. Also consider the significance of the specific letters or grades on the report card.

Rescue

To dream that you are being rescued or rescue others, represents an aspect of yourself that has been neglected or ignored. You are trying to find a way to express this neglected part of yourself. Alternatively, it symbolizes an unconscious cry for help. Perhaps you are too proud in your waking life to ask for assistance.

In particular, to dream that you rescue someone from drowning, indicates that you have successfully acknowledged certain emotions and characteristics that is symbolized by the drowning victim.

Reservoir

To see a filled reservoir in your dream, symbolizes pent up or repressed emotions. If the reservoir is empty in your dream, then it indicates that you have expended all your energy and emotions on others. You need to focus on yourself for a change.

Restaurant

To dream that you are in a restaurant, suggests that you are feeling overwhelmed by decisions and choices that you need to make in your life. Alternatively, it indicates that you are seeking for emotional nourishment outside of your social support system.

Résumé

To see a résumé in your dream, suggests that you are evaluating your own abilities and performance in some situation. Depending on how you feel about the résumé, it is telling of whether or not you feel you have what it takes for the task at hand.

Retire

To dream of retirement, represents issues you have with getting old. Retirement may also refer to a transition or phase. Alternatively, the dream may be a metaphor for something that you need to "retire" or put to rest.

Reunion

To dream that you are attending a reunion, suggests that there are feelings from the past which you need to acknowledge and recognize. Or perhaps the dream is highlighting how you have already incorporated the certain aspects or qualities of the people in your dream reunion.

Revenge

To dream that you are taking revenge, suggests that you are experiencing some emotional imbalance. You are harboring some repressed emotions.

To dream that someone is taking revenge on you, signifies fear and distrust.

Reverse

*Please See Backward.

Revolution

To dream that you are part of a revolution, suggests that major changes are occurring within yourself. You are experiencing some major emotional turmoil that needs to be confronted and resolved. Alternatively, the dream symbolizes your view of the world and your future.

Rewind

To dream that something is rewinding, represents your desires to turn back time and redo certain things over again. It may denote regrets and remorse. You need to stop living in the past and look toward the future. Alternatively, the dream may be a reminder of where you came from and how you got to be where you are today. Give appreciation to those who have helped you along the way.

Rhinoceros

To see a rhinoceros in your dream, suggests that you need to forge ahead toward your goals. Do not take "no" for an answer or let any obstacles sidetrack you from your destination. You need to be more aggressive.

Rib

To see your ribs in your dream, suggest that you are shielding yourself from heartbreak. In the biblical sense, the rib is symbolic of your spouse.

Ribbon

To see a ribbon in your dream, signifies innocence, playfulness, festivities, frivolity and girliness. Consider the type of ribbon and how it is tied. Also consider the color of the ribbon for additional significance. For example, a blue ribbon is associated with being the best. Pink ribbon is symbolic of breast cancer awareness. Yellow ribbon signifies the pending return of a loved one from the military. And a red ribbon symbolizes AIDS awareness.

Rice

To see grains of rice in your dream, symbolize success, prosperity, luck, fertility and warm friendships.

To dream that you are eating rice, denotes happiness and tranquility in the home.

To dream that you are cooking rice, signifies the new responsibilities that will bring you much joy.

Rich

To dream that you are rich, signifies pride and self confidence. You will experience much success through your perseverance. The dream may also refer to someone named "Rich" or "Richard".

Rifle

*Please See Gun.

Right

To dream of the right side, represents conscious reality, deliberate action and rational thoughts. It may also be a pun on the rightness of an idea, decision, or plan. The dream is telling you that you are doing the right thing or that you are on the right path. Alternatively, the dream may mean that you need to stand up for your "rights". Or it may be a metaphor for your right leaning political views.

Ring

To see or receive a ring in your dream, symbolizes emotional wholeness, continuity, commitments and honor. If the ring is on your finger, then it signifies your commitment to a relationship or to a new endeavor. You are loyal to your ideals, responsibilities, or beliefs.

To see a broken ring in your dream, indicates that your loyalty is called into question. Someone is attacking your sense of loyalty. It also implies disappointments and separation.

To dream that you lose a ring or someone has stolen your ring, represents insecurity. You may be losing interest in some relationship or issue.

Riot

To see or participate in a riot in your dream, suggests that you need to stand up for yourself. You need to speak up and address what is bothering you. Alternatively, the dream signifies a loss to your individuality. You are involved in a situation that is destructive to your well being.

Rip

To rip something in your dream, indicates dissatisfaction with the direction that a project or situation is going. Alternatively, the dream may be a pun on "rip off" or "to rip on someone" as in to insult or bad mouth them. Consider if these scenarios parallel your waking situation.

To see something rip in your dream, suggests that you are overestimating the strength of something. In particular, to dream that your notebook is ripped, means that you lack confidence in your ability to write and convey your thoughts. Perhaps you are having difficulty accepting your flaws and imperfections. Alternatively, the dream may be a metaphor to signify the acronym for "R.I.P."

River

To see a clear and calm river in your dream, indicates that you are just going with the flow. You are allowing your life to float away. It is time to take a more decisive role in directing your life. Alternatively, a river symbolizes joyful pleasures, peace, prosperity and fertility. If you are crossing a river in your dream, then it represents an obstacle or issue that you need to deal with in order to move closer toward your goal. It is also reflective of a new stage in your life. If the river is muddy, then it indicates that you are in turmoil.

To see a raging river in your dream, signifies that your life is feeling out of control. You are feeling emotionally unsettled. Alternatively, a river means you are ready to confront life's challenges and life's twists and turns.

To dream that a river is comprised of flowing red chili, refers to the raw emotion, and intense passion or anger that is flowing through you and yearning to be expressed.

To dream that you are bathing in a river, represents purification and cleansing.

Roaches

*Please See <u>Cockroach</u>.

Road

To see a road in your dream, refers to your sense of direction and how you are pursuing your goals. If the road is winding, curvy, or bumpy in your dream, then it suggests that you will encounter many obstacles and setbacks toward achieving your goals. You may be met with unexpected difficulties. If the road is dark, then it reflects the controversial or more frightening choices which you have made or are making.

If the road is smooth and bordered by trees or flowers, then it denotes a steady progress and steady climb up the social ladder. If the road is straight and narrow, then it means that your path to success is going as planned.

To see an unknown road in your dream, represents a path that has not been ventured. You are setting a new precedence for something.

To dream that a threatening creature is on a road, parallels a hostile situation/person you are encountering in your waking life. It is an obstacle that you need to overcome, no matter how intimidating the situation or person may appear.

Road Rage

To dream that you have road rage, indicates that your emotions are out of control. You feel that someone is out to get you. You need to find a better way to express your feelings or you or someone will get hurt.

Road Signs

To see road signs in your dream, represent some advice and message that your unconscious is trying to convey. The road sign may be trying to guide you toward certain decisions. Consider what the road sign is saying and how you need to apply its message to an aspect of your daily life.

*Please See <u>Stop Sign</u> or <u>U-Turn</u>.

Roadkill

To see roadkill in your dream, represents unavoidable death. The death may be a symbolic death representing an end to a habit, behavior or idea. It is time to let go of old habits and put those ideas to rest, as you are only prolonging the inevitable. Alternatively, roadkill suggests that there is some issue in your past that is hindering your pursuit of your goals.

To dream that an animal is about to become roadkill, indicates loss of control in some aspect of your life. Consider the type of animal that is hit for clues as to what aspect of your life is out of control.

Roadrunner

To see a roadrunner in your dream, represents mental agility. You tend to run toward one idea after

253

another. At the same time, you also have the ability to stop at a moment's notice to consider your next plan of action.

Robot

To see a robot in your dream, indicates that you are going about life in a mechanical, methodical and rigid way. You have lost the ability to express your feelings. Alternatively, a robot symbolize the way you view your working life.

Rocket

To see a rocket in your dream, indicates that your plans or ideas will soon be taking off in a big way. You are experiencing a higher level of awareness. All your hard work is paying off. Alternatively, you feel that things are going too fast. If a rocket is taking off, then it is symbolic of male sexuality.

Rocking Chair

To dream that you or someone is sitting in a rocking chair, signifies a life of ease, comfort and relaxation. You have no worries.

To see an empty rocking chair in your dream, represents sadness or quiet contemplation.

Rocking Horse

To see a rocking horse in your dream, indicates that you are feeling stuck in some area of your life. You are not making any progress toward your goals. Alternatively, a rocking horse may be memories of your childhood.

Rocks

To see a rock in your dream, symbolizes strength, permanence, stability and integrity, as conveyed in the common phrase "as solid as a rock". The dream may also indicate that you are making a commitment to a relationship or that you are contemplating some changes in your life that will lay the groundwork for a more solid foundation. Alternatively, a rock represents stubbornness, disharmony and unhappiness.

To dream that you are climbing a rock, signifies your determination, ambition and struggle. If the rock is particularly steep, then it refers to obstacles and disappointments.

*Please Also See <u>Stones</u>.

Rodeo

To dream that you are at the rodeo, suggests that you need to take control of your animalistic forces and primal urges.

Rogue

To dream that you are going rogue, indicates that you are pushing the limits. You are lacking restraint and control in your life.

Roller Blades

To dream that you are on roller blades, suggests that you are moving rapidly through life with tremendous ease and determination. You are experiencing a sense of liberation and freedom.

Roller Coaster

To dream that you are riding a roller coaster, represents life's frequent ups and downs in your waking life. You are experiencing erratic behavior brought on by yourself or a situation.

Rolling Credits

To see rolling credits in your dream, represents recognition for your work. You are looking for acknowledgement for a job well done.

To see your name in the rolling credits in your dream, symbolizes your confidence in your own ability.

You believe that you can succeed in whatever you pursue.

Romance

To dream of romance, suggests that you need to be more affectionate in your waking life. Perhaps you are longing for more romance in your personal relationship.

Rome

To dream that you are going to Rome or are in Rome, signifies love, death, destiny or fate. Consider the phrases "Rome wasn't built in a day" or "when in Rome, do as the Romans do" or "all roads lead to Rome". Think about how these adages are applicable to some aspect of your walking life.

Roof

To see a roof in your dream, symbolizes a barrier between two states of consciousness. You are protecting or sheltering your consciousness, mentality, and beliefs. The dream provides an overview of how you see yourself and who you think you are.

To dream that you are on top of a roof, symbolizes boundless success. If you fall off the roof, then it suggests that you do not have a firm grip and solid foundation on your advanced position. If you are re-roofing in your dream, then it suggests that you need to raise your goals and set your sights higher.

To dream that the roof is leaking, represents distractions, annoyances, and unwanted influences in your life. New information is slowly revealing itself to you. Something is finally getting through to you. Alternatively, the dream means that someone is imposing and intruding their thoughts and opinions on you.

To dream that the roof is falling in, indicates that your high ideals are crashing down on you. Perhaps you need to rethink the high expectations or goals you have set for yourself.

Room

To dream that you are in a room, represents a particular aspect of yourself or a specific relationship. Dreams about various rooms often relate to hidden areas of the conscious mind and different aspects of your personality. If the room is welcoming or comfortable, then it signifies opulence and satisfaction in life. If you see a dark or confined room, then it denotes that you feel trapped or repressed in a situation.

To dream that you find or discover a new room, suggests that you are developing new strengths and taking on new roles. You may be growing emotionally. Consider what you find in the discovered room as it may indicate repressed memories, fears, or rejected emotions. Alternatively, such rooms are symbolic of neglected skills or rejected potential.

To dream that you are in an empty white room, indicates a fresh start. It is like a blank canvas where you want to start life anew. Alternatively, the dream means that you are trying to isolate yourself. You do not want any outside influences.

To dream of a yellow room, suggests that you need to use your mind. You are feeling stimulated mentally.

*Please See Also <u>Bathroom</u> or <u>Kitchen</u>.

Rooster

To see a rooster in your dream, symbolizes masculinity, pride, valor, cockiness and arrogance. It indicates that you or someone is being a show-off with little or no regards for others. Alternatively, the dream highlights your eccentricities or wittiness. The dream may also be a pun on the penis.

To hear a rooster in your dream, signifies bragging and self-glorification.

To see roosters fighting in your dream, suggests that you are involved in some bitter rivalry.

Roots

To see plant or tree roots in your dream, symbolize the depths and core of your unconscious mind and soul. It represents your values and belief system. Alternatively, roots denote your family ties and bonds. You may be searching into your past. Or perhaps you need to get to the root of some problem in your waking life.

To dream that you are pulling up roots, suggests that you are ready to move on from the past. You have to let go of the relationship that is holding you back.

Ropes

To see a rope in your dream, represents your connection and attachment to others. It is symbolic of what is holding your relationship together. Alternatively, a rope signifies bondage, restriction and captivity.

To dream that you are walking on a rope, indicates that you are in a very precarious situation. You need to proceed carefully and weigh all the pros and cons of your decisions.

To dream that you are climbing up a rope, represents your determination to succeed and overcome adversity. It may be analogous to your climb to the top. If you are climbing down a rope, then it indicates that you are experiencing disappointments and decline in some professional progress.

To dream that you are tied up in ropes, suggests that you are letting your heart guide you, despite your better judgment.

Rosary

To see or hold a rosary in your dream, symbolizes comfort, solace, or satisfaction. It is also connected to the act of giving and asking.

Roses

To see roses in your dream, signify faithfulness in love and the coming of joy in some are of your life. Roses also symbolize love, passion, desire, femininity, unity, and romance, particularly if they are red roses. If you see a white rose, then it symbolizes virginity, pureness, and secrecy. It you see a yellow rose, then it refers to infidelity, jealousy, or friendship. According to Freud, the rose represents the female genitalia.

To see withered roses in your dream, refers to the parting or absence of a loved one. Alternatively, it is symbolic of death or an end to something.

To smell roses in your dream, denote happiness and pleasure. The dream is telling you that you need to slow down and smell the roses or else you will miss out on some opportunity or event in your life.

To see thorny roses in your dream, suggest that you are having difficulties or issues in your personal relationship. Alternatively, the dream indicates that you need to overcome some sticky or prickly situation before you can reap the benefits, as represented by the rose.

Rubber

To see rubber in your dream, represents your adaptability and versatility to various situations. Alternatively, the dream may be a metaphor for a condom. Perhaps you dream relates to a sexual issue.

To dream that you or someone is hit with a rubber object, indicates that things literally bounce off of you. You are unaffected by what is going around you or what others are saying about you.

Rubber Band

To see or use a rubber band in your dream, suggests that you need to be more accommodating to others. You need to expand your attitude, imagination and way of thinking.

To dream that a rubber band snaps, indicates that you have outstretched yourself into too many responsibilities. You may be overextended.

Rubber Duck

To see or play with a rubber duck in your dream, represents your playful attitude or your child-like emotions. You are lacking depth and compassion in the way you are expressing your feelings. In other words, your emotions are very superficial and shallow.

Rubik's Cube

To see or play with Rubik's cube in your dream, represents a problem or challenge that you are being confronted with in your walking life. You are looking for order. If you solve the cube, then it suggests that will overcome your problems.

Ruby

To see a ruby in your dream, symbolizes passion, vitality and sexual desire. Be cautious in affairs of the heart as they may be fleeting. Alternatively, consider the proverb, "wisdom is better than rubies", which means that wisdom and knowledge is better than wealth and money. The dream may also be a metaphor for someone who is named Ruby.

To see ruby slippers in your dream, represent your path to spiritual enlightenment. You need to venture out on a journey in order to find who you are as a person.

Rules

To dream that you are breaking the rules, indicate you feelings of frustrations. You feel that someone or something is treating you unfairly. Alternatively, the dream indicates that you need to stand up for yourself and assert your opinion. Sometimes you need to go against the system.

To dream that you are obeying the rules, symbolize integrity.

To dream that you are making rules, suggest that you need more discipline in your waking life.

To dream that you are disputing the rules, symbolize internal conflict and personal struggles.

Rumor

To hear a rumor in your dream, signifies a hidden message from your unconscious. Alternatively, the dream may be telling you that you should not believe everything you hear. You need to do your own research and get a firsthand account on things before making a judgment call.

To spread a rumor in your dream, signifies your personal insecurities.

Runaway

To dream that you are a runaway, indicates that you are struggling with issues of belonging and acceptance. Alternatively, the dream means that you are refusing to confront some issue or situation.

Running

To dream that you are running away from someone, indicates an issue that you are trying to avoid. You are not taking or accepting responsibility for your actions. In particular, if you are running from an attacker or any danger, then it suggests that you are not facing and confronting your fears.

To dream that you are trying to run but cannot make your feet move as fast as you want them to, signifies lack of self-esteem and self-confidence. It may also reflect your actual state of REM paralysis during the dream state.

Runway

*Please See Catwalk.

Rust

To see rust in your dream, signifies neglect, disappointments, depression or old age. Rust also suggests that you are not utilizing your talents and potential.

RV

To see an RV in your dream, means that you are feeling empowered. Alternatively, the dream is a metaphor to enjoy life to the fullest.

Rye

To see rye or fields of rye in your dream, symbolizes prosperity in your future.

To see or eat rye bread in your dream, refers to a cheerful and tranquil home.

S

To see the letter "S" in your dream, suggests that there is something that needs your attention.

Sabotage

To dream that you have been sabotaged, indicates that there is something that you are ignoring or overlooking in your waking life.

To dream that you are sabotaging something or someone, indicates that an overwhelming anxiety is threatening the boundary between your unconscious and your ego. You are feeling conflicted between right and wrong. Alternatively, the dream means that you need to get rid of your old attitudes and former ways of thinking.

Sacrifice

To dream that you are being sacrificed, signifies your tendency to punish yourself. The dream may parallel waking sentiments where you feel that others do not appreciate your talents and efforts or that you are not being recognized for what you have given up. Alternatively, the dream means that you need to eliminate certain aspects of your life and make time and space for more productive and rewarding experiences.

To see an animal being sacrificed in your dream, indicates that you are ready to give up your basic, carnal desires for spiritual pursuits and enlightenment.

Sad

To dream that you are sad, suggests that you need to learn from your disappointments and just be happy. Try not to dwell on the negative. The dream may be a reflection of how you are feeling in your waking life.

Saddle

To see a saddle in your dream, suggests that you need to freely pursue your goals. Go for it and do not let anyone hold you back from achieving your goals.

To dream that you are sitting on a saddle, indicates that you will rise to a position of prominence and power. You need to exercise more control over someone or some situation.

Sadism

To dream of sadism, indicates repressed anger, often from childhood. You may still be punishing yourself for your misdeeds or past actions.

Sagittarius

To dream that someone is a Sagittarius, represents your high ideals. You are outspoken, adventurous, goal-oriented and optimistic in your thinking. The dream may mean that you are trying to break from your routine.

Safari

To dream that you are on a safari, represents freedom from societal norms and rules. You are trying to break free from the confines of civilization.

Safe

To see a safe in your dream, indicates that you are hiding your sense of self worth and self value. It also refers to your security and secrets. Alternatively, the dream may also be a pun on feeling "safe".

To see an empty safe, signifies loss or lack.

Safety Pin

To see a safety pin in your dream, indicates that a situation is on the verge of falling apart causing anxiety or fear. You feel that the livelihood of the relationship depends on you.

Sailing

To dream that you are sailing, represents how your life is going and how you are able to handle life's problems. You are in control of your life. The dream may be metaphor that things are "smooth sailing." If you are sailing through the rough seas, then it means that you will overcome life's difficulties. If you are sailing against the wind, then it indicates that you are experiencing some struggles in your waking life.

Salamander

To see a salamander in your dream, represents your ability to survive through shame, misfortune, and/or embarrassment. You will persevere through some adversity. Alternatively, the dream denotes your ability to resist temptations.

Salary

To dream about your salary, symbolizes the results of your hard work. You need to take advantage of the opportunities. It is also an indication of your level of confidence and strength.

Sale

To dream that something is on sale, represents opportunities that are readily available to you. Alternatively, it indicates that you are underestimating yourself in some area.

Saliva

To see saliva in your dream, symbolizes sexual and sensual appetites. You are harvesting some creative energy.

To dream that you are spitting out your saliva, implies that you are experiencing some anxieties about losing control, either physically or emotionally.

To see the saliva of an animal in your dream, denotes intense feelings of anger and rage.

Salon

To dream that you are at the salon, indicates your concerns with your looks. You may be overly conscious about your appearance and beauty. Perhaps you are trying too hard to impress others. The dream also suggests deception and cover-up of some situation. Alternatively, it may denote a new outlook toward life.

Salt

To see or taste salt in your dream, represents a new found flare in your waking life. You are experiencing increased worth and a higher sense of zest and vigor. Alternatively, salt symbolizes dependability, truth, and dedication. Also consider the phrase of throwing salt on an open wound. The dream may thus elude to some painful or difficult memory.

To dream that you are salting meat, symbolizes longevity. There is something that you want to hold on to and preserve.

To dream that you are throwing salt over your shoulder, represents protection or luck.

Salute

To salute someone in your dream, represents your yield to authority. You need to accept your status in life and where you stand.

To dream that someone salutes you, signifies respect and reverence.

Sand

To see sand in your dream, signifies a shift in perspective or a change in your attitude. Consider the familiar phrase, "the sands of time" in which it may be suggesting that you are wasting your time or letting time pass you by. If the sand is wet, then it indicates that you are lacking a sense of balance in your life.

Sand Castle

To dream that you are building a sand castle, refers to your delusions of grandeur. You do not have a solid foundation needed for success.

Sandbox

To see or play in a sandbox in your dream, suggests that you are taking a situation too seriously. You need to lighten up and enjoy the experience. Alternatively, the dream refers to your childish or juvenile behavior.

Sandpaper

To see or use sandpaper in your dream, suggests that you need to smooth over some rough spots in your situation or relationship. Alternatively, it may indicate that you are a little too abrasive or harsh in your words or attitude.

Sandwich

To see a sandwich in your dream, suggests that a lot of pressure and stress is being put on you. It also reflects your ability to do two things at once. Alternatively, a sandwich is just a sandwich sometimes.

To see or eat a fish sandwich in your dream, indicates conflict between your spiritual beliefs and what is practical.

Santa Claus

To see Santa Claus in your dream, indicates that you need to be more giving, accepting, and/or forgiving. You need to acknowledge and tend to some aspect of yourself. Alternatively, the dream means that you are reflecting on the good and bad things that you have done.

To dream that you or someone is dressed as Santa Claus, suggests that you need to treat others as you would like to be treated. Put yourself in someone else's shoe and determine how they might feel.

Sap

To see sap in your dream, signifies physical health, vigor, and energy. It may also represent someone who is excessively gullible or sentimental.

Sapphire

To see a sapphire in your dream, represents protection, heaven, and divinity. Alternatively, you may be getting to the truth of something. Perhaps, you have unlocked an aspect of your unconscious. The sapphire may also refer to a person who is born in September.

Sari

To see or wear a sari in your dream, signifies covert sensuality, simplicity and adaptability. The dream may have exotic connotations. Alternatively, a sari may be a pun on being "sorry".

Sasquatch

*Please See Bigfoot.

Satellite

To see a satellite in your dream, symbolizes global communication and how we are all dependent on each other.

Saturn

To see Saturn in your dream, represents discipline, constraints, and limitations. It is a reflection of your conservative attitude. Alternatively, the dream refers to the cycles of life and how it brings about destruction and rebirth.

Sauce

To see or taste some sort of sauce in your dream, represents your sense of wisdom and intellect. Consider the color and flavor of the sauce for additional significance.

The dream may also be a pun on being "saucy". You need to be more bold and direct with your feelings or opinions even though it may not seem to be an appropriate time.

Saw

To see or use a saw in your dream, indicates that you need to quit doing something. There is something in your life that you need to cut out. The dream may also be a pun on something you saw or are seeing. Alternatively, sawing may be analogous to some sexual act.

To see an electric saw in your dream, signifies your ability to get down to the core of the problem. You know how to get to the point quickly.

Sawdust

To see sawdust in your dream, suggests that you need to clear up an emotional wound that was recently opened.

Saxophone

To see or play a saxophone in your dream, indicates that there is something you need to express from deep within your soul. Perhaps you have made a deep connection with someone.

Scab

To see a scab in your dream, symbolizes a time of healing. If you are picking at the scab, the it suggests that you are interfering in the healing process. You need to let things be and let things take their natural course. Alternatively, the dream may be a pun for a person who is a scab or someone who is breaking a strike.

Scale

To see a scale in your dream, signifies a decision that you need to make. Alternatively, the scales mean that you need to look at a situation from a rational perspective. Don't be so black and white about everything. Consider the gray area in the situation.

To dream that you are standing on a bathroom scale, represents concerns about your weight and your image. You are preoccupied with your physical shape and appearance. Perhaps you need to stop comparing yourself to the standards of others.

To see fish scales in your dream, represent your protective barrier. You have put up a defensive wall around yourself. If you are descaling a fish, then it means that you are starting to break down your emotional barriers.

Scanner

To see or use a computer scanner in your dream, represents your lack of originality and your tendency to mimic other's ideas and beliefs. Alternatively, it signifies the processing, transfer, and sharing of information. The dream may also be a metaphor that you need to "scan" and examine your options before making a decision.

To hear a police scanner in your dream, indicates an unrest within your unconscious that needs your immediate attention. Your intuition telling you that something is wrong.

Scarecrow

To see a scarecrow in your dream, indicates depression. You are going through some crisis in your life.

Scared

To dream that you are scared, indicates that you are experiencing feelings of self-doubt, incompetence, and lack of control in your waking life. Perhaps you are having second thoughts about a decision you have made. Anger often masquerades as fear, so also consider issues about which you are angry about in your waking life.

Scarf

To see a scarf in your dream, symbolizes self-restrictions. You may be too controlling of your emotions instead of expressing them. Alternatively, you feel that your voice is being muffled.

To dream that you are wearing a scarf, suggests that you are separating your mind from your body. You may be relying too much on how you think, rather than how you feel or vice versa. Alternatively, the dream means that you need to tell yourself that it is mind over matter.

Scavenger Hunt

To dream that you are in a scavenger hunt, indicates that you are lacking something in your waking life. You are looking for fulfillment of your needs or wants. Consider exactly what you are looking for.

School

To dream that you are in school, signifies feelings of inadequacy and childhood insecurities that have never been resolved. It may relate to anxieties about your performance and abilities. If you are still in school and dream about school, then the dream may just be a reflection of your daily life and has no special significance.

Alternatively, a dream that takes place in school may be a metaphor for the lessons that you are learning from your waking life. You may be going through a "spiritual learning" experience.

To dream that you are looking for a school, suggests that you need to expand your knowledge and learning. To dream that you are at a new school, means that you are feeling out of place in some situation. Or perhaps there is a new lesson that you need to learn.

To dream that your childhood school is in ruins, suggests that you are dwelling on some unresolved childhood issue. Alternatively, the dream represents the passage of time. You need to look toward the future instead of reliving the past.

*Please See Also Teacher.

School Bus

To see a school bus in your dream, suggests that you are about to venture on an important life journey needed for your own personal growth.

To dream that you drive a school bus, indicates that you like to take charge of others and watch out for their best interest.

Scientist

To dream that you are a scientist, signifies experimentation, invention, or eccentricity. You need to think outside the box. Alternatively, the dream suggests that you need to look at some problem more objectively and rationally. Perhaps you need to detach yourself from a situation or relationship.

Scissors

To dream that you are using scissors, denotes decisiveness and control in your waking life. You need to get rid of something in your life. It also represents your ability to cut things or people out of your life. Perhaps you are being snippy about some situation.

To see a pair of scissors in your dream, indicates that your focus is being divided into too many directions.

Scoreboard

To see a scoreboard in your dream, represents how you are doing in life and how you compare to others. How are you measuring up? Consider the significance of the specific numbers or digits on the scoreboard.

Scorpio

To dream that someone is a Scorpio, signifies self-control, determination, tenacity, healing and transformation. You have the ability to get down and penetrate to the core of a matter. Alternatively, the dream indicates some sexual matter.

Scorpion

To see a scorpion in your dream, represents a situation in your waking life which may be painful or hurtful. It is also indicative of destructive feelings, "stinging" remarks, bitter words and/or negative thoughts being expressed by or aimed against you. You may be on a self-destructive and self-defeating path. The scorpion is also a symbol of death and rebirth. You need to get rid of the old and make room for something new. Alternatively, the scorpion represents a person who is born under the astrological sign for Scorpio.

To see scorpions floating in water, suggest that you need to let go of some pain and learn to accept the situation. You may be going through the three-step process of denial, acceptance, and finally moving on.

Scrapbook

To see a scrapbook in your dream, represents old feelings and memories. They symbolize the past and things that you have put behind you or have forgotten.

To work on a scrapbook in your dream, indicates that you need to incorporate some aspect of your past into a waking situation.

Scratch

To dream that you are scratching yourself, symbolizes a minor irritation or frustration. Perhaps something that started out as minor may have the potential to become worse. Or somebody may have hit a sore spot in you.

To see a scratch in your dream, suggests that you are feeling anxiety about having to start over or begin something "from scratch".

Scream

To dream that you are screaming, symbolizes anger and fear. You are expressing some powerful emotion which you have kept pent up inside. If you try to scream, but no sound comes out, then it indicates your sense of helplessness and frustration in some situation. No matter how hard you try to get someone's attention, they cannot hear you. The dream highlights your difficulty in communicating with this person. You need to immediately identify your fears or feelings and confront this situation in real life. Alternatively, your inability to scream may be a form of REM paralysis.

To hear or dream that someone is screaming, indicates that some friend or family member is in need of your help.

Screw

To see a screw in your dream, represents your feelings of being taken advantaged or that you are messing things up. You are overlooking the little details that keeps and holds everything together. Alternatively, a screw may be a metaphor for having sex.

Screwdriver

To see a screwdriver in your dream, indicates the need to hold some situation or relationship together. Consider also if there someone in your life who is "all screwed up" or whom you would like to "put the screws on"?

Scrubs

To wear scrubs in your dream, refers to your caring, supportive and giving nature. The dream may be a metaphor that you need to literally clean up your act and get back on track. You need to organize aspects of your life before you can progress forward.

Scuba Diving

To dream that you are scuba diving, represents your desire to delve deep in to your unconscious. You are ready to confront your base feelings and explore your repressed thoughts. Alternatively, the dream indicates that you are trying to get to the bottom of a current situation or the root of your problems or feelings.

Sculpture

To see a sculpture in your dream, indicates that you are refusing to accept things as they really are. You are afraid that you are not presenting yourself in a positive light or image.

Sea

To see the sea in your dream, represents your unconscious and the transition between your unconscious and conscious. As with all water symbols, it also represents your emotions. The dream may also be a pun on your understanding and perception of a situation. "I see" or perhaps there is something you need to "see" more clearly. Alternatively, the dream indicates a need to reassure yourself or to offer reassurance to someone. It brings about hope, a new perspective and a positive outlook on life no matter how difficult your current problems may be.

To dream that you are lost at sea, suggests that you are drifting around in life without any direction. You are feeling overwhelmed by emotions.

Sea Horse

To see a sea horse in your dream, represents the power of your unconscious. You have a new perspective or different outlook in life. If the sea horse is invisible, then it suggests that there is an emotional issue that you are not acknowledging or recognizing.

Seafood

To see or eat seafood in your dream, indicates recognition and a mergence of your spirituality with your conscious being. You are acknowledging and fulfilling the needs of your unconscious. The dream may also be a pun on "seeing food" and thus the symbolism of "food" is also applicable.

*Please See Also Food.

Seagulls

To see seagulls in your dream, indicate a desire to get away from your problems or the demands of your walking life. You may be wasting away your potential and unused skills. Alternatively, a seagull symbolizes your strengths. You are able to cope with life's changes with grace and understanding. The dream may also be a pun on "see go" and thus indicate something that you need to let go or see go.

Seal

To see a seal in your dream, indicates your playfulness, prosperity, good luck, faithfulness, success, security in love and spiritual understanding. You have the ability to use and incorporate differing. Alternatively, the dream symbol may also be a pun and indicate you need to put closure on some situation as in "sealing the deal".

Séance

To see or be part of a séance in your dream, represents your intuition and awareness. You need to assess some hidden information within your unconscious. Gain more insight into some situation and look beyond what is in front of you. Stand back and look at the big picture. Alternatively, the dream is a way for you to cope with issues of death.

Seashells

To see seashells in your dream, represent security and protection. You are not showing your true self or real feelings. In protecting yourself from getting hurt, you are also becoming reclusive and emotionally closed off.

Seasick

To dream that you are seasick, represents emotions that are dragging you and weighing you down. You need to get rid of these feelings.

Seasons

To dream of the seasons, signify a passage of time and the phases and periods in your life. In particular, if the seasons are changing rapidly through your dream, then it suggest that you are undergoing an important transformation and deep spiritual development in your life. Consider the specific season for additional meaning.

Seat

*Please See Chair.

Seatbelt

To wear a seatbelt in your dream, suggests that you need to work on controlling your emotions. Try to stay compose and do not fall apart in any situation.

To dream that you are having trouble putting on your seatbelt, indicates that you are worried about what is ahead in your future.

Seaweed

To see seaweed in your dream, suggests that you need to rely on your intuition and trust your instincts.

Secret

To dream that you or someone has a secret, represents hidden power. It suggests that something is emerging from your unconscious.

Secret Admirer

To dream that you have a secret admirer, suggests that there are some unknown aspects of yourself that you need to find out about and incorporate into your character. Alternatively, the dream may be drawing your attention to someone who is interested in you. Or perhaps the dream is telling you to be more aware of your surroundings.

To see seeds in you dream, symbolize fertility, heritage, potential, and continuity of life. Now is the time to start a new venture. Alternatively, a seed relates to the human psyche and soul. An idea has been planted in your mind and new a experience is being created.

Seesaw

To see or dream that you are on a seesaw, represents the ups and downs of your emotions and of your life in general. A seesaw also signifies indecisiveness and lack of initiative. Alternatively, the dream may refer to your childhood memories. You may be acting too carefree in some waking issue or situation.

Segway

To see or ride a Segway in your dream, suggests that you need to exercise more balance and control in your waking life. You need to approach your goals at a steady and even pace.

Selling

To dream that you are selling something, indicates that you are undergoing changes in your waking life. You may be experiencing difficulties in letting go or parting with something. Learn to compromise. Alternatively, the dream may be a pun that you are "selling" yourself short.

Semen

*Please See Sperm.

Sepia

To dream in sepia hues, indicates feelings and thoughts from the primal aspects and less developed parts of your unconscious.

September

To dream of the month of September, signifies a positive outlook with good luck and fortune.

To dream about the events of September 11, 2001 represents your anger and fears. It brings you back to a time where you feel vulnerable and helpless. Alternatively, the dream denotes a highly stressful time in your life.

Sequins

To see or wear sequins in your dream, represent your desires to be noticed. You want to be in the spotlight. Alternatively, the dream indicates that things are not always what it seems. Consider the phrase "all that glitters is not gold." Don't be fooled by what is on the outside or how things may appear to be.

Serenade

To dream that you are being serenaded, represents emotional and spiritual fulfillment.

To dream that you serenade someone, signifies your love for life. You are trying to bring joy and positivity to those around you. Alternatively, the dream suggests that you need to vocalize your love more and express your romantic side.

Seven

Seven signifies mental perfection, healing, completion, music and attainment of high spirituality. The number seven may also refer to the seven deadly sins, the seven days of the week, or seven chakras. Alternatively, the number seven indicates uniqueness and eccentricity.

Seventeen

Seventeen symbolizes soul.

Seventy

Seventy signifies completeness and perfection. You are enjoying life.

Sewer

To see a sewer in your dream, signifies putrid conditions and old relationships. Something needs to be cleaned up or immediately changed. You need to let go of your outdated ideas and beliefs.

To see a sewer pipe in your dream, represents the flow of unconscious material being suppressed deeper and deeper. You need to address these issues before it overflows.

Sewing

To dream that you are sewing, suggests that you are trying to make amends with others. There may be a situation or relationship that needs to be repaired. Perhaps you are creating a new self-image and taking on a new attitude. Alternatively, sewing represents fertility, growth, and emotional maturity.

Sex

To dream about sex, refers to the integration and merging of contrasting aspects of yourself. It represents psychological completion. You need to be more receptive and incorporate aspects of your dream sex partner into your own character. Consider the nature of the lovemaking. Was it passionate? Was it slow? Was it wild? The sex act parallels aspect of yourself that you wish to express. A more direct interpretation of the dream, may be your libido's way of telling you that it has been too long since you have had sex. It may indicate repressed sexual desires and your needs for physical and emotional love. If you are looking for a place to have sex, then the dream may be analogous to your search for intimacy and closeness. You want to rekindle some relationship. If you dream of having sex in a public place, then the dream implies that others are talking about your private relationship.

To dream about sex with someone other than your spouse or significant other, suggests dissatisfaction with the physical side of your relationship. On the other hand, it may be harmless fantasy. In such situations, you may find that you are less inhibited sexually. Perhaps you need to bring the same sense of adventure into your existing relationship.

To dream that you are having sex with an ex or someone who is not your current mate, denotes your reservations about embarking in a new relationship or situation. You may feel nervous about exposing yourself and are feeling a resurgence of those old emotions and feelings that you felt back when you and your ex were together. If you are approaching your wedding date, then is not uncommon to experience especially erotic adventures with partners other than your intended spouse. This may be due to the intensity of the sexual passion with your fiancé. It also relates to the new roles that you will be taking on and the uncertainty that that may bring.

To dream that you are having sex with a stranger, represents uncertainty about what is ahead. Alternatively, the dream allows you to experiment freely without having any hang ups, emotional baggage or preconceived notions associated with a person you would know. In such a scenario, you are able to let loose and express your desires, passions and emotions.

If you are heterosexual and you dream that you are having sex with someone of the same sex, then it represents an expression of greater self love and acceptance. You need to be in better touch of your feminine or masculine side. The dream does not necessarily imply homosexual desire.

To dream that you are having sex with a celebrity, indicates your drive to be successful. You are striving for recognition. Consider what movies your associate this celebrity with for clues as to where and what you want to achieve success in.

To see your parents having sex in your dream, indicate that you are seeing similar aspects between their relationship and your current relationship. Most of us cringe at the thought of our parents having sex, so this dream imagery is really trying to get your attention. Consider your parents' real life relationship together and what you can learn from it.

To dream that you are the opposite sex, suggests that you need to incorporate certain qualities of the opposite sex. Ask yourself, how do you feel being a man or a woman? In what ways can you incorporate those feelings into your waking life.

Shack

To see a shack in your dream, represents your undeveloped self. You need to expand your Self. Alternatively, the dream may also be a pun on "shacking up".

Shadows

To see you own shadow in your dream, signifies an aspect of yourself which you have not acknowledged or recognized. It may be a quality about yourself or a part of you that you are rejecting or want to keep hidden. These qualities may not necessary be negative, but can be creative ones. Alternatively, the dream may mean that you are in someone else's shadow. You are constantly being overlooked and are fed up with it.

To see a shadowy figure in your dream, represents characteristics which you have not acknowledged or incorporated into your own personality. Alternatively, it symbolizes the young, the helpless or the under-developed.

Shaking

To dream that you are shaking, suggests that you are getting rid of your old habits and former ways of thinking. You need to get rid of the old in order to welcome in the new and better. Shake things up a bit. Alternatively, shaking is symbolic of fear.

Shampoo

To see or use shampoo in your dream, indicates that you need clear out your old attitudes and old ways of thinking. You may also need to take a different approach toward some situation or relationship. Alternatively, shampoo represents self-growth and you desire to present a new image of yourself to others.

To dream that you are shampooing someone else's hair, represents issues of dependency and hopelessness.

Shamrock

To see a shamrock in your dream, symbolizes your need to be or feel protected.

Sharing

To dream that you are sharing something, symbolizes your generosity toward others. Perhaps you need to be more generous with your feelings. Alternatively, the dream may be a metaphor for the "shares" you have in the stock market. You are expressing concern over your finances.

Shark

To see a shark in your dream, indicates feelings of anger, hostility, and fierceness. You are undergoing a long and difficult emotional period and may be an emotional threat to yourself or to others. Perhaps, you are struggling with your individuality and independence, especially in some aspect of your relationship. Alternatively, a shark represents a person in your life who is greedy and unscrupulous. This person goes after what he or she wants with no regards to the well-being and sensitivity of others. The shark may also be an aspect of your own personality with these qualities.

Shave

To dream that you are shaving, suggests that you are making a minor life-changing decision. Some aspect of your daily routine is being altered. Alternatively, it may represent your severe attitude or some sort of self-punishment. It can also have sexual connotations.

To dream that someone is shaving your leg, represents a loss of your independence. You are relying on others to get you through some difficult times. You need to build up your self-confidence and self-esteem.

To see someone shaving in your dream, indicates that there is some conflict in your self-image. Perhaps what you portray or project does not match who you really are inside.

To dream that you are shaving your head, indicates a desire to reveal more of yourself. If you leave some hair on your head, then it suggests that you are not completely prepared to let others see who you really are. You are still afraid what people might think. The few clumps of your hair serve as some sort of safety net. Alternatively, shaving your head represents humbleness and humility.

Sheep

To see sheep in your dream, indicates docility and conformity. You lack creativity, individuality and initiative to venture out on your own. You tend to go along with the group. Alternatively, seeing a sheep signifies your compassion. The dream may also be a metaphor on being sheepish. Perhaps you have done something wrong.

To see a black sheep in your dream, symbolizes greed and temptation. The dream may also be a metaphor for someone who represents the black sheep in your family. Perhaps it is you who is the non-conformist.

Sheet Music

To see sheet music in your dream, represents sensuality and harmony, especially in some waking relationship. Perhaps you are lacking these qualities in your relationship.

Shell

To see a shell in your dream, signifies your inner desire to be sheltered, nourished and protected from life's problems. It also indicates that you are closing yourself off emotionally. You are keeping your feelings inside.

Ship

To see a ship in your dream, denotes that you are exploring aspects of your emotions and unconscious. The state and condition of the ship is indicative of your emotional state. If you dream of a cruise ship, then it suggests pleasant moods. If you dream of a warship, then it means that you are experiencing feelings of aggression.

To dream that you are sailing the high seas in a ship, denotes that you are still standing tall despite the emotional turmoil occurring in your life.

To dream that a ship has crashed or sunk, suggests that you are feeling emotionally out of control. You are expressing some fear or uncertainly within your emotional state. You are afraid of losing something close to you because of certain difficulties.

To dream that you abandon ship, indicates that you need to move on and let go. Your emotion may be holding you back. Alternatively, consider the phrase "jumping ship", to indicate changing of sides.

Shirt

To dream of a shirt, refers to your emotions or some emotional situation. The shirt you wear reveals your attitude and level of consciousness about a particular situation.

To dream that you are giving a shirt to someone, may be a metaphor for "giving the shirt off your back". It refers to your self-sacrifice and generosity.

To dream that you are shirtless or that you lost your shirt, signifies financial worry, monetary lost or risky endeavor.

Shiver

To shiver in your dream, indicates that you are experiencing some deep seeded fears from the unconscious. The dream may also highlight your emotions and how cold and rigid you are behaving.

Shoelace

To dream that your shoelaces are untied, indicate that you are unprepared for some task at hand. Perhaps you are not ready to move forward in a relationship or endeavor. Alternatively, the dream may mean that you are living under limited means. Consider the phrase a "shoestring budget".

To dream that you are tying your shoelaces, suggest that you are getting ready for a challenge. Or you are ready to move forward with your goals or a decision.

Shoes

In general, shoes represent your approach to life. Wearing shoes in your dream, suggests that you are well-grounded or down to earth. It also represents your convictions about your beliefs. If you are changing your shoes, then it refers to your changing roles. You are taking a new approach to life. If you forget your shoes, then it suggests that you are leaving behind your inhibitions. You are refusing to conform to some idea or attitude.

To see old and worn shoes in your dream, indicates that you will find success through hard work and diligence. You have come to terms about who you are.

To see new shoes in your dream, suggests that you are overconfident in your success. Alternatively you may be on a life path that is unfamiliar to you.

To find shoes in your dream, suggests that you have regained your foothold on life. You are back on the right path again.

To dream that you are wearing inappropriate shoes for the occasion or for the activity at hand, means that your progress and path in life will be long, hard and laborious. It may also indicate that you are heading in the wrong direction. Perhaps you need to reevaluate your goals. If you dream that your shoes do not fit or that they pinch and hurt, then it means that you are questioning your goals. You are doubting the direction of the path you are taking.

To dream that you are not wearing any shoes, indicates that you have low self-esteem and a lack of confidence in yourself. You are dealing with issues about your self-identity. It also represents poverty, lack of mobility, or misunderstanding. Alternatively, to dream that you are not wearing shoes, represent your playful attitudes and relaxed, carefree frame of mind. You have a firm grasp and good understanding on a situation. If you dream that you lose your shoes, then it suggests that you are searching for your identity and finding yourself.

To see baby shoes in your dream, symbolizes purity, innocence, vulnerability, tenderness and the desire for love. If you are planning to have or already have a baby, then it suggests that the baby will or has grounded you. After all, with a baby to tend to, you find yourself rooted at home most of the time and not being able to go out as much.

Shooting

To see a shooting in your dream, indicates that you have a set goal and know what to aim for in life. Your plans are right on target!

To dream that you shoot a person with a gun, denotes your aggressive feelings and hidden anger toward that particular person. If the person you shoot is a stranger, then it indicates that you are rejecting unknown aspects of yourself that you do not understand.

To dream that someone is shooting you with a gun, suggests that you are experiencing some confrontation in your waking life. You may be feeling victimized in some situation.

Shooting Star

To see a shooting star in your dream, is a sign of self-fulfillment and advancement. A shooting star is also symbolic of a new birth and big changes in your life.

Shopping

To dream that you are shopping, symbolizes your needs and desires. It also represents opportunities and options that you come across in life. Consider what you are shopping for and what needs you are try to fulfill. In particular, to dream that you are shopping for food and groceries, signifies your hidden attempt to buy the attention of others. If you are shopping for clothes, then it suggests that you are trying to put forth a new image.

To dream that you cannot find what you are shopping for, suggests that you are trying to find a solution to some life problem.

Shopping Cart

To see or use a shopping cart in your dream, indicates that you are reaping the rewards and benefits of your hard work. Alternatively, to push a shopping cart in your dream, suggests that you need to search out more options for some aspect of your life. Remember that you have choices and you do not need to settle. If the shopping cart is empty, then it suggests that you are coming up empty in some endeavor or plan.

Shorts

To dream that you are wearing shorts, indicates that you are ready to be more open and reveal a little more about your inner persona. Alternatively, the image of shorts refers to your youth and playful attitude. The dream may also be a metaphor that you are selling yourself short.

Shoulders

To see your shoulders in your dream, symbolize strength, responsibility and burdens. Perhaps you feel that you have too much responsibility to bear and are overburdened by circumstances in your life. Alternatively, shoulders represent your ability to offer support and nurturance others.

Shovel

To see a shovel in your dream, suggests that you are seeking knowledge, insight, and inner intellect. You are on a quest for a new understanding of your true Self. Alternatively, a shovel means that you are trying too hard in finding the truth to a problem.

To dream that a shovel is broken, indicates that you are frustrated with work.

Shower

To dream that you are taking a shower in clear, fresh water, symbolizes spiritual or physical renewal and forgiveness. You are washing the burdens out of your life. Alternatively, the dream may be a metaphor that you are "showering" someone with gifts or love.

To dream that you are taking a shower in muddy, dirty water, signifies misfortune and losses.

To dream that you are showering with your clothes on, means that even though you may change your outer appearances, it does not change who you are on the inside. Alternatively, your dream indicates that you are unwilling to let your guard down. You are still keeping up a protective barrier between you and others.

Shredder

To see or use a shredder in your dream, indicates that there is something that you are trying to hide or protect. Perhaps you are in denial about something. Also consider the significance of what you are shredding.

Shrimp

To see or eat shrimp in your dream, suggests that you are feeling overpowered and insignificant. You feel like you want to hide from the world and be left alone for awhile.

Shrink

To dream that you are shrinking, suggests that you lack self-confidence and self-esteem. You may be feeling embarrassed, insignificant or unimportant in some situation. Perhaps you feel that you have been overlooked by others. Alternatively, the dream may refer to a time were you were young and small and thus, symbolic of your childhood.

To see others shrink in your dream, indicates their insignificance. This may also be a pun on a psychologist and your need to consult one.

To see objects shrinking in your dream, indicate that they are not as important as they once were.

Sick

To dream that you or others are sick, denotes discordance and trouble in your life. It may signal a part of yourself that needs to be healed, either physically or mentally. Perhaps you are wallowing in your own self-pity. You need to quit feeling sorry for yourself.

Sickle

To see a sickle in your dream, is symbolic of your labor and hard work. The symbol may also be a pun on "sicko".

Sign

To see a sign in your dream, indicates that you need help. You need some direction and guidance in your life. Pay attention to what the sign says and what it is pointing you to do. Perhaps the dream is highlighting "a sign of the times".

Sign Language

To communicate in sign language in your dream, suggests that you need to find other ways to get your opinion heard since no one is listening to you.

Signature

To see your signature in your dream, represents your agreement and acceptance for a particular condition or situation. It is also an indication of your seal of approval. You are taking charge and accepting responsibility of a situation.

Silk

To see or feel silk in your dream, represents luxury, smoothness, and softness.

To dream that you are wearing silk, suggests prestige. You will never lack the necessities of life.

Silver

To see silver in your dream, symbolizes the moon, intuition and the feminine aspects of yourself. It signifies tranquility and understated confidence.

Silver color represents justice and purity. It is symbolic of some protective energy.

Singer

To see a famous singer in your dream, represents a divine influence. It indicates harmony and glorification of the human spirit. Consider also your general impression of this singer and how those specific qualities may be triggered by someone or some situation in your waking life.

Sink

To see a sink in your dream, represents your feelings and your ability to control your emotions. You may need to cleanse yourself of past feelings and start fresh. Consider also the common phrase "everything but the kitchen sink" which refers to a situation where you have almost everything that you can possible want or need. The symbol may also be a pun on "sinking" or drowning.

Sinking

To dream that you or something is sinking, suggests that you are feeling overwhelmed. Someone or something is pulling your down. You may be experiencing low self-esteem and confidence. Alternatively, the dream means that some important and significant stage in your life may be coming to an end. Consider what is sinking and its significance.

*Please See Also <u>Drowning</u>.

Sirens

To hear sirens in your dream, signify a situation or problem that is giving you much stress. The sirens may serve to get your attention and focus on the problem at hand.

Sister

To see your sister in your dream, symbolizes some aspect of your relationship with her, whether it one of sibling rivalry, nurturance, protectiveness, etc. Your sister may draw attention to your family role. Or the dream may also serve to remind you that someone in your waking life has characteristics similar to your sister. Alternatively, your sister may be a metaphor for a nun. In this case, she may represent some spiritual issues.

If you do not have a sister and dream that you have one, then it signifies feminine qualities that you need to activate or acknowledge within your own self. Pay attention to the actions and behavior of your dream sister.

Sitar

To see or hear a sitar in your dream, signifies passion, joy and healing. The sitar is also symbolic of the Indian culture.

Sitting

To dream that you are sitting, indicates your indecision. You do not know what you want to do about something. It also suggests that you are idling and wasting your life away.

Six

Six is indicative of cooperation, balance, tranquility, perfection, warmth, union, marriage, family, and love. Your mental, emotional, and spiritual states are in harmony. It is also indicative of domestic bliss.

Sixteen

Sixteen symbolizes innocence, naiveté, vulnerability, and tenderness. It also indicates some spiritual cleansing and destruction of the old and birth of the new. Alternatively, the dream may represents a coming of age for you.

Consider the significance of "sweet sixteen".

Sixty

This number is associated with time. It may refer to time running out or longevity.

666

To see the digits 666 in your dream, represents the devil and all things evil. Its appearance in your dream may point to some illicit activity or some wrong doing.

Size

To dream about the size of something, represents the importance or lack of importance that you attach to certain objects or persons. The larger something is, the more important it is. Conversely, the smaller something is, the more trivial it is. Size also relates the degree of power you are exerting and the power others have on you. Perhaps the dream indicates that you are "sizing" someone up. According to Freudian school of thought, the size of an object, signifies the size of someone's penis, perhaps your own or your lover.

Skateboard

To see or ride a skateboard in your dream, indicates that you have the gift of making any difficult situation look easy. You carry yourself with style, grace and composure in the hardest of situations. Alternatively, the dream signifies your free and fun-loving side.

Skating

To dream that are skating, symbolizes your ability to maintain a balance in your life. You are progressing through your life's path and working toward your goal. Alternatively, the dream may be a metaphor that you are "skating" over some matter. In other words, you are just getting by. Perhaps you are trying to avoid some issue or not devoting enough attention to a problem.

To dream that you are skating on ice, indicates satisfaction with a current project. Consider also the phrase "skating on thin ice" to suggest that you may be on the verge of overstepping your boundaries or taking certain risks in your waking life.

Skeleton

To see a skeleton in your dream, represents something that is not fully developed. You may still in be the planning stages of some situation or project. Alternatively, a skeleton symbolizes death, transformation, or changes. You need to get to the bottom of some matter. The skeleton may also be a metaphor for "skeletons in your closet." Do you have something to hide?

To see someone depicted as a skeleton, signifies that your relationship with them is long dead.

Skiing

To dream that you are skiing, suggests that you are pushing yourself and putting your mental and/or physical ability to the test. You are your own fiercest competitor.

Skillet

*Please See Pan.

Skin

To dream of your skin, represents protection or shield of your inner self. It serves as a physical boundary and how close you let others get to you. Alternatively, your skin indicates that you are being too superficial or shallow.

To dream that your skin is covered with rashes or other skin deformities, signifies your fear of facing a harsh reality. You are afraid of making a wrong impression. The dream may also be a pun that you are making a rash decision. If you dream that your skin has been burned, then it implies that you are unwilling let down your guard. Your line of defense has been compromised. This dream may also be a metaphor that you are "getting burned" or humiliated by someone or some situation.

To dream that your skin is orange, signifies self-love. You are content with who you are.

To dream that your skin is different color, suggests that you are not being true to yourself. Look up the specific color for additional meaning. If your skin is darker than your true skin, then it may mean that you are trying to hide or blend into the background. If it is lighter than your true skin, then it symbolizes fear. Alternatively, it may be a sign of sickness. Perhaps a call to the doctor is in order.

Skinny

Please See Thin.

Skipping

To dream that you are skipping, suggests that you need to be more light-hearted. You may need to take a friendlier approach toward a situation. Alternatively, the dream may be a metaphor that you have skipped something important.

Skirts

To dream that you are wearing a skirt, represents the signals and hidden messages that you are conveying or sending out. It also symbolizes femininity and your sense of sexuality. The dream may also be a metaphor on an issue that you are "skirting" around over and not confronting head on.

If you are a man and dream that you are wearing a skirt, then it indicates that you need to acknowledge the emotional aspects of your personality.

Skull

To see a skull in your dream, symbolizes danger, evil or death. Alternatively, a skull represents the intellect or secrets of the mind. You are keeping certain things hidden.

To dream that a skull is talking to you, suggests that aspects of yourself that you have suppressed or rejected is starting to come back to the surface. These aspects will not be denied any longer and must be dealt with on a conscious level.

To dream that a skull is trying to swallow you, indicates that you are literally being consumed by some danger. You are letting evil or death take over your life.

Skunk

To see a skunk in your dream, suggests that you are driving people away or turning them off. Alternatively, the dream indicates that your suppressed anger is on the verge of exploding. You are not expressing your true feelings even though you do not agree with a decision.

Sky

To look up at the clear blue sky in your dream, denotes hope, possibilities, creativity, peace and freedom of expression. As the saying goes "the sky's the limit." If the sky is cloudy and overcast, then it foretells of sadness and trouble.

To see a green colored sky in your dream, symbolizes high hopes. The strange color of the sky helps to instantly draw your attention to it. The color green and the sky itself both represent hope, nature or creativity. So these are the qualities that you need to focus on. It is also indicative of a positive outlook and prosperous future.

To see a red colored sky in your dream, represents looming danger. Alternatively, it suggests that something is coming to an end. If the sky is white, then it symbolizes desires. If you dream of a colorful sky in your dream, then it denotes romance.

To dream that the sky is falling, represents your fear of the unknown. You feel that your hopes and dreams have been shattered. Perhaps you have been too idealistic and the dream is an attempt to bring you back to reality.

To dream that something is falling out of the sky, signifies your pessimistic attitude. You are losing perspective on a situation. If the object is getting closer and casting a shadow on you, then it indicates that you are being ignorant about some situation. You need to get out from under the shadow and gain a different perspective on things.

Skydiving

To dream that you are skydiving, represents your high ideals. Sometimes you need to compromise your ideals and be more realistic of your expectations.

Skyscraper

To see a skyscraper in your dream, represents your high ideals, creativity, accomplishments and imagination. You always aim high at whatever you do. The skyscraper is seen as a metaphor for the foresights and achievements of man. Alternatively, the dream represents the phallus.

Skywriting

To see skywriting in your dream, represents a spiritual message. It signifies a connection and union between the spiritual realm and the physical realm. You are looking for some reassurance.

Slap

To dream that you are slapped, indicates carelessness. You either feel unappreciated or betrayed.

To dream that you slap someone, suggests that you are harboring some repressed anger and deep-seeded rage.

Slave

To dream that you are a slave, suggests that you are not taking charge of your own life. You may be a slave to your job, to your family, to some habit, or to some obsession.

Sled

To see a sled in your dream, signifies childishness.

To dream that you are sledding, represents your fun-loving personality and open-minded perspectives on life.

Sledgehammer

To see or use a sledgehammer in your dream, suggests that you need to break down the walls that you have created around you.

Sleeping

To dream that you are sleeping, denotes peace of mind. Alternatively, it means that you are ignorant of the conditions and circumstances around you. If you are sleeping with a stranger, then it suggests that you are avoiding some issue or situation that is being symbolized by the stranger. Perhaps you are refusing to recognize a negative or hidden aspect of yourself. Sleeping may also be synonymous with death in that it beckons renewal and new beginnings.

To see someone sleeping in your dream, is a reflection of yourself and your own unconscious mind. It is telling you that you may not be alert or informed about a particular situation.

Sleeping Beauty

To see Sleeping Beauty in your dream, symbolizes eternal beauty. The dream may also be trying to tell you that you are oblivious to some situation. There is something that you are completely overlooking.

Sleepover

To dream that you are at a sleepover, indicates that there is a situation that you are refusing to see or accept. You need to be more alert and pay attention to what is going around you. Alternatively, the dream suggests that you need to let your guard down and learn to be more open and receptive.

Sleepwalk

To dream that you are sleepwalking, suggests that you are feeling emotionally detached from others. You are out of touch with what is happening around you.
Alternatively, the dream means that you are stuck in a routine where you are doing things by rote. There is a lack of excitement and energy in your life. You are just going through the motions.

Slide

To dream that you or somebody is on a slide, indicates that you are experiencing some instability in your waking life. You have lost your grip on a situation or relationship.

To dream that you are sliding, represents a loss of control.

Slime

To see or feel slime in your dream, represents your inability to place your trust in someone. The dream may be a metaphor for someone is a slimeball.

Slingshot

To see or play with a slingshot in your dream, represents the negative aspects of your childhood. You are feeling defensive about something. The dream may be brought about by some waking conflict that mimic your experiences from childhood.

Slippery

To dream that you are walking on slippery ground, indicates a lack of progress in some endeavor. You need to rethink your course. Alternatively, it symbolizes caution. You need to be careful in what you say and do; otherwise you might get yourself into trouble.

Slot Machine

To see or play a slot machine in your dream, suggests that you need to be more careful with your spending. Or you need to allocate your time and energy to something more productive. Alternatively, a slot machine symbolizes luck and chance. Perhaps the dream is telling you to take a gamble on something. Go for it.

Sloth

To see a sloth in your dream, indicates your passivity in a situation. You need to assert yourself and make your presence known. The sloth is also symbolic of gentleness, laziness or lack of ambition.

Slow Motion

To dream that you are moving in slow motion, suggests that you are feeling powerless, anxious or frustrated. You are currently going through a hard time in your waking life and experiencing tremendous stress, which is almost immobilizing you.

Slugs

To see slugs in your dream, indicate that you are progressing through life in a slow, steady, and persistent manner. Perhaps you are moving painfully slowly toward a goal. Alternatively, the dream may be a pun on "feeling sluggish".

To dream that slugs are coming out from inside your body, suggest that you are having difficulties expressing some aspect of your emotion. Consider where in your body are the slugs coming out from.

Slumber Party

*Please See Sleepover.

Small

To dream that someone or something is smaller than usual, represents feelings of insignificance, helplessness and unworthiness. Alternatively, you may be literally trying to "knock" this person down to size. Perhaps it suggests that you or someone in your life has an inflated ego and need to be taught a lesson.

To dream that you are small and everyone is normal sized, suggests that you are suffering from low self-esteem and/or a sense of helplessness. Perhaps you are being overlooked.

Smell

To smell something in your dream, indicates your past experiences and feelings you associate with that particular smell. Your dream is trying to convey a feeling with a familiar smell or scent. Alternatively, the scent may be part of your real environment which you have incorporated into your dream.

Smile

To dream that you or others are smiling, means that you are pleased with your achievements and approve of the decisions you have made. You will be rewarded for the good things you have done for others. Alternatively, a smile indicates that you are in search of something or someone that will make you happy.

Smog

To see smog in your dream, symbolizes your negative emotions. You may be feeling upset and fearful of a situation or relationship. Alternatively, smog suggests that you have not fully understood a situation to make an informed decision.

Smoke

To see smoke in your dream, indicates some sort of trouble that is entering your life. You are suffering from confusion and anxiety. In particular, if the smoke is black, then it means that you are not seeing some situation or problem clearly.

Smoking

If you do not smoke in waking life and dream that you are smoking, then it indicates that you are trying to shield yourself and others against your emotions. You have trouble letting others in. The dream may also be a metaphor for an addictive relationship or habit in your waking life.

Smoothie

To make or drink a smoothie in your dream, is analogous to how your life is going. It is a "smooth" road ahead for you.

Snails

To see a snail in your dream, suggests that you are being overly sensitive. You are feeling inhibited, but desire to be more outgoing and energetic. Alternatively, a snail suggests that you are making steady progress toward a goal. You need to go at your own pace.

Snake

To see a snake or be bitten by one in your dream, signifies hidden fears and worries that are threatening you. Your dream may be alerting you to something in your waking life that you are not aware of or that has not yet surfaced. Alternatively, the snake may be seen as phallic and thus symbolize temptation, dangerous and forbidden sexuality. In particular, to see a snake on your bed, suggests that you are feeling sexually overpowered or sexually threatened. You may be inexperienced, nervous or just unable to keep up. If you are afraid of the snake, then it signifies your fears of sex, intimacy or commitment. The snake may also refer to a person around you who is callous, ruthless, and can't be trusted. As a positive symbol, snakes represent healing, transformation, knowledge and wisdom. It is indicative of self-renewal and positive change.

To see the skin of a snake in your dream, represents protection from illnesses.

To see a snake with a head on each end in your dream, suggests that you are being pulled in two different directions. You are feeling overburdened and do not know whether you are coming or going. Your actions are counterproductive. Perhaps the dream represents some complicated love triangle. Alternatively, the dream signifies your desires for children. If you see a two-headed snake in your dream, then it refers to cooperation and teamwork in some relationship.

To dream that you are eating a live snake, indicates that you are looking for intimacy or sexual fulfillment. Your life is lacking sensuality and passion. If you vomit or throw up the snake, then it may mean that you are overcompensating for something that is lacking in your life. You may be rushing into something.

Sneakers

To see or wear sneakers in your dream, suggest that you are approaching through life with ease and little obstacles. It also denotes comfort and satisfaction with yourself and who you are. Alternatively, the dream indicates that you lead an active life and are always on the go.

Sneeze

To dream that you sneeze, indicates a life of ease and joy. Alternatively, it suggests inner healing.

Sniper

To dream that you are a sniper or are being attacked by one, represents hidden aggression that you need to acknowledge. You need to express your anger in a more controlled and healthy manner.

Snoring

To dream that you or someone is snoring, indicates that you are completely oblivious to what is going on around you. Life is passing you by. The dream may also be a reflection of your waking surroundings. You have incorporated the actual sound of snoring (by you or by your sleep partner) into your dream scenario.

Snorkeling

To dream that you are snorkeling, suggests that you are exploring your emotions and trying to understand why you feel the way you do about certain things. It may also indicate that you are looking back at past emotions and what you can learn from those experiences.

Snow

To see snow in your dream, signifies your inhibitions, unexpressed emotions and feelings of frigidity. You need to release and express these emotions and inhibitions. Alternatively, snow means that you are feeling indifferent, alone and neglected. If the snow is melting, then it suggests that you are acknowledging and releasing emotions you have repressed. You are overcoming your fears and obstacles.

To see dirty snow in your dream, refers to a lost in innocence, impurity and uncleanness. Some aspect of yourself or situation has been tainted.

To dream that you are watching the snow fall, represents a clean start and a fresh, new perspective. It is indicative of spiritual peace and tranquility.

To dream that you are playing in the snow, indicates that you need to set some time for fun and relaxation. Alternatively, the dream means that you need to take advantage of opportunities that arise; otherwise such opportunities will disappear.

To dream that you find something in the snow, suggests that you are exploring and accessing your unused potential, abilities, and talents. You have uncovered some hidden talent and ability within yourself. It may also refers to a need to forgive.

Snow Globe

To see a snow globe in your dream, signifies your desires for peace and serenity. Consider the scene depicted inside the snow globe and the corresponding significance. The dream may indicate that you are longing for some aspect of your past.

To dream that you are inside the snow globe, suggests that you are feeling stuck in your life. You feel that you are in a rut doing the same thing and going to the same places. Alternatively, the dream means that you are not expressing your emotions. You are keeping too much inside and as a result, you are feeling trapped.

Snowboarding

To dream that you or someone is snowboarding, indicates that you are overcoming your fears. You are utilizing your skills.

Snowflake

To see a snowflake in your dream, represents purity and perfection. It also signifies your individuality and uniqueness.

Snowman

To see a snowman in your dream, suggests that you are emotionally cold or frigid. Perhaps you have been a little cold-hearted and insensitive. Alternatively, a snowman is symbolic of playfulness, holiday cheer and time of togetherness.

Soap

To see soap in your dream, indicates that you need to wash away some of your past emotions or memories. You may also be feeling emotionally dirty or guilty and are trying to wash away the shame. Perhaps you need to confess something.

Soap Opera

To dream that you are in or watching a soap opera, indicates that your life is like a drama. Perhaps you are identifying with a character in the soap opera. Also consider the title of the soap opera. For example, "All My Children" may refer to some drama you are experiencing with your children. "Guiding Light" suggests that you need more spirituality in your life.

Soccer

To dream that you are playing soccer, suggests that you are suppressing your sexuality or aggression and expressing it in a more socially acceptable manner. From a Freudian perspective, sports generally serve as a disguise for attitudes about sex as a aggressive act. Hence soccer can be seen as a pun on "sock her". Alternatively, the game of soccer parallels to how you function and how you run your life when confronted with challenges. You need to be able to think quickly on your feet, if you are going to succeed. The soccer game also reflects you competency, integrity, strengths and weaknesses.

Socks

To dream that you are wearing socks, signifies warmth and comfort. Alternatively, to see socks in your dream indicate that you tend to yield to other's wishes. You are flexible and understanding in your thinking.

To see a single sock in your dream, is a pun on hitting someone or being hit. Or perhaps the dream means that you have been hit with some surprising information or news.

Soda

To drink soda in your dream, indicates that you need to be more bubbly or vivacious. Liven up! Alternatively, the dream suggests that you need to be refreshed or rejuvenated.

Sudoku

To see or play Sudoku in your dream, suggests that you are being faced with a mental challenge and complex problem. Consider the significance of the number or numbers highlighted. The dream may point to financial worries and how you are trying to make the numbers work for you.

Sofa

Please See <u>Couch.</u>

Soil

To see or be in contact with soil in your dream, symbolizes growth and fertility. It also represents a solid foundation for life. You need to approach your goals with practicality. If the soil is hard and dry, then it indicates that you are not being true to yourself. You are trying to hide under a hard shell. The dream may also be analogous to something that is "soiled" or tainted.

Solar System

To see the solar system in your dream, suggests that you are lacking direction in your life. You have a wandering mind. If applicable, look up the specific planet for additional significance in the Dream Moods dream dictionary.

Soldier

To see or dream that you are a soldier in your dream, signifies discipline, structure, rigidity and your staunch attitude. You are imposing your opinions and feelings on others. Alternatively, a soldier means that you are preparing yourself to do battle over an issue. You feel the need to defend your beliefs, values and opinions.

To dream that you are an ex-soldier, represents your ability to yield in your decisions and your way of thinking. You need to change your approach toward your goal.

Sommelier

To dream that you are a sommelier, represents your role in someone else's decision making process. You are good at offering your advice to others.

To see a sommelier in your dream, indicates that you are looking for advice on some decision or the direction you should take in life.

Son

To see your son in your dream, signifies your ideal, hopes, potential, and the youthful part of yourself. On the other hand, to see your son in your dream may not have any significance and is simply mirroring your waking life. The dream may also be a pun on "sun".

If you don't have a son and dream that you are searching for him, represents the undeveloped masculine aspect of your own self. You need to acknowledge the youth and child in you.

Songs

To hear or write songs in your dream, indicate that you are looking at things from a spiritual viewpoint. Your future will be filled with happiness and wealth. Consider the words to the song that you are dreaming about for additional messages.

Sorcerer

To see or dream that you are a sorcerer, represents your talents, inner strengths, and creative ability. Your mind is squarely set on achieving your goals.

Sores

To dream that you have sores on your body, suggest that you are keeping in some negative emotions and attitudes that need to be released and expressed. Consider the symbolism of the body area where the sores are located. Perhaps the dream is an indication that you are still feeling "sore" and resentful about some situation or relationship.

To feel sore in your dream, indicates that you are feeling worn down by some emotional issue.

Sorority

To dream that you are in or join a sorority, signifies personal growth and social changes that you are experiencing in your life. You need to expand your awareness and knowledge. The dream is also symbolic of the bounds of sisterhood and togetherness. If you are in a sorority in your waking life, then the dream may just be a reflection of the waking relationship and bear no special significance.

Soul

To dream that you have a lack of soul or no soul, suggests that you are feeling spiritually lost. You need to find yourself and find what will makes you feel whole as a person.

To dream that your soul is leaving your body, represents your feelings of self-guilt. You may have compromised your own beliefs and values. Perhaps you are feeling numb and out of touch with those around you. It is time to change some vital part of your waking life in order to feel fully alive and whole again.

Soup

Similarly to food, to dream about soup, represents emotional hunger or nourishment. In addition, soup also signifies comfort and healing. Consider the contents inside the soup and its symbolism.

Sour

To taste something sour in your dream, refers to some resentment in your emotional state of mind. The dream may be analogous to a relationship that is going "sour."

South

To dream of the direction south, indicates life, expectations, and questions. Alternatively, the dream may symbolize love, passion and warmth. Or the dream may be a metaphor that a plan has "gone south" or gone awry.

South Pole

To dream that you are in the South Pole, represents the challenges and hardships in your waking life and your ability to endure it all.

To dream that you live in the South Pole, symbolizes your survival skills.

Soybean

To see or eat soybean in your dream, implies that you are expressing some health concern. Perhaps, you need to adapt a healthier lifestyle. Alternatively, the dream suggests that there is some decision or situation that you are thinking hard about. In Spanish, "soy" means "I" and thus the dream could be a pun on the self.

Space

To see or dream that you are in space, represents exploration and independent thinking. You are broadening your horizons and view. Alternatively, the dream may be a metaphor that you are "spacing out". You need to return your concentration back on your future and goals. Or the dream may be a pun on your need for more "space" in a relationship or situation.

Spaceship

To see a spaceship in your dream, symbolizes your creative mind. It denotes a spiritual journey into the unknown and signals self-development and self-awareness. Alternatively, the dream suggests that you need to take on a different perspective, no matter how bizarre or unusual it may be.

Spaghetti

To see or eat spaghetti in your dream, symbolizes longevity, nourishment and abundance. Alternatively, eating spaghetti indicates that you find yourself entangled in some messy relationship or uncomfortable position. Perhaps you are not sure how to end a relationship or situation.

Spanking

To dream that you are spanking someone, suggests that you need to work on your childish rage and tantrums.

Sparkle

To see sparkles or see something sparkly in your dream, indicates an aspect of your life that is in need of your attention. The dream may also be a metaphor that you are feeling "sparks" in some new relationship. Alternatively, the dream suggests that things are not always what it seems. Consider the phrase "all that glitters is not gold." Don't be fooled by what is on the outside or how things may appear to be.

Speakers

To see speakers in your dream, indicates that you are demanding to be heard. The dream may be telling you that you need to project your voice. Your opinion matters.

Speech

To give a speech in your dream, indicates that you need to vocalize your feelings and thoughts. You need to communicate something important and/or urgent. Alternatively, the dream may be highlighting your fear and nervousness of speaking in public, especially if the speech goes wrong or if the audience is unruly.

To dream that there is no one listening to your speech, suggests that you are not being acknowledged for your work or achievements. Perhaps you are feeling ignored, neglected, or overshadowed.

To hear a speech in your dream, suggests that your inner feelings are being made known to those around you. Consider what is said in the speech. If you hear a politician give a speech, then it represents egotism, deceit or pride.

Speed

To dream that you are taking speed, indicates that you are putting yourself in a dangerous situation, particularly if you do not use speed in your waking life. The dream may be a pun on "speediness". Perhaps you need to move more quickly.

Speed Bump

To see or go over a speed bump in your dream, indicates that you need to slow down. You may be moving too fast in some relationship or some aspect of your waking life. Alternatively, speed bumps represent minor obstacles you are facing in your life.

Speeding

To dream that you are speeding, indicates that you are compelled and driven to complete something. As a result, you may be pushing people away. Alternatively, the dream suggests that you are moving too fast in some relationship or situation. Perhaps you need to slow down.

Speeding Ticket

To get a speeding ticket in your dream, indicates that you are rushing through some decision or rushing into a relationship. You need to slow down. Alternatively, the dream may be telling you that life on the fast line is not all that is cracked up to be.

Speedometer

To see a speedometer in your dream, is analogous to the pace of your life. Are you living life on the fast lane or are you moving at a snail's pace? Consider the numbers for additional significance.

Spell

To dream that you are under a spell, indicates that someone has a powerful influence on you. You may be taken for a ride or being manipulated in some waking situation. Alternatively, the dream is a commentary on your waking relationship and how deeply intertwined you are within a relationship.

Spending

To spend money in your dream, suggests that you are emotionally spent. You are wasting your time on a relationship or on someone who is not worth your time, energy or love.

To dream that you are watching your spending, indicates that you are holding back your emotions. You are having second thoughts about a relationship.

Sperm

To see sperm in your dream, symbolizes masculinity and fertility. It also refers to the potential for growth and development.

Sphinx

To see a sphinx in your dream, signifies fear of the unknown. Alternatively, it represents some cold, hard emotion. You lack any sort of feeling.

Spice

To dream of spice, suggests your need for variety in your life. You need to look at a situation/relationship from a different perspective or angle.

Spiders

To see a spider in your dream, indicates that you are feeling like an outsider in some situation. Or perhaps you want to keep your distance and stay away from an alluring and tempting situation. The spider is also symbolic of feminine power or an overbearing mother figure in your life. Alternatively, a spider refers to a powerful force protecting you against your self-destructive behavior. If you kill a spider in your dream, then it symbolizes misfortune and bad luck.

To see a spider spinning a web in your dream, signifies that you will be rewarded for your hard work. You will be promoted in your job or recognized for your achievement in a difficult task. Spiders are also a symbol of creativity due to the intricate webs they spin. On a negative note, spiders may indicate a feeling of being entangled or trapped in a sticky or clingy relationship. It represents some ensnaring and controlling force. You feel that someone or some situation is sucking the life right out of you. Alternatively, if a spider is spinning a web in your dream, then it could be a metaphor for the world wide web and global communication.

To see a spider climbing up a wall in your dream, denotes that your desires will be soon be realized.

To dream that you are bitten by a spider, represents a conflict with your mother or some dominant female figure in your life. The dream may be a metaphor for a devouring mother or the feminine power to possess and entrap. Perhaps you are feeling trapped by some relationship.

To eat a spider or dream that a spider is in your mouth, symbolizes your control over a situation. You are not afraid to exert your dominance in a relationship.

Spill

To dream that you spill something, represents your carelessness and inconsideration of someone's feelings. You are not paying enough attention to those around you and as a result are offending and upsetting them. Alternatively, the dream may be a metaphor for something that you are dying to say, as in "spill it."

To dream that you spill some food, indicates that you need to eliminate that food from your diet.

To dream that you spill a drink at a party, symbolizes your social ineptness and awkwardness in a social situation.

Spin The Bottle

To play spin the bottle in your dream, suggests that you need to take a chance at love.

Spinach

To see or eat spinach in your dream, indicates your need to be reenergized or revitalized. It is synonymous with strength and power. Alternatively, the dream may simply be telling you that you need to eat better and lead a more healthier lifestyle.

Spine

To dream about yours or someone else's spine, represents your support system, your strength, stamina and responsibilities. You need to keep your head high even in difficult times. Alternatively, the spine suggests that you need to stay true to your own convictions and be firm. The spine is symbolic of strength. The dream may be one of the contrary and thus suggests that you are "spineless."

Spinning

To dream that you are spinning, signifies confusion. You are feeling out of control. Alternatively, the dream means that you are going nowhere.

To dream that something is spinning around you, indicates that you are feeling overwhelmed by circumstances beyond your control.

Spiral

To see a spiral in your dream, indicates that some situation in your waking life is spinning out of control. Alternatively, a spiral represents your creative power and new idea. You are surrounded with creative energy.

Spit

To spit in your dream, signifies an aspect of yourself that you need to get rid of. Spitting represents anger, spite and contempt. Alternatively, the dream implies that you have something that you want to say. Spit it out!

Splits

To dream that you are doing the splits, signify some struggle or division within your social circle. There is some disagreement and dissension that needs to be addressed. The dream may also be a pun to "split", as in to leave or get out of a situation. Perhaps, the dream is telling you to go.

Sponge

To see or use a sponge in your dream, suggests that you are receptive and are able to easily absorb new knowledge and information. The dream may also be a metaphor that you are "sponging off someone" or that someone is "sponging" off you. Perhaps you are becoming too dependent and need to find your own path.

Spoon

To see a spoon in your dream, refers to a reciprocal relationship where you need to give and receive nourishment. You or someone is being given special treatment. Also consider the phrase "born with a silver spoon in your mouth" to mean that you have a life of privilege.

Sports

To dream that you are playing a sport, signifies the learning of rules, recognition of your talents, and the achieving of your goals. It also highlights the importance of cooperation, harmony, and teamwork. Perhaps the dream is a pun on how you need to be more of a "sport". Alternatively, playing sports represent your perspective about sex as an aggressive act.

To dream that you are watching a sports competition, represents two opposing viewpoints or conflicting opinions.

To play or watch extreme sports in your dream, suggests that you may be pushing yourself too hard. You need to consider the risks involved and if it is still worth it to pursue further.

Spotlight

To dream that you are in the spotlight, indicates your need to be noticed and to be the center of attention. Perhaps you are feeling overlooked in your waking life and the dream is a compensatory one.

Spring

To dream of the season of spring, signifies hope, new beginnings and creative endeavors. It is also a symbol of warmth, virility and fruitfulness.

To see a water spring in your dream, symbolizes your emotional energy and expressiveness. You make your feelings and opinions known. Alternatively, a water spring denotes your ability to draw on your inner resources.

To see a metal spring in your dream, indicates that you are feeling tense. You are under some tremendous pressure. Alternatively, the dream may also be a metaphor on your need to "spring" into action.

Spy

To dream that you are a spy, indicates your mistrust of others and your tendency to be in everyone's business and affairs. Perhaps you have recently stumbled upon some information that was not meant for your eyes.

To dream that someone is spying on you, represents your impulsive behavior. This dream may also serve as a warning that you are being watched, investigated, or evaluated. Someone is looking over you.

Square

To see a square in your dream, signifies strength, solidity and stability. Alternatively, a square indicates that you are limited in expressing yourself. Consider the pun on "being too square". Perhaps you are being too conventional, unhip or dull. To see a square in your dream may also mean that you are "back to square one". You need to start over and go back to the beginning.

Squeeze

To dream that you are squeezing something, suggests that you need to make more space for other things in your life. You need to stop dwelling on your past emotions and clear them away. Alternatively, the dream may mean that you are putting the "squeeze' on somebody. You or someone may be feeling pressured or stressed. The dream may also be a pun on your "main squeeze" or your mate. Perhaps the dream trying to comment about the relationship.

Squid

To see a squid in your dream, suggests that you are feeling unconsciously threatened. Your judgment may also be clouded. Perhaps you are not seeing things too clearly at the moment. Alternatively, a squid symbolizes greed. You go after what you want without any regard for others.

To dream that you are eating squid, indicates that you are feeling self-conscious and worrying about how others perceive you. You may be find it easier to isolate yourself instead of risking judgment from others.

Squint

To dream that you are squinting your eyes, suggests that there is some situation or relationship that you need to examine closer. A situation may be unclear or hazy. You are confused about some aspect of this situation. Alternatively, the dream indicates that you are refusing to see the facts of a situation or are in denial about something.

Squirrel

To see a squirrel in your dream, indicates that you are involved in a loveless, pointless relationship or an unprofitable business project. You are pursuing empty and fruitless endeavors. Alternatively, seeing a squirrel in your dream, suggests that you are hoarding something. You are holding on to too much and need to learn to let go. On the other hand, a squirrel means that you need to reserve your time and energy.

To dream that you are trying to run over squirrels with a lawn mower, suggest that you are trying to change your beliefs and alter your ideas in order to conform to others. You are looking for some form of acceptance.

To dream that you are feeding a squirrel, denotes that comfort will come about through hard work, diligence and prudence.

Stage

To dream that you are on a stage, represents your behavior, manipulation of and relationships with others. It is telling of your interactions with society. You are putting up an act and not being who you really are. There is a saying that goes, "all the world is your stage" and the dream may thus refer to your desire to be the center of attention. Also consider how your stage performance parallels a waking situation.

To dream that you are on a side stage, reflects your introverted personality. This dream is telling you that you need to be more confident and self-assured.

Stain

To see a stain in your dream, symbolizes a superficial and reversible mistake in your life. Consider and analyze the substance, color and location of the stain. If you cannot remove the stain, then it represents guilt or your unwillingness to forgive and forget.

Stairs

To dream that you are walking up a flight of stairs, indicate that you are achieving a higher level of understanding. You are making progress into your spiritual, emotional or material journey. The dream is also analogous to material and thoughts that are coming to the surface.

To dream that you are walking down a flight of stairs, represents your repressed thoughts. You are regressing back into your unconscious. It also refers to the setbacks that you are experiencing in your life. If you are afraid of going down the stairs, then it means that you are afraid to confront your repressed emotions and thoughts. Is there something from your past that you are not acknowledging?

To dream that you slip or trip on the stairs, signify your lack of self confidence or conviction in the pursuit of some endeavor. If you slip going up the stairs, then it means that you are moving too fast toward attaining your goals. If you slip going down the stairs, then it suggests that you are moving too quickly in delving into your unconscious. You may not be quite ready to confront your unconscious or repressed thoughts.

To see spiral or winding stairs, signify growth and/or rebirth.

Stamps

To see stamps in your dream, represent a need for communication. Consider what is depicted on the stamp and the amount. A stamp may also be a pun on "stamping" your feet. Perhaps, you need to show more fortitude, enthusiasm and confidence in some waking situation.

To see a stamp collection in your dream, signifies issues and concerns with money and/or security.

Standing

To dream that you are standing, suggests that you are asserting yourself and making your thoughts and feelings known. Be proud. You need to make a "stand".
Alternatively, the dream means that you are detached from your surroundings.

Staples

To see staples in your dream, indicate that you need to organize your life and keep things in order. Learn to sort out your feelings and express them. The dream may also be a pun on the "staples" or basic essentials of your life.

Starfish

To see a starfish in your dream, suggests a period of healing and regeneration. Alternatively, it indicates that you have many options to weigh and decisions to make.

Staring

To dream that you are staring at something or someone, indicates that you need to take a much closer look at some situation or relationship. Perhaps you need to approach a situation from another perspective or viewpoint. Alternatively, staring represents your passivity. It is time to start taking action.

To dream that someone is staring at you, suggests that you are hoping someone would look your way more often. It may also represent anxiety or pride.

Stars

To see stars in your dream, symbolize excellence, success, aspirations or high ideals. You are putting some decision in the hands of fate and luck. Perhaps you are being too "starry eyed" or idealistic. Or the stars may represent a rating system. You are you trying to evaluate a situation or establishment. Alternatively, the stars signify your desire for fame and fortune.

Static

To feel static in your dream, depicts your magnetic personality and how you are able to draw things to you. Alternatively, the dream may represent friction, stemming from disagreements or from different ways of doing things.

To hear static in your dream, indicates that there is a lack of clarity and understanding.

Something is not being communicated properly or clearly.

Statue

To see people you know as statues in your dream, symbolize a lack of communication with that person You feel that the relationship is inflexible, unyielding or going nowhere. Alternatively, it may represent someone you idealize and admire. You are putting someone on a pedestal. Perhaps the dream is analogous to their statuesque and nice figure.

To dream that you are a statue, signifies that your true self is out of touch with reality.

To see a weeping or crying statue in your dream, represents some miracle. You have accomplished something that you thought was impossible. Alternatively, the weeping statue symbolizes passion and devotion.

Steak

To dream that you are eating a steak, represents your animal instincts. The dream may be telling you to trust your instincts or that you need to utilize your instincts more. The dream could also be a pun on "stake", as in having a claim to something.

Stealing

To dream that you are stealing, suggests that you are feeling deprived. The locale (at home, the office, at school, etc) of where the stealing takes place is indicative of your neediness. Alternatively, stealing signifies unrealized and unfulfilled goals. You may have set your goals too high.

Steam

To see or hear steam in your dream, denotes your intense emotional state regarding an issue or situation. You are headstrong about proceeding forth on an issue. Perhaps you are angry with someone or at something as in the metaphor "letting out steam". Alternatively, it signifies a new idea or some "steamy" situation.

Steel

To see steel in your dream, symbolizes toughness, willpower, determination and strength. The dream may also be a pun on stealing.

Steering Wheel

To see a steering wheel in your dream, represents control over the direction you are taking in life.

Stencil

To see or use a stencil in your dream, indicates a lack of freedom in some aspect of your waking life. You are bounded by barriers and obstacles. Someone is not letting you do what you want or be who you are. Alternatively, stenciling means that you are looking for some guidance and direction in some decision.

Stepfather

To see your stepfather in your dream, symbolizes authority and protection. Consider also your waking relationship with your stepfather and how aspects of his character may be incorporated within yourself. If you do not have a stepfather in real life, then the dream may represent some unresolved issues and tension with your actual father.

Stepmother

To see your stepmother in your dream, suggests that you are trying to cope with a mothering figure in your life. You are either feeling smothered or neglected. If you do not have a stepmother in real life, then the dream may represent some unresolved issues and tension with your actual mother. Or the dream could be a pun that you or someone is "stepping" all over your mother. Show her some appreciation and compassion for all the work that she does.

Stethoscope

To see or use a stethoscope in your dream, suggests that you need to pay better attention to some health advice. You need to improve your diet and take better care of yourself.

Stew

To make or eat stew in your dream, signifies aspects of yourself that are being joined together as a whole. In particular, to see or eat beef stew in your dream, indicates that you need to incorporate aspects of your childhood into your adult life. You need to be more light-hearted. Alternatively, the dream may also be a pun on someone who is named Stew/Stu.

Stick

To see a stick in your dream, symbolizes the phallus and your attitude toward sex. Alternatively, the dream may be a pun on a "sticky" situation or how you need to "stick up" for yourself and your beliefs.

Sticker

To see stickers in your dream, suggest your tendency to hold on and cling to your childhood. Pay attention to what is depicted on the sticker as it may offer you a clue to what particular aspect of yourself you are refusing or having trouble letting go. Alternatively, the dream refers to a sexual innuendo and may be on pun on "stick her".

If the stickers in your dream are scented, then consider what the scent reminds you of and the memory it brings back. There may be an unresolved issue from your past. If the stickers are squishy or have a tactile quality, then the dream maybe telling you that you need to take a more hands on approach in addressing the unfinished issues in your childhood.

Stigmata

To dream that you or someone has stigmata, refers to the sacrifices you made and the difficulties you endured. Time will heal the pain. Alternatively, it symbolizes your passion and the intensity of what you believe in.

Stilts

To dream that you are walking on stilts, indicate that you are feeling insecure. A situation or relationship is unstable. You are doing your best trying to balance various aspects of your life.

To dream that you fall off a pair of stilts, suggest that you should not put all your trust in one person.

Sting

To dream that you are stung, represents some hurtful action or remark. The dream may be a pun on some "stinging remark". Although, you are not letting it show how it has affected you, the pain is making its way into your dreamscape. Alternatively, the dream may also be a metaphor for being in love.

Stingray

*Please See <u>Manta Ray.</u>

Stitch

To dream that you have stitches, represent your responsibility in keeping and holding a situation or relationship together. You fear that this situation or relationship is falling apart and it is up to you to mend it. Consider also the symbolism of where the stitches are on the body for additional significance.

To dream that you are stitching, indicates that you need to take extra care in adding your personal care and special touch to some situation.

Stock Market

To dream about the stock market, represents the ups and downs of your life. You are one who is willing to take risks.

To dream that the stock market crashed, indicates a major blow to your hopes and dreams. Your goals are being sidetracked.

Stockings

To wear stockings in your dream, represent your sense of understanding. You are well-grounded and supported by those around you. If the stockings are torn or have a run, then it signifies lacking self esteem and reduced self confidence. The dream may also be a pun on the word "stalking". Are you devoting too much attention to someone or something?

To see someone put on stockings, relates to some sexual situation.

To see a Christmas stocking in your dream, symbolizes expectations and a need for recognition and acknowledgement. On the other hand, the dream means that you need to be more giving.

Stomach

To see your own stomach in your dream, refers to the beginning of new changes in your life. The dream may highlight the difficulties you have with accepting these changes. It is also indicative of how you can no longer tolerate or put up with a particular situation, relationship, or person, as in being able to "stomach" something. Alternatively, the stomach is often seen as the center of emotions. Thus the dream may be about how you process or handle your emotions.

Stonehenge

To see Stonehenge in your dream, suggests that you are undergoing some spiritual enlightenment. Light has been shed on something that was once confusing. Alternatively, the dream is symbolic of a mysterious and powerful force.

Stones

To see a stone in your dream, symbolizes strength, unity, and unyielding beliefs. Look at the shape, texture and color of the stone for additional significance. If the stones are rough, then it represents your quest in recognizing and developing your self-identity. Part of this quest is to also become aware of your unconscious and suppressed thoughts. Consider the common phrase "etched in stone" which suggest permanence and unchanging attitudes. Some stones also carry sacred and magical meanings. Alternatively, stones relate to issues of moral judgment and/or guilt. Or the dream may also be a metaphor for "being stoned" or under the influence of drugs.

To dream that you are carrying a bag of stones, refers to your inner strength and fortitude that you have yet to unleash and reveal to others.

To dream that you are throwing stones, suggests that have a tendency to look at the faults and shortcomings of others without looking at yourself first.

For various cultures, stones have spiritual significance. Consider the Black Stone of Mecca which is believed by Muslims to allow for direct communication with God. For the Irish, the Blarney Stone is seen as a gift of eloquence.

Stop Sign

To see a stop sign in your dream, suggests that you need to stop what you are doing and rethink about the situation before moving forward. You need to proceed with care and caution. Alternatively, a stop sign signifies barriers and difficulties in your path.

To dream that you run a stop sign, indicates that you are not considering the consequences of your action. It may also refer to your reckless habits.

Stoplight

To see a stoplight in your dream, suggests that you feel you are being held back from pursuing your goals. Your forward progress is being controlled by someone or by some outside forces. In other words, you are not in control of your own life. Alternatively, the dream represents the pressure to succeed or else be left behind. If the traffic is green, then it indicates that you have been given the go-ahead to follow whatever path you have chosen or whatever decision you have made.

Store

To see or be in a grocery or convenience store in your dream, suggests that you are emotionally and mentally strained. Alternatively, the dream means that you are brainstorming for some new ideas or looking at the various choices out there for you. The dream may be a pun on something that is in "store" for you. It could signify the inevitable.

*Please Also See Market.

Stork

To see a stork in your dream, symbolizes motherly love, faithfulness, new birth or fertility. Perhaps you are expecting a new baby into your family. The birth may also be a symbolic birth to mean the fruition of some idea. Alternatively, the stork represents creativity and cleansing.

Storm

To see a storm in your dream, signifies some overwhelming struggle, shock, loss or catastrophe in your waking life. The storm also represents unexpressed fears or emotions, such as anger, rage, turmoil, etc. On a more positive note, the storm symbolizes your rising spirituality. It may signal rapid changes ahead for you.

To dream that you take cover in a storm, foretells that whatever disturbance or problems is occurring in your life will quickly blow over. Consider also the phrase "weather the storm", which refers to your ability and strength to withstand whatever comes.

Stove

To see a stove in your dream, symbolizes a developing awareness. If the stove is broken and does not light, then it refers to an emotional issue you are facing in some waking relationship. You may be neglecting this relationship. Alternatively, the dream means that you need to focus your attention to something that you have placed on the back burner.

Strait Jacket

To see or wear a strait jacket in your dream, indicates that you are feeling limited or restricted in some aspect of your life. You are feeling helpless.

Stranger

To see a stranger in your dream, signifies a part of yourself that is repressed and hidden. Alternatively, it symbolizes the archetypal dream helper who is offering you insight and advice.

To dream that you are kissing a stranger, represents acknowledgement and acceptance of the repressed aspect of yourself.

Strangle

To dream that you or someone else is being strangled, indicates that you are repressing or denying a vital aspect of your expression.

Straw

To see or use a straw in your dream, indicates that you may have been taking some things for granted. Once you pay more attention to the people around you, you will find that you will have stronger and more meaningful bonds with them. Alternatively, the dream means that you need to better direct your feelings and express it in a healthy way. Or perhaps the dream may be a metaphor for "the last straw". You have reached your breaking point.

To dream that you are buying straw, suggests that you are trying to buy your way into a situation or relationship.

Strawberry

To see or eat strawberries in your dream, signify your sensual desires and temptations. Strawberries are often associated with feminine qualities and female sexuality. Alternatively, to see strawberries in your dream, indicate that your ideas and goals will soon be realized.

Street

To see a street in your dream, symbolizes your life's path. The condition of the street reflects how much control you have over the direction of your life. Consider also the name on the street as it may offer some significance or advice to the meaning of the dream.

To see or travel on side streets in your dream, refer to a need to explore an alternative way of life.

*Please See Also Road.

Stress

To dream that you are under stress, reflects the actual stress that you are experiencing in your waking life. The stress has carried over into your dream state where even in your sleep, you are unable to relax. The dream may call attention to some setbacks, obstacles, self-doubts, or criticism that you are facing in some waking situation or relationship. You are on the verge of breaking down and need to take some leisure time off to distance yourself from these issues.

Stretcher

To dream that you are lying on a stretcher, indicates your need to be rescued from some situation or relationship. Perhaps you need to take time out and confront your emotional demons.

To see a stretcher in your dream, suggests that there is trouble ahead for you in the near future.

295

Stretching

To dream that you are stretching, suggests that you are in need of some relaxation. Alternatively, the dream may be a metaphor that you are "stretching" yourself too thin, either financially, physically, emotionally or time-wise.

Strike

To dream that you are going on strike, suggests that you are feeling under-appreciated. Perhaps you feel that you are being forced to do something that you don't really want to.

String

To see a string in your dream, represents binding, cohesion, or joining, depending on the context of the dream. It relates to the strength of your involvement in a project, situation, or relationship. Perhaps, you are having concerns about your ability to hold some situation or relationship together. Alternatively, the dream indicates that you need to use your position and leverage to get what you want. Consider the phrase "pulling strings."

To dream that you are tying a string, indicates something you have forgotten to do.

To dream that you are untangling a string, suggests that there is some issue in your waking life that you need to straighten.

Stripes

To see stripes in your dream, suggest that you are making a bold and daring statement. Horizontal stripes represent your directness and straightforwardness, while vertical stripes indicate that you are a non-conformist. In particular, black and white vertical stripes signify your close-mindedness and limited way of thinking.

Stripping

To dream that you are stripping, indicates repression of your personal and physical desires. You are yearning for greater self-expression and exploration of your sexuality. Alternatively, the dream may be a pun on being "stripped" of something that you valued or cherished.

Stroke

To dream that you have a stroke, refers to your inability to function in a certain situation of your waking life. You may be dealing with issues of acceptance/rejection and approval/disapproval.

To see someone suffering from a stroke, represents your own repressed fears. Consider how aspects of that person has been repressed within your own self.

Stuck

To dream that you are stuck, represents a feeling of helplessness and not being able to escape from life's problems or stresses. You have lost confidence in yourself and in your ability to move ahead in your life. Your lack of clear goals and low self-esteem may be a common cause for such dreams.

Student

To dream that you are a student, indicates that you need better understanding of something. There is some learning you need to do in order to get ahead in life. If you are a student in real life, then the dream may just be a reflection of who you are and bear no significance.

Studying

To dream that you are studying, signifies that your intellect and knowledge will catapult you into a path of success and wealth. Alternatively, studying indicates that you need to study more or increase your self-knowledge.

Stuffed Animal

To see a stuffed animal in your dream, represents an immature attitude. You are trying to escape from your daily responsibilities and problems. Alternatively, a stuffed animal indicates your need to relax and be less serious. You need to let your mind and body to rejuvenate. A stuffed animal may also mean security, love, comfort, support and unconditional or unquestioned love.

To dream that a stuffed animal is choking you, indicates that something that was originally emotionally comforting is now giving you much stress. You are feeling emotionally restricted and unable to communicate how you feel especially in matters of the heart.

Stump

To see a tree stump in your dream, indicates that something or someone is preventing your growth or forward progress. Alternatively, the dream may be a pun on "being stumped" on some problem or issue. The dream may be offering a solution to your problem.

Stun Gun

To dream that you have been hit by a stun gun, suggests that you are in need of a jolt or a shot of energy in your life. Alternatively, the dream is a warning that you need to stop and think about what you are doing. Perhaps you need to be knocked into your senses.

Stutter

To dream that you stutter, indicates your inability to make yourself heard and express yourself clearly. You are hiding how you really feel.

Alternatively, the dream suggests that you are nervous about what you are saying.

Styrofoam

To see Styrofoam in your dream, indicates that you are undergoing some form of transition in your life. In particular, to see a Styrofoam cup in your dream, suggests that you are feeling somewhat insecure or instable in a relationship.

Submarine

To see a submarine in your dream, indicates that you are cautiously exploring your emotions and unconscious feelings. You are guarded about certain emotional issues. Alternatively, the submarine indicates that you need to adapt a different perspective and new understanding of an issue. The submarine is a metaphor that you need to get down to the core of some situation or problem.

Subtitle

To have subtitles in your dream, indicate that what you are saying in your dream lacks clarity. The subtitles are drawing direct attention to what you are trying to say and convey. Or the dream is highlighting a lesson or advice that you need to take with you when you wake up.

Subway

To dream that you are in the subway, denotes that you are reaching your goal via unconscious methods. By recognizing the hidden aspects of yourself, you are able to move forward in life. Alternatively, a subway suggests that you are making a hasty decision.

Suffocating

To dream that you are suffocating, signifies that you are feeling smothered or oppressed by some situation or relationship. Something or someone is holding your back. You are experiencing a lot of stress and tension.

To suffocate someone in your dream, indicates that you want to dominate or overpower this person in your waking life. This person may also represent an aspect of your own self that you are trying to control.

Sugar

To see or eat sugar in your dream, represents the pleasures and enjoyment that you are denying yourself in your life. Sometimes, you need to indulge yourself and not worry about the consequences.

To see a sugar cube in your dream, suggests that you need to lighten up and quit being so serious.

Suicide

To dream that you commit suicide, represents your desperate desire to escape from your waking life. You may be harboring feelings of guilt that you cannot get over and thus turning the aggression on yourself. You need to start approaching problems from a different angle. Alternatively, the dream suggests that you are saying good-bye to one aspect of yourself and hello to a whole new you. It is symbolic of a personal transformation or a new stage in your life.

To see someone commit suicide in you dream, highlights your concerns for that person. Consider what characteristics and qualities in that person you may be trying to "kill" and annihilate in your own self. Perhaps you hope that you are not like this person and are making attempts to get rid of those traits within your own self.

Summer

To dream about summer, represents growth, knowledge, high productivity, tolerance and maturity. You are expanding your realm of understanding. It is important to keep your hope alive.

Sumo

To see a sumo wrestler in your dream, suggests that you are throwing your weight and power around. You are not afraid to let others know that you are in charge.

To watch sumo wrestling in your dream, indicates that you are dealing with a big problem in your waking life. You feel that the problem has a stronghold on you.

Sun

To see the sun in your dream, symbolizes peace of mind, enlightenment, tranquility, fortune, goodwill, and insight. It also represents radiant energy and divine power. Generally, the sun is a good omen, especially if the sun is shining in your dream. The sun may also be a metaphor for your "son".

To dream that the sun has a creepy, harsh glare, represents a significant disruption or serious problem in your life. The sun is considered a life-giver and thus, any abnormalities and peculiarities to the sun's appearance represents some sort of pain or chaos occurring in your waking life.

Sunburn

To dream that you have a sunburn, indicates that there is an emotional situation or problem that you can no longer avoid. Some urgent matter is literally burning through to your soul and demanding your immediate attention.

Sundae

To see or eat a sundae in your dream, symbolizes joy, pleasure, togetherness and satisfaction with your waking life. You are happy with how things are going in your waking life and are giving yourself a sweet reward. The dream may also be a pun on Sunday. Perhaps there is some occasion or appointment that you need to remember on Sunday.

Sunday

To dream about Sunday, signifies spiritual enlightenment, relaxation and appreciation.

Sundial

To see a sundial in your dream, indicates that something in your waking life does not feel quite real. You may be trying to live up to unrealistic expectations or goals.

Sunflower

To see a sunflower in your dream, symbolizes warmth, abundance, longevity, and prosperity. The sunflower also serves to point you in the right direction and is a source of spiritual guidance. Even through difficult times, you will persevere. Alternatively, the sunflower denotes haughtiness. You may be deceived by the false appearance of someone.

Sunglasses

To dream that you are wearing sunglasses, indicates your poor perception of some issue. You tend to be pessimistic and see the dark or negative side of things. Perhaps you don't want to see or be seen.

Sunrise

To see the sunrise in your dream, represents new beginnings, renewal of life and energy, and fulfillment of your goals and purpose. You are about to embark on a new adventure in your personal life.

Sunscreen

To see or apply sunscreen in your dream, suggests that you are refusing to see the truth in some matter. You are rejecting some advice or message. Alternatively, the dream is symbolic of an emotional wall that you are putting up. You feel the need to protect yourself against negative influences.

Sunset

To see the sunset in your dream, indicates the end of a cycle or condition. It is a period of rest, contemplation and evaluation.

Suntan

To dream that you have a suntan, signifies the shadow aspect of yourself and your primal instincts and natural senses. It is also indicative of hard work. You are owning up to your duties and responsibilities.

To dream that someone else has a suntan, suggests that you are not properly acknowledging a quality or aspect of that person within your own self.

Super Soaker

To see or play with a super soaker in your dream, suggests that you are directing your aggression toward one person. You are upset at this person, but are not expressing your anger in an appropriate manner. Alternatively, the dream may be analogous to the sexual act. Or the dream may be a pun on "soak her".

Superhero

To dream that you are a superhero, represents your above-average talents, ideas, and other hidden abilities that you may not realize you possessed. Alternatively, the dream parallels some extraordinary problem or issue that you are trying to deal with in your waking life. You need to approach the issue head on.

Superman

To see Superman in your dream, represents the heroic male figure in your life. It is also a symbol of power, strength, and masculinity.

To dream that you are Superman, suggests that you are taking on too many responsibilities. You feel that you are going above and beyond your expectations. Because of Superman's ability to fly, perhaps you are expressing an unconscious desire to fly off and get away from it all.

Supermarket

*Please See Market.

The Supremes

To see the Supremes in your dream, signifies your achievements. The Supremes may also be a metaphor for being supreme or being at the top of some situation or circumstance.

Surfboard

To see or ride a surfboard in your dream, suggests that you are going with the flow of things. You have giving in to the existing rhythm and are just along for the ride. The dream may trying to tell you that you need to take more initiative in where you want to go and what you want to do. Alternatively, riding a surfboard refers to your leisurely pursuits.

Surfing

To dream that you are surfing, parallels the ups and downs of some emotional situation or relationship. You may feel overwhelmed. One minute you can be in control of your emotions and the next minute you are not. Alternatively, the dream means that you are going with the flow.

Surgery

To dream that you or someone else is undergoing surgery, signifies the opening of the Self and/or the need for emotional healing. You need to "cut out" or eliminate something from your life. Alternatively, a surgery suggests that you are feeling the influence of some authority figure. You are being swayed to act and behave a certain way. A more literal interpretation of this dream may reflect your concerns about upcoming surgery or about your health.

Surrender

To dream that you surrender, suggests that you need to rid yourself of past emotions and habit. It is time to let go. Alternatively, the dream indicates that you are giving up something important. Perhaps you are having second thoughts.

Surrogate

To dream that you or someone is a surrogate, indicates that you are trying to compensate for something that is missing in your life. You are looking to replace or substitute a missing aspect of your life.

Surroundings

*Please See Landscape.

Sushi

To see or eat sushi in your dream, indicates that you need to acknowledge your spiritual side. It is food for thought. Alternatively, sushi means that you need to adapt a more healthier lifestyle.

Suspended

To dream that you are suspended from school, indicates that you are feeling disconnected. You may be questioning your identity and who you are. Perhaps you are questioning your future. Alternatively, the dream refers to feelings of guilt and shame from your actions. You need to clear your conscience.

Suspenders

To see or wear suspenders in your dream, indicates that you are doing your best to hold yourself up in some situation. Alternatively, the dream may be a pun on being left hanging.

Swallow

To dream that you swallow something, indicates that you are holding back your feelings or words. You may feel unable to express your anger. Alternatively, the dream may be a metaphor that you need to swallow your pride in some situation.

To see a swallow in your dream, symbolizes purity, renewal, never-ending joy and fresh beginnings.

Swamp

To see a swamp in your dream, symbolizes the repressed and dark aspects of yourself. You may be feeling insecure. The dream may also be a pun on feeling swamped from work, a relationship, or other emotional burden.

To dream that you are walking through a swampy area, foretells that you will find yourself in an adverse situation. You may experience setbacks and disappointments in love. Alternatively, walking through a swamp in your dream, denotes the attainment of prosperity and pleasure through dangerous and underhanded means.

Swan

To see a white swan in your dream, symbolizes grace, purity, beauty, dignity, wealth and prestige. Something or someone that may initially be unappealing can turn out to be quite attractive. It is important not to prejudge a situation or person based on the surface.

To see a black swan in your dream, signifies mystery and the unknown. It represents something that is alluring, yet forbidden.

Swap Meet

To dream that you are at a swap meet, suggests that you are feeling undervalued or under-appreciated. You are selling yourself short. Consider the symbolism of the item you are buying and how you feel about it in the dream. Alternatively, the dream may be interpreted literally and represents something occurring in your life that needs to be "swapped" or exchanged.

Swastika

To see the swastika in your dream, symbolizes hatred, evil, cruelty, and destruction. It is commonly associated with the Nazis.

Swearing

To dream that you are swearing, suggests that you need to stop allowing others to harass you. You need to stand up for yourself and don't allow yourself to be taken advantage of.

To hear someone swear in your dream, indicates that you have overlooked an urgent matter or situation. Perhaps someone is in need of rescue from some circumstance and it is your job to protect them.

Sweat

To dream that you are sweating, suggests that you are experiencing some overwhelming anxiety, stress, fear, or nervousness in your life. This dream may serve to remind you that in order to achieve success, you need to endure the struggle and efforts that go along with success. Alternatively, sweating signifies a kind of cleansing or ridding of bad karma. You may be going through an emotional cool-off period.

Sweatshop

To dream that you are in a sweatshop, signifies your waking unhappiness and discontentment at work. Alternatively, you may also be feeling undervalued or stifled in some area of your life.

Sweater

To see or wear a sweater in your dream, symbolizes warmth and love. You have a strong connection to your family and home life. Alternatively, a sweater represents innocence, immaturity, and/or naive thinking.

To dream that you are knitting a sweater, symbolizes your creativity. It may also indicate that you need practice patience.

Sweeping

To dream that you are sweeping, implies that you are clearing your mind of emotional and mental clutter. Get rid of all the minor annoyances in your life and focus on the more important things. You need to take a new stance and have a fresh attitude toward life. Alternatively, sweeping means that you are ignoring some important facts and are going against what your gut and intuition is saying.

Sweet

To taste something sweet in your dream, suggests that life is going well for you. You are expressing your satisfaction with life. Alternatively, the dream may be giving approval to move forward with some decision or action. Sometimes, you need to indulge yourself and not worry about the consequences.

Sweets

To see or eat sweets in you dream, represent indulgence, sensuality, and forbidden pleasure. Perhaps you have been depriving yourself of some joy or pleasure and the dream is a way for you to reward yourself. Alternatively, the dream symbol is a metaphor for your sweetie or the special someone in your life.

Swelling

To dream that you are swelling up, symbolizes a growing problem or issue. You need to address the situation before it gets out of hand. Consider the object or body part that is swollen for additional significance. Alternatively, the dream may be a pun on something that is going "swell". Or it may be a metaphor of your over-inflated ego.

Swimming

To dream that you are swimming, suggests that you are exploring aspects of your unconscious mind and emotions. The dream may be a sign that you are seeking some sort of emotional support. It is a common dream image for people going through therapy.

Swimming Pool

To see a swimming pool in your dream, symbolizes relaxation, calmness, luxury and ease. You need to take a break. Alternatively, a swimming pool suggests that you need to acknowledge and understand your feelings. It is time to dive in and deal with those emotions. You need to cleanse yourself and wash away those past hurts.

To see an empty swimming pool in your dream, suggests that you are literally feeling empty and devoid of emotions.

To dream that the swimming pool is filled with trash, indicates that you are leading a lifestyle of excess. You need to tone it down and discard some of the negative emotions in your life.

Swimsuit

To dream that you are wearing a swimsuit, suggests that you are feeling exposed or emotionally vulnerable. Consider how you feel in the swimsuit. If you are comfortable in the swimsuit, then it signifies a life of ease, relaxation and leisure. If you feel uncomfortable, then it represents a lack of self confidence. If you are wearing a swimsuit in an inappropriate occasion, then it has similar significance as being naked in a dream.

Swing

To dream that you are on a swing, suggests that you are experiencing great satisfaction and freedom in your waking life. It also symbolizes cycles and movement. Alternatively, a swing signifies a desire for sexual variety. The dream may be a pun on being a "swinger."

To see a swing set in your dream, indicates memories from childhood. You want to escape from your current responsibilities and be worry free.

To dream that you are swinging, suggests that you are going back and forth in some situation or decision. You need to make up your mind.

Switch

To see a switch in your dream, represents the status of a situation or relationship in your life, depending on whether the switch is on or off. The dream may also be a pun on something that has been "switched", changed or exchanged.

In particular, to dream that a light switch is broken or that you cannot find the switch, indicates a lack of insight and perspective on a situation.

Swordfish

To see a swordfish in your dream, represents your ability to cut through your emotions and break through the emotional barriers. Alternatively, the swordfish symbolizes masculine sexuality.

Syringe

To see a syringe in your dream, symbolizes health issues, illness, or drug use. Alternatively, the dream may be a metaphor that you need to inject more enthusiasm, fun, or determination into your life. Consider also the contents of the syringe and how it would affect you.

From a Freudian perspective, the needle and its contents represent the penis and sexual intercourse.

Syrup

To see syrup in your dream, symbolizes sentimentality and nostalgia. Alternatively, the dream means that you have found yourself in a sticky situation. Or the dream may be a metaphor for some situation or something that is moving slowly.

T

To see the letter T in your dream, represents your stubbornness and your refusal to change your attitudes and opinions. Alternatively, the dream is analogous to a fork in the road and the two choices or directions.

Table

To see a table in your dream, represents social unity and family connections. If the table is broken, wobbly or not functional, then it suggests some dissension in a group. It may also refer to a sense of insecurity. Perhaps there is something you cannot hold inside any longer and need to bring it out in the open.

To dream that you are setting the table, suggests that you laying the groundwork for a plan or personal endeavor. It also implies confidence.

To see a round table in your dream, indicates evenness, sharing, cooperation, equal rights and opportunities for all. It also symbolizes honesty, loyalty, and chivalry.

To dream that you are lying on a table, indicates your need for nourishment and relaxation. It relates to health concerns and anxieties about your well-being.

To dream that a table is walking or moving by itself, signifies that you will undergo some changes in your life which will relieve you of some dissatisfaction.

Tackle

To dream that you are being tackled, represents obstacles that are standing in your way toward your goals. Something or someone is preventing you from achieving your goals.

Tadpoles

To see tadpoles in your dream, suggest that you have not reached your full potential. If you are a woman and dream of tadpoles, then the dream may indicate your desire to be pregnant.

Tag

To dream that you are playing tag, represents your level of determination and agility toward achieving your goals. If you are the one being chased, then the dream means that you are trying to dodge some responsibility. If you are the one who is doing the chasing, then it signifies your instincts and your determination to go after what you want. The dream may be telling you that "you're it!" You are the chosen one or the one that is chosen for the job.

Tail

To see only the tail of an animal in your dream, signifies annoyances and complications in a situation where pleasure was expected. If the tail is wagging, then it symbolizes excitement, thrills, and joy. If the tail is between the legs, then it represents fear and humiliation. Alternatively, the dream represents balance. Or it may be a pun on "being tailed" as in being followed or chased.

To dream that you have grown a tail, represents an aspect of the past that still lingers with you.

Tailor

To see a tailor in your dream, represents your abilities and creativity. The dream may also be a pun on the need to "tailor" your actions or behavior in order to fit in.

Talent Show

To dream that you are in a talent show, indicates that you are recognizing and using your potential and skills. You are acknowledging your abilities and moving toward a new stage in your life. Consider the reaction and behavior of the audience as they symbolize your social circle and support system. If the audience reacts negatively, then it suggests that your friends and family are not supportive of you. Conversely, if the audience reacts positively, then it means that you have a support system to lean on.

To dream that you are watching a talent show, suggests that you are not utilizing your full potential. You are watching your own talents go to waste.

Talking

To dream that you are talking does not have any significance unless it is unusual or bizarre. What are you saying specifically. Consider also if what you say evoke strong feelings or behavioral reactions. The dream may simply be highlighting your need improve your communication skills or learn to express yourself more clearly.

Tall

To dream that you are taller than someone, indicates that you may be looking down on that person. You feel that you are above him or her. Alternatively, the dream represents authority and pride.

To dream that others are taller than you, suggests that you have a tendency to overlook things. Perhaps you feel that a higher power is always looking over you and judging your actions. Alternatively, the dream denotes low self-esteem issues. You are looking down on yourself.

Tambourine

To see or play a tambourine in your dream, symbolizes the rhythm and beat of your life. You are in control of the various aspects of life that you partake or join in.

Tango

To dream that you are dancing the tango, signifies sensuality, intensity, and drama. Perhaps you need to exhibit these qualities in your work or relationship. Also consider the proverb "it takes two to tango" which refers to mutual cooperation and teamwork.

Tanker

To see a tanker in your dream, represents the need to defend yourself and stand up for your beliefs, even if it means being confrontational or violent. Alternatively, the tanker symbolizes a threat. You are expressing your anger and feelings in a hurtful and volatile way and not letting anything or anybody stand in your way toward your goals.

Tanning Bed

To see or lay on a tanning bed in your dream, symbolizes your vanity and your preoccupation with beauty. Alternatively, the dream may be calling attention to your primal instinct or dark side.

Tap

*Please See <u>Faucet.</u>

Tap Dancing

To dream that you are tap dancing, indicates that you need to keep up with life or else you will be left behind. The franticness and speed of the tapping parallels how chaotic or calm your life is.

To see someone tap dancing in your dream, represents the rhythm of life.

Tape

To see or use tape in your dream, represents your limitations. On the other hand, the dream may be telling you that you need to show more restraint in some aspect of your life.

Tape Measure

Please See <u>Measuring Tape.</u>

Tape Recorder

To see or use a tape recorder in your dream, suggests that there is a message that you need to absorb and incorporate in your daily life. Alternatively, it indicates that there is a past message that you may have overlooked.

Tapeworm

To have or see a tapeworm in your dream, forewarns of poor health. You need to reevaluate your diet and lifestyle.

Tar

To see tar in your dream, signifies your dependency on something or someone. You need to be more self-reliant. Tar is also symbolic of the unconscious and the negative aspect of the Self.

In particular, to dream that you are tarred and feathered, symbolizes pent up anger, hostility and shame. You are punishing yourself.

Tarantula

To see a tarantula in your dream, represents your dark and sinister side. A tarantula is also symbolic of a woman figure in your life.

Target

To dream that you are shooting at a target, indicates that you have your sights clearly set on a goal. The dream may also be trying to motivate you along. If you missed the target, then it symbolizes missed chances, missed opportunities, or missed judgment calls. If you hit the target, then the dream is telling you that you are on the mark or that you are on the right track.

Tarot Cards

To dream of a tarot reading, indicates your current situation and state of mind. You are open to exploring your unconscious thoughts and feelings. Pay attention to what the Tarot Cards reveal. Consider the following general meanings of the four Tarot suits: The Wands represent fire, inspiration, spirituality, action, initiative, and the Psyche. The suit of the Swords signify air, determination, strength, faith, and conquering of fear. The Cups symbolize water, emotions, purity, and your outlook toward life and the future. The Pentacles denote finances, social influence, worldly knowledge, and your connection with nature and earth.

Tart

To see or eat a tart in your dream, suggests that things are going well for you. Alternatively, the dream may also be a pun for a woman who looks like a tart? If you are a woman, then the dream may mean that you need to loosen up a little bit and not be so uptight.

Tassels

To see tassels in your dream, signify some spiritual transition.

Taste

To taste something bad in your dream, suggests that you need to reconsider some situation, relationship or decision. Give it a second chance. For specific taste, please see Sour, Sweet, Salty in the Dream Moods dream dictionary.

Tattoo

To dream that you have tattoos, represent your sense of individuality and the desire to stand out in a crowd. You want to be unique and different from everybody else, particularly if you do not have any tattoos in real life. Consider also what the tattoo is and what significance it has in your life. It may represent something that has left a lasting impression on you. Alternatively, to dream that you have a tattoo, suggests that a waking situation or decision is having a much longer lasting effect that you had expected.

To dream that you are a tattoo artist, suggests that your exotic tastes and strange experiences may turn off those around you. If you are a tattooist in real life, then the dream is just a reflection of who you are.

Taurus

To dream that someone is a Taurus, represents determination, practicality, stubbornness, perseverance and willpower. Perhaps you need to incorporate these qualities into yourself. It also refers to your love of beauty and your gentleness. Alternatively, the dream points to some issues with your neck or throat.

Taxi

Please See Cab.

Tea

To dream that you are making or drinking tea, represents satisfaction and contentment in your life. You are taking your time with regards to some relationship or situation. Alternatively, the dream signifies tranquility, serenity, calmness, and respect.

To dream that you are reading tea leaves, means that you need to look pass the superficial and get to the core of the situation.

To attend or watch a tea ceremony in your dream, signifies unity, togetherness, respect and family.

Teacher

To see your teacher (past or present) in your dream, suggests that you are seeking some advice, guidance, or knowledge. You are heading into a new path in life and are ready to learn by example or from a past experience. Consider your own personal experiences with that particular teacher. What subject was taught? Alternatively, a teacher relates to issues with authority and seeking approval. You may be going through a situation in your waking life where you feel that you are being treated like a student or in which you feel you are being put to a test.

To dream that you are a teacher, indicates that you are in a position of disseminating your knowledge and wisdom to others. The dream may imply how you are "teaching someone a lesson" and giving them a hard time about something. If you are a teacher in real life, then the dream is just a reflection of who you are and is about your work.

To dream that you are having sex with a teacher, implies that there are still things you need to learn when it comes to sex.

Please See Also School.

Ten

Ten corresponds to closure, great strength, and gains. It also refers to the law or to the ten commandments.

Tear Gas

To come in contact with tear gas in your dream, suggests that you are feeling suffocated and smothered by some relationship. You need to cleanse yourself and get rid of past pain.

Teasing

To dream that you are being teased, suggests that you are behaving or acting inappropriately in some waking situation. You are not taking your actions seriously. Alternatively, the dream indicates that you are feeling victimized by others or by circumstances. Teasing may also be a metaphor for someone who is being "a tease", perhaps even yourself.

To dream that you are teasing another person, indicates that you are having a problem accepting an aspect of your own character as represented by the person being teased. They may highlight your own insecurities and self-doubt.

Teenager

If you are beyond your adolescence and you dream that you are a teenager, then the dream suggests that you are acting immaturely. An aspect of yourself may still need some developing in order to achieve fulfillment. Alternatively, to dream that you are a teenager, suggests that you are struggling for your independence and autonomy.

Teeth

To dream that you have rotten or decaying teeth, forewarns that your health and/or business is in jeopardy. You may have uttered some false or foul words and those words are coming back to haunt you.

To dream that your teeth is gleaming, signifies happiness and fulfilled wishes.

To dream that you are brushing your teeth, refers to your level of confidence, your struggles and your aggressiveness. You need to look out for yourself and your own interest. Perhaps, you feel that your position is shaky.

Telephone

To see or hear a telephone in your dream, signifies a message from your unconscious or some sort of telepathic communication. You may be forced to confront issues which you have been avoiding. Alternatively, the telephone represents your communication and relationship with others. If there is no dial tone or the phone is left off the hook, then the dream indicates that you are shutting yourself out. You are experiencing difficulties in getting your thoughts and feelings across.

To dream that you do not want to return a call or answer a ringing telephone, indicates a lack of communication. There is a situation or relationship that you are trying to keep at a distance. To dream that the telephone is constantly ringing, means that some message is not coming through properly.

To dream that you are having a telephone conversation with someone your know, signifies an issue that you need to confront with that person. This issue may have to do with letting go some part of yourself. If you are put on hold, then the dream is a metaphor for being taken for granted or being unable to freely express yourself.

To dream that you dial the wrong number, means that you are experiencing difficulties in relating to others. You have trouble expressing yourself and over-think things.

Telephone Book

To see or use a telephone book in your dream, suggests that "you need to reach out and touch someone". Perhaps there is someone from your past that you need to reconnect with. Or the dream may be a metaphor telling you that there is some issue that you need to "address".

Telephone Number

To see a phone number in your dream, suggests that you need to make contact with someone or reach out for help.

To dream that you cannot remember or find a phone number, suggests that you need to start being more independent and responsible.

To dream that you cannot dial a phone number correctly, suggests that you are having difficulties in getting through to someone in your waking life. Consider whose phone number you are trying to dial. Perhaps he or she is not taking your advice or listening to what you have to say.

To dream that you are giving someone your telephone number, means that you need to take the initiative and reach out to others. You need to make the first move.

Teleportation

To teleport in your dream, represents your desires to escape your current situation or to move more faster and easier through it. You may be expressing some frustrations with how your waking life is proceeding and the slow speed that it is moving at.

Telescope

To see a telescope in your dream, suggests that you need to take a closer look at some situation. It may also indicate that you are going through a period of uncertain changes. As a result, you are feeling anxious. Alternatively, the dream may be a metaphor and that you need to extend or reach out to something or someone.

To dream that you are looking through a telescope at the stars and planets, signifies pleasurable but costly journeys.

Television

To dream that you are watching television, represents your mind and its flowing thoughts. The dream reflects how you are receiving, integrating, and expressing your ideas and thoughts. The programs you dream of watching are an objective view of the things that are in your mind.

To dream that you are on TV, suggests that there is something that you want to broadcast to the whole world. You have the desire to express yourself. Alternatively, the dream means that you are trying to take a more objective view on your life issues.

To dream that the television is broken or that the picture is fuzzy, suggests that you are looking at a problem all wrong. You need to re-evaluate an issue.

Temperature

To dream that you or someone is taking your temperature, suggests that you need to keep your temper in check. If the temperature is high, then it indicates that feelings of anger or hatred or threatening to come to your consciousness. If the temperature is low or normal, then it indicates that you are able to remain calm and cool under pressure.

Temple

To see a temple in your dream, represents inspiration, spiritual thinking, meditation and growth. It is also symbolic of your physical body and the attention you give it. Perhaps you need to pamper yourself. Alternatively, the dream suggests that you are looking for a place of refuge and a place to keep things that are dear to you.

Ten Commandments

To dream of the ten commandments, suggest that you will be rewarded if you behave and follow the rules.

Tennis

To dream that you are playing tennis, represents changes or challenges in your life. You need to actively assert yourself and prove yourself time and time again. Alternatively, playing or watching tennis indicates that you are unable to commit to a situation or decision. You are literally going back and forth between two choices. Perhaps the dream is trying to tell you that "the ball is in your court." It is your turn to make the next move.

Since one of the score in tennis is denoted as "love", then the game of tennis may be a metaphor for a romantic relationship or a courtship.

Tent

To dream that you are in a tent, indicates that you need a temporary change to your daily routine. You need to take time off and get away from the daily grind. Alternatively, the dream may mean instability and insecurity in your current situation. You do not want to settle down.

Dreaming that you are in a tent, may be a pun on your "in-tent" or intentions.

Termite

To see termites in your dream, represent an attack to your soul or to your being. Alternatively, the dream refers to the end of a phase in your life.

Terrorist

To see or dream that you are a terrorist, suggests that your frustrations is giving way to your violent tendencies. You are feeling disempowered, resentful, and frustrated. You need to redirect your energy in a more positive manner.

Test

To dream that you are taking a test, indicates that you are being put to the test or being scrutinized in some way. If you fail the test, then it suggests that you are feeling inadequate or insecure about some aspect of your waking life. If you ace the test, then it means that you are prepared and ready for the task at hand. There is also the notion that if you visualize success, than you will achieve success. Thus, this dream may be a "practice exercise" for you to visualize success in your real life. Alternatively, the dream may be a pun on "feeling testy" and irritated.

Testicles

To see testicles in your dream, symbolize raw energy, power, fertility or sexual drive. The dream may refer to anxiety about your sexual prowess. Alternatively, it indicates that you will need a lot of nerve to achieve some task.

Tetris

To dream that you or someone is playing Tetris, indicates that you are juggling various responsibilities in your life. You are overwhelmed with trying to fit everything into your busy schedule. The dream is analogous to sorting out and organizing the different aspects of your life.

Text Message

To dream that you are sending a text message, represents your connection to others and your network of friendships. The dream may also elude to romance.

Thanksgiving

To dream about Thanksgiving, represents togetherness, family reunions, festivities, and your sense of community. The dream is a reflection on your life and the connections that you have made. Alternatively, this dream may be a metaphor that you need to thank somebody. You may be indebted to someone. Consider also your own associations and traditions with Thanksgiving.

Theater

To dream that you are in a theater, signifies your social life. Consider how the performance parallels to situations in your waking life. Observe how the characters relate to you and how they may represent an aspect of yourself. You may be taking on a new role. Alternatively, the dream is a metaphor that you are being too theatrical or too melodramatic. Are you being a drama queen?

To dream that you are laughing and/or applauding in a theater, indicates that you are choosing pleasure and instant gratification over working on future goals.

To dream that the theater is on fire, signifies risky new projects that you are tying to undertake.

Theme Park

Please See Amusement Park.

Thermometer

To see or read a thermometer in your dream, represents your emotions, whether you are frigid, emotionally cold, warm, or hot. It also symbolizes your reaction to a situation or relationship.

Thief

To dream that you are a thief, suggests that you are afraid of losing what you have. Perhaps you feel that you are undeserving of the things you already have. Alternatively, to dream that you are a thief indicates that you are overstepping your boundaries in some situation or relationship.

To dream that you are a witness to a theft or a victim of theft, indicates that someone is wasting your time and/or stealing your energy and ideas. Perhaps you feel robbed in some way.

Thigh

To see your thigh in your dream, symbolizes stamina and endurance. It refers to your ability to perform and do things. If you are admiring your thigh in your dream, then it signifies your adventurous and daring nature. However you need to be careful with your conduct.

Thirst

To dream that you are thirsty, symbolizes an unmet need. There is an emotional void in your life. Or you may be seeking for some inspiration, motivation or just an extra push.

To quench your thirst in your dream, indicates that you have the ability to succeed and fulfill your desires.

Thirteen

Thirteen is a paradoxical number which means death and birth, end and beginning, and change and transition. It is symbolic of obstacles that are standing on your way and that you must be overcome. You must persevere and work hard and persevere in order to succeed and reach your goals. To many, the number thirteen represents bad luck.

Thorns

To see thorns in your dream, suggest that there is a prickly situation that you need to overcome. Thorns also symbolize past trauma or some physical suffering. You may be putting up your defenses. Also consider if someone is being a pain or a "thorn by your side."

Thread

To see thread in your dream, symbolizes your life path and destiny. It also represents a connection to your thoughts and ideas. Consider also the color of the thread for additional significance.

Three

Three signifies life, vitality, inner strength, completion, imagination, creativity, energy, self-exploration and experience. Three stands for a trilogy, as in the past, present, and future or father, mother, and child or body, mind, and soul, etc. Dream of the number three may be telling you that the third time is the charm.

Throat

To see your throat in your dream, symbolizes the ability to express yourself and communicate your thoughts and ideas.

To dream that you have a sore throat or have throat problems, suggest that you are having problems saying what you really think. You are having difficulties experiencing how you feel and conveying your thoughts. You may feel threatened or vulnerable when you express yourself. Alternatively, your dream may be telling you that you need to swallow your pride.

Throne

To dream that you are sitting on a throne, symbolizes power, leadership and authority. You are in control of all aspects of your life. Alternatively, a throne represents your achievements and goals.

To see an empty throne in your dream, signifies your unwillingness to accept some responsibilities.

Throw

To dream that you are throwing something, indicates that there is someone or something that you need to rid yourself of from your life. Consider the object that you are throwing. Alternatively, the dream may be a pun that you are "throwing" or fixing a game or situation. Are you working against the objective?

Thumb

To see a thumb in your dream, indicates that you need to get a grip on things. It is symbolic of power and ability. If you are giving the thumbs up, then it represents approval and that you are "okay" to proceed. If you are giving the thumbs down, then it means disapproval.

To dream that you have no thumbs, denotes poverty and loneliness.

To dream that you have an abnormally large thumb, signifies a rapid rise to success.

To dream that your thumb has a very long nail, signifies that some negative force is luring you toward some illicit activity.

Thunder

To hear thunder in your dream, signifies a violent eruption of anger and aggression. Alternatively, thunder is an indication that you need to pay attention and learn some important life lesson.

Thyme

To see thyme in your dream, indicates that you need to muster up more courage. It may also be a pun on "time". Perhaps you feel that time is running out for you or that there is some deadline that you need to be mindful of.

Tiara

To see or wear a tiara in your dream, symbolizes feminine power and mystique. You know how to use your femininity to get your way.

Tic Tac Toe

To dream that you are playing tic tac toe, represents your strategy for success. You need to line up your plan in order to achieve success. Alternatively, the dream symbolizes X's and O's or hugs and kisses.

Ticket

To see a ticket in your dream, represents the price you need to pay to attain your goals. You have decided on your path in life. A ticket signifies the start of a new endeavor. Consider also the type of ticket. A bus or train ticket symbolizes the price you pay to get ahead in life, while a movie ticket represents your need to be more objective in a situation.

To dream that you lose a ticket, denotes confusion and ambiguity in the direction of your life.

Tickle

To dream that you are being tickled, indicates a need for humor and laughter in your life. You are taking things too seriously. Alternatively, the dream may be a metaphor for someone that "tickles" your fancy.

Ticks

To see or be bitten by a tick in your dream, indicates that something or someone is slowly draining the energy and strength out of you. A relationship, your job, or a situation is sucking the life and energy out of you. Ask yourself what in your life is causing you much exhaustion. Alternatively, the dream may be a pun on being "ticked off" and thus represent your feelings of being annoyed or irritated.

Tie

To see or wear a tie in your dream, represents your obligations and relational bonds. The dream may also be a pun on feeling tied down to a situation or relationship. If the tie is loose fitting around your neck, then it suggests that you have some unfinished business to tend to. If the tie is too tight-fitting, then it denotes that you feel trapped or suffocated in a situation or condition.

To dream that you are tying something, represents your network and connection to others. Alternatively, the dream may be a metaphor of your family ties.

Tiger

To see a tiger in your dream, represents power and your ability to exert it in various situations. The dream may also indicate that you need to take more of a leadership role. Alternatively, the tiger represents female sexuality, aggression, and seduction.

To dream that you are attacked by a tiger, symbolizes repressed feelings or emotions that you are frighten you of.

To see a caged tiger in your dream, suggests that your repressed feelings are on the verge of surfacing.

To see rugs made of tiger skins, symbolize a life of luxury and ease.

Tightrope

To dream that you are walking on a tightrope, indicates that you are in a very precarious situation. You need to proceed carefully and weigh all the pros and cons of some important decision.

Time

To dream about time, indicates your fears of not being able to cope with the pressures and stresses of everyday life. If time is flying or moving slowly, then it is analogous to aging and growing old.

To dream that you do not have enough time, signifies stress, anxiety and fear. You may feel that time is running out in a business or personal matter.

Time Travel

To dream about time travel, indicates your wish to escape from your present reality. You want to go back into the past or jump forward to the future to a period where your hopes are realized. This dream also represents your romantic tendency and or your desire to romanticize everything.

Tiptoe

To dream that you are tiptoeing, highlights your grace and poise in a situation or circumstance. You have a careful understanding of the smaller and minor details in your life. Alternatively, the dream indicates your reservation and hesitance in pursuing toward some path.

Tires

To see tires in your dream, suggest that you are dwelling too much in the past and need to move on toward the future. It also refers to your emotional health and your ability to bounce back from adversity. You are able to carry yourself from one situation to another with confidence.

To see or dream that you have a flat tire, indicates that you are feeling emotionally drained and weary. Your goals are temporarily hindered and as a result, you are unable to progress any further.

To dream that your tires have no more tread, suggests that are unable to get any traction toward achieving your goals.

To see tire tracks in your dream, denote that you are stuck in a rut.

Tissue

To see or use tissue in your dream, indicates that it is time to let go of the past and move on. You need to confront your current problems in order to progress forward.

Toast

To see or eat toast in your dream, signifies your appreciation for the simple things in life. If the toast is burnt, then it suggests that your passion may consume you.

To make a toast in your dream, suggests that you need to look at the brighter side of things. Consider what you are toasting to. The dream may be a pun for something that is toast or done. Or it may mean being toasted or intoxicated.

Toaster

To see a toaster in your dream, suggests that you are quick witted and quick-thinking. It refers to your continuous flow of ideas.

Toes

To see your toes in your dream, represent the way you move and walk through life, either with grace and poise, or the lack of. It also signifies your path in life. Alternatively, toes represent the minor details of life and how you deal with them.

To dream that your toe nails are growing, symbolize an extension of your understanding in a particular matter.

To dream that you lose or gain a toe(s), suggests that you are lacking determination and energy needed to move forward in some situation.

To dream that you hurt your toe or that there is a corn or abrasion on it, means that you are feeling anxious about moving forward with some pan or decision.

To dream that someone is kissing your toe, indicates that someone is trying to reassure and reaffirm your progress forward. They are motivating you to do better.

Toga

To see or wear a toga in your dream, signifies serenity, peace, love and fate.

Toilet

To see a toilet in your dream, symbolizes a release of emotions. You need to get rid of something in your life that is useless. Seeing a toilet in your dream may also be a physical manifestation brought about by a full bladder. The dream is attempting to get you up and to the bathroom. If you are cleaning the toilet, then it means that you are starting to shed your outer wall or lose your inhibitions.

To see a clogged toilet in your dream, suggests that you are holding and keeping your feelings to yourself. Your emotions have been pent up too long and you need to let go of the negative feelings.

To see an overflowing or flooded toilet in your dream, denotes your desires to fully express your emotions.

Toilet Paper

To see or use a roll of toilet paper in your dream, represents the aftermath of some emotional release. You are ready to heal from your emotional outburst.

To dream that your house has been toilet papered, suggests that your personal space has been violated. You feel victimized emotionally. If you are toilet papering someone else's house, then it indicates that what may be seemingly harmless can have serious repercussions.

Toilet Seat Cover

To see or use a toilet seat cover in your dream, means that you are not ready to address your emotions directly. Something or someone is still preventing you from fully letting go of your feelings.

Toll Road

To dream that you are on a toll road, signifies the price you have to pay in order to get ahead in life. There is no such thing as a free ride.

Tomatoes

To see a tomato in your dream, symbolizes domestic happiness and harmony.

To dream that you are eating tomatoes, foretells of good health.

Tongs

To see or use a pair of tongs in your dream, suggest that you need to keep your distance from some matter or situation. It is time to mind your own business.

Tongue

To see your own tongue in your dream, represents the things you say and express. You may have either said too much or you may need to express yourself more. If you dream that your tongue is unusually long, then it suggests that you are not being truthful and are lying to yourself about something. If your tongue is sore or looks unusual, then it indicates that you are talking negatively about somebody. The dream may also be a metaphor that you are tongue-tied. You are nervous about verbalizing or communicating some feeling or thought.

To dream that your tongue is hairy or that there is hair on your tongue, indicates that you are regretting what you said. Something you said could be leaving a strange taste in your mouth.

To dream that you rip someone else's tongue out, indicates that you are extremely upset with something that this person has said, but you are not able to appropriately express your anger. Because you tend to keep your emotions inside, it is finding expression in your dreams in a violent way.

To dream that someone is sticking out their tongue at you, refers to some sexual connotation. The tongue is sometimes connected with sexuality and maybe seen as a phallic symbol. Alternatively, the dream symbolizes some sort of insult.

Tonsils

To see your tonsils in your dream, suggest that you are ready to share an aspect of yourself.

Tools

To see or use tools in your dream, represent your self-expression, skills and abilities. You are using the resources that are available to you. It is also a symbol of masculinity. Perhaps you need to create and move toward a different direction. Alternatively, to see tools in your dream, suggest that a situation or relationship is in need of some damage control or attention. According to the Freudian school of thought, tools are symbolic of the penis and thus tools being used refer to intercourse.

The tool in your dream may also be a pun on how you are acting like a tool or that someone who is a tool. The dream may also be telling you that you are being taken advantaged of or that you are blindly following others.

Toothbrush

To see or use a toothbrush in your dream, suggests that you are feeling defensive about any criticism directed towards you. You are putting up a shield or barrier to protect yourself from potential hurt. Alternatively, the dream means that you are preoccupied with your appearance and are worried about how others perceive you.

Toothpick

To see a toothpick in your dream, suggests that you are too picky. Perhaps you are dwelling too much on minor flaws, faults, and other small issues.

To dream that you are using a toothpick, indicates that you are unable to verbalize some emotion or feeling. Your words are stuck in your mouth.

Top

To see or spin a top in your dream, represents idleness. You are not going anywhere in life and are wasting your time away on frivolous pleasures.

To dream that you are on top, signifies your goals, aspirations and ideals. You are seeking higher understanding and knowledge.

Topaz

To see a topaz in your dream, signifies calmness, warmth and relaxation. You need to restore balance in your life. Alternatively, topaz symbolizes faithfulness, friendship and forgiveness.

Topless

To dream that you are topless, signifies your way of showing and exhibiting love. You may be inviting love toward your direction.

Torch

To see a torch in your dream, represents self confidence, ability to succeed, enlightenment and spiritual confidence.

To dream that you are carrying a lit torch, symbolizes love. The dream may be a metaphor that you are carrying a torch for someone or that you have some sort of crush on them. Alternatively, the dream denotes your struggles and desires to break free.

Tornado

To see a tornado in your dream, suggests that you are experiencing some extreme emotional outbursts and temper tantrums. Is there a situation or relationship in your life that may be potentially destructive?

To dream that you are in a tornado, means that you are feeling overwhelmed and out of control. Your plans will be filled with much complications and you will be met with a series of disappointments.

To see several tornadoes in your dream, represent people around you who are prone to violent outbursts and shifting mood swings. It may also symbolize a volatile situation or relationship.

Torpedo

To see a torpedo in your dream, suggests that you need to be more direct and honest with your feelings. Or on the other hand, you may be too direct and blunt. The torpedo also has phallic connotations and signify masculine aggression or power.

Tortoise

To see a tortoise in your dream, symbolizes perseverance, determination, and longevity. You need to take some chances in order to get ahead in life. The opportunities for advancement are opened to you, but you need to take the next step. Alternatively, the tortoise represents the need to be sheltered or protected from life's problems.

Torture

To dream that you are being tortured, indicates that you are feeling victimized or helpless in some relationship or situation. You feel that you cannot do anything. Alternatively, the dream suggests that you may exhibit some sadomasochistic desires.

To dream that you are torturing someone or see others being tortured, suggests that you are punishing yourself for your own negative or bad habits. You are projecting yourself onto the person or animal being tortured. Consider the symbolism of who is being tortured. Alternatively, the dream indicates repressed feelings of revenge which you are not able to act on in your waking life.

Totem Pole

To see a totem pole in your dream, represents your need to feel protected. It is symbolic of strength and power. Alternatively, a totem pole symbolizes respect and familial solidarity.

Toucan

To see a toucan in your dream, denotes paradise, relaxation and ease. This dream symbol may also appear as a pun on "two can". In other words, two can do it. It is about a partnership, collaboration or teamwork. You cannot do everything yourself, but two can do it.

Toupee

*Please see Hairpiece.

Tourniquet

To dream that you are using a tourniquet, indicates that you are feeling drained. You need to concentrate your energy on your strengths and not your weaknesses.

Tow

To dream that you are towing a vehicle or heavy object, suggests that you are overworked and overburdened. You feel that others are not pulling their own weight at work, at home, or in a personal relationship. You also feel that you are giving more than you are receiving.

Tow Truck

To see a tow truck in your dream, represents your burdens and responsibilities. Alternatively, it signifies an aspect of your life where you need a little assistance. You need someone to help "pick" you up and get you on the right track again.

To dream that you are driving a tow truck, means that you feel others are overly dependent on you. You are feeling burdened or overwhelmed.

Towel

To see or use a towel in your dream, suggests that you need to deal with your emotions in order to move forward in your life. You need to find some sort of a resolution. Alternatively, it represents completion, a fresh start and new transition.

Toxins

*Please See Poison.

Toys

To see or play with toys in your dream, symbolize childhood, domestic joy and harmony. You may be searching for the comfort and security of home. It also represents playful attitudes and your childish ways. Alternatively, the dream may be a metaphor that you are "toying" with somebody's feelings, especially if you are playing together with someone in the dream. Perhaps you are leading someone on.

To dream that you are giving away toys, denote that you are being acknowledged for your good deeds.

To see or play with broken toys in your dream, suggest that you are trying to make the best out of a negative situation. If you or someone breaks a toy, then it indicates a lack of joy, harmony, or security in your life. You are no longer deriving as much joy from some aspect of your life as you used to. Consider the type of toy and its significance to you.

Track

To dream that you are tracking something or someone, suggests that you need to get in touch with some aspect of yourself. The dream may be a pun for some goal, person, or ideal which you have lost track of.

To dream that you are being tracked, indicates that you need to be more careful and stand up for yourself. You need to be on guard and on the defensive.

Tractor

To see or ride a tractor in your dream, represents your resourcefulness and ingenuity. You set your sights on something and you go for it.

Traffic

To dream that you are in traffic, signifies the frustrations that you are experiencing in your life. Things are not going as smoothly as you would like it to. You feel stuck at where you are in life.

To see traffic in your dream, indicates the hustle and bustle of everyday life. Sometimes you feel like you are just going with the flow. Things have become too routine.

To dream that you are directing traffic, implies that you have power and control over the path or destinations of others. The dream may be highlighting your anxieties about exercising that control.

Traffic Cone

To see traffic cones in your dream, suggest that you need to slow down. You may be experiencing some delays or setbacks toward your goals. Perhaps the dream is telling you that you need to take a different approach.

Traffic Light

To see a traffic light in your dream, suggests that you feel you are being held back from pursuing your goals. Your forward progress is being controlled by someone or by some outside forces. In other words, you are not in control of your own life. Alternatively, the dream represents the pressure to succeed or else be left behind. If the traffic light is green, then it indicates that you have been given a seal of approval to follow whatever path you have chosen or whatever decision you have made.

Trailer

To see a trailer in your dream, suggests that you are feeling overburdened. You are carry more weight on your shoulders than you need to. The dream may also indicate that you are more of a follower than a leader.

Train

To see a train in your dream, represents conformity. You are just going along with what everyone else is doing. Alternatively, a train means that you are very methodical. You need to lay things out specifically and do things in an orderly and sequential manner. In particular, if you see a freight train, then it refers to the burdens and problems that you are hauling around. It is also symbolic of manual labor. If you see a passenger train, then it relates to mental work. If you see or play with a model train in your dream, then it indicates that you want more control and power over your own life and where it is headed. Dreaming of trains may also be a metaphor that you are "in training" for some event, job or goal.

According to Freud, a train is analogous to the male penis.

To dream that you are on a train, symbolizes your life's journey. It suggests that you are on the right track in life and headed in the right direction. Alternatively, the dream means that you have a tendency to worry needlessly over a situation that will work out in the end.

To see or dream that you are in a train wreck, suggests chaos. The path to your goals are not going according to the way you planned it out. You are lacking self-confidence and having doubt in your ability to reach your goals.

To dream that you are the engineer, signifies that you are in complete control of a particular situation in your waking life.

To dream that you miss a train, denotes missed opportunities. It also suggests that you are ill-prepared for a new phase in your life. You may be procrastinating or putting things off that should have already been completed.

Trainer

To see or dream that you have a personal trainer, suggests that you need to push yourself to do better in all that you do. Do not take the easy way out. Alternatively, the dream indicates that you are seeking guidance and help in improving your self-image.

To see or dream that you are a dog trainer, indicates that you need to keep your negative behavior in check. You need to show more restraint.

Trampoline

To dream that you are jumping on a trampoline, represents your resilience and your ability to bounce back from difficult and emotional situations.

To see a trampoline in your dream, symbolizes the ups and downs of life.

Transfusion

To dream that you have a blood transfusion, indicates that you need to be revitalized and reenergized. You may be lacking inspiration and need some new motivation in life.

Transparent

To dream that something is transparent, indicates feelings of vulnerability. You are able to see things and see through people and their motives. Thus the dream may be symbolic of your actions and your true intentions. Alternatively, if something is transparent, then it represents clarity and understanding.

Transsexual

To dream that you are transsexual, symbolizes your anxieties or ambivalence about masculine/feminine roles or passive/aggressive behavior. You may be reluctant in dealing with these issues. If you are considering or awaiting transsexual surgery, then the dream may represent your anxieties and fears about the surgery, recovery, and life after surgery.

To see a transsexual in your dream, indicates that the masculine and feminine aspects of your Self have been damaged. You may be unwilling to confront your shadow self.

Transvestism

*Please See <u>Cross Dressing</u>

Trap

To dream that you are setting a trap, indicates that you are trying desperately to hold onto a relationship, to some old habits or to your former ways. Alternatively, the dream signifies your readiness to take action.

To dream that you are trapped or caught in a trap, suggests that you are feeling confined and restricted in your job, career, health, or a personal relationship. You may be in a rut and are tired of the same daily monotony.

Trapeze

To see a trapeze act in your dream, signifies a carefree attitude toward life. You are trying to escape from your daily responsibilities and take some time out to relax. Alternatively, the dream represents your high aspirations and ideals.

To dream that you are swinging on a trapeze, indicates a desire or wish for sexual variety and adventure. Alternatively, the dream symbolizes indecisiveness. You are going back and forth on some choice.

Trash

*Please See Garbage.

Traveling

To dream that you are traveling, represents the path toward your life goals. It also parallels your daily routine and how you are progressing along. Alternatively, traveling signifies a desire to escape from your daily burdens. You are looking for a change in scenery, where no one has any expectations of you. Perhaps it is time to make a fresh start. If your travels come to an end, then it symbolizes successful completion of your goals.

To dream that you are traveling in a car filled with people, signifies new friends and exciting adventures.

Treadmill

To dream that you are on a treadmill, indicates that you are stuck in the same old routine. You are not going anywhere despite your hard work and efforts. It is time to break free from the monotony.

Treasure Chest

To see a treasure chest in your dream, represents your hidden talents. It also refers to a sense of security and belonging. You are content with where you are in a situation or relationship.

To dream that you are looking inside the treasure chest, suggests that you are trying to recapture something valuable from your past.

Treasures

To dream that you find treasures, indicate that you have unveiled some hidden skill or talent. It also symbolizes your self-worth and what you have to offer to the world. Alternatively, the dream may be a metaphor for something or someone that your value or "treasure".

To dream that you are burying treasure, suggests that you are thinking ahead to the future. Perhaps there is some talent or skill that you want to keep secret from others.

Tree House

To see or dream that you are in a tree house, indicates that you are trying to escape from your waking problems. You are blocking off the harsh reality of daily life.

To dream that you are building a tree house, suggests that you are working hard to realize your hopes and goals. The dream is about self-development and maximizing your own potential.

Trees

To see lush green trees in your dream, symbolize new hopes, growth, desires, knowledge, and life. It also implies strength, protection and stability. You are concentrating on your own self-development and individuation.

To dream that you are climbing a tree, signifies achievement of your career goals and attainment of higher positions in life. The speed at which you climb the tree will parallel the speed of your achievement of these goals.

To dream that you chop or cut down a tree, indicates that you are wasting your energy, time, and money on foolish pursuits. Alternatively, the dream may be a comment on your sexual fear or guilt.

To see a falling tree in your dream, means that you are feeling off balance and out of sync. Perhaps, you are off track and headed in the wrong direction.

To see a withered or dead tree in your dream, indicates that your hopes and desires have been dashed. You are experiencing some instability and setback in your life. Alternatively, the dead tree represents infertility or a lack of virility. Perhaps it signal an end to a familial line (as in a family tree).

To see bare trees in your dream, indicate used up energy. You have put your all into some relationship or project and now you are exhausted. Perhaps you are even feeling depressed. Alternatively, the dream signifies the cycle of life or the passage of time.

To see crows perched on the dead tree, symbolizes the end of some cycle or behavior. It is representative of death.

Trespass

To dream that you are trespassing, suggests that you are forcing your beliefs on others. You are also being overly attentive or overly possessive, especially in a relationship. You need to give someone their breathing room.

Trial

To dream that you are on trial, indicates that you need to be more accepting of yourself and less judgmental of others. You may be too harsh on yourself or of others. Alternatively, a trial suggests that you are feeling guilty about something in your waking life.

Triangle

To see a triangle in your dream, symbolizes your aspirations, potential and truth. It represents your spirituality: the body, mind, and spirit. If the triangle is pointing upward, then it signifies the masculine while a downward pointing triangle signifies the feminine. Alternatively, seeing a triangle serves as some sort of warning or caution, especially if the triangle is yellow. The dream may also be a metaphor for a love triangle in your waking life.

Trick

To play a trick on someone in your dream, indicates that you are not being honest with yourself. You are trying to divert attention elsewhere, other than yourself. Alternatively, the dream may be a metaphor for "turning tricks."

To dream that you have been tricked, suggests that your plans are about to backfire.

Tricycle

To see a tricycle in your dream, symbolizes simplicity and a carefree nature. You are experiencing an alleviation from tension and stress.

Trip

To dream that you trip on something, indicates that something is out of order in your life. Things are not going as smoothly as you want, especially when you are faced with obstacles. The dream may forewarn that you are about to make a mistake in some waking decision.

To dream that you are going on a trip, suggests that you are in need of a change of scenery. You are feeling overworked and need to take time out for yourself for some fun and relaxation. Alternatively, the dream means that you are looking to explore a different aspect of yourself.

To dream that you are on a business trip, suggests that you are having a difficult time trying to relax and being at ease. You may be feeling overwhelmed.

Triplets

To see triplets in your dream, suggest that you need to consider the physical, the emotional and the spiritual aspects of a situation or decision. Also think about the significance of things that may appear in threes in your waking life.

Trophy

To see a trophy in your dream, symbolizes recognition for your hard work. The dream may be trying to motivate you.

Truck

To see a truck in your dream, suggests that you are overworked. You are taking on too many tasks and are weighed down by all the responsibilities. Pregnant women often dream of trucks or driving trucks. This may be a metaphor of the load they are carrying or an expression of their changing bodies.

Trumpet

To see or hear a trumpet in your dream, signifies some sort of warning or danger that you have found yourself in. It may be a way for your subconscious to get your attention.

Trunk

To see a trunk in your dream, represents old memories, ideals, hopes, and old emotions. It indicates issues and feelings that you have not dealt with.

To see the trunk of a car in your dream, signifies the things that you are carrying around with you.

To see the trunk of a tree in your dream, signifies your personality, your character, and your inner sense of well being. It is symbolic of your backbone and the things that hold you up. If the trunk is thick and large, then it denotes that you are a strong, rugged and durable person. If the trunk is thin and narrow, then it suggests that you are a highly sensitive person.

Truth Or Dare

To dream that you are playing truth or dare, indicates that you need to hold true to your words and do what you say you are going to do.

To dream that you have to tell the truth, then it means that you need to come clean about something that has been nagging on your mind. You need to release some guilt or clear your conscious.

To dream that you dare someone to do something, suggests that you are being too dominating. If someone dared you to do something, then it indicates that you will find yourself in some embarrassing or compromising position.

T-Shirt

To see or wear a T-shirt in your dream, suggests that you need to take it easy and relax. Alternatively it represents your honesty and genuineness, especially in your personal relationships. Consider also if there is a design or saying on the T-shirt.

Tuba

To see or play a tuba in your dream, indicates that there is an important message that you need to convey. Alternatively, the dream suggests that you want to make your presence known and stand out from the crowd.

Tug Of War

To dream that you are playing tug of war, suggests that you need to balance various aspects of your personality. You need to learn to compromise.

Tulips

To see tulips in your dream, indicate fresh new beginnings. You are loving life! Tulips are also symbolic of faith, charity, hope, perfection, idealistic love and fertility. Consider the pun "two lips". Perhaps it is hinting to a kiss?

Tumbling

To see or dream that you are tumbling, represents your ability to balance aspects of your life. You are able to land on your feet and overcome difficulties with grace. Alternatively, the dream signifies carelessness. Tumbling may also be a metaphor that you have taken a "tumble" or a misstep.

Tumor

To dream that you or someone has a tumor, suggests that some repressed memory or feeling remains unsettled and is threatening to emerge into your consciousness. You need to confront these issues. Consider where in the body is this tumor is located for additional symbolism.

Tuning Fork

To see or use a tuning fork in your dream, suggests that you are "in tune" with your conscious or your instinct. Keep on doing whatever you are doing.

Tunnel

To see a tunnel in your dream, represents the vagina, womb, and birth. Thus it may refer to a need for security and nurturance.

To dream that you are going through a tunnel, suggests that you are exploring aspects of your unconscious. You are opening yourself to a brand new awareness. Alternatively, it indicates your limited perspective as in the phrase "tunnel vision". Are you being close minded or narrow minded in some issue?

To see the light at the end of a tunnel, symbolizes hope. You will navigate through life and all its difficulties with great success. Alternatively, it also indicates the end of your journey and the realization of your goals.

Turban

To see or dream that you are wearing a turban, suggests that you are feeling confined by what society considers normal.

Turkey

To see a turkey in your dream, indicates that you are being foolish.

You are not thinking clearly. Alternatively, a turkey is symbolic of Thanksgiving and thus, a time of togetherness and family.

To see a sick or dead turkey in your dream, denotes an attack to your pride.

To see a flying turkey in your dream, foretells of a rapid rise from obscurity to a position of prominence.

To dream that you are hunting or shooting a turkey, suggests that your success is achieved through dishonest and underhanded means.

Turquoise

To see turquoise in your dream, symbolizes luck, success and fortune. The turquoise possess healing energy and acts to unify forces between the spirits of the earth and the air. Alternatively, the dream indicates an evil or negative force that you are trying to ward off.

As a color, turquoise is symbolic of healing power and natural energy. It is often associated with the sun, fire, and masculine power. If you have negative feelings toward this color, then it indicates that you are shutting off your emotions and not letting people in. You fear change.

Turtle

To see a turtle in your dream, symbolizes wisdom, faithfulness, longevity, and loyalty. It also suggests that you need to take it slow in some situation or relationship in your life. With time and patience, you will make steady progress. Alternatively, a turtle indicates that you are sheltering yourself from the realities of life. You are putting forth a hard exterior and not letting others in. As a result, you are feeling withdrawn.

To dream that you are being chased by a turtle, indicates that you are hiding behind a facade, instead of confronting the things that are bothering you. .

Tutu

To see or wear a tutu in your dream, symbolizes your femininity or issues with your feminine side. You are struggling with gender roles and what is acceptable. Alternatively, the dream may be a pun on the number 2 or 22. Consider the significance of the number in your waking life.

Tuxedo

To see or wear a tuxedo in your dream, represents culture, sophistication, and/or grace. It refers to a cultivated passion and your desires for the finer things in life. Alternatively, a tuxedo suggests that you want to amount to something in your life. You want to make a name for yourself and establish your reputation.

Tweezers

To see tweezers in your dream, indicate that you need to look at a situation much more closely. There is something that requires precision and accuracy.

Twelve

Twelve denotes spiritual strength and divine perfection. It also represents cycles and repetition.

Twenty

The number twenty indicates that you are in need of support. Perhaps you are feeling withdrawn and isolated. The dream may signify having 20:20 vision. You are seeing something more clearly now.

Twenty-One

The number twenty-one represents a turning point in your life and your full transition into adulthood. It is also associated with the responsibilities that you need to own up to. Alternatively, twenty-one suggests that you will be lucky at a game of blackjack.

Twenty-Four

The number twenty-four symbolizes rewards, happiness, love, money, success and creativity. It also refers to your associations with people of high position and power. The number may be telling you that you are being too arrogant in love or in success. Alternatively, the number twenty-four may imply time, as in 24 hours or all day.

Twilight

To see the twilight in your dream, refers to some old habit, condition, or situation.

Twins

To see twins in your dream, signify ambivalence, dualities or opposites. It also represents security in business, faithfulness, and contentment with life. It may also mean that you are either in harmony with or in conflict between ideas and decisions.

To see twins fighting in your dream, represent a conflict between the opposites of your psyche. One twin signifies emergence of unconscious material and suppressed feelings, while the other twin represents the conscious mind. There is some situation that you are not confronting.

Twisty Tie

To see or use a twisty tie in your dream, suggests that you need to put closure on a relationship or situation. It is time to move on. The dream may be analogous to how you are wound up or how your thinking is "twisted".

Twitter

To twitter in your dream, represents your desires to stay connected with others. Perhaps you are expressing concerns about losing touch with someone around you. If you are following someone on twitter in your dream, then it may mean that you need to learn to think for yourself. You need to be a leader instead of a follower. Alternatively, if you dream that others are following you on twitter, then it highlights your leadership skills.

Two

Two stands for balance, diversity, partnership, marriage cooperation, soul, or receptivity. It can also symbolize double weakness or double strength. The world is seen as being made up of dualities and opposites, as in the male and female, mother and father, light and dark, heaven and hell, yin and yang, etc.

Typewriter

To see a typewriter in your dream, indicates that you need to open the lines of communication with someone in your life.

Typing

To dream that you are typing, symbolizes your communication skills. It may indicate the difficulties you have in verbally expressing your thoughts. Alternatively, the dream may be a pun on a "type" of something. Perhaps you are being typecast or that you are looking for your type.

U

To see the letter "U" in your dream, is a pun on "you" and how you act and behave in your waking life. Consider what you are doing and how you are feeling in the dream for additional significance.

U-Turn

To make a u-turn in your dream, indicates that you are altering the course of your life. You are changing directions and starting on a completely different path. Alternatively, the dream means that you have made a wrong decision or choice.

To see a no u-turn sign in your dream, suggests that you cannot take back what has already been done. There is no turning back on the choices you have made.

Ultrasound

To dream that you are getting an ultrasound, signifies a new and developing phase in your life. Perhaps you are starting a new relationship, switching jobs or relocating. The dream may also reflect your actual concerns about a pregnancy or your desires to have children.

Umbrella

To see an umbrella in your dream, symbolizes emotional security. You are putting up a shield against your emotions and are trying to avoid dealing with them. If the umbrella is leaking, then it indicates that you are unprepared with facing your problems.

To dream that you cannot open you umbrella and it is raining, then it suggests that you are open to confronting your own feelings and letting your emotions come to the surface.

Uncle

To see your uncle in your dream, represents some aspect of your family heritage and trait. It also symbolizes new ideas and emerging awareness. Consider the idiom "say uncle" to mean surrender or admit defeat.

Unconscious

To dream that you are unconscious, indicates your helplessness and inability to function in some given situation. You are not prepared for the major changes that are happening around you. Alternatively, being unconscious suggests that you are oblivious to your surroundings or ignorant of some situation. The dream may be a pun on your unconscious mind and its suppressed content.

Undead

To see the undead in your dream, represents your fears and the rejected aspects of yourself. You are refusing to acknowledge those negative parts. If you are being chased or are surrounded by the undead, then it symbolizes unresolved issues that you are not confronting. Things that you thought or assume were put to rest is coming back to haunt you.

To dream that you are undead, represents your inability to express yourself. You are feeling disconnected with others. Alternatively, the dream suggests that you have relapsed back to your old habits and ways.

Underarm

*Please See <u>Armpit.</u>

Undercover

To dream that you are undercover, indicates that you are hiding your true feelings or true nature. Perhaps the dream is trying to tell you that you are being someone that you are not.

Underwater

To dream that you are underwater, suggests that you are being overcome with emotions and are in over your head regarding some situation. You need to gain greater control of your life.

To dream that you are breathing underwater, represents a retreat back into the womb. You want to return to a state where you were dependent and free from responsibilities. Perhaps you are feeling helpless, unable to fulfill your own needs and to care for yourself. Alternatively, breathing underwater is analogous to being submerged in your own emotions.

Underwear

To dream that you are in your underwear, signifies a situation that has created a loss of respect for you. Alternatively, it symbolizes some aspect of yourself that is private. If you feel ashamed of being seen in your underwear, then it indicates your hesitance in revealing your true feelings, attitudes, and other hidden habits/ideas. If you are not bothered by being in your underwear, then it suggests that you are ready to reveal or expose something that was previously hidden.

To dream that you are not wearing any underwear, signifies fear that your secrets will be revealed.

To dream that someone is in their underwear, signifies an embarrassing and inexplicable situation. Alternatively, the dream means that you are seeing this person for who he or she really is.

To see dirty or torn underwear, suggests that you are not comfortable in your own skin and have feelings of inadequacy. You are uncomfortable about your sexuality and are overly critical about yourself.

Undress

To dream that you are undressing, suggests that you need to reveal your true feelings and be open about them. Alternatively, undressing indicates your connection and comfort level with your sexuality.

To see someone undressing in your dream, indicates that you need to be aware of other people's feelings. If you are undressing someone else, then it suggests you are trying to gain a better understanding of that person.

Unibrow

To dream that you have a unibrow, indicates that you are feeling insecure about your physical appearance. Alternatively, the dream suggests that you are not expressing your feelings enough. Perhaps you are keeping too much of your emotions inside. There is something you are trying to hide.

Unicorn

To see a unicorn in your dream, symbolizes high ideals, hope and insight in a current situation. It also symbolizes power, gentleness, and purity. Alternatively, it may represent your one-sided views.

Unicycle

To dream that you are riding a unicycle, signifies that you are in total control of a situation and are exercising authority in both personal and business matters.

Uniform

To dream that you or someone is in uniform, signifies your need to belong or be part of a group. Alternatively, the dream may suggest that you are conforming too much to the beliefs of others. Learn to think for yourself and be your own person.

In particular, to see a nurse's uniform in your dream, indicates cleanliness, compassion, and properness. To see a school uniform, means how you are identifying with your school and your classmates. It may bring attention to some issue you have at school. To see people in strange uniforms, signify disruption and chaos.

Up

To dream of being or moving up, suggests that you are emerging from some depressing or negative situation. You may be feeling high or euphoric. The dream may also compensate for your waking feelings of sadness. Alternatively, it signifies that your ego is inflated. Or that you are experiencing upward mobility or progressing toward your goals.

According to Jung, the dream parallels some material or repressed thoughts that may be emerging from your unconscious.

Upside Down

To dream that you are upside down, suggests that there is some situation or problem in your waking life that you need to straighten you. It may also mean that your initial assumptions were completely opposite of what you thought.

Uranus

To see Uranus in your dream, represents originality, unconventional thinking, independence, freedom, and individualism. You may be rebelling against some situation in your waking life. Alternatively, Uranus indicates that something unexpected is about to occur.

Urination

To see urine in your dream, represents the feelings you have rejected. Alternatively, the dream may be a pun on your "pissy" attitude.

To dream that you are urinating, symbolizes a cleansing and a release of negative or repressed emotions. Depending on your dream context, urination is symbolic of having or lacking basic control of your life. You are literally "pissed off" and not expressing yourself in a positive or constructive manner.

To dream that you are urinating in public, symbolizes a lack of privacy in some personal matter. Alternatively, the dream mean that you are trying to establish your boundary and "mark your territory."

Utopia

To dream about utopia, symbolizes your ideals and your strive for perfection. The dream may be warning you against trying to achieve unattainable goals. You are expecting too much out of others. Alternatively, the dream is one of wish-fulfillment where you wish that all your difficulties problems are gone. You are looking for an escape from your daily life.

V

To see the letter V in your dream, symbolizes victory, success or peace. As a Roman Numeral, it could represent the number 5.

Vacation

To dream that you are on vacation, indicates that you need a break to recharge your energies and revitalize yourself. You need to break out of your daily routine and do something different. Alternatively, dreaming of a vacation represents your achievements. You are giving yourself a pat on the back and are deserving of a reward for your hard work.

To dream that you are having a bad or awful vacation, suggests that you are not able to escape from the daily responsibilities of your waking life. You are having difficulties coping with life's problems and issues.

Vacuum

To see a vacuum in your dream, refers to feelings of emptiness. You may be experiencing a void in your life. Alternatively, the dream indicates that you need to clean up your act and your attitude. It is time to rid yourself of your outdated ideas and negative habits.

To dream that you are vacuuming, signifies a loss of control. You feel that you are being sucked up by some problem. Alternatively, the dream represents your desires to keep up appearances. Things may look fine on the surface, but some problem still persists underneath.

Vagina

To see your vagina in your dream, suggests issues with your femininity and you sexual needs/urges.

Valentine

To dream that you are sending valentines, indicate your need to express more love and affection.

To dream that you are receiving a valentine, represents your likeability, compassion and good-hearted nature.

To see a box of valentines in your dream, signify that an old lover may come back into the picture.

Valet

To dream that you are a valet, indicates that you are lacking your own direction in life. You are always helping others with their goals.

To dream that a valet parks your car, suggests that you are letting other people dictate your direction in life. Or you are putting the goals of others ahead of your own.

Valley

To dream that you are in a valley, symbolizes fertility, abundance, or your need to be sheltered and protected. If you are entering or walking through a valley, then it is analogous to your issues of death and dying. This death may be symbolic as in an end to something in your life. Alternatively, the dream represents life's struggles and hardships before you can achieve some spiritual enlightenment or epiphany.

Vampire

To see a vampire in your dream, symbolizes seduction and sensuality, as well as fear and death. The vampire represents contrasting images of civilized nobility and aggression/ferocity. It may depict someone in your waking life whose charm may ultimately prove harmful. Deep down inside, you know that this person is bad for you, yet you are still drawn to him or her. Vampires also sometimes relate to decisions about sex and losing your virginity. Alternatively, to see a vampire suggests that you are feeling physically or emotionally drained. The vampire may also be symbolic of someone who is addicted to drugs or someone in an obsessive relationship.

To dream that you are a vampire, signifies that you are sucking in the life energy of others for your own selfish benefit.

Van

To see or drive a van in your dream, symbolizes convenience and/or practicality. Consider the load that you are carrying and what you can handle. Don't stress yourself out.

Vandalism

To dream that you commit vandalism, signifies repressed anger. You feel that you are being treated unjustly.

To witness vandalism in your dream, represents your passive aggressive tendencies. The dream is telling you that you need to express yourself more constructively.

Vanilla

To taste or smell vanilla in your dream, indicates a welcoming experience or inviting situation. Alternatively, it symbolizes purity and innocence.

Vanish

Please See <u>Disappear</u>.

Vase

To see a vase in your dream, symbolizes the womb and all things feminine. You are open to criticism or suggestions. Alternatively, the dream represents creativity. If the vase is ornate, expensive, or fancy, then it indicates that you like to be the center of attention.

To dream that a vase is cracked or broken, represents past, forgotten, or lost love.

Vasectomy

If you are a man and dream that you have a vasectomy, then it indicates that you are expressing some dissatisfaction about your sex life. Alternatively, it suggests some self-doubt or issues with your self-image.

VCR

To see a VCR in your dream, refers to something that needs to be documented or recorded. There may be something that you have overlooked. A VCR also refers to memories and lessons of the past and the insights that you can still gain from it. The dream may also be calling attention to the impression you leave behind and what others may think of you.

Vegetables

To see vegetables in your dream, signify your need for spiritual nourishment. It may also indicate that you are lacking in a particular nutrient. Look up the specific vegetable for additional interpretation.

To see withered vegetables in your dream, denotes sadness. The dream may also be a metaphor that you are "vegging". You need to get up and be more active.

Vegetarian

If you are not a vegetarian in your waking life and dream that you are a vegetarian, then it refers to your strict self discipline. Alternatively, the dream may also mean that you are lacking substance in some are of your life.

Veil

To dream that you or someone is wearing a veil, represents something that you wish to hide or conceal. Things may not be what it appears to be. In particular, if you are a man and dream you are wearing a veil, then it signifies the feminine aspects of your character. Perhaps, you need to acknowledge your feminine side. Alternatively, a veil symbolizes humility, coyness or innocence.

Veins

To see your veins in your dream, represent a challenge that will test your character and ability. The dream also suggests that you should not take things for granted, especially if they seem to come easily.

Velvet

To dream that you are wearing velvet, signifies distinction and honor. It also represents you sensuality and emotions.

To dream that you are wearing velvet pants, signifies your sensual side.

Vending Machine

To see a vending machine in your dream, represents the things that are just outside of your grasp or reach. You need to invest a little more effort before your goals come to fruition. Consider what is inside the vending machine for further significance.

Venereal Disease

To dream that you have a venereal disease, indicates some sort of contamination, either physical or emotional. You may feel vulnerable or victimized in a waking relationship. Alternatively, the dream signifies a fear of sex or an imbalance in sexual energy.

Venom

To come in contact with venom in your dream, represents pent-up anger and hostility you may be expressing or experiencing from others. Perhaps, your feelings of hate are beginning to show through. Alternatively, the dream is indicative of a lack of self-esteem, lack of self-love, or insecurities you have.

Ventriloquist

To see a ventriloquist in your dream, symbolizes deception, fraud or some treasonable matter affecting you in a negative way.

To dream that you are a ventriloquist, signifies dishonorable conduct and deception towards people who trusted you. There is a part of yourself that you are not revealing. Alternatively, the dream means that you are trying to influence, manipulate, or control people around you.

Venus

To see Venus in your dream, symbolizes love, desire, fertility, beauty, and femininity. It also represents the things you value and cherish in life.

Venus Flytrap

To see a Venus flytrap in your dream, symbolizes the devouring female. It refers to a powerful or overbearing woman in your life. Alternatively, the dream may be a metaphor that you are feeling "snappy."

To dream that you are being eaten by a Venus flytrap, indicates that you are being overwhelmed by some dominant female in your waking life.

Vertical

To dream of a vertical line or something that is vertical,

symbolizes the spiritual realm and the supernatural.

Vest

To dream that you are wearing a vest, represents your compassion for others. Alternatively, the dream may be a pun on being "vested" in something or someone.

Veterinarian

To see a veterinarian in your dream, indicates that you need to tame your instinctive behavior and unconscious self so that it is more socially acceptable.

Vibrate

To feel a vibration in your dream, suggests that you need to pay more attention to your intuition and to your emotional side. Alternatively, the dream refers to some sexual need.

Victim

To dream that you are a victim, suggests that you are being oppressed and overpowered by others. Such dreams suggest that you are feeling powerless and helpless in a waking situation. Alternatively, the dream indicates that you are unwilling to take responsibility for your choices.

Video Camera

To dream that you are using a video camera, suggests that you need to be more objective in your decisions. Focus on the task at hand and try not to let your emotions cloud your judgment.

To dream that someone is using a video camera, indicates that you are reflecting back on your past and old memories. You may be trying to learn from previous mistakes or relive the good and bad times.

Video Game

To dream that you are playing a video game, represents your ability to manipulate others into doing what you want them to do. Alternatively, playing video game suggests that you are trying to escape from the problems in your real life, instead of confronting it. Consider the type of video game for additional insights.

To see or dream that you are a character in a video game, suggests that you are feeling controlled and manipulated by others. You feel that you have no control over your actions or are not taking responsibility for them.

Videotape

To watch a videotape in your dream, indicates that you need to stop and relax. Take a break from life and let your mind rest. Consider the title of the videotape or what you are watching and determine how it relates to your waking life. It may also represent past memories or repressed thoughts that are playing out as the dream videotape.

If you are rewinding the videotape, then it suggests that you are experiencing regret or remorse over your past actions.

If you are forwarding the videotape, then it suggests that you are trying to escape from some current situation.

Viking

To see a Viking in your dream, indicates that you are feeling violated or conflicted in some way. You are facing a confrontational situation.

To dream that you are a Viking, represents exploration of your unconscious thoughts. It also means that you are taking a chance at some emotional relationship.

Vinegar

To see or drink vinegar in your dream, suggests that you are feeling sour about some situation. It may denote a relationship that has gone sour. Alternatively, the dream may be telling you to make the best out of a bad situation. You are worrying too much.

Vines

To see vines in your dream, represent your hopes, ambitious thoughts or ideas. Alternatively, vines symbolize a clingy relationship. Perhaps you feel trapped and are searching to break free. Your emotions could be holding you back.

To see grape vines in your dream, symbolize rewards, prosperity, and spirituality. Grape vines signify sexuality and sensuality.

Violence

To see violence in your dream, indicates unexpressed anger or rage. You need more discipline in your life. If you enjoy the violence, then it points to your aggressive or sadomasochistic tendencies. The dream may also reflect repressed memories of child abuse. In particular, to dream that the violence is directed to yourself, represents self punishment and guilt. You may be feeling helpless or vulnerable in some area of your life. Violence toward others in your dream, suggests that you may be fighting or struggling against aspects of your own Self.

Violet

The color violet denotes high spirituality, religious aspiration, purification, affection, gentleness, charm, and peacefulness. You have a sense of intuitive understanding and special intimacy.

To see violet flowers in your dream, signify passion, joy and bliss. It also indicates enlightenment, spirituality and humility. Alternatively, the dream represents your shyness. You tend to hide in the background.

Violin

To see or hear a violin in your dream, symbolizes peace and harmony in your waking life. If the violin is broken, then it signifies separation, sadness, and bereavement.

To play a violin in your dream, denotes honor, distinction and refinement. You will be well recognized for your work.

Virgin

To dream that you are a virgin, symbolizes purity and potential. Note that the dream may not necessarily mean actual physical virginity, but could also represent emotional innocence. In particular, if you are not a virgin but dream that you are one, then it signifies past regret or remorse. You need to stop dwelling on the past and look toward the future.

To dream that someone is a virgin, indicates integrity and honesty. You may have an ideal that you are tying to attain.

Virgo

To dream that someone is a Virgo, denotes cautiousness, purity and perfection. You are detail-oriented and are always striving toward perfection. Alternatively, the dream symbolizes release of emotions.

Virus

To dream that you have a computer virus or a bug, refers to something in your life that is out of control. It may parallel something in your life that has come to a crashing end.

To dream that you have a viral infection or contracted a virus, suggests that you are experiencing an unpleasant change or an emotional breakdown in your waking life. The virus may be symbolic of your inability to cope with a situation and you see that being sick is a way out. On a more direct note, the dream may signal you to pay close attention to your health, especially to the area of body revealed in the dream.

Vitamins

To see or take a vitamin in your dream, indicates that you need to strengthen your willpower and stand up for yourself. Alternatively, taking vitamins point to your waking eating habits and that you need to add certain nutrients to your diet.

Voice Mail

To dream that you have a voice mail, symbolizes some important advice that you may have overlooked, but need to heed. Pay attention to the message and how it applies to your waking life.

Voiceless

To dream that you are voiceless, represents a loss of identity and a lack of personal power. You are unable to speak up and stand up for yourself.

Voices

To hear voices in your dream, signify a message from the unconscious or spiritual realm. Alternatively, the dream may be a metaphor that you need to "voice" your opinions more loudly. Speak your mind!

Volcano

To see a volcano in your dream, indicates that you are unable to control your emotions, particularly if the volcano is erupting. You are ready to burst. The outcome may be damaging and hurtful, especially to those around you. If the volcano is dormant, then it represents past issues that have been resolved and put to the rest.

Volleyball

To dream that you are playing volleyball, represents your indecisiveness and your inability to commit. Alternatively, playing volleyball indicates the importance of cooperation and teamwork. You need to learn to rely on others instead of doing everything yourself.

Volume

To dream that you are turning up the volume, suggests that you are demanding to be heard. No one is paying attention to what you are saying. You are feeling overlooked or overshadowed in some waking situation.

To dream that you are turning down the volume, indicates that there is something that you are refusing to hear. You may be rejecting what your inner voice or instinct is trying to convey.

To dream that the volume is too loud, indicates that you are forcing your opinions and views on others. You are too overbearing and/or confrontational.

To dream that the volume is too low, suggests that you are not paying enough attention to what someone is trying to tell you. You are not picking up on the cues. Alternatively, the dream signifies missed opportunities or feeling left out.

Vomiting

To dream that you are vomiting, indicates that you need to reject or discard an aspect of your life that is revolting. There are some emotions or concepts that you need to confront and then let go.

To see someone vomiting in your dream, signifies the false pretenses of people who are trying to take advantage of you.

Voodoo

To dream that you are practicing voodoo, suggests that you are unconsciously trying to ward off some surrounding negative energy.

To see a voodoo doll in your dream, represents a primitive and shadowy aspect of yourself.

Vote

To dream that you are casting a vote, signifies your desire to belong to a larger group or to develop an aspect of your character on a more public level. You or someone is looking for support, approval and acceptance. The dream may also mean that you are speaking your mind and letting your voice be heard. You are demanding a say in how you should live your own life.

Vulture

To see a vulture in your dream, suggests that your past experiences will provide you with invaluable insight into a current situation or problem. Learn from your past. Alternatively, a vulture indicates that you or someone is being opportunistic. Someone is watching you and is waiting for you to take a misstep. You feel that someone is taking advantage of you or is using you. Consider the metaphor of someone who is a "vulture". Sometimes, a vulture is a symbol of death or doom.

W

To see the letter "W" in your dream, is a reiteration of "you". You need to focus on you and only you.

Waffle

To dream of eating a waffle, indicates that you need to come down from your lofty ideals and approach life from a more pragmatic perspective. The dream may also be a metaphor that you are "waffling" or undecided over some matter.

To dream that you are waffling over a topic, suggests that you need to think things more clearly and learn to express yourself with more assurance and conviction.

Wagon

To see a covered wagon in your dream, is symbolic of difficulties and difficulties that you are carrying with you. It signifies your thrifty nature and your unwillingness to take risks. The dream may also be a metaphor that you have "fallen off the wagon". You have broken a resolution or promise to yourself.

To see a red wagon in your dream, represents childhood joy and light-hearted fun.

To see an empty and abandoned wagon in your dream, signifies loss and dissatisfaction with the current state of your life.

Waist

To notice your waist in your dream, suggests that you are concerned about your diet or weight. The dream may also be a pun on "wasting" time, money, or some aspect of your life.

Waiter/Waitress

To dream that you are a waiter or waitress, indicates that you are too busy catering to the needs and demands of others, instead of your own. You feel that you are underappreciated as you wait on others hand and foot. You need to be more assertive and stand up for yourself. Consider the quality of service that you are giving for additional significance.

To see a waiter in your dream, indicates that you need to be nurtured and to feel special. The dream may also be a pun to be patient. Learn to wait.

Waiting

To dream that you are waiting, is indicative of issues of power/control and feelings of dependence/independence, especially in a relationship. Consider how you feel in the dream while you were waiting. If you are patient, then you know things will happen at their own pace. If you are impatient, then it means that you are being too demanding or that your expectations are too high.

Alternatively, the dream may denote your expectations and anxieties about some unknown situation or decision. You are experiencing a sense of anticipation or uneasiness.

Wake

To dream that you attend a wake, refers to your grieving process. You need to find closure. It is okay to seek the support in order to help you get through a difficult time. Alternatively, the dream suggests that it is time to celebrate the positive qualities of someone who is no longer in your life.

To dream that you are waking up in your dream, indicates that something is missing or lacking in your life. There is an aspect of your life that you are not utilizing to its fullest potential. You are not recognizing your abilities. The dream is literally telling you to open your eyes and wake up! Alternatively, waking up in your dream may be a signal of a lucid dream.

Walkie Talkie

To see or use a walkie talkie in your dream, suggests that you need to be both receptive and communicative in some waking work situation or personal relationship. Remember that communication is two-way. You need to learn to speak and to listen. The clarity of the message is symbolic of how poorly or how well you are communicating your feelings, ideas, or thoughts. Alternatively, the dream is a metaphor telling you that if you walk the walk, you need to talk the talk.

Walking

To dream that you are walking with ease, signifies a slow, but steady progress toward your goals. You are moving through life in a confident manner. Consider your destination.

To dream that you have difficulties walking, indicates that you are reluctant and hesitant in proceeding forward in some situation. You may also be trying to distance yourself from certain life experiences. The difficulty in walking is a reflection of your current situation and the obstacles that you are experiencing.

Wallet

To see your wallet in your dream, symbolizes yourself identity or financial security.

To dream that your wallet has been stolen, indicates that someone may be trying to take advantage of you. Perhaps someone has "stolen" your heart away.

To dream that you lost your wallet, suggests that you need to be more cautious and careful about your spending and finances. You need to be more responsible with your money. Alternatively, losing your wallet, indicates that you are losing touch with your true identity. You are experiencing some anxiety over changes and uncertainties happening in your life. If you find a wallet, then it indicates that you have regained financial stability.

To see an empty wallet in your dream, represents financial worries. Alternatively, it refers to an emotional void or inner emptiness.

Wallpaper

To dream that you or someone is hanging up wallpaper, signifies that you are putting up a barrier or some sort of shield between yourself and others. It also suggest that you are covering something up or that you are hiding a secret. Alternatively, the dream may mean something that needs beautifying. Consider the color and pattern of the wallpaper, as it will offer clues as to the kind of barrier, secret or feeling that you are putting up.

To dream that you are peeling or stripping off wallpaper, denotes that you are beginning to let your guard down. You are breaking down your barrier one layer at a time. It also indicates that you are revealing aspects of yourself that have been kept well hidden.

Walls

To see a wall in your dream, signifies limitations. obstacles and boundaries. There is a barrier obstructing your progress. Alternatively, the wall indicates that you are too accustomed to your old habits and way of thinking. You feel stuck.

To dream that you jump over a wall, suggests that you are able to

338

confront tough obstacles and get around barriers with success and ease.

To dream that you demolish or break down a wall, indicates that you are breaking through obstacles and overcoming your limitations. It also means that you desire some freedom and independence. If you see a wall crumble, then it suggests that you have risen above your problems and overcame your barriers.

To dream that you are building a wall, refers to a bad relationship or childhood trauma. You are trying to keep others out for fear of getting hurt again. Alternatively, the dream suggests that you have accepted your limitations.

To dream that you are hiding behind a wall, suggests that you ashamed in acknowledging your connections.

To dream that you are being thrown or shot through a wall, means that you need to literally breakdown those walls that you have put up around you. You need to venture out and explore.

To dream that a house has no walls, represents a lack of privacy. You feel that everyone is looking over your shoulder or up in your business.

Walnut

To see walnuts in your dream, indicate that too much mental activity is being expended towards a task at hand. You are wasting your time. Alternatively, walnuts represent joy and abundance.

To dream that you crack a walnut, foretells that your expectations will collapse.

Walrus

To see a walrus in your dream, represents your display of

dominance in some situation or relationship. You are always on the lookout for anybody who is trying to out-maneuver, out-rank, or out-wit you. Alternatively, the walrus represents your protective shell and thick-skin. You do not let the comments/criticism of others get to you.

For Eskimos and Native Americans in the North, the walrus symbolizes supernatural ability and power.

Wand

To see or wave a wand in your dream, represents your power and influence over others. You are only limited by your imagination. If someone else is holding the wand, then it signifies their power over the situation.

War

To dream of a war, signifies disorder and chaos in your waking life You are experiencing some internal conflict or emotional struggle which is tearing you up inside. Alternatively, the dream indicates that you are either being overly aggressive or that you are not being assertive enough. Perhaps you need to be prepared to put up a fight in some area of your life. On a more direct level, the dream may be reflection of current wars around the world and your personal feelings about it.

Warehouse

To see a warehouse in your dream, represents stored energy or hidden resources. The warehouse also refers to memories. Alternatively, the warehouse means that you are putting your ambitions and goals on hold.

To see an abandoned or empty warehouse, indicates that your inner resources have been depleted. You need to take some time off to restore your energy and replenish your resources.

To dream that you are leasing or renting an empty warehouse, represents your receptiveness and your open-mindedness to new things.

Warning

To receive a warning in your dream, indicates that something in your waking life is in need of your attention. The dream may serve to make you stop and rethink the consequences of your action or decision.

To dream that you are warning someone, suggests that you need to recognize the dangers or negatives of some situation. You need to bring this to the surface.

Warrant

To dream that a warrant is being served on you, indicates that you will be involved in some important matter or decision. Consider the type of warrant that is being serves. If it is a search warrant, then you need to take a second look at your motives and actions. If it is an arrest warrant, then you need to stop what you are doing and take a different course of action.

To dream that a warrant is served on someone else, refers to a misunderstanding.

Warthog

To see a warthog in your dream, suggests that you need to take charge of your life.

Warts

To dream that you or someone has a wart, suggests that you need to learn to acknowledge the beauty within you. The dream also

339

indicates self-punishment. You are unwilling to forgive yourself.

Washing

To dream that you are washing yourself, indicates that you are proud of your social life and personal endeavors. You may even receive some recognition and prestige. Alternatively, the dream represents the cleansing away of unhappy experiences or neglected emotions in your life. You are ready to make a fresh new start.

To dream that you are washing your feet, indicates that you are ready to make a big change in your life.

To dream that you are washing your hands, suggests that there is a worrisome issue that you need to work through. Alternatively, the dream suggests that you are not taking responsibility for some matter. You need to let go of old emotions and past relationships. It is time to get the negativity out of your system.

To dream that you are washing your car, suggests that your problems will soon pass. You are ready to go through life with a fresh new outlook and attitude.

Washing Machine

To see or use a washing machine in your dream, suggests that you need to resolve issues of the past in order to be able to make a clean, new start for yourself.

Wasp

To see a wasp in you dream, signifies evil, anger and negative feelings. Alternatively, the wasp represents someone who is a WASP or White Anglo-Saxon Protestant. Perhaps you are dealing with some aspects of society or politics.

To dream that you are stung by a wasp, indicates that there is some hatred directed toward you. It also refers to envy.

To dream that you kill a wasp, signifies your fearlessness in fighting off your opponents, while maintaining your ethics and rights.

Waste

To see waste in your dream, indicates that you are overexerting yourself or investing too much of your energy on something that may not be worthwhile. Alternatively, the dream may be telling you that you are being wasteful and thus need to reevaluate certain aspects of your life. You are literally wasting away. The dream may be a metaphor for "being wasted" or intoxicated.

Watch

To see or wear a watch in your dream, suggests that you need to be more carefree and spontaneous. Your life is too structured. Or you are feeling limited and constrained. Alternatively, the watch symbolizes the ticking of the human heart and thus is indicative of the emotional side of your life. The dream may also be a metaphor to indicate that you need to "watch out".

To see a broken watch in your dream, indicates that you are unsure of your own feelings or how to express yourself. You are experiencing an emotional standstill. Alternatively, a watch suggests that you have poor time management. You have lost track of what you have to do.

Watching

To dream that you are watching something, indicates your passiveness. You lack initiative to take a position or to take action. It may reflect upon your real life and how you are watching life pass you by, instead of participating it. You need to take more initiative. Alternatively, the dream symbolizes your neutrality in some situation. You do not want to take a side. The dream may also be a metaphor warning you to "watch it!"

To dream that you are being watched, suggests that you are feeling confined in your work environment or personal relationship. You are lacking privacy and feel you are being scrutinized or criticized.

Water

To see water in your dream, symbolizes your unconscious and your emotional state of mind. Water is the living essence of the psyche and the flow of life energy. It is also symbolic of spirituality, knowledge, healing and refreshment. To dream that water is boiling, suggests that you are expressing some emotional turmoil. Feelings from your unconscious are surfacing and ready to be acknowledged. You need to let out some steam.

To see calm, clear water in your dream, means that you are in tune with your spirituality. It denotes serenity, peace of mind, and rejuvenation.

To see muddy or dirty water in your dream, indicates that you are wallowing in your negative emotions. You may need to take some time to cleanse your mind and find internal peace. Alternatively, the dream suggests that your thinking/judgment is unclear and clouded. If you are immersed in muddy water, then it indicates that you are in over your head in a situation and are overwhelmed by your emotions.

To dream that water is rising up in your house, suggests that you are becoming overwhelmed by your emotions.

To hear running water in your dream, denotes meditation and reflection. You are reflecting on your thoughts and emotions.

To dream that you are walking on water, indicates that you have total control over your emotions. It also suggests that you need to "stay on top" of your emotions and not let them explode out of hand. Alternatively, the dream is symbolic of faith in yourself.

Water Cooler

To see or use the water cooler in your dream, suggests that you are literally bottling up your emotions. You are looking for safe and controlled release. Alternatively, a water cooler indicates that you are seeking spiritual nourishment or just conversation. Consider the phrase "water cooler talk".

Water Gun

To see or play with a water gun in your dream, signifies you passive aggressiveness. You are expressing your anger in such a playful way that others do not recognize or acknowledge your true feelings. You are having difficulties expressing your real feelings.

Water Lily

To see a water lily in your dream, signifies grief, sorrow, and bereavement.

Water Park

To dream that you are in a water park, indicates that you are expressing an emotional high point. You are feeling emotionally satisfied and fulfilled.

Water Skiing

To dream that you are water skiing, represents an uplift in your spirituality and increase in your self-confidence. You are experiencing a new sense of freedom and calm.

Waterbed

To see a waterbed in our dream, suggests that you are slowly acknowledging aspects of your unconscious. You are recognizing certain unexpressed energy, particularly issues dealing with sexuality, fear, aggression, etc.

Waterfall

To see a waterfall in your dream, is symbolic of letting go. You are releasing all those pent up emotions and negative feelings. Alternatively, the dream represents your goals and desires. In particular, if the waterfall is clear, then it represents revitalization, regeneration and renewal.

To dream that you are at the bottom of the waterfall, suggests that you are feeling emotionally overwhelmed. You are experiencing difficulties in coping with your feelings.

Watermelon

To see a watermelon in you dream, represents emotions of love, desire, lust, and fiery passion. Pregnant women or women on the verge of their menstrual cycle often dream of watermelons due to their changing or bloated bodies. Alternatively, watermelons mean summertime ease, leisure, and relaxation.

Waves

To see clear, calm waves in your dream, signify renewal and clarity. You are reflecting on some important life decision that needs to be made. Alternatively, if you are riding a wave, then it indicates that you are trying to get a handle on your emotions. Waves also symbolize potential and power.

To hear waves crashing in your dream, indicates tenderness and relaxation. It also brings about feelings of sensuality, sexuality and tranquility.

To dream that you are caught in a tidal wave, represents an overwhelming emotional issue that demands your attention. You may have been keeping your feelings and negative emotions bottled up inside for too long. You may be holding back tears that you are afraid to express in your waking life. On a positive note, the tidal wave symbolizes the clearing away of old habits. If you are carried away by the tidal wave, then it means that you are ready to make a brand new start in a new place.

To see muddy, violent waves in your dream, indicate a fatal error in an important decision.

Waving

To dream that you are waving to someone, represents your connection to that person. You are trying to gain their recognition or get their attention. Perhaps there is a certain aspect of this person that you need to incorporate into your own self. The dream may also signify your need to develop deeper and closer friendship ties.

Wax

To see wax in your dream, indicates that there is too much activity going on in your life. There is too much chaos going on. You need to slow down and take a breather. Alternatively, the dream may be a metaphor suggesting that you are impressionable and easily influenced.

To dream that you are waxing something, suggests that you are ready to move forward in some project or endeavor. You have gained the approval of those around you.

To see dripping wax in your dream, represents your hidden passionate emotions and spiritual cleansing.

Weapons

To see or hold a weapon in your dream, indicates a need to defend and protect yourself emotionally and/or physically. You are experiencing some conflict in your waking life. Alternatively, the dream may indicate your hidden desire to hurt someone or something. Your dream provides a safe haven for expressing these desires. In dreams, weapons also often have sexual connotations.

Weasel

To see a weasel in your dream, represents your lack of trust in others. It may also mean that you are acting or being deceitfully.

Weather

To dream about the weather, signifies your emotional state of mind. Stormy or windy weather implies conflict and aggression. Rain and hail represents depression and sadness. And rainbows and sunshine signify hope and happiness. Alternatively, weather may be a pun on "whether" you should do this or that. Perhaps you are trying to decide between two options.

To dream that the weather is ever-changing, signify the passage of time.

To dream that you are reading the weather report, means that you are about to make some major move. Alternatively, it indicates a decision that you need to make.

Weather Vane

To see a weather vane in your dream, indicates unpredictability and versatility. Alternatively, the dream suggests that are going around in circles. The dream may also be a pun on being vain or doing something in vain.

Weaving

To dream that you are weaving something, suggests that you are trying to piece together some information. You need to incorporate various components together and look at the picture as a whole. Alternatively, weaving symbolizes your creativity.

Web

To see a web in your dream, represents your desire to control everything around you. Alternatively, it suggests that you are being held back from fully expressing yourself. You feel trapped and do not know what to do or where to go. The dream may also be symbolic of your social network of acquaintances and associates or it may represent the world wide web.

Wedding

To see a wedding in your dream, symbolizes a new beginning or transition in your current life. A wedding reflects your issues about commitment and independence. Alternatively, your wedding dream refers to feelings of bitterness, sorrow, or death. Such dreams are often negative and highlight some anxiety or fear. If you dream that the wedding goes wrong or ends in disaster, then it suggests that you need to address some negativity immediately.

To dream that you are attending a wedding, consider how you feel at the wedding. If you are upset or sad, then it means that you are unhappy about the current status of your life. If you are happy, then you are embracing a new change in your life.

To dream that you are getting married to your current spouse again, represents your wedded bliss and happiness. It highlights your strong commitment to each other. It may also signify a new phase (such as parenthood, new home, etc) that you are entering in your life.

To dream that you are planning a wedding to someone you never met, is a metaphor symbolizing the union of your masculine and feminine side. It represents a transitional phase where you are seeking some sort of balance between your aggressive side and emotional side. The dream may also indicate that two previously conflicting aspects are merging together as one.

If you are getting married and have dreams of your pending wedding, then it highlights the stress of organizing a wedding. Conflicts over wedding details, tension with family and in-laws, fear of commitment, and loss of independence may all cause wedding anxiety dreams. Research has shown that up to 40% of brides and grooms have dreams about their ceremony and things going perfectly.

*Please See Also <u>Marriage</u>.

Wedding Dress

To wear a wedding dress in your dream, indicates that you are evaluating and assessing your personal relationship.

If you or someone is wearing a wedding dress in an inappropriate situation, then it suggests that you are feeling inferior or unworthy.

Wednesday

To dream about Wednesday, indicates that you are in misery or agony over something. You feel conflicted about a decision and are stuck in the middle. Wednesday is often referred to as "hump day". Thus the dream may be a form of encouragement; you are at the halfway point of some endeavor.

Weeds

To dream that you are weeding, suggests that you need to rid yourself of the negativity in your life in order to move on and grow as a person. It is time to release past grudges and build on future relationships.

To see weeds in your dream, indicate that you are feeling neglected, overshadowed or cast to the side. Weeds may also represent friendships or relationships that have gone awry.

To dream of cannabis, denotes a loss of control. You are trying desperately to escape. The dream may be a reflection of waking drug use.

Week

To dream about the week, signifies your sense of time management. The dream may also be a pun on being "weak".

Weeping

To dream that you are weeping, indicates some deep sadness in your waking life. You are suppressing your sad feelings and they are now manifesting in your dream. Bottling up these feelings are not always healthy.

Weight

To dream of your own weight, represents your self-worth, self-esteem, influence or power of persuasion. It is also indicative of the burdens you carry in life. Alternatively, weight represents your preoccupation with your physical shape and appearance. The dream may also be a pun for "wait".

To dream that you are losing weight, indicates that you are no longer being weighed down by some responsibility or emotional burden. It is as if something has been lifted off your shoulders.

To dream that you are overweight or that you are gaining weight, suggests that you are feeling over-burdened and pressured. You are carrying too many responsibilities.

To dream that you are underweight, implies that you need to work harder at something. The dream may also be telling you that you are way out of your league in some situation.

Weightlifting

To dream that you are lifting weights, represents your strength and power. Do not underestimate what one person can do. Alternatively, the dream is a metaphor that you are flexing your muscle. You want others to know that you are in charge.

Welfare

To dream that you are on welfare, indicates that you are feeling shameful of your life circumstances. Alternatively, the dream may be a pun on being "well" and "fair". It may also be a pun on your "well being".

Well

To see a well in your dream, represents your hidden abilities and talents that have not yet come to the surface or not yet recognized. The well is also symbolic of the depth of your emotions. It may serve as a depository for your emotions and how you are trying to suppress them. Alternatively, the dream may be a pun on how you are doing "well".

To dream that you fall into the well, indicates losing emotional control.

To dream that the well is dry, suggests that there is an emotional void in your life. You feel empty inside and need to be fulfilled.

Werewolf

To see a werewolf in your dream, indicates that something in your life is not what it seems. It is symbolic of fear, repressed anger, and uncontrollable violence.

To dream that you are a werewolf, suggests that some aspects of your personality are hurtful and even dangerous to your own well-being. You are headed down an undesirable path. Alternatively, a werewolf refers to your repressed instincts.

West

To dream of going west, represents fulfillment, opportunities, and growth. Alternatively, west symbolizes death, old age or an ending of something.

Wet

To dream that you are wet, indicates that you are overcome with emotions. It also signifies a spiritual cleansing, rebirth or renewal. Alternatively, the dream may imply sexual arousal.

Wet Suit

To see or wear a wet suit in your dream, suggests that you are slowly and safely exploring your inner feelings and emotions. You are a point where you are comfortable in acknowledging your vulnerabilities and feelings.

Whale

To see a whale in your dream, represents your intuition and awareness. You are in tuned with your sense of spirituality. Alternatively, a whale symbolizes a relationship or business project that may be too big to handle. You are feeling overwhelmed. The dream may also be a pun on "wailing" and a desire to cry out about something.

Wheelbarrow

To see or use a wheelbarrow in your dream, represents hard work, labor, and difficulty. The wheelbarrow also symbolizes your body and the way that you are moving about through life. Consider what is inside the wheelbarrow for clues as to where you are headed.

Wheelchair

If you do not use a wheelchair in your waking life and dream that you are in a wheelchair, then it suggests that you need to stop depending on others. A situation or relationship has made you feel helpless. Alternatively, a wheelchair indicates that you are literally letting others push you around. You need to start standing up for yourself.

If someone is able-bodied in real life, but you dream that they are in a wheelchair, then it suggests that he/she is in need of your help. They may be afraid to ask you directly and have been dropping hints which your unconscious may have picked up on.

Wheels

To see spinning wheels in your dream, signify completion or continuation of a familiar situation. The dream may be telling you that your life and daily routine is becoming too repetitive. You are going around in circles and headed nowhere. You need to be more spontaneous! Alternatively, the dream symbolizes forward motion and the ability to proceed toward your goals.

To dream that you lose a wheel from a vehicle, indicates that you are feeling lost. You do not know what direction to go or where you are headed.

To dream that you are inventing the wheel, refers to your high aspirations. Alternatively, the dream may suggests that you are over-thinking things.

Whip

To see a whip in your dream, signifies punishment, unhappiness shame and guilt. It may indicate some abusive situation or unfortunate circumstance. Alternatively, the whip means that you need to exercise more control over your life. You need to have more discipline or be more obedient. The dream also may be a metaphor for something that you need to "whip" up.

To dream that you are whipping someone, suggests that you are in control. You are aware of the power you have and may even be exploiting that power. The dream may also have sexual connotations. Perhaps your sex life is in need of a little excitement. Alternatively, the dream may also be a pun on "being whipped", as in either having someone who would do anything for you or that you yourself are the one who is "whipped".

Whiplash

To dream that you have whiplash, indicates that you are butting heads with someone in your waking life. You are experiencing a conflict at school, work, family, or personal relationship. It may also be a pun on "a pain in the neck". Perhaps you or someone is being a pain.

Whirlpool

To see a whirlpool in your dream, signifies emotional turmoil.

Whispering

To hear whispering in your dream, suggests that you need to pay closer attention to something or listen to someone more carefully. Alternatively, whispering represents your insecurities and anxieties. You feel that people are talking about you behind your back.

To dream that you are whispering, indicates that you are lacking conviction in what you are saying. Perhaps you have something to hide or are afraid of fully expressing yourself.

To dream that someone is whispering in your ear, suggests that you need to pay closer attention to something or listen to someone more carefully. Alternatively, it represents your insecurities and anxieties that people are talking about your behind your back.

Whistle

To hear a whistle in your dream, represents a warning. There is something that requires your immediate attention. Alternatively, a whistle marks an end to a period of time or phase in your life.

White

White represents purity, perfection, peace, innocence, dignity, cleanliness, awareness, and new beginnings. You may be experiencing a reawakening or have a fresh outlook on life. Alternatively, white refers to a clean, blank slate. Or it may refer to a cover-up. In Eastern cultures, white is associated with death and mourning.

Wife

To see your wife in your dream, signifies discord and unresolved issues. Pay attention to how you feel in the dream as it may highlight feelings that you are not expressing in your waking life. If you do not actually have a wife, then your dream wife symbolizes the feminine aspects of yourself. Perhaps you may even be expressing a desire to be in a committed relationship. Or the dream may just be a reflection of your waking life and bear no real significance.

Wig

To dream that you are wearing a wig, symbolizes deception, incompetence, false impressions, pretentiousness and falsehood. You are trying to pass other people's ideas, work and opinions as your own. You need to start thinking for yourself. Alternatively, the dream may be a metaphor that you are "wigging out" or making a big deal over some trivial matter.

To dream that you lose a wig, indicates that you have completely lost your mind.

Wild Hog

To see a wild hog in your dream, symbolizes ferocity, strength, and courage. You are expressing a desire

347

to escape from your daily life and your responsibilities.

To dream that you are hunting a wild hog, indicates your need for some balance in your life. You are trying to suppress your desires for independence.

Will

To dream that you are making or writing a will, indicates that you are looking ahead to the future. You are starting a new phase in your life. Alternatively, the dream suggests that a decision you have made is final. You cannot be swayed. The dream may also a pun on your *will*ingness and determination to do something. Or the dream symbol may represent someone in your life named Will.

To dream that something is left for you in a will, represents characteristics or qualities that you can learn or adopt from your descendents.

To dream that a will is being read, suggests that you are ready to reap the benefits of your hard work. Alternatively, the dream means that you are being rewarded for your past efforts.

Willow

To see a willow tree in your dream, symbolizes mourning and sadness. It also denotes a loss of someone or something. Alternatively, the willow represents survival or rebirth.

Win

To dream that you win at something, indicates that you will succeed in some task. You are experiencing new found confidence in your abilities. The dream may serve to offer you encouragement and motivation. Alternatively, the dream symbolizes a sexual conquest.

Wind

To dream that the wind is blowing, symbolizes your life force, energy, and vigor. It reflects changes in your life. Alternatively, the dream suggests that you need to pick up your pace and work on achieving your goals more quickly and efficiently.

To dream of strong or gusty winds, represent turmoil and trouble in your life. You are experiencing much stress in some waking situation.

Windmill

To see a windmill in your dream, symbolizes the power of the mind. It is indicative of your emotional state of mind. Alternatively, a windmill refers to your resourcefulness.

Window

To see a window in your dream, signifies bright hopes, vast possibilities and insight. If the window of a house is dark, then it indicates a loss to your perception or vitality.

To dream that you are looking out the window, signifies your outlook on life, your consciousness and your point of view. It also refers to your intuition and awareness. You may be reflecting on a decision. Or you need to go out into the larger world and experience life. If you are looking in the window, then it indicates that you are doing some soul searching and looking within yourself. It is time for some introspection.

To see shut windows in your dream, signify desertion and abandonment.

To see a shattered and broken window in your dream, represents your distorted view and skewed outlook on life. It is also refers to a state of vulnerability.

To dream that you are fixing or replacing a broken window, indicates that you are reassessing your view and outlook on life. You are gaining a new perspective on things.

To see a tinted window in your dream, represents your need for privacy. You are keeping some aspects of yourself hidden. You also want to remain ambiguous.

To dream that you are washing windows, suggest that you need some clarity in some matter. Something is not clear.

Window Shopping

To dream that you are window shopping, suggests that you are being excluded from life's luxuries. You are feeling inadequate or unqualified. Alternatively, the dream indicates that you are looking for something that is lacking in your life. You feel unsatisfied or unfulfilled with the current direction of your life.

Windshield

To look through the windshield in your dream, represents what is ahead of you and the choices you make. It may also indicate that your approaching your goals in all the wrong way.

To dream that your windshield is broken or cracked, indicates that you have a skewed perspective or outlook on things. You are experiencing many setbacks in the pursuit of your goals.

To dream that your windshield is fogged up, suggests that you are not really expressing how you really feel.

To dream that your windshield is dirty, indicates that you are confused or unclear about where you are headed in life.

Wine

To dream of drinking wine, symbolizes festivity, celebration, companionship, satisfaction and success. You are content with the way your life is going. The dream may also be a pun on "whining" and how you like to whine about things. In particular, to dream that you are drinking red wine, signifies excess and sensuality. If you are drinking communion wine in your dream, then it represents some spiritual celebration or ceremony.

To dream that you are breaking wine bottles, signify overindulgence in your desires and passion. Alternatively, the dream symbolizes the masculine.

Wink

To dream that someone is winking at you, indicates that they are up to something. You are involved in some insider information. Alternatively, the dream may signal romance.

Winter

To dream of winter, signifies ill-health, depression, and misfortune. The dream may be analogous to how you are feeling - emotionally cold and frigid. For some, winter may mean a favorite time of the year signaling the holiday season of fun, joy, togetherness and giving. Alternatively, winter is a time of reflection and spiritual introspection.

Wipe

To dream that you are wiping something, suggests that you are ready to make a clean start. You want to start anew.

To see or use wipes in your dream, indicate that you need to rid yourself of the negativity existing in your life. Consider the type of wipes. If you are using disinfecting wipes, then it means that you need to make a fresh, clean start. If you are using baby wipes, then it suggests that you need to eliminate your immature behavior or attitude.

Wish

To dream that you are making a wish, indicates that there is something that you are longing for and missing in your life. It signifies your accomplishments and hopes for the future. The dream may also be trying to reinforce your waking achievements. Alternatively, the dream may be metaphor that you are "wishy washyness" and indecisiveness. You need to be more decisive and assertive.

Witch

To see a witch in your dream, represents evil and destruction. It may point to your negative ideas of anything feminine and your experiences with dangerous or heartless women. Alternatively, a witch may be a symbol of goodness, power and enchantment depending on your feeling toward your dream witch.

Witchcraft

To dream about witchcraft, signifies some inner transformation or changes. It may also suggest that something or someone is manipulating you and your surroundings.

Witness

To witness to something in your dream, represents your need to be more observant. You need to examine something more closely and look at a situation more objectively. Alternatively, the dream suggests that you are watching life pass you by. Perhaps you are emotionally detached or feel you are an outcast of society.

To dream that you are testifying as a witness, indicates that you need to be accountable for your actions.

Wizard

To see a wizard in your dream, suggests that you are trying to hone your skills and exercise your power.

Wolf

To see a wolf in your dream, symbolizes survival, beauty, solitude, mystery, self-confidence and pride. You are able to keep your composure in a variety of social circumstances and blend into any situation with ease and grace. You are also a loner by choice. Negatively, the wolf represents hostility, aggression, or sneakiness. It may reflect an uncontrollable situation or an all-consuming force in your life. This could point to an obsession, an addiction or something that is beyond your control.

To see a white wolf in your dream, signifies valor and victory. You have the ability to see the light even in your darkest hours.

To dream that you kill a wolf, indicates betrayal. Certain secrets will be revealed to you.

To hear a wolf howling in your dream, represents a cry for help from somebody in your waking life.

Woman

To see a woman in your dream, represents nurturance, passivity, caring nature, and love. It refers to your own female aspects or your mother. Alternatively, a woman indicates temptation and guilt. If you know the woman, then it may reflect concerns and feelings you have about her.

To see an old woman in your dream, indicates your concerns about aging and growing old. Alternatively, the old woman may be an archetypal figure to symbolize feminine power.

Womb

To dream that you are still in the womb, suggests that you are regressing into a period of time when you were safe and completely dependent. You may be trying to escape from the demands of your daily life.

To see the womb in your dream, represents creation, childbirth, fertility and new beginnings The dream is also symbolic of fresh new ideas.

Wonton

To see or eat wontons in your dream, symbolize warmth, family and togetherness. Alternatively, the dream may be a pun on a "wanton" or immoral act or behavior.

Wood

To dream of wood, suggests that you are feeling dead and emotionless inside. Your behavior is too automated. You are not fully thinking things through. Alternatively, the dream may be a pun on "getting wood" or sexual arousal.

To dream that you are carving or shaping a piece of wood, indicates a power-giving act or creative gesture. You are molding or shaping the course of your own life. Alternatively, the carved wood symbolizes spirituality and vital energy.

Woods

To see the woods in your dream, represent life, fertility, rejuvenation, and spring. Alternatively, the woods symbolize the unknown and the unconscious. You need to open yourself up to discovering your potential and your instinctual nature.

To dream that you are walking through the woods, signify your return to an aspect of yourself that is innocent and spiritual. If you are walking out of the woods, then the dream may be a literal depiction of being "out of the woods" or being in the clear of some situation.

To dream that you are lost in the woods, indicates that you are starting a new phase in your life. You are expressing some anxiety about leaving behind what is familiar to you.

To dream that the woods are dry or dying, suggests that there is a situation in your life that has not yet been resolved. You are overwhelmed with a problem or issue.

Wool

To see wool in your dream, symbolizes warmth and coziness. You are seeking protection from loved ones. Alternatively, the dream indicates that you are being naive or gullible about some situation. Consider the phrase "having the wool pulled over your eyes". Perhaps you have been tricked or duped.

Words

To see random words in your dream, signify some confusion in your thought process. Your mind is too cluttered. Alternatively, the dream may be a pun on how "you have my word", as in a promise to be kept.

Work

To dream that you are at work, indicates that you are experiencing some anxiety about a current project or task. The dream may also be telling you that you need to "get back to work". Perhaps you have been slacking off and need to pick up the pace. Stop procrastinating. Alternatively, the dream reflects your success.

To dream that you are at your former work, suggests that there is an old lesson that you need to learn and apply to your current situation.

To dream that you have been replaced at work, represents your concern about your current job security. You feel that you are in a precarious position at work or in some group project.

World

To dream that it is the end of the world, suggests that you are under a tremendous level of stress. You may be feeling vulnerable or helpless in some situation.

To dream that you are saving the world, signifies confidence in your abilities and belief in yourself. You have a positive perspective on life and in where you are headed. Don't let someone or something prevent you from progressing forward or question your abilities.

Worm

To see a worm in your dream, represents weakness, degradation, filth and general negativity. You have a very low opinion of yourself or of someone in your life. The dream may also relate to self-esteem issues or a skewed self image. Alternatively, dreaming of a worm may be a metaphor for someone who is untrustworthy or slick.

To dream that the worm is crawling on your body, indicates that you feel someone around you is taking advantage of you and feeding off your kind heartedness.

Wound

To dream that you are wounded, signifies grief, anger, or distress. You need to slow down and take time to heal. Consider the location, size and type of wound. Alternatively, the dream may be metaphor that you are all "wound up" or tense about some situation.

Wrapping

To dream that you are wrapping something, indicates that you are trying to hide the truth You are involved in a cover-up. Alternatively, the dream suggests that you are trying to present the ugly truth in a way that is easier to accept. Consider what you are wrapping and the color or pattern of the wrapping paper. The dream may be a pun on "rapping" and your need to speak up about something.

Wreath

To see a wreath in your dream, symbolizes honor, celebration, continuity or completeness. Alternatively, a wreath represents sorrow and mourning. You are wallowing in self-pity. The dream also signals the end of some relationship.

To give a wreath to someone, signifies the bond you have with that person.

Wrench

To see or use a wrench in your dream, indicates your desire to fix a situation or relationship. You feel that it is your job to repair and put things back in order.

Wrestling

To dream that you are wrestling, suggests that you are grappling with a problem in your personal or professional life. You are dealing with ideas and habits that need to be brought back into control.

Wrinkle

To see a wrinkle in your dream, represents your feelings of getting older or wiser. It also symbolizes the things you have learned from your past experiences.

Wrist

To notice your wrist in your dream, represents your ability to combine fun and excitement with productivity at the same time. You are able to grab the attention of others and get them involved.

To see an injured or bandaged wrist in your dream, indicates a loss in productivity. You are in an imbalanced or one-sided relationship. In particular, if your wrists that are injured, then it implies that you are not reaching out to others enough. Alternatively, the dream suggests that you are taking more than you give.

Writing

To dream that you are writing, signifies communication with someone or with your conscious mind. Alternatively, writing refers to an error in judgment or a mistake that you have made. The dream may also be a metaphor that you are "right" or that your political views are right leaning.

To see ancient writings in your dream, suggests that there is something you need to learn and understand from the past.

X

To see an X in your dream, signify something that is forbidden. You are being prevented to do something.

To dream of a treasure map marked a big X , indicates that your goals are in sight and you will soon be greatly rewarded.

X-Ray

To dream that you are being x-rayed, denotes that you are being deceived by a person or situation. You need to look beneath the surface of the person or situation. On the other hand, the dream means that you are working through a problem or issue that has been troubling you.

To dream that you have x-ray vision, suggests that you need to look pass the surface and focus on what is inside. Perhaps the dream is trying to tell you that looks aren't' everything.

Xylophone

To see or play a xylophone in your dream, indicates concerns for the environment. You need to be more environmentally conscious. Alternatively, the dream represents your ambition and your drive.

Y

To see the letter Y in your dream, indicates some decision that you need to make. It may represent a fork in the road or a path that you need to choose. The letter Y may also be a pun on "why". Perhaps there is something that you need to start questioning.

Yacht

To see a yacht in your dream, symbolizes wealth, pleasure, and luxury. You are free or worry and in pursuit of a life of ease. You want to devote more time to recreational pursuits. Just take it easy for a while.

Yak

To see a yak in your dream, represents your uniqueness and dependability. The yak may also be a pun on "yakking" too much. Maybe you should stop talking and listen more.

Yam

To see or eat yams in your dream, signify sensuality and virility.

Yard

To see a neat and well-kept yard, reflects your ability to maintain and organize aspects of your outside life, such as work and your social activities.

To see a messy and unkempt yard, denotes that aspects of your life are out of your control.

Yard Sale

To hold or be at a yard sale in your dream, indicates that you are recycling past experiences and finding use for your old skills and ideas. You are learning from your past and making productive use of the lessons you have learned.

Yardstick

To see a yardstick in your dream. symbolizes rigidity and an unyielding personality. Alternatively, a yardstick represents good judgment and acceptance.

Yarn

To see yarn in your dream, symbolizes your connection and creativity. Alternatively, yarn in your dream means that you are stuck in a rut. You are going about your daily life in the same old tired pattern. If the yarn is tangled and knotted, then it implies that you are experiencing some emotional distress or confusion in a situation.

Yawning

To dream that you or someone is yawning, suggests that you are lacking emotional and intellectual stimulation. You are also lacking energy and vitality in your life.

Yearbook

To see your yearbook in your dream, represents the old friends or old flames that you have lost touch with over the years. The dream may also serve to bring you back to a time where you had less responsibilities and less worries. Consider if anybody signed your yearbook and the messages written as it may provide some important advice to follow.

Yellow

The color yellow has both positive and negative connotations. If the dream is a pleasant one, then the color yellow is symbolic of intellect, energy, agility, happiness, harmony, and wisdom. On the other hand, if the dream is an unpleasant one, then the color represents deceit, disgrace, betrayal, cowardice and sickness. You have a fear or an inability to make a decision or to take action. Your desire to please others is at the risk of sacrificing your own needs and happiness. As a result, you are experiencing many setbacks.

To dream of a yellow room, suggests that you need to use your mind. You are feeling mentally stimulated.

Yes

To dream that you are saying "yes", symbolizes reaffirmation or acceptance of a condition, situation or decision. The dream may also be giving you permission to do something that you are having doubts about in your waking life.

Yesterday

To dream about yesterday, indicates that you need to stop reliving the past and learn to let go. Focus on the future. Alternatively, the dream symbolizes past regrets.

Yeti

To see a yeti in your dream, suggests that you need to learn to find balance between your reasonable, rational side and your emotional, instinctual nature.

Yew Tree

To see a yew tree in your dream, symbolizes mourning and death. The dream may also be a metaphor to mean "you", the dreamer.

Yin Yang

To see the yin yang in your dream, symbolizes a balance of opposites. It represents the feminine and the masculine, the spiritual and the physical, and the emotional and the rational.

Yodel

To hear yodeling in your dream, represents a cryptic message from your unconscious. Listen carefully to the tones and syllables.

To yodel in your dream, represents the connection between your mind and your heart.

Yogurt

To see or eat yogurt in your dream, suggests that you need to learn to behave appropriately for the different situations and various circumstances you find yourself in.

Yolk

To see an egg yolk in your dream, represents life, ideas, and creativity.

Young

To see young people in your dream, indicates a fresh outlook on your life. It may also represent a more youthful aspect of yourself. Perhaps you need to be more playful and carefree.

To dream that you are young again, indicates that you are behaving childish or immaturely. Alternatively, it represents your failed attempts to rectify past mistakes. You are dwelling too much on past regrets and lost opportunities. It is time to move on toward the future.

Yoyo

To see or play with a yoyo in you dream, signifies the ups and downs of your life. Alternatively, the dream indicates that you are not taking life's issues and problems seriously enough. You see things too trivially.

Z

To see the letter "Z" in your dream, suggests that you need to get more "Zzzz's" or rest.

Zebra

To see a zebra in your dream, represents perfect balance, unity and harmony. It also indicates that opposites attract. Alternatively, a zebra suggests that you are spending too much time in trivial matters. You need to establish a clear timeline and lay your groundwork for success.

Zero

Zero symbolizes nothingness and emptiness. You are experiencing a void in your life. The symbol may also share the same significance as a circle and thus denotes infinity, eternity, completeness, absolute freedom and holiness. Alternatively, the dream forewarns that you are going around in circles and headed nowhere. Perhaps your actions have been counterproductive. It also represents timelessness and the super-conscious.

*Please See Also Circle or Number.

Zig-Zag

To see zig-zags in your dream, represent your erratic behavior. It may also indicate that you are being defensive about something.

Zipper

To see a zipper in your dream, implies sexuality and sexual innuendos. If you are unzipping, then it indicates that you are opening up. If you are zipping up, then it suggests that you are closing yourself off emotionally.
Alternatively, the dream may be a pun that you need to keep your mouth "zipped." You are talking too much.

To see a broken or stuck zipper in your dream, refers to your difficulties in expressing your sexual desires or feelings. You are frustrated about not being able to resolve a situation or problem. You may also have difficulty in maintaining your composure, especially in an awkward or public situation.

Zits

*Please see Pimples.

Zombie

To see or dream that you are a zombie, suggests that you are physically and/or emotionally detached from people and situations that are currently surrounding you. You are feeling out of touch. Alternatively, a zombie means that you are feeling dead inside. You are just going through the motions of daily living.

To dream that you are attacked by zombies, indicate that you are feeling overwhelmed by forces beyond your control. You are under tremendous stress in your waking life. Alternatively, the dream represents your fears of being helpless and overpowered.

Zoo

To dream that you are at a zoo, symbolizes loss of freedom. Alternatively, a zoo suggests that your abilities and talents are going unnoticed. You or an aspect of your life feels caged in. The zoo may also represent chaos and confusion as implied by the common phrase "this place is a zoo!" You may need to tidy up some situation in your life.

Your Personal Dream Dictionary

List your own personal dream symbols. Remember that DreamMoods.com is continuously updated with new symbols. So if you can't find a word, make sure to check the website. Or you can also email your symbol to dictionary@dreammoods.com for inclusion in a future update of the online dream dictionary.

dream moods™

what's in **YOUR** dream?

dream moods

Printed in Great Britain by
Amazon.co.uk, Ltd.,
Marston Gate.